MIKE
THE MEMOIRS OF THE RT. HON. LESTER B. PEARSON
VOLUME TWO
With a foreword by the Rt. Hon. Jean Chrétien

One of Canada's most dynamic prime ministers, Lester B. Pearson lived a life that took him from a childhood in rural Ontario to the apex of international politics. In the second volume of his memoirs, he provides a first-person account of the busy and challenging decade that followed his entry into politics in 1948.

Completed after Pearson's death under the supervision of his son Geoffrey, this volume recounts his involvement in Canadian politics and diplomacy as a Member of Parliament and Secretary of State for External Affairs during the early years of the Cold War. It offers his perspective on issues such as the formation of NATO, Canada's involvement in the Korean War, and the diplomacy that ended the Suez Crisis and earned Pearson the Nobel Peace Prize in 1957. Two appendices, taken from his diaries, show him hard at work at the United Nations during the Korean crisis.

Mike captures Pearson's intellect, his sense of humour, and his humanity, offering an inside look at the moments that shaped the twentieth century. This new edition features a foreword by Pearson cabinet minister and former prime minister Jean Chrétien.

LESTER B. PEARSON (1897–1972) was Canada's fourteenth prime minister.

Mike

THE MEMOIRS OF
THE RT. HON. LESTER B. PEARSON

VOLUME 2
1948–1957

Edited by
JOHN A. MUNRO and ALEX I. INGLIS

With a foreword by the Rt. Hon. Jean Chrétien

UNIVERSITY OF TORONTO PRESS
Toronto Buffalo London

© University of Toronto Press 2015
Toronto Buffalo London
www.utppublishing.com
Printed in the U.S.A.

First published in 1973.

ISBN 978-1-4426-1565-6

♾ Printed on acid-free, 100% post-consumer recycled paper

Library and Archives Canada Cataloguing in Publication

Pearson, Lester B., 1897–1972, author
Mike : the memoirs of the Rt. Hon. Lester B. Pearson ; with a foreword by
the Rt. Hon. Jean Chrétien.

Volumes 2–3 edited by John A. Munro and Alex I. Inglis.
Originally published: Toronto : University of Toronto Press, ©1972–1975.
Includes bibliographical references and indexes.
Volume 2. 1948–1957.
ISBN 978-1-4426-1565-6 (volume 2 : paperback).

1. Pearson, Lester B., 1897–1972.   2. Canada – Politics and government –
1963–1968.   3. Canada – Politics and government – 1957–1963.   4. Canada –
Politics and government – 1935–1957.   5. Prime ministers – Canada –
Biography   I. Munro, John A., 1938–, editor   II. Inglis, Alex I., 1939–, editor
III. Chrétien, Jean, 1934–, writer of foreword   IV. Title.

FC621.P4A3 2015   971.064'3092   C2015-904821-4

University of Toronto Press acknowledges the financial assistance to its
publishing program of the Canada Council for the Arts and the
Ontario Arts Council, an agency of the Government of Ontario.

 Canada Council   Conseil des Arts
for the Arts   du Canada

 ONTARIO ARTS COUNCIL
CONSEIL DES ARTS DE L'ONTARIO
an Ontario government agency
un organisme du gouvernement de l'Ontario

Funded by the   Financé par le
Government   gouvernement
of Canada   du Canada    Canada

FOREWORD to the 2015 Edition

THE RT. HON. JEAN CHRÉTIEN

On 8 April 1963, Lester Pearson became prime minister of Canada and I was elected to the House of Commons for the first time. Mr Pearson was sixty-six years old, the son of a Methodist minister from Ontario, and a Nobel Peace Prize winner. He had lived in grand embassies and dined with Churchill, Roosevelt, and de Gaulle. I was twenty-nine, the son of a factory machinist from French-speaking, Roman Catholic Quebec, and a small-town lawyer. Our worlds were completely different and I never imagined he would be the kind of guy I'd go fishing with. From the first day I met him, however, the distance between us quickly evaporated.

I always joked that I came to Mr Pearson's attention because of his love of baseball. One day he asked me if I would pitch the annual softball game that used to take place between the politicians and the press corps. Though I had never been much of a sports star, I did well enough, and to our coach's great delight, we won. Not long afterwards he made me his parliamentary secretary!

Parliamentary secretaries don't have any formal or legal role, they're just there to be of help in any way they're asked. However, in those days the post was usually a sign that you were considered to be ministerial material and on your way to the Cabinet. But two developments almost blocked me.

The first happened in 1964 when I was asked to consider returning to Quebec to run for the provincial Liberals in a by-election in Shawinigan. I was tempted. It was the early days of the Quiet Revolution,

Quebec City was an exciting place to be, and Premier Jean Lesage himself told me that he needed someone of my youth and experience on his team, which was as close as he could come to guaranteeing me a position in his government.

When rumours reached Ottawa, Mr Pearson called me into his office and asked me if they were true. "Yes," I replied, "I'm thinking of going."

Those were difficult days for him. He was trying to help French Canadians across Canada and combat the incipient separatist movement in Quebec, but he was in a minority situation, the Conservatives were impeding a lot of his initiatives (including the introduction of a Canadian flag and official bilingualism), and there were a spate of scandals involving his Quebec ministers. "Jean," he asked, "do you believe in Canada?"

"Of course I believe in Canada," I said, somewhat taken aback. "If you wish, I will not go, Prime Minister."

"No, don't make that decision right away," he said. "Go home and take a week to think about it."

I went back to Shawinigan and consulted with my wife Aline and nineteen of my friends. Seventeen advised me to go to Quebec City, because all the activities that mattered locally – schools, hospitals, welfare – were provincial responsibilities. That was my own inclination, I must admit. But Aline and two of my closest advisers, Fernand D. Lavergne and Marcel Crête, convinced me otherwise. Though Mr Pearson didn't promise me anything, he was obviously grateful.

By 1965 I was often mentioned favourably in the Quebec press as an active, "new guard" Liberal and my name kept showing up in their short lists of potential Cabinet ministers. But a second obstacle presented itself when Mr Pearson decided – against my advice, I might add – to call an early election in the hope of securing a majority government.

At one point I was out campaigning with him in his riding, Algoma East, when he told me of a new development. The Liberals had recruited three exceptional candidates in Quebec: the well-known union leader Jean Marchand, the distinguished journalist Gérard Pelletier, and a law professor with a radical reputation named Pierre Elliott Trudeau. "What do you think of them coming with us?" Mr Pearson asked me.

I thought it was a good idea and would help rebuild the party in Quebec. "But I have a problem with this guy Trudeau," I added. "We'll never get him elected anywhere."

"You know, Jean," Mr Pearson added, "this might mean that you won't come into the Cabinet as quickly as hoped."

I understood his situation. "Prime Minister," I said, "if you have better people than me, you should promote them before me."

After the election, which produced another minority, he made Marchand a minister right away, but he surprised everyone by bypassing Pelletier, Trudeau, and myself and appointing Jean-Pierre Côté, an older, likeable MP with powerful supporters in Cabinet.

I was standing near the Prime Minister's office when Mr Pearson spotted me and called me in. "Jean," he said, "you're mad at me because I named Côté a minister instead of you."

"I cannot be mad at you, Mr Pearson," I said, though of course I was very disappointed, "because I'm not in a position to question your judgment." Besides, he could disarm anyone with a pat on the back and his warm charm.

"Someday you will understand, Jean," he said. "I'm going to appoint you parliamentary secretary to Mitchell Sharp in Finance. You will learn things there, and I hope you will become the first French-Canadian Minister of Finance. If I had taken you into the Cabinet today, in the traditional French-Canadian portfolio of Postmaster General that I've given to Côté, it might not lead you to greater things."

Though I can't be sure if his words were merely kindness, they turned out to be prophetic. He subsequently told me how struck he had been that, when all the Liberal MPs, English- or French-speaking, were asked to indicate which committees they wanted to join, I was the only one who had ticked the Finance and Banking Committee as my first choice.

Mr Pearson must have received good reports of my work from Mitchell Sharp, for he summoned me to his office one morning in 1967 and gave me good news. On April 4 I was sworn in as Minister without Portfolio attached to Finance, along with two other future prime ministers: John Turner and Pierre Elliott Trudeau. In January 1968 he elevated me to Minister of National Revenue.

The Pearson government may have looked chaotic, but it wasn't a case of weak management or lack of direction. He was very, very tough in controlling his ministers, and he knew what had to be tackled. Contrary to the public impression, Mr Pearson was much less consensual than Mr Trudeau. There would be great storms during the Cabinet meetings, with ministers pounding the table and raging at each other. Eventually the Prime Minister would say, "It's time to go to lunch, so I'll take care of the matter." He had his own views and, for the most part, he just did what he wanted to do.

Though not every minister was strong, history has confirmed the strength of people such as Mitchell Sharp, Walter Gordon, Allan

Foreword by the Rt. Hon. Jean Chrétien

MacEachen, Paul Martin Sr, Lionel Chévrier, and Guy Favreau. They were full of experience and ideas, and though that sometimes made for a fractious and leaky group, with plenty of their ideological and political battles showing up in the press the next day, they normally rallied around Mr Pearson whenever he was in trouble. His diplomatic skills allowed him to perform calmly when trapped in a crisis, and his cheery awkwardness made everyone want to come to his rescue. People felt warm towards him, they respected his values and his humanity, and we all thought he was a great man.

It was a tumultuous era, and the problems that overtook him were controversial, often emotional ones. There were also the normal difficulties of minority governments, compounded by a Leader of the Opposition who was highly irresponsible. John Diefenbaker always seemed in an angry mood – as though Mr Pearson had interrupted his God-given destiny to be prime minister – and he exploited the bad luck of some Liberal ministers by exaggerating their so-called scandals.

Lester Pearson shaped my vision of what Canada could and should be, both at home and on the world stage. He once said to me, "The biggest mistake ever made in Canada was when Queen Victoria chose Ottawa over Montreal as the national capital. It was a bad move because Ottawa was an English city." And he was determined to right that wrong. He began the effort to make the capital the lively, bilingual centre it is today and to ensure that federal services became available in both official languages.

Mr Pearson loved Canada, and he loved it passionately. He knew from his rich international career that a democratic and liberal country's true worth is measured by how tolerantly it treats its minorities and how generously it shares its wealth. He set up the Royal Commission on Bilingualism and Biculturalism and the Royal Commission on the Status of Women. He fought tooth and nail, and with great personal bravery, for a distinctive Canadian flag. He introduced the Canada Student Loan Plan that made a university education possible for so many more Canadians. He sought to make the Canadian immigration process blind to race and religion. He brought in the Canada Pension Plan and Medicare over the objections of the entrenched interests.

Like all Canadians, each in their own way, I owe Mr Pearson a tremendous debt of gratitude. He profoundly changed our lives and our country for the better. Canada is the best! *Vive le Canada*!

FOREWORD

When my father died on 27 December 1972 he had completed first drafts of the first four chapters of this volume of his memoirs and had done some work on the United Nations and Suez chapters. At the beginning of November, suspecting he might be gravely ill, he turned to the third volume (1958–68) and worked on the first part of the period until a few days before his death. His research associates, John Munro and Alex. Inglis, continued to work on the manuscript of the second volume, to which he had hoped to return.

We took two decisions in January. The first was to complete the second volume. The second was to keep it in the first person. Fortunately, in addition to the draft material left by L.B. Pearson, there were other major sources of first person material, as the editors explain in their introduction. John Munro and Alex. Inglis agreed to edit this material, at the request of the trustees of the estate, and Professor Blair Neatby and Mr Christopher Young agreed to join me as advisers to the editors.

The resulting volume is not the volume L.B. Pearson would have written, although the first four chapters and most of chapter six were close enough to completion to stand as his handiwork. He was an inveterate reviser of manuscripts. The diary and other material would have been shaped and moulded to fit his later perceptions and memories. He would have reflected on experience, as he does in chapters one and two, and of course he would have added new material, perhaps on Canada-United States relations and on the Department of

External Affairs, where he had so many friends whom he would have wished to recall. But still, very little in this volume, whether written in 1950 or in 1972, is not from his pen.

As these pages show, L.B. Pearson was a man of the world. But he was not worldly. He never lost the bearings he had acquired at home and in the small towns of Ontario. He was a nationalist, as any Canadian who moves around the world is likely to be, but he was deeply marked by the bitter fruits of the European nationalism of the 1930s. He saw no contradiction between pride in country and the pursuit of peace. Indeed, moving as he did on to the stage of world politics in the shadow of the atomic bomb, he found himself echoing the anti-war sermons his father had delivered after the war of 1914–18, at the same time as he worked with passion to avoid the mistakes of the era of appeasement. Public men deal with the problems of their times in the light of their own experience. L.B. Pearson was surprised in later years sometimes to be told that he had not acted in 1950 according to the canons of 1970. Yet no man was more conscious of change, and he was wont occasionally to don the robes of Cassandra. Pessimism would give way, however, to that buoyancy of spirit which, allied to good health and the favours of fortune, left little time for introspection.

Reflecting in November 1972 on his life, he wrote: 'No single man, no single group, indeed no single country can master today's challenges. You do the best you can, proud of the special opportunity you have been given, hoping that your achievements will have added something to your country's real strength and its people's happiness, and that your mistakes – of omission and commission – will be corrected by your successors.'

I would like to thank the editors for carrying this project forward in the spirit which L.B. Pearson would have wished; the Canada Council, the Molson Foundation, the Dominion Archivist, and the International Development Research Centre for facilitating their task, and those friends and former associates of my father who read and commented on parts of the manuscript.

GEOFFREY PEARSON

CONTENTS

꿍

ILLUSTRATIONS

Outside the East Block (*Life* Magazine)
With my leader, Louis St Laurent (Ville de Québec)
With Miss Manitoulin 1955 (*Manitoulin Expositor*)
The Pearson campaigners
With Eden and Acheson (United Nations)
With Nehru (Punjab Photo Service)
With Dulles, Lie, and Eisenhower (United Nations)
With Khrushchev and Bulganin
Tedious hours at the UN (United Nations)
President of the General Assembly (United Nations)
Consulting Foster Dulles (Leo Rosenthal)
Agonizing with Dag Hammarskjöld (United Nations)
MPs *v.* the Press Gallery (Newton Associates)
Relaxing with my grandchildren (*Life* Magazine)
Grandfather during the 1965 campaign (*Toronto Star*)
A proud mother (Ron Vickers Ltd)
With my wife and the Nobel medal (Capital Press)

INTRODUCTION

From 10 September 1948 to 17 June 1957 Lester Pearson was Canada's Secretary of State for External Affairs. He has referred to these years, when he was at the height of his international career, as the most exciting period of his life. With twenty years' experience as a professional diplomat for his training, he became one of the world's statesmen.

In the aftermath of war, Canada had a special place in the international community; a position of power and authority and influence that she had not had before and which, in large measure, she has since lost. L.B. Pearson was keenly aware of both the responsibilities and the opportunities which accompanied that position. He made sure that his country accepted those responsibilities and took full advantage of the opportunities to make a better world and thus a better Canada.

In the first volume of *Mike*, Mr Pearson set out to tell his own story. In this volume he continued to do so, but before he was able to finish this important work, he died. With the authority of the Pearson family and estate, the editors, who had worked closely with Mr Pearson in the preparation of his memoirs as his research associates, undertook to see the manuscript to completion. In doing so, it was determined that the work should remain as a volume of memoirs and not become biography. To that end they adopted as their first principle the rule that, unless the story could be told in Mr Pearson's own words, it would not be told at all. The editors were fortunate to have good sources to draw upon: the draft manuscript that Mr Pearson had prepared; the transcripts of lengthy interviews done by the Canadian

Broadcasting Corporation for the television programmes 'The Tenth Decade' and 'First Person Singular' (providing much of the reflective judgment that otherwise would have been lost); Mr Pearson's diaries in which he described events as they happened; his comments and instructions on certain research papers which had been prepared for him by the editors; his letters, reports, memoranda, speeches, and other writings; and, finally, the editors had the enormous benefit of almost daily consultations with Mr Pearson in the two years preceding his death. In the course of working intimately with him, they were left with little doubt as to the form Mr Pearson wanted these memoirs to take.

This volume of the Pearson memoirs, then, is the result of the editors' weaving together these various sources. They hope that in doing so they have come as close as possible to telling the story as Mr Pearson would have done. In addition to normal stylistic editing, they have had to take upon themselves the responsibility for writing some passages of the book. They have, however, been rigorous in enforcing the rule that they would only write 'bridging' material: that is, passages which in factual background tie two or more pieces of Mr Pearson's from different sources into a united whole. They have at all times guarded against writing in their own judgments on people and events. Wherever such judgments and reflections occur, the reader can be assured that they are Mr Pearson's.

Based on these criteria, the chapters of this book came about in the following way. Chapter 1 was written entirely by Mr Pearson. Chapter 2 was prepared in draft form by him but considerably reorganized by the editors. Chapters 3 and 4 were written by him but altered in accordance with his instructions. Chapter 5 was compiled from Mr Pearson's diaries, lecture material, correspondence, and transcripts. Chapter 6 was based on Mr Pearson's early draft with excerpts from diary entries and some transcript material added. Chapters 7 and 8 were based on a research paper, diary entries, speeches, CBC transcripts, and correspondence. Chapter 9 was from his diary and transcripts in accordance with his instructions. Chapters 10 and 11 were from his own preliminary draft on Palestine, extensive instructions in the form of marginal comments on a research paper, plus diary entries, correspondence, lecture material, official documents, and transcripts. The two appendices are from Mr Pearson's diary. An attempt was made to incorporate this material into the text of the Korean chapters, but it proved too unwieldy. At the same time, the detail of diplomatic negotiations and of Mr Pearson's role at the United Nations made it important, at least for the more specialized reader, that the material be published.

In bringing these sources together the editors have freely transferred contemporary descriptive material into the past tense. They have, however, been careful not to allow contemporary opinions and judgments to appear as though they were later reflections. Wherever such judgments occur they are indeed later reflections.

In performing these tasks the editors appreciate highly the support, guidance, and advice of their Advisory Committee, composed of Mr Geoffrey Pearson, Mr Christopher Young, and Professor Blair Neatby. The editors are similarly grateful to a number of individuals who acted as consultants on various chapters, notably Mr John Holmes and Mr Escott Reid, and also Mr Arthur Menzies, Mr George Ignatieff, and Dean F.H. Soward. Mr Mark Collins has provided valuable service as the editors' research assistant. Mr Pearson's private secretary, Annette Perron, has continued to render the memoirs that faithful service which is her hallmark. Miss Lois McIntosh, Mr Pearson's secretary when he was Secretary of State for External Affairs, came out of retirement to work on the project. To these ladies and to Mrs Paulette Popowick, the editors are grateful for their work on the manuscript and the many extra tasks they have undertaken. The editors are especially grateful to Mr Archibald A. Day, who for this volume, as for its predecessor, acted as stylistic consultant. The work of Mr Rik Davidson and Mrs Rosemary Shipton of the University of Toronto Press is also appreciated.

Finally, the editors wish to say a word of thanks to Mrs Pearson. Without the knowledge that they had her trust and confidence, their task would have been impossible. We hope that, of all people, she will derive pleasure from these pages.

JOHN A. MUNRO
ALEX. I. INGLIS

ON PARLIAMENT HILL

outside the East Block

WITH MY LEADER

the Right Honourable Louis St Laurent

Opposite page

CONSTITUENCY DUTIES

top – with Barbara Lewis, 1955
bottom – the Pearson campaigners

WORLD LEADERS

top – Anthony Eden and Dean Acheson
bottom – Pandit Nehru

top – Foster Dulles, Trygve Lie, and President Eisenhower
bottom – Nikita Khrushchev, Nikolai Bulganin

AT THE UNITED NATIONS

above – the way it is
opposite – President of the General Assembly

SUEZ DIPLOMACY

– consulting Foster Dulles

– the inscription reads:
'to be or not to be' for the UN Force?
With deep gratitude, Dag Hammarskjöld

RELAXATIONS

top – MPs *v.* the Press Gallery, 1954

left and above – with my grandchildren

THE NOBEL PEACE PRIZE

top – a proud mother
bottom – with my wife and the Nobel medal

MEMOIRS

ᘒ1ᘒ

POLITICS AND POLITICIANS

This volume covers my years as Secretary of State for External Affairs, a period that began on 10 September 1948, when, in the presence of Canada's outgoing and incoming Prime Ministers, I was sworn in by the Acting Governor General on a Bible later presented to me by Mr King with a friendly inscription to encourage me in the days ahead. It was not 'Forgive us our trespasses as we forgive them that trespass against us.' My ministerial career ended on 17 June 1957, when Mr St Laurent and his colleagues made the slow march to Rideau Hall to present their resignations to the Governor General after the defeat of the government in the election. We were determinedly cheerful, if still a shade unbelieving, as the twenty-two years of Liberal rule in Canada came to an end. I had no doubt myself about the change that had occurred in my status because my wife, practical as always, had suggested that, as I now had more time for domestic chores, I might pick up some hamburger on the way home.

In writing about these years, I will naturally be dealing almost entirely with external affairs, and more particularly with my relation to them as the responsible Canadian Minister. Foreign policy was my work in the government; in Parliament and in the country I was concerned with domestic matters only to a relatively minor degree, in part because foreign affairs, at least until 1956, were largely non-partisan. My participation in parliamentary and political conflicts came gradually. I had quite enough to do in my own field, since this was a busy and exciting time for Canada internationally.

My entry into the government as a front-bench Minister must have
seemed to my new political colleagues a sudden and surprising ascent.
At the beginning, however, the change to me did not seem startling.
It felt like being promoted from general manager to president in the
same company: 'External Affairs, Ltd.' It took me some little time to
realize fully the political implications of my new position, although
the transition from official neutrality to political affiliation was not
really difficult.

As a civil servant, I had had, of course, no connection with any party;
but I was in no doubt about the support I could give to the basic policies and principles of the Liberal party which I was now joining. Nor
was I in any doubt about the quality of its leadership. For Mr St Laurent, under whom I would be serving, I had a deep admiration and
respect. I was happy to join a party that had provided as Prime Ministers Alexander Mackenzie, Sir Wilfrid Laurier, Mackenzie King, and
Louis St Laurent – alternating English-speaking and French-speaking
Canadians. I thought of that alternation in terms of the contribution
it had made to Canadian unity and progress. The Conservative party
had never been able to find this kind of succession in choosing its
leaders.

I believed strongly in the postwar foreign policies of the Liberal government. I was proud of the place Canada had gained in the world by
her services in the war against the Nazis and by the part she had played
with her allies in trying to organize the peace. I was also impressed by
the way in which Canada's postwar domestic problems had been faced.
Historically, I felt that Liberalism had given wise leadership in the progress of Canada from dependent colony to united independent nation.
To me this development did not mean that we were severing our ties
with Britain or France. We could enjoy national freedom while maintaining our special connection with Britain and the new Commonwealth. I was also in strong sympathy with Liberal policies advocating
greater social security and justice without which those individual rights
and freedoms, which must be preserved, would lose most of their meaning. In short, I thought of the Liberals as the party of social welfare,
popular progress, and the achievement of nationhood, of the Conservatives as historically the party of the status quo and the British connection. I was comfortable in my new political home.

In later years, it was occasionally thrown at me that I had always
been a Conservative by inclination and had betrayed that preference
because of personal ambition when offered the position as Secretary of
State for External Affairs. This charge goes back, I suppose, to the days

when I lived in Toronto where I had more Conservative than Liberal friends – Roland Michener, George Drew, Gordon Graydon, or Jim Macdonnell. There could have been no other basis for the notion. It is also true, however, that as a civil servant I had always been quite comfortable and happy in my relationships with my political masters of both parties. I did not instinctively interpret politics in terms of party; and this no doubt was one factor delaying my more immediate partisan indoctrination. I had certainly been brought up in an atmosphere of small 'l' liberalism, even if one of my parents called himself a Conservative.

Once sworn in as a Minister, even though not yet elected to Parliament, I was a member of Canada's central governing body, the Cabinet. I well remember my first Cabinet meeting. It was not as impressive as I had expected. Mr St Laurent, who was Minister of Justice and Acting Prime Minister, was in the chair. I was late in arriving – one of the very few times in my life when I was guilty of that fault, for my normal weakness is to be too early for everything. Mr St Laurent was speaking when I entered the sacred portals, and I did not know where to sit. I just stood there awkwardly – a new boy waiting to be told where to go. This was not the way a great occasion should begin. In a second or two, however, though it seemed to me interminable, Mr St Laurent stopped speaking and pointed to a seat at the bottom of the table. There was no welcoming speech, no obvious realization by my Cabinet colleagues that here was a most important accession to their ranks.

I sat down, prepared to make my first contribution to the government of Canada by participating in the discussion of that question of national or international significance which I assumed was under way. I was far from prepared. It was a capital case. Under the law, the death sentence imposed had to be submitted to Cabinet for confirmation or commutation. The Solicitor General put the case for and against commutation at considerable length. In other issues in Cabinet, the Prime Minister would listen to the discussion, summarize it, give his own view, and announce or reserve a decision. In capital cases, however, every Minister has to state his position. So I made my first Cabinet intervention. A few minor matters were then dealt with, ending with the appointment of the honorary colonel of a militia regiment. This did not seem to me an affair of national concern although perhaps relevant to the fortunes of the Liberal party in that particular area with an election in the offing. All in all, it was not the introduction to Cabinet government which I had expected.

I could attend Cabinet meetings from the day of my ministerial ap-

pointment. I could not, of course, take my place in Parliament until I
became an elected member. So I was soon engaged in trying to sell myself to the people.

Mr King and Mr St Laurent had decided to speed up the appointment of Thomas Farquhar to the Senate, where there was an Ontario
vacancy. This would open the seat in Algoma East, and I was to seek
the Liberal nomination for the by-election to fill it. It was good, but by
no means safe, Liberal territory. From its establishment in 1904, five
of the eight members before Mr Farquhar had been Conservative, as
was the sitting provincial member.

Before worrying about getting elected, however, I would first have
to be accepted at a constituency nominating convention as the Liberal
party candidate. To discuss the convention and matters relevant to my
nomination, the secretary of the riding Liberal executive, Farquhar
Anglin, came to Ottawa. We discussed the situation and Anglin
thought I would be accepted by the convention without too much difficulty, especially if I could pay them a visit beforehand to meet as
many of the Liberals as possible. I was glad to do this, remembering
Mr King's advice a few days before to go to Algoma as soon as I could
and meet 'everybody.' He emphasized how important it was that a
member keep in the closest touch with his constituents and that I
should begin that process by campaigning every day before the by-
election once I had secured the nomination. I should never forget, he
told me, that, as a Minister of the Crown, I had a very special obligation to those who elected me. I was their member, hence their servant.
It was good advice.

Campaigning in Algoma East had its own difficulties. It was a large
area, 20,000 square miles or so, extending from Manitoulin Island to
the CNR transcontinental line, and from a few miles east of Sudbury to
a few miles west of the Soo. It was sparsely populated with no single
large community, and therefore not easy to cover. There were the
further disadvantages that I lived in Ottawa, with duties that took me
throughout Canada and, indeed, the world, and that I had no residence
in the district where I was elected nor had I any earlier connection with
it. Over the years, however, I did my very best to keep in close touch
with my constituency and to be a good representative of my electors.
In return, they gave me their continuing support, encouragement, and
friendship for which I shall always be deeply grateful.

Anglin and I were on our way north the night after his arrival in
Ottawa and after I had been given a thorough briefing on everything
and everybody in Algoma East. The next day was one I shall never

forget. We got off the train at McKerrow, a station on the edge of the constituency on the line from Sudbury to Sault Ste Marie. Senator Farquhar, as he now was, met us and we began the day's drive along Highway 17, stopping at every village or town, even at some farms, where I met and was inspected by local Liberal worthies. It was my first experience of rural main-streeting. Though somewhat doubtful about my reception as a visiting dignitary, and even worse, as a diplomat, I soon got into the swing of things, and began to enjoy this new experience. I have always liked people as persons, if not so much en masse. I found it easy and pleasant (my background and training, as well as my nature, helped me) to talk to people in the village store, or at the street corner.

I was well sponsored on this first day's journey into political life. Senator Farquhar was well liked, highly respected, and knew everybody. We would greet everyone we met; or if we were just driving by, we waved. They knew who he was but, as he said, people find things out up here very quickly 'so you wave too.' By the end of the day, I had become both a fairly relaxed talker when we stopped and a vigorous waver as we went by. We drove many, many miles before the sun went down. Then, at the end of the day, I saw a farmer making his way home across a field close to the road. So, naturally, I waved; the Senator's arms, however, remained still. He approved of my enthusiasm but said: 'You can stop waving now, we're out of the constituency.' It was another lesson in politics – conservation and selectivity of effort.

The nominating convention was held at Espanola on 24 September 1948. It was well attended. I was given a friendly reception and my nomination was unopposed. I confess, however, that I was very nervous in making my acceptance speech for I had never before spoken on such an occasion or to such an audience.

The by-election campaign which followed gave my wife and me a good opportunity to meet the electors and of this we took full advantage. When it was over we had visited every settlement and, it seemed to me, had shaken hands with every voter in Algoma East.

The Conservative party decided not to oppose me, at least until the next general election, but the left-wing CCF and the right-wing Social Credit parties waged vigorous campaigns, especially the Social Crediters. Their candidate was a colourful resident of Blind River, John Fitzgerald, secretary of the Social Credit League of Ontario and the son-in-law of a lumber magnate of that area. Fitzgerald worked hard, emphasizing the value of his local affiliations, but I won without too much difficulty. It was the first of eight electoral victories, and the one in which, notwithstanding the absence of a Conservative opponent, I received my smallest majority.

The high spot in the campaign was the visit of Mr St Laurent, to see how his protégé was getting along. It was, I think, his first political appearance outside Ottawa since he had succeeded Mr King as party leader. The visit was to include a church supper at Little Current on Manitoulin Island. In a sense, this was a most unusual initiative. Although part of my constituency had a strong Catholic and French-speaking element (indeed, in some of the lumber camps the Pope and Sir Wilfrid Laurier, who to them was still the Liberal Leader, were the two most important men in the world), Manitoulin Island, apart from the Indian reservations, was strongly and conservatively Anglo-Saxon, Masonic, and Orange Protestant.

My local supporters on this largest of all fresh-water islands, and certainly one of the most beautiful, must have wondered how a devout French-Canadian Catholic would fare in the crowded basement of a United Church. They had nothing to worry about. I knew Mr St Laurent and I knew church suppers. He enjoyed himself thoroughly, charmed everyone, and made a moving little speech about brotherhood and goodwill among all Canadians. I was very proud of my leader that night, as I was to be so often later, as the finest possible embodiment of Canadian unity. I am certain that, to the Manitouliners who met and heard him speak, Quebec was closer than it had ever been before.

I always had a particular interest in the welfare of my Indian constituents, whom I met for the first time in the by-election. There was a considerable number of them, in several bands, and I was able to help them in various ways, whether in arranging for better educational facilities or in getting new instruments for a brass band whose music made up in volume whatever it may have lacked in harmony.

The largest Indian band was at Wikwemikong on a peninsula at the eastern end of Manitoulin Island. It was a well-organized community and had retained much of its culture, pride, and tradition. The material standard of life, however, was low and there was little opportunity for rewarding employment, a factor which, here as elsewhere, weakened their morale and hopes. Later, Mrs Pearson and I were inducted into the band during a colourful ceremony conducted by its chief, Joe Peter Panguish, whom I got to know quite well. At the close of the 1953 election, as I remember, my wife and I were receiving the results in Espanola. She was particularly interested in the Wikwemikong returns since we had been given an especially warm reception there a few days before. I found the results highly satisfactory: Pearson 110, my opponent 4, or something like that. But my wife is a perfectionist and did not share my joy. Her reaction was: 'I wonder who those four could have been.'

The by-election was not a very severe challenge for me, politically or physically. By nine-thirty on election night the results were in. I had won my first election. My confidence was renewed in the wisdom and common sense of the people who could choose so wisely! After a short celebration, Farquhar Anglin, who had been my very efficient campaign manager, drove us to Sudbury, about fifty miles away, to catch the midnight train for Ottawa, whence I was to fly to France next day and rejoin the diplomatic world by taking over the leadership of the Canadian Delegation to the UN Assembly, meeting that year in Paris. We ran into one of the worst fogs possible outside of Sudbury, and barely managed to catch the train. It was an exciting end to a very exciting day.

Though this by-election, as I have said, was not too difficult, the result was reassuring. Harold Nicolson wrote in the third volume of his *Diaries and Letters*: 'A good candidate should be convinced that he is more intelligent, far more honourable and infinitely more valuable to his country than any of his opponents. I have never been adept at that sort of thing. However convinced I may be of the rightness and inevitability of a given political doctrine, I am temperamentally unable to give even a faint breath of fanaticism to my conviction.' He might have been writing about me.

If my by-election success gave me more confidence in myself as a candidate, that confidence was soon to be put to a sterner test.

My next political exposure came in November 1948, when I took part in a by-election meeting at Orono, in Ontario. From there I went to Port Arthur for another meeting the next day. C.D. Howe was to shepherd me on both occasions. The Orono rally was a rowdy, rousing political affair with the redoubtable Senator 'Billy' Fraser, a vigorous party orator and a gifted tub-thumper, in the chair. He spoke first, got the people shouting and cheering for the Liberal cause, and in the process used some insulting, if witty, language about the Tory Opposition. I had not been exposed to this kind of thing before and thought it pretty dreadful, until I got caught up myself in the partisan excitement. Then my turn came to speak. I was going to talk about the United Nations or something in the field of foreign affairs, but I soon found myself attacking the Tories and their 'Bay Street Colonels,' a pejorative phrase the Liberals were using to smear the Conservative Leader, George Drew, and his party lieutenants.

After the meeting we drove back to Toronto's Malton Airport which we reached about one in the morning. A blizzard was raging, and we had to fly through it in a small private plane to reach Port Arthur. That hardened old campaigner, 'C.D.,' afraid of nothing, strapped himself in, and almost before we took off into the wild blue yonder, or rather the wild white yonder, was sound asleep. We got to Port Arthur about 4 o'clock in the morning, drove to a hotel, had two or three hours sleep, and then took part in a breakfast meeting. 'This political life,' I reflected, 'is tougher than I expected; there's obviously more to becoming a Minister for External Affairs than going off to Paris to a United Nations Assembly.'

જ

Politics and politicians deserve far more respect in our democratic society than they receive. A politician, however, is vulnerable and exposed. He is the trustee of the hopes and worries, the desires and demands of those who elect him. He lives and works under conditions of maximum exposure. Any sin of omission or commission is bound to secure wide publicity and savage criticism. To blame it on the government or on politics is an inevitable, almost an automatic, democratic reaction. At times this is a healthy reaction. But often it is merely an excuse for the critic's neglect of his public duty or, especially if he is a publicist or an academic, an opportunity to demonstrate his own superior wisdom and knowledge. My own experience has given me a great respect for those who discharge their political responsibility by working for the party of their choice, and especially for those who do so by serving, or seeking to serve, in Parliament or in other legislative bodies. There can be no prouder achievement than to be chosen by one's fellow citizens to speak and work for them in a freely elected assembly. When politics and politicians are disparaged and referred to contemptuously, especially by those who are in default of their own duties as citizens, then democracy itself is diminished; it is even more diminished when the politician himself betrays the trust of those who elected him. This rarely happens in our country, although the insinuations and sneers of ill-informed critics would lead us to believe that it is common. As for me, I shall always feel proud and privileged that I was a Canadian politician, and that I made so many friends among politicians of all parties.

On 26 January 1949 I was introduced to the House of Commons as the new Member from Algoma East. Introduction of a new member is, at least to the initiate, a very impressive ceremony. After a few minutes' nervous waiting outside the chamber, my sponsors, the Prime Minister and C.D. Howe, appeared and, grasping me firmly by the arms, led me to the Speaker's Chair where Mr St Laurent, using a form of words with which I was to become very familiar in years to come, asked that I be allowed to take my seat. The Speaker graciously agreed, and I went to my place in the front row, reserved for Cabinet ministers. I received the friendly desk-thumping given to new members on these occasions. Of course, it was louder on the Liberal side but, in retrospect, I am sure that even there some of the older members must have thought it strange that this new man who, until his recent appointment, had never been in politics at all, should have moved at once from the official gallery to the front benches. Some indeed may have felt, and understandably, that the party establishment did not seem to value very greatly long and faithful parliamentary service when this could happen. If there were any such feelings, I was never made conscious of them, then or afterwards, for I received nothing but kindness and friendship from my parliamentary colleagues.

My maiden speech came a few days later, on 4 February. I knew that I should begin by talking about my constituency as the most delectable place this side of heaven and by thanking the gods for the privilege of having been chosen to represent it in Parliament. Having made this contribution to tradition, and indeed to my own sentiments, I went on to speak about foreign policy in a non-partisan way. I got a very good hearing across the aisle until I came to negotiations for the NATO pact then in progress. The Conservative party and its new leader, George Drew, had not yet declared themselves specifically in favour of Canada's membership in NATO. I expressed disappointment at their hesitation and, departing from my text (or as MPs always say, 'my notes,' since it is against the rules to read from a text), asked rhetorically: 'Are any of us playing politics with peace at this time?' That was an offensive and unfortunate observation for a new member to make, especially in his maiden speech and on a subject, external affairs, which was relatively non-partisan. The Opposition's attitude changed very quickly and Gordon Graydon, one of my oldest friends in the House, interrupted me with a derogatory comment. My reception across the aisle from then on was correct but not particularly sympathetic, and with good reason. I got the usual notes of congratulations afterwards but not those I might have received, on a maiden speech, from my friends in the Opposition. However, Jim Macdonnell was charitable enough to write: 'That was a very fine speech except for one most unfortunate lapse.'

I have often wondered why I threw in this gratuitous and provocative remark. I think it must have been because subconsciously I realized that I was speaking like a civil servant or a professor and that if I was ever going to be accepted as a politician, as a good member of my own party in the House of Commons, I should make at least one partisan thrust. The fact that I always regretted it was merely another indication I was clearly not a born politician.

I was certainly not a natural or eloquent parliamentary speaker. For me, as for many others, the House of Commons was an intimidating rather than an inviting place in which to speak. This was not simply because the acoustics were bad or the setting was awkward for the speaker. The main reason, for me at least, was that much of the debating seemed artificial, a kind of play-acting. The words were for the record, not uttered in hope that they would change the mind of anyone. Minds were, with very rare exceptions, already convinced. There was no real challenge in most debates, and I did not have that interest in the classic cut and thrust of partisan exchange dear to so many others, the disappearance of which is lamented by parliamentary romantics. I could share the excitement and glee of a successful verbal assault on the opposition, or become aroused and belligerent when we were under attack – always, of course, unfairly. I could also appreciate the sense of participation in history on a great parliamentary occasion, or be impressed by a debate on matters of genuine principle or vital importance. But I was not, I fear, a House of Commons man in the popular sense of the term. That, I suspect, is largely because I came into the House close to my fiftieth birthday, because I had never been a private member who over the years could come to share in full the life and the atmosphere of the chamber and the lobbies. Politics and Parliament were not in my blood, at least not as they were with many members of the House. Moreover, as a Minister and especially as a Prime Minister, my attendance in the Commons had to be limited. There was so much other work to be done, so many people to be seen, so many meetings to attend. Indeed, it often seemed that to talk in the House was not relevant or important enough to be given priority over other and graver business of government.

వ

It was one thing to campaign successfully in one's own constituency, without any Conservative Opposition, or in a more typical by-election with all parties contending; it was something else to take part in a national campaign, with all-out local and national opposition trying to unseat the government, and you with it.

My first general election followed soon after my personal success of October 1948. Mr St Laurent, after sampling the political weather in a Western tour, decided the heavens were propitious for an election when the people and press affectionately began to call him 'Uncle Louis.' The old Parliament was therefore dissolved and 27 June 1949 was set as the date for electing the new. Now I would learn what electioneering really meant and whether the decision I had made a few months before to leave the Civil Service was rash. Defeat would mean unemployment for me. There was no certainty that the Liberals would win now that Mackenzie King, the old magician, had departed.

There was no single great issue in this election of 1949. We talked about the success of the government in soldiers' re-establishment and in reconstruction after the war, and about the national economy. Everyone feared there would be a great depression when the men came home from overseas, and that the government would never find enough jobs for them. But these fears were groundless, and this was a great advantage for the Liberals.

I had a basic speech for my national appearances on which I would ring the changes as local conditions dictated. I would say how proud I was to have been asked to join the government of a man like Mr St Laurent, whom I lauded as a great Canadian and a fine man. I gave my definition of Liberalism and praised the government for its Liberal achievements. Naturally, I made the record of those achievements sound like a march to national glory and salvation. I would try then to answer some of the opposition attacks on the government's record: 'It is becoming increasingly clear, as the campaign goes on, that the people of this country will repudiate the vague, contradictory, and unfounded attacks now being levelled at the government. Canadians will ignore the absurd irrelevancies of the Tory appeal, will refuse to be impressed by the extravagant and desperate promises of a group hungry for power. We know, on the other hand, that the electors will give a vote of confidence and support to the government which led Canada through the long and critical years of war, and, with brilliant results, through the difficult years of postwar readjustment and reconstruction. The years ahead will not be easy, new problems are cropping up, but the people of this country are not going to entrust their solution to rash and inexperienced and grasping hands.' I was learning the language.

After praising the government and chastising its critics, I would go on to a non-partisan account of Canada's new foreign policy, and our role at the United Nations and elsewhere in the search for peace and security. This was the subject, no doubt, about which my audience expected me to be more impressive and knowledgeable than on the virtues of Liberalism and the record of the government.

The wind-up would be a plea to keep our country united, prosperous, and free by rejecting the insidious appeal of the Opposition and by voting Liberal. It all came down to the following:

'There is a choice and a challenge before us, as Canadians, in this election. I know that the people will make the choice of tried and trusted government and meet the challenge to that government from the left and from the right. On the fringes of the right are the hard-faced reactionaries and on the fringes of the left are the wild-eyed revolutionaries. It has been the experience of other countries that the right and left tend to become the victims of their own extremists. That is the great menace to democratic government today, the menace from extremes. If you believe in the middle way, you will vote Liberal, because that is the way of safety and progress. Indeed, the best testimony to this fact is the campaign being conducted by the Tories and the CCF, both of whom are attempting to disguise their own essential doctrines by covering them with Liberal garments. They keep prowling around our beaches in the hope of stealing our clothes while we are in swimming. They haven't been able to do that but they have produced some imitation garments which hang uneasily on them. If you read again the Conservative platform you will see what I mean. Policies and principles of social security, agricultural security, economic security, and political security, which they regarded with a cold and jaundiced eye when they were produced first by Liberal governments many years ago, they now put forward as their own discoveries.

'In the democratic world today, along with extremism, indeed arising to some extent out of it, is the parallel danger of instability, of government by groups uneasily joined together. Here again in Canada we are fortunate. In the centre, in our country is one strong, united national party. That party is marching forward in the centre of a road leading in the right direction.

'So on June 27th the people of Canada will vote for the party that stands for stability without stagnation, for unity without uniformity, for freedom without licence, and for progress.'

A few weeks before the election a Conservative friend, Jim Macdonnell, had told me that his party was trying to persuade a particular gentleman to run against me and, if successful, it would mean the end of my short political career, something which, he generously added, he would personally regret. The Tories did persuade their chosen candidate to run. He was Grant Turner, whose family had been prominent in the business and community life of Manitoulin Island for many years and who was himself a highly respected resident of Little Current, where the family retail business was located. It was a very vigorous, but clean and gentlemanly campaign. Indeed, it was the beginning of friendly relations with the Turner family which continued during my years as member for Algoma East. The Opposition, as they did in all subsequent elections except 1965 when they themselves brought in an outside celebrity, concentrated on my 'foreign' status and lack of roots in the constituency.

But they failed. I even had a majority in Mr Turner's home town. In this election I had a strong national tide running in my favour, while, personally, I had managed to convince my constituents that I was sincere in my desire to serve them as a member, that I was interested in local problems, and was no stuffed-shirt diplomat, aloof from their concerns. If I was a Minister with an important, even a somewhat glamorous portfolio, External Affairs, I was also an elected representative of the people with a constituency to look after. I learned that if I forgot my constituency duties I might soon be ejected from my ministerial and diplomatic responsibilities.

I was once given a good lesson on this score during a visit to my constituency. I was chatting with some villagers in front of the general store and telling them about a recent visit to Washington, where their member had the honour of signing the North Atlantic Treaty for Canada. It had been a historic occasion and I felt that my listeners had been suitably impressed by my account of it, when one elderly farmer drawled: 'Yes, that was a fine thing you did down there in Washington, a fine thing for Canada, but it won't help you much around here if you don't get us a new post office.' Thereafter, I tried always to remember that the United Nations and the village post office were both to be treated seriously. My memory was at least good enough for an Opposition speaker to claim some years later that, if I were elected to Algoma East once again, I would have a dock right around Manitoulin Island and a government-financed stockpile of uranium at Elliot Lake which would top the highest hill.

We decided to await the results of my first general election at the village of Massey, where the returning officer lived, at Beauchamp's, a small but, in my view, the best inn of all the north country. I had been visiting polls throughout the day, ending with one in Massey where I was accosted by a voter with the discouraging remark: 'You're a nice fellow, Mr Pearson, but I don't think you are going to be our member.

You shouldn't have been sent up here, so far from home, and almost a stranger to us.' This rather depressed me and I was nervous as we began one of Mr Beauchamp's good dinners; not so nervous, however, as my brother who with his wife had come up from Boston for the big day and who kept assuring the rest of us, desperately, that everything would be all right. It was.

The first returns were brought in by my local manager as we were dining. Ernie Macdonald handed me the slip with a grin, but warned that we could not hope to do so well in all the polling stations. This was a very small one at a nearby mine where only seven had voted. They were all 'Pearson' – a shut-out!

While I found my first national election an interesting experience, I always enjoyed much more the local or regional campaigning. Once I came to know Algoma and the north country, political visits there acquired for me the appeal of the familiar and the friendly. The electioneering was decent and civilized, with little of personalities or mudslinging. My national political responsibilities as a member of the government, however, forced me to spend less time in my constituency and more in travel throughout the country, both during and between elections. I was fortunate to have as a secretary Mary Macdonald, a very friendly, outgoing person who enjoyed meeting new people. She became the bulwark of my political life and soon knew everyone in the constituency, to my great advantage.

When I became Leader I could spend only a day or two in my own constituency during an election. But my friends there were steadfast in their support, and my organization worked all the harder in my absence. I never ceased to be grateful for my good fortune in having Algoma East as my political home. I was glad that I was a member for a rural constituency and not one in a big city. Apart from my special feeling for this particular district, it was more satisfying for me to serve as the member of a rural riding, one of farm and bush, of mine and lake and lumber camp, of new lively industrial towns and of old sleepy villages. All of this is found in Algoma East. It was enjoyable and heartwarming to talk to the people there even in the midst of political controversy and competition.

Politics, of course, is not all problems and pressures. There are lighter moments to be enjoyed, especially if one is blessed with that greatest of all gifts for the politician, a sense of humour. In my political tours and electoral campaigns there were tribulations and troubles but there were also many laughable incidents and situations.

In Algoma East politics and elections were taken seriously. Particularly on Manitoulin Island, meetings, however small, were conducted with due dignity and formality. On occasions, in some little red schoolhouse, there might be no more than a dozen or so present, half of whom would be on the platform and on the programme. Once, in my early days, when the audience and the performers were about equally divided, I ventured to suggest to the chairman that it might be more sensible if we just sat around and talked informally. 'Not at all. This is a meeting and we have a programme.' So we went through the prescribed ritual, as if I were addressing a large rally in a coliseum. At the beginning we sang 'O Canada.' Oh, the innumerable times I have listened to that somewhat mournful dirge, or, when rendered in the right way, that stirring anthem! At the end there was 'God Save The Queen.' Nothing can alter that music, for better or for worse. In between, I was formally introduced, along with other platform guests. I spoke. I was thanked. The meeting adjourned.

At one of my smallest gatherings I was once thanked by a gentleman whose passion was not politics but monetary theory. This was his great opportunity to explain his views on the subject in public to a Cabinet Minister, and this he did for thirty minutes. I felt I should now get up and thank him in turn.

Introductions were usually shorter than this, but not always. The shortest and best I have ever experienced was at a constituency meeting when the chairman, a taciturn and weather-beaten farmer, spoke: 'I have been asked to introduce Mr Pearson, who has been asked to speak to us. I have. He will.' This chairman became a very good friend of mine. His homespun and even rough manner concealed a shrewd brain and a nice wit. He once explained modern economics to me from his own experience as an impoverished farmer on very poor land. When I asked him if he did all the work or had a hired man to help, he answered that he could not afford permanent help but would pay a hired man as long as possible, by which time he would be bankrupt and would then sell his farm to his employee. The former owner would then become the farm labourer until he had accumulated enough money to buy back the farm. And so they could go on indefinitely. I resisted the temptation, after I became Prime Minister, to put Bill on the Board of the Bank of Canada.

Algoma people were invariably hospitable and friendly – even if they voted against you. Each visit to a community at any hour of the day called at the very least for 'coffee and doughnuts.' During a campaign this might mean eating every hour or two. Once at the end of a day of travelling and speaking, greeting and eating, my wife and I found ourselves at a meeting of party officials from the various sections of the constituency. The survey of campaign progress was over by ten o'clock or so, and the moment for another snack had arrived, when the chairman said: 'Is there anything else to bring up?' My wife who, as was her custom, had been attentive but silent all day, spoke up, to general surprise and pleasure: 'Yes, I would like to bring something up.' 'What is it?' asked the chairman with respectful interest. 'Twelve cups of coffee and eight doughnuts!' That remark got greater publicity than any of the wise and weighty political observations I had made during the day.

As a member of the government, I had responsibilities outside Algoma East, more particularly in nearby constituencies, of which the closest were Algoma West, Nickel Belt, and Sudbury. I customarily participated in election campaigns in these ridings which, as in most of northern Ontario, kept returning Liberal Members of Parliament. More important, my Liberal parliamentary neighbours, veteran politicians, were generous in their help to me, especially when as a novice I needed that help most. One of these colleagues was Leo Gauthier, the member for Nickel Belt, a very experienced politician and a campaigner who knew all the tricks of the trade. In the play of politics, he was a rough diamond, but a valuable one, with a natural eloquence and an earthy sense of humour which had great appeal at political meetings. He did his best, with only limited success, to show me how to inspire the faithful and convert the sceptics by exalting the party and all its works, while destroying the opposition with devastating attacks in either or both of our own official languages. I remember particularly one Saturday evening during the 1953 campaign when I was with him in Sudbury. We were attending a baseball game where Leo had arranged for me to throw out the first ball which he would hit and a local Liberal dignitary would catch. This was a great coup on his part for there would be four or five thousand present and it would be invaluable advertising for the Liberal candidate. The Tories and the Socialists would be furious.

I surprised him, however, by saying that I did not think much of the idea, which no doubt confirmed his feeling that I did not know very much about politics. On this occasion I was certainly wrong. 'This is a wonderful idea, so what's worrying you?' asked Leo. 'Well, you know, people don't like to have a baseball game held up by expectant politicians, especially during an election.' 'Nonsense,' he replied, 'it will be just fine. I know my people.' So we went out to the field, went through our drill, and walked off. I thought we had a pretty cool reception and said so on the way to our seats: 'Leo, that wasn't very successful.' A round, fat man and a jovial extrovert, he gave me a wide smile: 'Don't be silly, that was a triumph, not a single boo!' Everything in politics is relative. To him, if three politicians in an election campaign, two of them candidates, could delay a ballgame for ten minutes without a boo from the bleachers, that was most encouraging – silence spelt success.

ᕮ

Later, as Leader of the Opposition, and then Prime Minister, I ranged politically far beyond my constituency or my region. I had the major part to play in four national campaigns – 1958, 1962, 1963, 1965. On these occasions my itinerary would be arranged with a punctilious regard for detail that would have done justice to a major military operation. The precise plans for meetings, stops, speeches, broadcasts, consultations, and all else now essential for a national campaign had to be minutely arranged in advance, while provision also had to be made for last-minute emergency alterations.

I could write reams about the working of these plans: the crises and the foul-ups, the successes and the surprises, the pleasures and the frustrations, the jeers and the cheers, and my own worries that I was not doing better as a circus performer and hot gospeller. I had none of the gifts of the demagogue. I was no passionate rouser, nor did I ride easily on waves of popular feeling. I had none of the gifts of the actor who can play on people's emotions and produce the mass frenzy that leads not only to irrational support for good causes, but also for causes evil and dangerous. I have always suspected and distrusted those who could arouse the masses by working on their emotions, turning favour into frenzy, support into hysteria, and normally rational human beings into howling mobs. I have always disliked and feared the demagogue and his relentless quest of power.

I have never forgotten what an inspired madman like Hitler could do to an entire people. I can still hear the fanatic shouts of hysterical approval in response to his demoniac appeals. There is a drama about politics which often invites, indeed at times requires, a histrionic response and an emotional reaction by the politician, especially the politician in a position of leadership. This is legitimate and important. I only wish that I had had more talent as a politician and had been able to make more of an event or of a situation than I may in truth have felt about it. But the exaggerated appeal to fanaticism, to a false and deceptive hope, or to a vision which cannot possibly be realized and can result only in disillusionment – this kind of thing, so common in today's politics, I have always disliked and distrusted, almost as much as I have abhorred the marketing of politicians and policies as though they were detergents or deodorants. These tactics can be effective, no doubt, in producing an electoral triumph. They can also be dangerously effective in cheapening or even destroying democracy which must rest not alone on freedom of choice but even more on a well-informed sense of responsibility.

The dedicated and hard-working people who do the organizing work from headquarters had a fondness for sending me to speak in places where either I or my parents had once lived and where, it was assumed, the Pearson name would be known, and not unfavourably. Since both my father and grandfather had been Methodist ministers when the rule of pastoral change every three or at most every four years was strict, I naturally had a personal or hereditary association with many Ontario cities, towns and villages. We made the most of this, as of course did the local party people who welcomed me, always hoping that I would be there on a Sunday so that I could preach in the 'Pearson' church (on world peace but not on party politics, of course) or, at least, read the lesson. These ties to the past were occasionally stretched to the breaking point.

Once I took part in an election rally at Newtonbrook where I was born, a village then but now a suburb of Toronto. The fact that I left Newtonbrook with my parents at the age of six weeks did not prevent my friends from proudly displaying a banner, 'Welcome, Lester Pearson, Home Town Boy.' A cynical member of my staff once observed that my mother must have been a truly miraculous person to have given birth to me in so many different places! If I was greeted somewhat excessively by the banner in Newtonbrook, the balance was restored a few days later when I arrived at a Holiday Inn in another town where I was to spend the night. It was edifying to read the message in glittering lights on a sign at the entrance: 'Welcome Liberace and our Prime Minister.'

Second billing was also my lot when I was campaigning with a local celebrity on a platform or on main street. This was invariably true if my companion was a sports hero. I once spent an afternoon during the 1963 election with Red Kelly, a great hockey star, who was seeking election, at my urging, in York West. While motoring from one meeting to another, we noticed some youngsters playing ball in a vacant lot. We both thought it would be fun, and might interest our press entourage, if we stopped for a few minutes to watch. We also stopped the game because Red was soon recognized, and was surrounded by excited youngsters clamouring for his autograph. He was somewhat embarrassed that no one took any notice of me, and asked one small boy, happily contemplating Red's signature, 'Don't you want Mr Pearson's too?' The reply put me in my place: 'Mr Pearson, who's he?' Even as Prime Minister, I had to accept that in the autograph market it would take five 'L.B. Pearsons' to get one 'Red Kelly.' My sporting experience helped me to accept this evaluation.

I cannot mention the subject of campaigning with celebrities without referring to the greatest expert of them all, Joey Smallwood, Premier of Newfoundland. To be under his sponsorship, seeking votes in Newfoundland, is an unforgettable experience, and, in the fifties and sixties, a successful one for anybody who left things in his hands, as I did. He was the producer, director, and leading man, and I was the supporting cast, though often manœuvred by the star to the front of the stage. I certainly had no reason to quarrel with this arrangement. It worked out well for our party and for me, and Joey worked as hard, in his own way, to win our federal elections as he did to win his own in his province. He was the kind of politician around whom stories naturally collect; I cannot refrain from adding to the collection.

Joey was a spellbinder and he knew it. So I let him do the talking, not that I could do anything about it anyway. His introduction was usually longer than my speech as he explained what a great man I was and what clowns or villains the opposition were. Above all, how wonderful it was to be a Newfoundlander living in the best place in the world, now better than ever, thanks to Confederation, Liberalism, and Mr Pearson's Liberal government. This kind of introduction always had the desired result of ensuring that I got a good reception for my own brief remarks. I remember especially a television interview in St John's during one campaign. The Premier decided that he would take the place of the interviewer. Joey was certainly qualified to do so, for he was an experienced and skilled radio and television performer. It was the easiest half-hour I ever had before the camera, and may have been my most successful. Mr Smallwood introduced me in a few flattering sentences and then asked the first question. This took ten minutes or so, more statement than question, at the end of which came the query, 'Do you agree with me on my assessment?' My reply had to be 'Yes, indeed,' for it had been a paean of praise for our party, its record, and its leader. Two more statement-questions and my hearty agreement, and the broadcast was over, with a 'Thank you' and 'Benediction.'

Smallwood was totally committed to politics, and knew everything about political tactics – especially, his envious opponents would say, the trickier kind. He used to smile at these accusations and put them down to jealousy. Never did I campaign in Newfoundland without a motorcade from the airport at St John's to the hotel with, naturally, many more cars than there were in the welcome for the Tory leader the week before. Then there would be a drive through the streets in an open car. On one occasion the weather was so atrocious, with cold and sleeting rain pelting down, that I assumed the drive would be called off. My mistake. We started at the appointed time with the leaders in the lead in an open car. Joey insisted that I sit up with him at the back so that everybody could look at me. So far as I could see 'everybody' was 'nobody' because the streets were empty. He assured me, however, that faces were pressed against every pane of glass and that I should wave and smile enthusiastically for their benefit. I felt foolish, and was miserably soaked and cold. At one point our road went through a cemetery and I thought that here, at least, I would be able to get down and crouch from the elements for a few moments. 'No, no,' said Joey, 'stay up there and wave. Some of your most faithful voters are in there.'

Mr Smallwood was not the kind of politician to concede that the Opposition had or deserved any chance of winning. Everybody was, naturally, on the side of progress, happiness, and Liberalism. Our crowds, therefore, were always the biggest, our meetings the most enthusiastic, our victory certain. He refused to concede anything to the Tories. Once in our procession from the airport he called my attention to the masses of people lining the street and to the cheers I was getting. The evidence on both counts was, I thought, far from conclusive, but it was a good welcome. Then our cavalcade had to halt momentarily. 'Look at them,' Joey exulted, 'they're all on your side. Everyone in St John's is. Everyone.' I called his attention to the scowling hostile face of a man on the curb, who seemed to be shaking his fist at us. 'Not everybody,' I demurred, 'look at that chap.' He did, but was not abashed. 'Well, we'll put him down as doubtful.' That was as far as he would go.

If I have concentrated on Newfoundland and Smallwood it is only because he was an especially colourful campaign character, as well as a politician who did much for the province and the people that he loved and served. Campaigning in other provinces brought further stories: the little boy who greeted me at one hotel with a sign 'I like Mike,' but a little uncertain about his instructions and even more about his letters, kept shouting 'I like milk'; and the old lady who once greeted me from the crowd, 'God bless you, John Diefenbaker.'

A national election campaign may have its lighter moments but it is a terrific test of stamina and endurance – physical, mental, and even moral. There were times when I felt that a D-Day landing against even the most murderous fire would be preferable. For eight weeks, day after day, night after night, meeting after meeting, parade after parade, visit after visit, the ordeal continues. The pressures increase, and your strength decreases until you begin to wonder whether you can see it through, counting the days, even the hours, with anticipatory longing until polling day will bring a blessed ending – a hoped-for victory, but even if defeat, release.

SOVEREIGNTY
IS NOT ENOUGH

The pendulum of historical judgment on events and conditions, on their nature and causes, customarily swings from one conclusion to the extreme opposite. The first judgment is often determined as much by immediate emotion as by evidence, or is based on official explanations perhaps motivated by immediate circumstance. Subsequently, the inevitable swing to revision takes place, leading to an entirely different conclusion by ignoring factors and feelings dominant at the time, which were often valid reasons for what took place and are certainly essential to an understanding of the period.

This is true of what we now know as the Cold War. The dangers to the peace and security of the West from Soviet aggressive and threatening policies, and the fears resulting therefrom, were, in my view, the main sources of the hostile confrontations during the postwar period and of the steps taken to organize collective action within and outside the United Nations for protection. Twenty-five years later, since the world is still intact and the forces we feared have acquired an aura of respectability and, some hope, 'settled down,' the revisionists can go to work to prove that there never was any threat to peace from the other side of the Iron Curtain, that the Kremlin was seeking only security by defensive measures, and that Stalin wished only for peaceful co-existence. It was the Pentagon, so it goes, in the interests of United States imperialism, which exaggerated, if it did not manufacture, the menace to peace from Communist imperialism. Washington kept the Cold War hot for its own power purposes. Canada and other western countries, therefore, were hoodwinked into seeking 'collective security' under United States leadership which was as unnecessary as it was unwise. We should have adopted the cautious attitude of Mac-kenzie King in the twenties and thirties, this time toward Washington, and should have remained uncommitted to either side in Cold War initiatives.

As one who went through these years in a position of some author-ity, I find this kind of criticism, or rationalization, if you will, singu-larly unimpressive. We did not accept United States Cold War analyses or tactics without examination and, when necessary, criticism. The idea that we were brainwashed by the Pentagon is nonsense. We recog-nized that the USSR had legitimate fears for its security and that certain United States statements and actions increased those fears. But the fact, the indisputable fact, remains that the main and very real threat to world peace during the first years of Cold War was the armed might, the aggressive ideology, and the totalitarian despotism of the Com-munist empire of the USSR and its satellite states under the iron hand of one of the most ruthless tyrants of all time. To ignore this danger, or to refuse to accept any commitments for collective action to meet it, while playing our part in positive action in the United Nations or else-where to bring about a better state of affairs, would have been demon-strably wrong and perilously short-sighted.

I do not wish to give the impression that in the altered conditions of today we can, or should, attempt to repeat certain initiatives taken – as I think quite successfully – in the decade after World War II. Circum-stances that may have occasionally called for Canadian interventions then do not exist today, even though there are certain conditions and principles that are unchanging.

On 13 January 1947 Mr St Laurent had given the Gray Lecture at the University of Toronto. In it he presented certain general principles and objectives which he thought, as I did when I succeeded him in the Department of External Affairs, were basic in the formulation and conduct of Canada's foreign policies. His list was not total. It took for granted one or two obvious purposes, such as protection of the national interest, the promotion of the greatest possible freedom in international trade, and recognition of the limitations and compulsions of geography. A major omission also was the need to ensure our survival as a sepa-rate state against powerful, if friendly, social and economic pressures from our American neighbour. This omission, no doubt, was oc-casioned by the fact that we were not as conscious of any threat from these pressures in 1947 as we became later. We had, I think, more pride in our country and a greater faith in its future. We were more self-confident, less fretful than later, when conditions changed, nationally and internationally.

What Mr St Laurent said in this lecture, however, remained a guide to me in the direction of Canada's foreign policies during the years when I was the Minister for External Affairs. For this reason I include here a few paragraphs from his speech:

1 *National Unity*
... our external policy shall not destroy our unity. No policy can be regarded as wise which divides the people whose efforts and resources must put it into effect. This consideration applies not only to the two main cultural groups in our country. It applies equally to sectionalism of any kind. We dare not fashion a policy which is based on the particular interests of any economic group, of any class or of any section in this country. Our history has shown this to be a consideration in our external policy of which we, more even than others, must be perpetually conscious. The role of this country in world affairs will prosper only as we maintain this principle, for a disunited Canada will be a powerless one.

2 *Political Liberty*
We believe that the greatest safeguard against the aggressive policies of any government is the freely expressed judgment of its own people. This does not mean that we have ever sought to interfere in the affairs of others, or to meddle in situations which were obviously outside our interest or beyond our control. It does mean, however, that we have consistently sought and found our friends amongst those of like political traditions. It means equally that we have realized that a threat to the liberty of western Europe. where our political ideas were nurtured, was a threat to our own way of life.

3 *The Rule of Law in National and International Affairs*
... respect for the rule of law has become an integral part of our external and of our domestic policy ...
... the freedom of nations depends upon the rule of law amongst states.

4 *The Values of a Christian Civilization*
No foreign policy is consistent nor coherent over a period of years unless it is based upon some conception of human values.

5 *The Acceptance of International Responsibility in Keeping with our Conception of our Role in World Affairs*
The growth in this country of a sense of political responsibility on an international scale has perhaps been less rapid than some of us would like ... If there is one conclusion that our common experience has led us to accept it is that security for this country lies in the development of a firm structure of international organization.

Mr St Laurent then went on to illustrate the practical application of these principles to certain aspects of our external relations, one or two of which seem less relevant now than they were in 1947:

1 The Commonwealth
... our relations with the British Commonwealth ... are ... a basic consideration in the external policy of this country.

We seek to preserve it as an instrument through which we, with others who share our objectives, can co-operate for our common good in peace as in war. On the other hand, we should continue to resist ... efforts to reduce to formal terms or specific commitments this association ... [and] oppose developments in our Commonwealth relations which might be inconsistent with our desire to participate fully in the task of building an effective international organization on a wider scale.

2 The United States
The relationship between a great and powerful nation and its smaller neighbour, at best is far from simple. It calls for constant and imaginative attention on both sides.

... our policy in regard to the United States has come with the passage of years to have two main characteristics. On the one hand, we have sought by negotiation, by arbitration, by compromise, to settle upon the basis of mutual satisfaction the problems that have arisen between us ... The other aspect of our relations with the United States is our readiness to accept our responsibility as a North American nation in enterprises which are for the welfare of this continent. In support of this assertion, there is a long and creditable record of joint activity. In making it, however, I must add that it has never been the opinion of any considerable number of people in Canada that this continent could live unto itself. We have seen our own interests in the wider context of the Western World. We have realized also that regionalism of any kind would not provide the answer to problems of world security. But we know that peoples who live side by side on the same continent cannot disregard each other's interests, and we have always been willing to consider the possibility of common action for constructive ends.

3 France
We have never forgotten that France is one of the fountainheads of our cultural life. We realize that she forms an integral part of the framework of our international life ... our objects in world affairs are similar. We in this country have always believed in the greatness of France, even at times when her future seemed most obscure ... We are aware of the heavy burden which invasion twice in a generation has laid upon France. We shall support her recovery not merely out of sympathy, but because we know that her integrity is a matter of great consequence to us.

4 International Organizations

No society of nations can prosper if it does not have the support of those
who hold the major share of the world's military and economic power. There
is little point in a country of our stature recommending international action,
if those who must carry the major burden of whatever action is taken are not
in sympathy. We know, however, that the development of international organizations on a broad scale is of the very greatest importance to us, and we
have been willing to play our role when it was apparent that significant and
effective action was contemplated.

It seems to me axiomatic, therefore, that we should give our support to
every international organization which contributes to the economic and
political stability of the world.

As Mr St Laurent's Deputy Minister and a civil servant, I had merely
to carry out government foreign policies, not to determine them except
in so far as any advice I gave might influence or impress the Minister
and the government. I was careful not to stray beyond the policies
adopted by the government in any representational or presentational
duties I was asked to perform at the UN and elsewhere, acting only
under instructions from my political masters. As Minister, however,
I had the direct responsibility for translating these principles into
policies, and I could also introduce and advocate policy proposals before the Cabinet. Here I was fortunate not only in the close relationship and identity of views which I had with the new Prime Minister
but also in international situations which provided opportunities for
Canada to play a positive and useful role in postwar developments.
Under Mr King my position would have been different. Indeed, before
his retirement Mr King had already indicated, at least to his diary, an
uneasiness over the tendency of Mr St Laurent (then Minister for
External Affairs) to take so much responsibility for the government
in the building of the new international structure at the United Nations,
and also in such matters as India's continuing membership in the Commonwealth as a republic. This was none of our business, thought
Mr King.

By the time I became Minister, however, notwithstanding Mr King's
private worries, Canada's role in foreign affairs, in contrast with that
of the thirties, had become active and innovative. This was greatly
assisted, indeed it was made possible, by the fact that Canadian public
opinion had come to realize that since Canada could not escape the effects of international storms by burying her head in the sand, she
should play a part in trying to prevent the storms by accepting international commitments for that purpose. This, however, could now be

done without imposing those strains on national unity that always, and rightly, preoccupied Mr King.

Indeed, the basic reason behind the cautious, non-committal policy of prewar Canadian governments lay in the profound differences of opinion on European affairs held by important sections of our countrymen. The doctrine of our foreign policy before 1939 (which we now reversed) – that of no commitments and a reluctance even to consult with other nations on the major issues which could threaten the peace – was a corollary of the first and guiding principle in the formulation of all Canadian policy – the maintenance of the unity of Canada as a nation. After 1945 this unity was not threatened but strengthened by our external activity. International commitments were also made easier to accept because there was a very general and valid fear of an aggressive Soviet Communist imperialism which threatened our basic values and which, it was thought, could be best countered and combatted by collective international action. We were now prepared to play our part in this action and were supported by public opinion in doing so.

Domestic critics have since complained that during these years we were at times guilty not only of exaggerating our influence and our rhetoric, of substituting posture for policy, but also, and this is more important, of becoming too closely identified with United States foreign policies and tactics. They added that we were more 'powder monkey' than 'peace maker' and had reduced our usefulness at the UN by tying ourselves to limited collective and continental defence arrangements dominated by the United States. Some critics, illogically, assailed us with the two-fold criticism that we short-circuited the UN by a too-close association with the United States in coalitions such as NATO, and at the same time were over-zealous to take on UN chores and obligations. They argued that we tried too often to play the part of honest and universal broker, compromiser, interpreter, bridge-builder, peacekeeper, or what you will, and that we had too many illusions about our importance as a 'helpful fixer.'

I had no illusions that the circumstances making an activist policy the right policy would remain unchanged. Some of the responsibilities of our postwar situation were temporary; but the opportunities were exceptional. The war which had weakened many other countries, and destroyed some, had left Canada economically strong and physically intact. It was this temporary situation, and our utilization of it, that made our international policies and actions more forthright than they would otherwise have been. This was unquestionably the proper role for Canada to play at that time. I have many times pointed out that we can exaggerate our influence and over-play our participation in international affairs. This does not require us, however, to depreciate our responsibilities.

Finally, there were those who complained that our foreign policy was too exclusively concentrated on North America and Europe, proceeding in the fixed and traditional channels; our policies were not adequately concerned with new, emerging areas of the world, with Asia and the Pacific, with Latin America and Africa. I do not believe this criticism of Euro-centricity, as it has been called, is justified. It is true that our political and economic growth, as we moved from dependent colony to independent confederation, had taught us to look across to Europe more often and more closely than to other parts of the world. Europe was not only the cultural homeland of most Canadians, it was the battlefield on which we first became nationally conscious and proud of our Canadian identity. This understandable concentration in the fifties, however, on the historic areas of Canadian interest and involvement, did not mean that we were unaware of the shiftings in world currents. It was clear that our deep and continuing concern with North America and Europe would have to be shared with an increasing interest in other parts of the world which were becoming more important not only for Canada but for the future of humanity. Later there were new problems of concern: race relations, the population explosion, environmental dangers, and many others. This was no time for a country's foreign policy to get stuck in conventional grooves.

Indeed, reconsideration first began when the violence of the Cold War had blown away so many of our earlier hopes and illusions. It was not long, for example, before it became clear that the UN, through the Security Council, could not guarantee the peace and security given priority in the Charter. Collective security could not, in fact, be organized on a basis of world-wide agreement. We knew that this harsh fact must lead to changes in our own policies, as it must in the development and authority of the United Nations. The Assembly clearly would have to take on new responsibilities for political security once the Security Council became ineffective. Regional or limited associations for collective defence and security such as NATO, consistent with the UN Charter, might have to be organized.

Canadian foreign policy, in short, had to be flexible in operation, within the limits imposed upon us by certain fixed factors such as geography, the imperative to maintain national unity, the nature of our federal system, our dependence on foreign trade. If flexibility in the conduct of foreign policy is essential for Canada, it is unwise, then, to lay down dogmatic priorities and postulates. This is especially true at a time of rapid and cataclysmic change, of the sudden emergence of international problems not even conceivable ten years before. In contemporary foreign policy, more than in most things, today's wisdom can quickly become tomorrow's folly.

ॐ

The postwar world was one of changing power relationships in which Europe was relatively much weaker and Canada much stronger than in earlier years. The most important change, however, was in the position of the United States, now the Western super-power and thus inevitably the leader of the free world at a time when we had good cause to think that this freedom was threatened. Britain and France had become lesser Great Powers, not too far above Canada in strength and resources. Britain, though remaining the heart of a new Commonwealth, was certainly no longer in a position to commit us by her decisions in vital matters of war or peace, as in 1914 and again in 1939. This made our relations with Britain easier, if less important. It was now the United States that had that power, a hard fact which brought us anxiety as well as assurance.

This was a dangerous and explosive decade, and certainly not a time for us to withdraw into ourselves even had we wished to. The danger of aggression from Communist imperialism, centred in Moscow with what seemed overwhelming military strength, together with the realization that, if peace was indivisible, war would be universally destructive, made it right and essential for a country in Canada's position to play this active international role at this point in its own and the world's history. It would have been unwise and perilous – and this remains true today – for Canada to minimize the importance of foreign affairs and diplomatic policy, and the value of a foreign service to make policy effective.

I am certain that, for Canada, isolation can never be a principle of policy, any more than can imperialist expansion. Everything that happens in the world affects us, and to a degree greater than most countries. Consequently, it is always foolish to assume that we can safely leave global matters of war and peace to the Great Powers while we modestly concentrate our energies on protecting our sovereignty and increasing our gross national product. Economic growth as a first objective of foreign policy is an uncertain trumpet sound to Canadians, scarcely stirring the blood or inspiring hope for a better country and a more secure world. Indeed, if every country gave this priority in its foreign relations, very little progress would be made toward the solution of those international problems which are essential for survival itself. If we withdraw into a foreign policy of narrow nationalism with economic growth as its main objective, Canada's voice might be heard but it would not impress.

To rely on 'sovereignty' for protection of our interests is more or less meaningless, certainly insufficient, in the conditions of today. In the last analysis, sovereignty is no protection unless you have the force and the will to back up your insistence on its recognition. Far more important is to use your sovereignty to protect and advance your own legitimate interests by establishing relations of friendship, good-will, and agreement with other countries so that insistence on the use of force will not be required. The protection of its interests and the promotion of its aims and objectives are, of course, a first concern and duty of any state. But the affirmation of sovereignty, though at times necessary, gives no real security.

In short, 'participatory internationalism' to maintain and strengthen world peace was a principal objective of Canada's national policy. We always asked ourselves not only 'What kind of a Canada do we want?' but 'What kind of a world do we want?' This world view was consistent with a proper regard for our own interests. We did not confuse short-term opportunities with long-run realities or allow our international preoccupations to obscure domestic concerns.

There was, however, a further reason for the broad and active internationalism of our foreign policy in those years. It helped us to escape the dangers of a too exclusively continental relationship with our neighbour without forfeiting the political and economic advantages of that inevitable and vitally important association. It permitted us also to establish a balance between our continental and our wider British Commonwealth, French, and other international connections. An axiom of Canadian external policy in prewar days had been to avoid situations where our Commonwealth and North American relationships came into conflict. This harmony could most effectively be achieved by participation with the United States in larger international groupings which would include our two mother countries, Britain and France. We hoped that the UN, on the world front, would be one of these, for political, social, and economic questions. Later on, NATO became a more effective, if more restricted, international political agency. But, in one form or another, for Canada, there was always security in numbers. We did not want to be alone with our close friend and neighbour. As a debutante on the world stage we were worried, not about rape, but seduction.

The Canadian people, nevertheless, even in those days of apprehended danger and need for international action to meet it, expected us to keep our specific international commitments and involvements within the limits of our resources. They also expected us to give special consideration to those questions having a direct interest and importance for us, especially those which arose out of our continental, Atlantic, and Commonwealth relationships. This we tried to do.

☞

As Secretary of State for External Affairs I adopted the attitude that the Canadian people should be kept fully informed of what was being done, subject to genuine but not contrived requirements of security. I welcomed and encouraged debates on international affairs in the House of Commons and the greatest possible use of its Committee on External Affairs, not merely for the examination of the administration and expenditures of the department (always of interest to an Opposition) but for a thorough exchange of views on Canadian foreign policies. In this way, I hoped that we might banish the legend that international affairs and diplomatic activities were so sensitive and specialized that they must be restricted to the enlightened few skilled in that art and practice and should be kept outside the purview of Parliament or the public at large.

Unfortunately, debates on foreign policy in Parliament more often than not were lifeless and dull. Indeed, they were not debates so much as a series of lectures, with the Minister opening and closing the programme. On these occasions the House of Commons was usually reduced to thirty or forty members, many of them transparently bored, while the members of the Press Gallery were usually conspicuous by their almost total absence.

A principal reason for this general indifference to international affairs was no doubt the non-controversial nature of so much of our foreign policy in those early postwar years. Usually there was a fundamental and general agreement with our broad lines of policy. It is hard to have a vigorous debate before a full and concerned House, without the cut and thrust of controversy. When there were strongly held and opposing views, as in Canada's policy at the United Nations over Suez in 1956, there was no lack of parliamentary interest or eloquence. Nevertheless, I used these parliamentary occasions to give the House all possible information on developments in Canadian foreign policies. I frequently appeared before the House Committee on External Affairs for the same purpose and, to reach a wider audience, made many speeches throughout the country.

While encouraging discussion based on knowledge and well-informed opinion, I often grew impatient with critics, the press, and other ostensible experts who argued that not only should the principles and broad lines of foreign policy be subject to the most searching debate and scrutiny before becoming accepted national policies, but that details of what was in hand at every stage of Cabinet or international discussions should be made public as they occurred. To me, diplomacy meant giving to the public full information on the principles determining our foreign policies and on the practices followed in applying those principles. Open diplomacy also meant the publication of agreements made or of commitments undertaken; but it did not mean the issue of a statement every day on the progress of negotiations, or on the Canadian position taken on every detail of negotiation. This would make give-and-take bargaining and reasonable compromise impossible. More often than not headline diplomacy, which is frequently political blackmail rather than diplomacy, must be avoided if agreement is intended.

From my considerable experience with international, federal-provincial, and intra-governmental negotiations, I have learned that quiet diplomacy, now so often disparaged, may have to be abandoned in exceptional circumstances and be replaced by political pressure together with complete publicity and frank disclosure. This exceptional weapon, however, is an admission of the failure of diplomacy. It is a recourse to normally undesirable public and political weapons to defend and to advance your case.

I agree with what Walter Lippman wrote in his column on 26 March 1950:

When statesmen become actors they not only stick to their parts in the show but, it may be added, they are stuck with their parts. They can be more and more of whatever they have been. But on pain of unpopularity they cannot appear to be a little bit less.

Thus by the hoop-la system of diplomacy – which some say is so wonderfully enlightening – every difficult issue, not infrequently a comparatively easy issue, is likely to become insoluble as each actor-statesman rises to such peaks of public righteousness that in public he cannot possibly descend again into common sense.

Then, there is no hope except to turn off the lights, to shut down the microphones, to take away the stage props, to wash off the make-up, to disperse the crowds and to let a few men absent themselves from publicity a while.

I would not like to leave the impression that during these years our performance on the international stage was above criticism. In the pursuit of our policies from 1945 to 1957 many of our actions and our words, especially at the United Nations, may have seemed to be more idealistic than practical. I admit that occasionally we succumbed to a tendency to sermonize on the subject of peace and international co-operation. While accepting the need to keep our feet on the ground while gazing at the stars, I felt it necessary to keep our eyes on the ulti-mate objective if we were to reach it, step by step. It was not a waste of time to talk about and advocate world peace and world federation or, on a less exalted level, an Atlantic Community or a permanent United Na-tions Peace Force – even when existing circumstances seemed to make a mockery of such idealism. I knew that peace was a policy as well as a prayer. I knew also that, even if politics was the art of the possible, the political arts could and should be practised without the loss of vision or idealism. I was not so naïve as to think that we could decisively, or even importantly, influence the policies of the Great Powers, but I hoped we could influence the environment in which they were pursued. My friend, Dean Acheson, wrote in his preface to my *The Four Faces of Peace* (American edition): 'Years ago Mr Pearson remarked that to be a Foreign Minister of a middle-sized nation put one in an enviable posi-tion. One was listened to and one's imagination had scope to fly, though not soar, before being brought back to earth by the weight of respon-sibility.' Perhaps I had, during my years as Secretary of State for Ex-ternal Affairs, unusual opportunities to fly, and even soar. It was that kind of time in Canada's history. But it is equally true that I was as conscious as any Minister of a Great Power of the weight of responsi-bility. True, our decisions might not have similar consequences, for good or ill, as those of the representative of a country with world in-terests and responsibilities. But we had always to keep in mind the ef-fect on our own country, not only of what we said and did, but also of what the powerful ones were doing. We tried to ensure that this effect was not harmful or, if it threatened to be so, to insulate ourselves from it, so far as that was possible. Very often it was not.

These were the views I held and the spirit in which I tried to carry out my duties as Minister for External Affairs. Canada's true national interests were in no way sacrificed to, or prejudiced by, our international activities. On the contrary, these interests were strengthened. Indeed, in few countries is there less likely to be a conflict between national interest and international policy, since in few are the requirements of interdependence so closely related to the maintenance of independence. I believe that this role, played not to spread ourselves or to gain prestige, but to discharge our proper international responsibilities, strengthened our feeling of national pride. This, in turn, contributed to national unity and to a deeper sense of national identity. We had come of age. The voice of Canada was now being heard and it was listened to seriously and with respect during these years.

ATLANTIC VISION

On Monday, 4 April 1949 we met in Washington to sign the North Atlantic Treaty – a solemn occasion in keeping with its importance. The national representatives considered, rightly, that a milestone had been reached in the search for security by collective action and through the acceptance of collective obligations and responsibilities. This was the culmination of many months of preparation. In that work Canada had played an important part, notably by emphasizing the importance of including in the treaty something which would underline the non-military character and purposes of what some others regarded as purely a military alliance. Thus we signed the North Atlantic Treaty on that pleasant spring day in Washington while the band of the US Marines played soft music, including two selections from *Porgy and Bess*: 'I got plenty of nothing' and 'It ain't necessarily so.'

I wish to make my position clear as I discuss the origins and development of the North Atlantic Alliance, which was, in effect, a recognition of the failure of the United Nations – or to be more precise, of the permanent members of its Security Council – to make effective the security provisions of the Charter. I never found anything inconsistent between my support for the United Nations and my strong belief in the progressive development of the North Atlantic countries into an international community with the maximum unity possible among them in political, economic, and defence affairs. I judged that this would be the best way to ensure our own security and prosperity, pending action on a larger scale in and through the United Nations. At the beginning of

the San Francisco Conference in April 1945 I had hoped that a United
Nations might be effective for this purpose. The realization soon came,
however, that any such hope was premature, as a deep gap opened
between the Western and the Communist worlds in methods and objectives. While Ambassador in Washington, I had reported to Ottawa
on reaction in the United States to Winston Churchill's Fulton, Mis-
souri, speech of 5 March 1946 in which he declared that an Iron Curtain had descended across Europe. To this report I added one or two of
my own early observations on Soviet policy:

'It may well be that Soviet policy is fundamentally defensive; an
effort to exploit a fluid postwar situation for all it is worth in the interest of their own domestic security; of squeezing the last ounce of
advantage out of their own relatively strong position. The Soviet
authorities may feel that they can now take with impunity steps which
would provoke a war if made ten years from now when an international
pattern has been re-established. They expect to encounter diplomatic
resistance and incur resentment; but nothing more, unless they go
beyond a line which has not yet been fixed and the boundaries of which
they hope themselves to be largely instrumental in determining. Once
determined, however, they will, as realists, not seek to go beyond it.
The risk would be too great.

'If this is, in fact, the motive of Russian policy, that policy becomes
understandable. Even the ill-will which it arouses outside Russia can be
used by the Russian rulers to strengthen their position at home. They
can and do complain of that ill-will as unwarranted and unfair and a
proof of the implacable hostility of the capitalist powers towards the
workers' and peasants' state; necessitating the maintenance of a huge
army, and justifying the sacrifices which this entails.

'There is, in my mind, only one effective reply to this Russian policy.
A Big Three Conference should be held where all the cards are placed
on the table; where all the issues will be faced and a genuine effort
made to resolve them. No such conference has yet been held, and it is
long overdue. Potsdam and Moscow were hasty, limited, and almost
half-hearted attempts, compared with what is really required. Such a
conference might have to remain in session for months, but should be
prepared to do so. The Foreign Ministers must be willing to take whatever time and make whatever efforts are required to clear away suspicions and differences and to bring about a definite understanding of
each other's desires and designs.

'If no real success is achieved at such a conference, then the United

States and the United Kingdom should convert the United Nations into a really effective agent to preserve the peace and prevent aggression. This means revising it radically. If the Russians veto such a revision, agreed on by others, a new organization must be created which, as the guardian of the peace of all nations, and not merely the English-speaking ones, can function without the Russians and, as a last resort, against them.

'All this is far removed from the more limited, but, I think, far less effective proposals of Mr Churchill for an English-speaking association. I am convinced, however, that this broader basis for a solution of our present difficulties would have a far better chance of acceptance in this country, and would provide a far stronger foundation for any effective organization of peace.'

There was, of course, no effective Western response to Soviet policy in these early years; it appeared that Moscow's advance would not stop as she brought under her control hundreds of thousands of square miles of territory in Eastern and Central Europe and more than 90 millions of people. There were Soviet-inspired crises in Berlin. Iran and Turkey were threatened, there was civil war in Greece, and, initially at least, a Soviet-dominated Communist régime in Yugoslavia. Soviet pressure on Norway was particularly disturbing, and political confusion, economic disruption, and a general postwar weariness in France and Italy threatened to bring about in these countries Soviet-supported communist takeovers. There was a general military impotence in the Western European countries and rapid demobilization in the United States, whereas the Soviet divisions seemed war-ready. Thus it is not surprising that there arose a very real fear of new aggressive moves by the Soviet Union westward across Europe to the Atlantic, moves directed by Stalin whose motives and attitudes were to be unveiled for us some years later by his successor, Nikita Khrushchev.

The North Atlantic Alliance was born of this fear, a fear intensified by the failure of every effort to bring about a more friendly and co-operative relationship with Moscow, both at the United Nations and in the Four Power machinery set up after the war to plan the peace settlement. That fear was brought to a head by the brutal takeover of Czechoslovakia in February and March 1948, and all that this seemed to portend.

Were we to sit and do nothing? Some of us had concluded that any attempt at wholesale revision of the UN Charter, and particularly of the veto power in the Security Council, would probably have served only to worsen the international situation by driving the USSR out of the UN and into complete isolation. We must work to strengthen the United Nations as our sole world organization but at the same time build a more limited but firmer structure for collective security, with those countries sharing our views. The North Atlantic seemed the obvious area for such an attempt. As early as 13 May 1946, when still Ambassador at Washington, I had pointed out in a lecture at Princeton University that membership in the United Nations need not impede this: 'We do not expect our membership in the UN to prevent our working out special arrangements with powers who wish to co-operate with us and which are consistent with our obligations under the Charter.'

On 4 July 1947 Mr St Laurent, with greater authority, told the House of Commons that there was room in the UN for closer associations for collective security which need not be 'inconsistent at all with the ideals of the world organization.' A few weeks later, on 13 August, Escott Reid, my second-in-command in the Department where I now was Deputy Minister, with the knowledge and approval of Mr St Laurent and myself, spoke to the Canadian Institute of Public Affairs at Lake Couchiching: 'Nothing in the Charter precludes the existence of regional political arrangements or agencies provided that they are consistent with the purposes and principles of the United Nations and these regional agencies are entitled to take measures of collective self-defence against armed attack until the Security Council has acted. The world is now so small that the whole of the Western world is in itself a mere region. If the peoples of the Western world want an international security organization with teeth, even though the Soviet Union is at present unwilling to be a member of such an organization, they do not need to amend the United Nations Charter in order to create such an organization.' They could do so, he said (consistent with the UN Charter), by creating 'a regional security organization' in which 'each member state could accept a binding obligation to pool the whole of its economic and military resources with those of the other members if any power should be found to have committed aggression against any one of its members.' The process of sounding out parliamentary and popular opinion on a North Atlantic security organization was under way – as is proper, indeed essential, in a democratic country – before policy is determined.

Before he retired from office Mr King was aware of these developments. He did not try to restrain Mr St Laurent in the expression of his views on collective security which, however, he felt were too greatly influenced by the department, more particularly by myself. While the Prime Minister favoured, in principle, the idea of a North Atlantic coalition, he thought that Canada should keep in the background, leaving the promotion and development of the idea to the Americans and the British, with Canadian support when necessary. He did not, however, express any disapproval, though he may have felt some uneasiness, at the important initiative taken by Mr St Laurent at the UN Assembly on 18 September 1947 in a speech which many have come to consider marked the beginning of the North Atlantic Alliance. I was with my Minister in New York at the time and discussed with him the ideas for this speech. I then spent most of the night in my hotel room writing a draft, the key paragraph of which read:

Nations, in their search for peace and co-operation, will not, and can not, accept indefinitely an unaltered council which was set up to ensure their security and which, so many feel, has become frozen in futility and divided by dissension. If forced, they may seek greater safety in an association of democratic and peace-loving states willing to accept more specific international obligations in return for a greater measure of national security. Such associations, it has already been pointed out, if consistent with the principles and purpose of the Charter, can be formed within the United Nations. It is to be hoped that such a development will not be necessary. If it is necessary, it will be most undesirable. If, however, it is made necessary, it will have to take place. Let us not forget that the provisions of the Charter are a floor *under*, rather than a ceiling *over*, the responsibilities of member states.

Those words gripped the attention of the world assembly, especially as the man who uttered them and the country he represented commanded respect. At once we were asked by many other delegations, especially by the British and American, to elaborate on them.

We did. We emphasized that what we had in mind was not a revision of the procedures of the Security Council, with its vetoes, but a more limited, collective security arrangement under Article 51 of the Charter, which affirmed 'the inherent right of individual or collective self-defence' of the United Nations members against armed attack. This arrangement, while not part of the UN structure, would be consistent with its principles.

During 1948 we became actively involved in diplomatic negotiations, especially with Washington and London, for an Atlantic security pact. These negotiations began on 10 March, when the British High Commissioner, Sir Alexander Clutterbuck (a man whose manner and appearance, almost a caricature of a British official, belied a very shrewd and sensible mind and a warm and kindly nature), delivered a 'top secret' message to Mr King from Prime Minister Attlee, urging secret talks 'without delay' between Canada, Britain, and the United States on the establishment of 'an Atlantic Security System.' Alarmed especially by increased Russian pressure on Norway, Attlee warned that 'failure to act now may mean a repetition of our experience with Hitler.' As I felt exactly the same way, I was delighted when Mr King at once accepted the Attlee proposal for confidential talks and assured the British High Commissioner of Canadian co-operation under 'the active leadership of the United Kingdom and the United States.'

I was the more pleased with this quick and positive response because earlier, on 14 January, when Mr Attlee appealed to our Prime Minister for Canadian support for a European coalition led by Britain against the 'Communist peril,' Mr King's reaction was much less positive. Some of his old fears were aroused by a sentence in Attlee's message: 'We should organize the ethical and spiritual forces of Western Europe backed by the power and resources of the Commonwealth and the Americas.' Anything even vaguely suggesting Commonwealth centralization was anathema to Mr King although, as I noted in a letter to Norman Robertson, our High Commissioner in London, on 29 January 1948: 'In general, I should say that his anxiety about Commonwealth commitments has been overshadowed by his anxiety over United Nations and United States commitments. In fact, the latter anxiety has become so strong, and with some reason, that he is beginning to counsel close contact with the United Kingdom, notably at Lake Success [the temporary headquarters of the UN, just outside New York], to make sure that we are not pushed too far by the United States. This, I have always been sure, was an inevitable development, but it has not proceeded to a point where the old fears do not occasionally emerge, even against the background of the newer and greater ones.'

A week after we received that first Attlee message, Foreign Secretary Ernest Bevin told the British House of Commons that Soviet hostility to the European Recovery Programme (the Marshall Plan) and its obstruction of a German settlement had convinced the British government to go ahead with plans for closer political and economic unity of the European countries and for their collective defence against aggression. Communist seizure of power in Czechoslovakia gave urgency to these plans. Indeed, on 1 March Mr Bevin was reported to have told the French Ambassador in London that Western Europe had about four weeks to put its house in order. As a result, the Treaty of Brussels was signed on 17 March 1948 by the United Kingdom, France, and the

Benelux countries. This was an important stage in the process of building collective security, and Mr King was quick to give it his full support. He stated in the House of Commons the day the treaty was signed:

... This pact is far more than an alliance of the old kind. It is a partial realization of the idea of collective security by an arrangement made under the Charter of the United Nations. As such it is a step towards peace, which may well be followed by other similar steps until there is built up an association of all free states which are willing to accept responsibilities of mutual assistance to prevent aggression and preserve peace.

May I read, in this connection, two articles of the Western Union agreement:

'Article III. The high contracting parties will make every effort in common to lead their people towards a better understanding of the principles which form the basis of their common civilization and to promote cultural exchanges by conventions between themselves or otherwise.

'Article IV. If any high contracting party should be the object of an armed attack in Europe, the other high contracting parties will in accordance with the provisions of Article 51 of the Charter, afford the party so attacked all the military and other aid and assistance in their power.'

Hon. members will, I am sure, also welcome the significant statement made to the Congress of the United States at noon today by President Truman in which, referring to the Brussels agreement which had just been signed, he spoke of the determination of the United States to help those five Western European nations to protect themselves.

The Canadian government has been closely following recent developments in the international sphere. The peoples of all free countries may be assured that Canada will play her full part in every movement to give substance to the conception of an effective system of collective security by the development of regional pacts under the Charter of the United Nations.

In the Department of External Affairs, we were ready for the talks proposed by the British Prime Minister on 10 March, having done a good deal of thinking about, and even some preliminary drafting of, an Atlantic security pact. Recent developments gave a sense of immediacy to our work, and we confined the consultations in Ottawa to a very small group. This no doubt allowed us to play a reasonably effective role in the negotiations. The price, however, of avoiding interdepartmental consultation and committees was that other departments of our government were never completely convinced of the treaty's value, especially its non-military aspects.

The talks, at this stage only between the United States, Britain, and Canada, began on the official level in Washington on 22 March. It was the commencement of a period of most intense and rewarding diploma-

tic activity. I attended the first meetings which were to be purely ex-
ploratory: should there be a separate Atlantic security pact for our
three countries, to which the European Atlantic powers could accede,
or should the United States and Canada become part of Western Union
through accession to the Brussels Pact? I preferred a modification of
the first – a three-power agreement on certain principles which, if acceptable to the other Atlantic countries, could be embodied in a treaty
which all would negotiate and sign. At the beginning, however, the
Americans seemed to favour an extension of the Brussels Pact to other
countries, including Italy, the United States, and Canada, or a simple
unilateral declaration that an attack on any Western European country
would be considered by the Americans as an attack on the United
States.

From the very first meeting we made our view clear that any pact,
however negotiated, should be broader and deeper than a military alliance. To quote Mr St Laurent in the House of Commons on 28 April
1948: 'Its purpose like that of "western union," would not be merely
negative; it would create a dynamic counter-attraction to communism –
the dynamic counter-attraction of a free, prosperous and progressive
society as opposed to the totalitarian and reactionary society of the
communist world.' It would set forth the principles of Western society
which we were trying not only to defend but to make the basis of an
eventually united world, and not simply make us part of an American
war machine against the Russians. The only possibility – and this remains true – of the North Atlantic Alliance enduring was to build it on
something more than just military co-operation. An alliance founded on
the fear of aggression and on the need to take defensive action against
aggression will disappear when the fear is removed. If our alliance was
to endure, it had to have political, social, and economic foundations –
if we could work these out. And by being idealists we were far more
realistic than those who opposed us on these questions.

When I returned to Ottawa after the first sessions, leaving our able
and experienced Ambassador, Hume Wrong, to represent Canada, I
found Mr King pleased at the course events were taking (I knew of Mr
St Laurent's reactions from telephone conversations), especially in our
advocacy of provisions for non-military co-operation in any Atlantic
pact. Encouraged, at Mr St Laurent's suggestion I presented to the
Prime Minister on 29 March a memorandum on a 'Security Pact for
the North Atlantic area.' This included the provisional agreement
reached by the officials in our Washington talks, and my own comments on that agreement. I pointed out that this agreement, naturally,

did not commit the three governments in any way, although, as things worked out, it did contain the basic features of what was to become the North Atlantic Treaty. To emphasize this, and from regard for the feelings of France and other North Atlantic countries not taking part in the first Washington talks, our draft agreement was in the form of a United States proposal only. It suggested that:

1 There should be a security pact for the North Atlantic area.
2 Pending its conclusion, the Brussels Pact should be extended to include the United States, Norway, Sweden, Denmark, and Iceland.
3 Italy should be included in both the Brussels and North Atlantic Pacts. (The British and Canadian representatives questioned the wisdom of this.)
4 Meanwhile the President of the United States should make a declaration of American intention to consider an armed attack against a signatory of the Brussels Pact as an armed attack against the United States. (I emphasized in my memorandum the far-reaching importance of this declaration of United States policy.)
5 There should be an Anglo-American declaration that the two countries would not countenance any attack on the political independence or territorial integrity of Greece, Turkey, or Iran and, in the event of such attack and pending the possible negotiation of some general Middle East security system, they would afford the states in question all the assistance in their power.
6 Invitations should be issued by the United States to the United Kingdom, France, Canada, Norway, Sweden, Denmark, Iceland, The Netherlands, Belgium, Luxembourg, Eire, Switzerland, Italy, and Portugal to take part in a conference for a North Atlantic Security Pact (with some political licence we ignored the geography of Italy and Switzerland) based on Article 51 of the Charter.

I was a minority of one in suggesting that Switzerland and Portugal should be left out. The others said that Portugal was essential for strategic reasons, while Switzerland should not be singled out for exclusion merely because her traditional neutrality made acceptance of any invitation most unlikely.

In addition to the guarantee of aid to a victim of military aggression – the core of collective security – there was also provision in the first tentative agreement for consultation among the signatories in case of a threat to the political independence or territorial integrity of any one of them. It was recognized that this so-called indirect aggression might be as great a menace to peace as an armed attack, but we judged that the obligation to consult was as far as we could go in dealing with a threat so difficult to isolate and determine. While the Americans thought that we should, at least, try to define indirect aggression and specify measures to deal with it, the British and ourselves considered that this would be a futile operation, doing more harm than good.

On our insistence that it should be made clear from the beginning that the pact must be more than military in scope, it was agreed that a paragraph should be included in the text of any treaty to the effect that the signatories would make every effort, individually and collectively, to promote the economic well-being of their peoples and to achieve social justice, thereby creating an overwhelming superiority of moral, material, and military force on the side of peace and progress. This was the genesis of the famous Article 2 of the treaty, which came to be known as the Canadian Article, and which has had a chequered and disappointing life.

After the three governments had considered the draft agreement, their officials met again in Washington on 30 March for further discussions. The official talks soon produced another document for submission to governments. The area of the agreement was now territorially limited, the pact was to be more closely associated with the UN Charter, and it was made clear that the obligation of mutual assistance was general, with specific measures to help defeat the aggressor to be decided by each government.

The United States administration had now to consult congressional opinion and, as a result, began to show some disposition to prefer a mere presidential guarantee of assistance to a selected group of states, a new Monroe Doctrine. In Ottawa we considered this inadequate and unsatisfactory as a basis for real and immediate collective security and for the ultimate development of an Atlantic community, the two objectives we always kept in mind. For one thing, there was no element of reciprocity in such a declaration. Indeed, it would emphasize European weakness and dependence on the United States. As I argued in a memorandum to the Prime Minister and to my Minister, on 12 April:

A unilateral guarantee smells of charity (in the worst sense of the word). The Western European democracies are not beggars asking for our charity, but are potential allies whose assistance we need in order to be able to defend ourselves. This is a point which will have to be made clear to the people of the United States and Canada. The difficulties of doing this in any case would be great but they will be increased if the United States gives a unilateral guarantee instead of entering into a multilateral security agreement.

Russia's allies in Western Europe now are not so much the Communists as the forces of despair, apathy, doubt, and fear. It therefore seems to me very important that the peoples of Western democracies should make what Mr Attlee has called a bold move to raise in the hearts and minds and spirits of all those in the world who love freedom that confidence and faith which will restore their vigour.

I asked Hume Wrong to emphasize these considerations, and also our worries, in the private discussions which he was continuing with our American friends. He should also give them no reason to think that we would join in any such United States declaration or make a separate one. This was no part of Canadian policy, which, in this matter, was not continental but Atlantic.

In one of my messages to Wrong, on 18 May, I said: 'the hopes that were inspired by the meetings that we attended some weeks ago seem now to have been largely dissipated and there is, I think, real danger of a reliance on old-fashioned alliance policies, dictated by purely military considerations. It would be disastrous, I think, if the Article 51 approach so hopefully begun should now be abandoned.' The Ambassador was not so alarmed as I, nor was he ever personally convinced that the non-military aspects of the proposed alliance were essential; but he passed on my feelings to those most concerned in Washington with whom he had those close and friendly personal relations which are the essence of effective diplomacy.

The British shared our anxieties on this point and also pressed the United States with, as I put it in a memo to the PM on 31 May, 'clear, forceful and well reasoned argument ... about the value of a formal treaty arrangement by the United States as contrasted with a mere unilateral guarantee.'

It was about this time that Paul-Henri Spaak, who was both Belgian Prime Minister and Foreign Minister, visited Ottawa, and I made my first contact with this brilliant man. He had discussions with Mr St Laurent and some of his colleagues at which I was present. I reported to Mr King on 20 April 1948: 'He, Spaak, was most anxious that a solid nucleus of United Western European States should be established which could become the basis for something larger. He would go very far in the subordination of European national interests to international action for security. For such action, according to Spaak, a European army and a European defence plan was necessary. The Europeans should take the necessary steps to unite themselves before they call on the United States for help. ... It is clear that Mr Spaak will prove an intelligent and energetic leader of the western states in their move toward unity. He will also be in the forefront, I think, when these European moves are transferred to the wider North Atlantic area.'

The days went by in Washington and with them the sense of urgency occasioned in particular by the coup in Czechoslovakia. Communist pressures on Norway and Finland eased, and the Soviets began to talk more about 'co-existence.' I regarded this 'appeasement offensive,' as I called it, with some suspicion as designed primarily to keep the Western democracies from building up and uniting their strength through an Atlantic treaty. Given their intelligence sources on our deliberations, this was undoubtedly so. Donald MacLean, then a Second Secretary in the British Embassy in Washington, attended these early official-level meetings and, I should imagine, reported immediately to Moscow; MacLean defected to the USSR in 1951. We had no MacLean inside the Kremlin, and so far as we could see the prospect of war stood ever on the horizon. Most reports, whether from Canadian, British, or American sources, seemed to confirm the high probability of further Soviet advances and of resulting conflict. One very interesting assessment came in a letter on 9 April from the Canadian Chargé in Moscow, John Holmes, who based his report on 'highly confidential conversations' with the British and United States Embassies in Moscow. It read, in part:

Both Embassies agree, however, that the USSR does not want to provoke a shooting-war until they have exhausted all their other tactics. They are not likely to want deliberately to provoke a shooting-war in the immediate future because for a number of reasons they expect to be in a better position in several years to sustain a hard fight. On the other hand they have relative advantages at the moment over their opponents which may be dissipated if they wait too long. *Herein lies the immediate danger.* If the Russians come to the conclusion that their Cold War methods will achieve no more success in the West and that the West is beginning to consolidate its strength so that it will become invincible, then *they may take the decision to strike while their striking force is still much greater than that of their opponents.* The decision as to whether or not to resort to war is under constant review. Because their recovery is still far from complete and because they have by no means used up all their other tricks, it is not likely that the Russians would deliberately start a war in 1948. It is more likely that they would do so in a year or two years' time.

On 16 April our Embassy in Moscow reported:

We in this Embassy cannot claim to have our fingers on the pulse of all the Russians but there has been sufficient evidence to substantiate the view that few people in the world are more apprehensive of an imminent war than those about us. The evidence is based on scattered conversations which have been had by members of our staff or of other missions, together with such phenomena as food shortages and the price of potatoes. The atmosphere of the market place is not a scientific index of the degree of war scares, but it is the best Soviet substitute for the stock market.

The United States was the key to any progress toward an Atlantic alliance, and at times we experienced considerable anxiety over the direction which policy might take within the State Department. In early May I wrote to Hume Wrong: 'I think that "Chip" Bohlen [Counsellor in the State Department] and those who feel like him [notably, George Kennan, Head of the State Department's Policy Planning Staff] are on the wrong track and that the idea that all that is required is to back Western Europe by some form of unilateral guarantee and by supplying arms is wrong and possibly dangerous. It is especially discouraging to hear talk at this stage about an Atlantic Pact provoking the Soviets. I have the unhappy feeling that the big moment has passed when a genuine regional security arrangement could be negotiated on a reciprocal basis under Article 51 and that the United States is now relapsing into policies which are both short-sighted and insufficient.'

Fortunately, on 11 June Senator Vandenberg, the powerful Republican Chairman of the Senate Foreign Relations Committee, introduced a resolution which, in effect, legitimized the March negotiations. It was adopted by a vote of 64 to 4, and stated that the objectives of United States foreign policy included:

1 Progressive development of regional and other collective arrangements for individual and collective self-defence in accordance with the purposes, principles, and provisions of the Charter.

2 Association of the United States by constitutional processes with such regional and other collective arrangements as are based on continuous and effective self-help and mutual aid, and as affect its national security.

3 Contributing to the maintenance of peace by making clear its determination to exercise the right of individual or collective self-defence under Article 51 should any armed attack occur affecting its national security.

The Vandenberg Resolution was of fundamental importance to everything that followed in the negotiation of the North Atlantic Treaty. It made us feel much more hopeful in Ottawa.

The next development was the beginning of discussions on 23 June between the United States and the Brussels Powers in which, somewhat to my surprise, we were invited to participate. Equally important was that Mr King agreed the invitation should be accepted. I went again to Washington for the first meeting of this larger group on 6 July. The next day I was in the happy position of being able to telegraph to Ottawa:

The talks here are going very well along lines which should be satisfactory to us. The Americans have apparently decided [perhaps we had helped them come to this decision] that the basis for any security arrangements should be broad and have emphasized that neither a military alliance of the old sort nor a unilateral guarantee is sufficient to achieve the purpose desired. Mr Lovett [the Under-Secretary of State] keeps referring to a 'North Atlantic system' and to the fact that arrangements agreed on should be positive and not merely negative; that co-operation should be wider than merely military and should be closely related to the principles and purposes of the United Nations.

Bob Lovett was talking 'Canadian.'

The inevitable working group was now set up in Washington to convert the ideas we had been discussing into new recommendations – principles into a pact. 'Chip' Bohlen, who seems to have fought a rear-guard action against the treaty until he was finally transferred to Paris, was chairman. Hume Wrong was again our representative.

Very little progress seemed to be made during the summer, although there were a number of meetings in the unbearable heat of that steamy, boiling city. The Americans, perhaps expecting a Dewey victory in their upcoming presidential elections, again became worried about the attitude of the Senate toward any broadly based Atlantic treaty and began to talk about a security pact which would have three parties, the United States, Canada, and the United States of Western Europe. This might be an ideal arrangement but we thought it completely unrealistic, as was the hope that a security commitment by North America could be used to force the unity of Western Europe. As usual, the administration made more concessions than necessary in an effort to assure a two-thirds majority in the Senate – the vote for ratification of the North Atlantic Treaty when it came was 82 to 13.

The French, for whatever reason, also became more negative as the summer went on. After a further visit to Washington for private talks I wired Georges Vanier, then our Ambassador in Paris: 'There is, I think, a real danger of the whole project being wrecked.' So I told him to talk some sense into his French friends who, of all people, should be the most enthusiastic about an Atlantic security system. Even Spaak, for all his brave and inspiring words in Ottawa, expressed anxiety in Washington about the danger of provoking the USSR by an Atlantic pact at this particular moment. I told our Ambassador in Brussels, Victor Doré, to see Spaak and remind him of the views he had expressed so eloquently in Ottawa, views which had made such an impression on us about the virtues and the value of an Atlantic alliance.

In September the worst of the summer heat was over. The talks also improved, though we were somewhat shaken by British objections to anything more than a short reference in the preamble to co-operation in the economic, social, and cultural fields. Their case was put by Gladwyn Jebb, then British representative on the Brussels Treaty Commission, who argued that there must be no provision in the pact itself that would complicate the work of the Organization for European Economic Co-operation and other European agencies in these non-military fields. Jebb has revealed in his memoirs that he was a 'two-pillar' man from the beginning. He and many others wanted a Western Europe which would be independent of the United States. In this, he had support from those groups in Washington who desired an Atlantic alliance that would be no more than a military alliance. An Atlantic alliance composed of two pillars, groups, or poles – one European, one North American – would have created an unenviable position for Canada in our relations with the United States. Wrong once again had to point out that we were not proposing specific action or new institutions but a commitment to co-operation and co-ordination of policies in order that conflict might be minimized.

The summer discussions resulted in the submission of another draft pact to the working group by George Kennan, who had been negative in his attitude to the treaty all along, and Jack Hickerson, the State Department's Director for European Affairs and one of the most positive about the treaty. We learned later that this draft had not been approved by their chiefs (a disconcerting tactic not uncommon in Washington). It attempted to summarize agreements and reconcile differences. It also introduced some entirely new features, including a three-tiered arrangement for membership with graduated obligations designed, among other things, to encourage all the European states to join the Brussels Pact and move toward a European federation, in return for which they would receive a security guarantee from the United States.

The Kennan-Hickerson memorandum, however, got little support from other members of the working group, none from us, and was withdrawn. Only Henri Bonnet, for France, seemed to approve it. Hume Wrong wrote: 'the State Department drafters are scratching their heads over what to do now.' They scratched until 9 September when the State Department came up with yet another draft which, it was agreed, should go to governments for consideration. It was not 'a draft of an agreement' but 'an agreed statement' on the nature of the problem and steps which 'might be practicable' to deal with it through a 'North Atlantic Security Pact.' This was an improvement over earlier documents, even though it did not include the draft of a treaty. As Wrong put it, 'A week of steady campaigning by the Brussels Powers and ourselves has led to the clarification of the conditions under which powers in addition to those participating in the conversations may adhere to the proposed pact. It is no longer necessary for European countries to adhere to the Brussels Pact in order to participate in a North Atlantic pact with full responsibilities and full privileges.' This, at least, was some progress.

I received this message on the day I was sworn in as Secretary of State for External Affairs. I now had additional responsibilities and an added incentive to do everything I could to bring the negotiations for a North Atlantic pact, which were proving increasingly difficult and complicated, to a successful conclusion. I hoped to make possible some progress toward the more important, if even more difficult and more remote, goal of an organized and functioning North Atlantic community. To be thus associated with our two mother countries, Britain and France, with our neighbour, the United States, now conscious of her Atlantic destiny, and with Germany, our military foe twice in this century, seemed to me to be both a Canadian and an international objective worthy of every effort. Looking back, and in the context of history, we have made some encouraging, indeed surprising, progress. But viewed against the compulsions, the dangers, and the revolutionary changes of our times which cry for early and drastic action to ensure man's security and even his survival, we have taken only a short and inadequate step.

My first public speech as a Cabinet Minister, on 21 September at Kingston, referred to North Atlantic treaty developments, and to aspects of the alliance basic to Canadian thinking and reflecting Canadian experience:

'The Canadian Government has taken these steps towards the creation of an effective regional security system with, I am sure, the overwhelming support of the people of Canada. The people of Canada have given this support knowing that Canada's participation in such a security system may require that, in an emergency, we share not only our risks but our resources. It would, for instance, be the task of a North

Atlantic security system, once it is established, to agree upon a fair allocation of duties among the participating countries, under which each will undertake to do that share of the joint defence and production job that it can do most efficiently.

'Such a sharing of risks, resources and obligations must, however, be accompanied by, and flow from a share in the control of policy. *If obligations and resources are to be shared, it is obvious that some sort of constitutional machinery must be established under which each participating country will have a fair share in determining the policies of all which affect all.* Otherwise, without their consent, the policy of one or two or three may increase the risks and therefore the obligations of all.

'During the last war ... the UK and the USA reserved to themselves the right to make the big strategic and political decisions ... It was the two great Western Powers – not all of the Western belligerents who appointed, for instance, the Supreme Commanders ... I feel sure that it would not be possible in any effective peacetime organization of collective security to accept the procedures which were adopted in the wartime organization of the grand alliance.

'It is, for instance, one thing for a group of states to accept common responsibilities, each taking its fair share in discharging them and, indeed, in adding or subtracting from them. It is, however, quite a different thing for one, two, or three states to make decisions which may have far-reaching consequences for all countries and all peoples, and then, one, two, or three of them ask other countries to jump in and help in solving the problems which those decisions have raised. There are times, no doubt, when the requirements for consultation and for co-operative decisions must be subordinated to the necessities of a grave emergency. But those occasions must be reduced to a minimum, before there can be any genuine collective action. *That is one reason why I hope that the North Atlantic Regional System for security and progress will soon be formed so that within its framework the decisions which affect all will be taken by all. Only then will the common responsibility for carrying out these decisions be clear and unequivocal.*'

As a Minister who believed passionately in international organization and collective action, but who was also a strong Canadian nationalist (I had no difficulty in reconciling the two), I often talked like this, both publicly and in private discussions and negotiations, especially with Americans. At times, however, it made me more popular in Oslo, say, than in Washington.

In my first ministerial memorandum to Cabinet, I recommended that we tell the other parties to the discussions in Washington that we were ready 'to enter into a Treaty ... along the general lines of the document of September 9, 1948' which appeared to meet the objectives of Canadian policy. My memorandum was given a close examination by my colleagues and a vigorous discussion took place, since it represented a highly important change in Canadian foreign policy. Agreement was given and our decision was then conveyed to the other governments.

There was still, however, difficult negotiating ahead. The meetings were now on the governmental level. The problem was to put agreed principles into a pact that could be signed, sealed, and delivered to the world. For this purpose, instead of a full-dress ministerial conference, the ambassadors, now with specific instructions from governments, were to resume their meetings in Washington. When their work was completed, and a treaty was ready for signature, a formal conference could be convened. It is possible that we made a mistake in agreeing to a conference of ambassadors in Washington. A conference of special representatives in London or Paris would have been less subject to United States pressures and might have produced a better treaty. As it was, Hume Wrong's job as our Ambassador in Washington was considerably complicated by his having to pursue a Canadian line in these multilateral negotiations which was often at variance with that of the United States.

Explicit instructions were sent to Mr Wrong on the necessity to include a definite obligation of mutual assistance – to consider a military aggression against one member state as an attack against all, subject always to national concurrence in any recommendations of the proposed Atlantic Council entailing economic or military action. We also maintained our insistence that any security treaty should have provisions for non-military co-operation. It must be more than a military alliance. These were matters on which we had already taken a firm position. On questions which were of greater concern to other governments than to ourselves, Wrong was given a greater flexibility.

The discussions began on 10 December. On the question of which countries should be covered by the agreement, however, it soon became clear that there remained differences of opinion not easy to resolve. Our own view, for instance, was that while we should make every effort to include Sweden and Ireland as Atlantic democratic nations, we did not think that the Mediterranean area should be covered by the treaty: Italy should not be a partner to the treaty, but should be given special assurances of our concern for her security; no such special assurances, however, should be given collectively to Greece, Turkey, or other countries. Our position was dictated by the view that there should be separate arrangements, in which the United States, Britain, and France could participate, for collective security in the Mediterranean. Nevertheless, we were flexible enough to go along with the majority which wanted Italy in from the beginning. While we were against including Algeria, our own enquiries in Paris confirmed that France was adamant in insisting it should be included in the North Atlantic Treaty area, so we also withdrew our objections here. As Mr St Laurent put it, 'Algeria was not a matter of great importance in relation to the main purposes of the Treaty, but France was essential.'

We were, of course, aware that the inclusion of Italy would increase pressure for adding Greece and Turkey later, which we opposed for reasons which I shall mention in the next chapter. We also worried about the inclusion of Portugal in a coalition of free democracies but accepted, reluctantly, the view of the Americans and British that strategic considerations must override ideological. As for Sweden, it was soon made clear that she would not abandon the neutrality which had kept her out of war for a century and a half, a neutrality which, in contrast with that of Norway and Denmark, had been respected in World War II, whatever the reason. It was wise, I thought, after ascertaining Swedish views informally, not to send a formal invitation or attempt to isolate Sweden in any other way from the other members of the proposed alliance. Our position was much appreciated in Stockholm.

I would, myself, have been delighted if Ireland had been a founding member of the Alliance. Once in Paris, where I was attending discussions on other matters, I tried to convince my Irish friends, Sean McBride and John Hearn, that they should take this course. Their reply was that the Irish government might be willing to do so, that they could see its advantages, but not so long as Ireland remained divided. The British naturally refused to recognize any connection between the two matters and neither the Americans, ourselves, nor anyone else was willing to press London on this delicate issue.

There was, of course, the question of non-military co-operation – of collaboration in political, economic, and social questions. One reason for our stand on this was, admittedly, political. We did not think that the Canadian people, especially in Quebec, would whole-heartedly take on far-reaching external commitments if they were exclusively military in character; nor should they be asked to do so. These domestic considerations, however, were reinforced by our dedication – felt, I admit, more strongly by me than by some of my ministerial and official colleagues – to the grand design of a developing Atlantic community, something which could never be realized through military commitments for collective security alone, urgent and important as these were at that time. Our effort to promote this grand design was an important chapter in the history of Canadian diplomacy.

On 10 September 1948, with the strong support of the United States delegation and the somewhat reluctant approval of the Brussels representatives, the Ambassadors' Committee in Washington had agreed on a text for inclusion in the treaty, eventually to become Article 2, which provided for 'the encouragement of efforts between any or all of the parties to promote the general welfare through collaboration in the economic, social and cultural fields.' To allay the fears of those who foresaw a duplication of established agencies for non-military co-operation, there followed a proviso against 'any duplication of, or prejudice to the work of other [economic] organizations in which the parties are or may be represented but shall, on the contrary, assist the work of those organizations.'

When, however, on 21 January 1949 Dean Acheson returned from private life to succeed General Marshall as Secretary of State, American opposition developed to our views about an 'Article 2.' Wrong and I, of course, were old and close friends of Acheson, who had been an Assistant Secretary of State from 1941 to 1945 and for two years, until July 1947, Under-Secretary of State. We knew him well and admired him greatly. We also knew that he was preoccupied with the problem of getting any treaty approved by the Senate. He impatiently dismissed our concern with non-military co-operation and the ultimate goal of an Atlantic community as typical Canadian moralizing that meant 'next to nothing.' It would only serve to dilute and weaken the argument that a critical emergency required an agreement for collective security through collective defence – an argument which the two key men in the Senate, Connally, the new Democratic Chairman of the Senate Foreign Relations Committee, and Vandenberg now supported. We were in the old familiar position of being at one end of a double negotiation between the State Department and the other countries on the one hand, and the US Senate Foreign Relations Committee on the other.

Nevertheless, I instructed Wrong on 7 February to press for something stronger than the first draft of Article 2. To that end I forwarded to him a memorandum from Escott Reid, 'Canadian Conception of the

Nature and Purpose of the North Atlantic Treaty.' Wrong was not much in sympathy with Reid's views on this subject or with the intensity of his expression thereof, so he warned me, 'We are now the only party to the negotiation that really favours the inclusion of anything in the Treaty about social and economic collaboration outside a general reference in the Preamble.' This was disturbing. It seemed that we were not going to have an easy time in preserving the present draft, let alone getting a stronger one.

I pressed London to help us, but the best I could get, for all Norman Robertson's ingenuity in putting our case, was an assurance of support for some 'economic clause,' not because they wanted it but, as they told our High Commissioner, to meet our wishes. Intervention with the Netherlands and Belgian governments brought more positive assurances of support, especially from Foreign Minister Stikker in The Hague. On 19 February I was delighted, and also surprised, to hear from Robert Schuman, the French Foreign Minister, for whom I had a high regard, that the French would support us 'à fond.' In the same month Mr St Laurent also had a talk with President Truman who seemed to understand and sympathize, if not with the Canadian Atlanticist viewpoint, at least with the realities of Canadian domestic politics. As a consequence, when Hume Wrong tried out our new and stronger Article 2 on the State Department, they were much more forthcoming than they had been a few weeks before, and on 24 February told us that they could accept the following text:

The parties will contribute to the further development of peaceful and friendly international relations by strengthening their free institutions and promoting conditions of stability and well-being. They will seek to eliminate conflict in their international economic policies and will encourage economic collaboration between any or all of them. They will make every effort to bring about a better understanding of the principles which form the basis of their common civilization.

This draft, which we were told had been approved not only by Acheson but by Senators Connally and Vandenberg, was, in essence, what we wanted. It was all we could expect. After consultation with the PM, I told Wrong that we approved the new text, which, with some minor changes, was what appeared in the treaty as signed.

I was happy at what we had achieved. I was also well aware that to put such an article in a treaty was one thing, to make it work was something else.

An interesting sequel to this story was provided some years later when, to my surprise, I read in Dean Acheson's *Present at the Creation* how he had 'defused' the Canadian draft of Article 2 by redrafting it to bring it into line with United States' objectives. In diplomacy, it is a good result when your victory is also felt by the other side to be a success. I was happy that Dean Acheson could report to the President that he had successfully dealt with the rather tiresome Canadians. In my turn I could report on 9 March to the Cabinet that 'As a result of representations by the Canadian Government Article 2 has been substantially strengthened' over the first draft.

The key article dealing with the obligation for mutual assistance in case of aggression was satisfactory; indeed it went further than some Congressional leaders would accept. One or two changes, not of great substance, were made to remove that difficulty. The inclusion of the words 'as it deems necessary' instead of 'as may be necessary' in reference to action taken to assist the victim of aggression, made clear that it was the responsibility of the individual state to make that decision, as, indeed, it was to decide whether an aggression had in fact been committed. We could understand Congressional preoccupation with this point.

After discussion on 10 March, the Canadian Cabinet approved the text of the treaty. By 16 March the other parties to the negotiation had also accepted the text. When the last comma had been agreed on in Washington, and the treaty approved in Ottawa, I sent the following message to Hume Wrong:

My colleagues in Cabinet have asked me to let you know how greatly they appreciate the work that you have done in representing Canada in the negotiations for the Treaty. They know how difficult these long negotiations have been and they realize how great the contribution is that you have made to their success.

May I add a personal and very sincere note of thanks and appreciation to you for the magnificent work that you have done. Without your skilful and experienced help, we would certainly not have had as satisfactory a Treaty as that which you will be signing for Canada. I am happy that my name will be associated with yours in that signature. It marks another stage in our joint progress from the days when we used to put our initials, together, on first year pass-papers in history at U of T.

On 28 March the treaty was submitted for debate to the House of Commons. The Prime Minister outlined the events leading up to the agreement. I explained in detail the significance of each article, and felt very privileged to be able to do so. On Article 5, the security commitment, I had this to say:

Under this treaty, then, each North Atlantic nation declares that it will in future consider an armed attack against any one of its allies as an armed attack against all. That does not mean that Canada would be automatically at war if one of our allies were attacked. We would, however, be bound, in company with the other members of the alliance, to take promptly the action which we deemed necessary to restore and maintain the security of the North Atlantic area.

I have heard no one suggest that the full weight of the North Atlantic alliance will be brought into play, over some minor event of little consequence. In whatever action is necessary, however, we agree to play our proper part in co-operation with the others to restore peace.

In the House there was practically no opposition to the treaty. The Leader of the Opposition, George Drew, was positive in his support. M.J. Coldwell, leader of the CCF, approved as did Solon Low for the Social Credit party. When the vote was taken only two were against. Thus I had the backing of an almost unanimous Parliament when Hume Wrong and I signed the treaty for Canada. This was one of the most satisfactory aspects of the whole negotiation, for I believed strongly that whenever possible in matters of foreign affairs party politics should end at the water's edge or at the national border. That was certainly the case with the policy which culminated in the North Atlantic Treaty.

On Friday, 1 April I flew to Washington with my wife. The next day I lunched with Dirk Stikker, attended Italian and British receptions for their Foreign Ministers, and was co-host with our Ambassador for a dinner at the Embassy. Our guest list was that mixture that I liked so much of personal and official friends. It included Oliver Franks, the British Ambassador; 'Scotty' Reston of the *New York Times*, who by this time had achieved the kind of position in Washington which enabled him to report accurately what political leaders said in their sleep; Jack Hickerson, who had been for so long one of our closest friends and most candid critics in the State Department, and who knew more about Canada than most Canadians; General Lemnitzer, later to be the chief of the NATO Forces; Congressman Eaton, born in Pugwash, NS, but now a Republican power in Congress on foreign affairs who liked to be considered there as the voice and true friend of Canada; Mrs Truxton Beale, eminent in Washington society as was another guest, the incomparable Mrs Nicholas Longworth, the elderly but vigorous and outrageously outspoken daughter of Teddy Roosevelt; and, finally, Escott Reid, who had striven so long with single-minded intensity to bring into being the perfect North Atlantic Treaty. If the treaty was not perfect, nevertheless, we felt that night something of historic importance had been achieved. It was a happy occasion, almost a celebration.

The next day was Sunday, 3 April, and my morning church service was a talk with that redoubtable human being and wise patriot, Ernie Bevin, whom I was later to get to know better; then, a Canadian reception for the visiting dignitaries followed by a small dinner given by Tommy Stone, Hume Wrong's second-in-command and my friend from boyhood days in Chatham. The Achesons were the guests and, in the cheerful and convivial atmosphere for which the Stone parties were famous on two continents, there was the customary genial, at times barbed but never poisoned, exchange of views and insults on the respective merits of Canadian and American negotiators, or of Canadian and American policies.

The ceremony of signature, the culmination of all that so many had worked for over so many long months, and for me the finale of my first exercise in ministerial diplomacy, took place at three o'clock on 4 April, a bright and pleasant spring day in Washington.

The Foreign Ministers of the signatory countries were welcomed by Secretary of State Acheson. His words, which I knew from experience, were always eloquently appropriate for any occasion, included: 'We are met together to consummate a solemn act. Those who participated in the drafting of this treaty must leave to others judgment of the significance and value of this act. They cannot appraise the achievement, but they can and should declare the purposes of their minds and hearts.'

So each of us in turn declared the purposes of our minds and hearts. We knew that those purposes were good, even if our words expressing them fell somewhat short of the Gettysburg Address. If, in my contribution, I was somewhat too optimistic about what we had done and were going to do, the occasion and the feeling of achievement which it reflected made this understandable. Indeed, we were all a bit euphoric on that April day. We were not even disturbed by the regrettable musical selections of the band of the United States Marines.

ᘓ4ᘘ

NATO AT WORK

The treaty had been signed. The work of organization had now to begin. We knew as early as the summer of 1949 from discussions with the British and Americans that we were going to have difficulty in implementing Article 2, at least in matters of economic co-operation. It is true that in the State Department Ted Achilles and Jack Hickerson were interested in exploring the possibility of a full Atlantic federal union and that they had received some backing in this from Acheson, who was prepared to examine a more limited first experiment. Escott Reid reported to me a luncheon conversation with Hickerson two days after the signing of the treaty: 'Jack Hickerson is now toying with the idea – I don't know how seriously – of what he calls an economic union between the US, the UK, and Canada. He defined an economic union to mean the free movement of goods and money but not of people.' To this end a tripartite committee, composed of Harry Labouisse for the United States, Don Matthews for Canada, and Sir Edwin Plowden for Britain, was created to co-ordinate the economic policies of the three countries. I do not recall that this committee ever actually accomplished anything. Nor do I believe that those who counted in the US and Britain ever took the idea very seriously; or, if seriously, for very long. I do know that in Canada our Department of Finance remained sceptical of ideas advancing Article 2. This was, in part, a direct consequence of our failure to consult Finance adequately before we began our campaign to establish in the treaty the basis for a larger Atlantic union. What they objected to, I think, was the Article 2 formula, *per se.*

Trade and Commerce and the Bank of Canada were, at best, doubtful supporters of the idea. More important, Atlantic union was objectionable to many of my own senior officials even as an ultimate goal. As Hume Wrong put it on 15 October 1951: 'The idea of the creation of a "political Commonwealth of the North Atlantic" is in present circumstances so remote from attainment that to discuss it as an aim of current policy is unrealistic.' Dana Wilgress, then High Commissioner in London, went further and wrote on 30 October 1951: 'I have long been mystified as to what exactly was the reason why we sponsored Article 2 of the Treaty' and 'I have never been able to take seriously the proposal for closer integration of the North Atlantic countries.'

Well, as Minister, I took it seriously and I was determined to do everything possible to bring about this closer integration through NATO, without, however, minimizing the difficulties ahead or losing sight of the more immediate and urgent need to establish collective security through collective defence. Without any illusions, I kept hammering away at the maximum possible application of Article 2 to further co-operation and unity within the Atlantic Alliance. I remained on the side of the angels, however remote they were.

At the initial Council meeting on 17 September 1949 in Washington, the Foreign Ministers of the member countries considered a structure facilitating collective defence as the first priority. The treaty had provided only for a Council, the members of which should set up such subsidiary bodies as might be necessary. While I certainly did not question the need for a defence structure, I was concerned that it should not prejudice the establishment of necessary machinery under other articles of the treaty. That first Council meeting set up a Defence Committee which was charged with the task of drawing up unified defence plans for the North Atlantic area. A Chiefs of Staff Military Committee was also established with its executive agency a 'Standing Group' of the Big Three (the United States, Britain, and France), and with Regional Planning Groups responsible for the development of regional defence plans and their submission, through the Standing Group, to the Military Committee. A Committee of Ministers to deal with financial and economic matters connected with defence, and a Military Production and Supply Board, responsible to that Committee, were created on 18 November.

The first meeting of the Defence Committee on 1 December 1949 agreed on a strategic concept for defence of the North Atlantic area and, subsequently, on a four-year defence plan or 'medium term defence plan' to implement it. Initially, it was something less than an integrated defence plan, consisting in the main of oft-repeated general statements concerning flexibility, co-ordination of political, economic, and psychological efforts of member nations, and the necessity for increased national defence forces. The advent of the Korean War changed this, and worn phrases were replaced by reasonably intelligent military preparations. SACEUR (Supreme Allied Commander Europe) was established, and General Eisenhower was appointed in theory by all the member governments but, in effect, by Washington. This was an appointment, however, that met with unanimous and enthusiastic approval and it gave the General, for the relatively short time he held it, a good opportunity to display his outstanding organizational and diplomatic qualities. He was the ideal man to be the first NATO Commander, and to put its multi-national headquarters, SHAPE (Supreme Headquarters Allied Powers Europe), on a firm foundation.

ॐ

I was still concerned that any programme on the military side of the Alliance be matched by progress on the non-military side. As I told the Canadian House of Commons early in November 1949: 'We have taken, I think, the first steps towards the widest possible military integration of the North Atlantic communities. What we must do now, I suggest, is to take as many steps as possible, as quickly as possible, towards the widest possible economic collaboration between the North Atlantic nations' and find out 'just what is involved in such collaboration.' The move toward European integration had begun and I felt it essential that it be reconcilable with the larger goal; that it be extended, as soon as possible, to the North Atlantic area.

Hume Wrong was therefore instructed to speak along these lines at the second Council meeting in Washington on 18 November 1949. Though he had some doubts that we would accomplish very much, our Ambassador spoke and was supported by the French and Norwegian delegates. Dean Acheson, irritated by this initiative, used his position as chairman to prevent the creation of a NATO working group on Article 2 and instead invited the Canadian government to submit specific proposals at a later meeting of the Council for its consideration. This put it strictly up to us. It also postponed any further consideration of the matter until the next Council meeting, at the earliest; and this no doubt was what Acheson wished. The suspicion was spread that, as Wrong put it: 'We are advocating the creation of a new international agency as an end in itself and not as a means to an end.' In fact, what we really wanted at this stage was a special study by experts on whether machinery for economic co-operation under Article 2 was desirable and, if so, how it should operate.

Responding to Acheson's request, an interdepartmental committee in Ottawa from the Departments of External Affairs, Finance, Trade and Commerce, and the Bank of Canada went to work on the problem but, when the Council met again in January 1950, we were not yet ready to report. In fact, our interdepartmental committee failed to produce a single concrete proposal for the implementation of Article 2, no doubt inspiring some ironic reflections in Washington and London. Still, we were not deterred. In April 1950, before the next meeting, I asked our ambassadors in the NATO countries to find out what the governments to which they were accredited would think of a statement on our part to the Council advocating some action under Article 2, or at least an examination and report on what could be done. The replies were not encouraging, except from Oslo and Rome. Nevertheless, I drafted a statement for use at the Council meeting in May, which got general approval in Ottawa. W.C. Clark, K.W. Taylor, and R.B. Bryce of Finance, however, continued to disapprove of these Canadian economic initiatives.

My statement to the Council concluded:

'The most important way for us to give effect to Article 2 is for each of our countries always to act in accordance with it. If the spirit is there, co-operation and elimination of conflict will follow readily enough. However, it will probably help us all to practise what we preach if, at our Council meetings, we have some pretty frank talks about each other's behaviour. I have in mind a mixture between a confessional and a Quaker meeting. Finally, I think we should consider, very seriously and without haste, what sort of machinery, if any, we should set up to give further effect to Article 2.

'We should examine first the question what use such machinery might serve. For this purpose I think we should set up a committee of perhaps half a dozen government officials from half a dozen countries, who are acknowledged experts in economic policies and economic machinery. The committee would study the possible economic application of Article 2 in the years beyond 1952 [the termination date of the Marshall Plan]. It would necessarily concern itself with the relationship between the economic pledges of Article 2 and other pledges of economic co-operation; in the Charter of the United Nations, in the General Agreement on Tariffs and Trade, in (I hope) the International

Trade Organization, in the Bretton Woods Agreements, in the Organization for European Economic Co-operation, and in the constitutions of other agencies. When we had considered the report of this group on the uses of Article 2, and on co-operation with non-signatory countries, we would be in a good position to decide whether or not we wanted to set up machinery and, if so, what sort of machinery we needed.'

This was a careful statement designed to allay fears that we were rushing NATO into economic activities for which it might not be suited, or which would overlap and conflict with the work of other international agencies.

British and American suspicions about Article 2 remained but at least I secured from the Council a direction to its committee of deputies, newly created, to report to the next meeting of the Council, in September 1950, on what further action could be taken to carry out the principles of Article 2. More important, a decision was taken that the United States and Canada should be associated with the Organization for European Economic Co-operation (OEEC) as a step toward providing continuing economic machinery linking both sides of the Atlantic. This could, of course, provide the kind of economic machinery which might have developed out of Article 2. Indeed, I once hoped that NATO might take over the work of OEEC in the field of economic collaboration, but political considerations led to a different result. I would have been quite happy if an enlarged OEEC, or an Organization for Atlantic Economic Co-operation, as it would have to be called, could have also become the vehicle for working out plans for Atlantic political as well as economic collaboration. This did not happen. OEEC, however, could be and was used to make any such action under Article 2 seem unnecessary and undesirable.

What we did get, in September 1951, was a Temporary Council Committee (known as TCC) with three distinguished and experienced members, Averell Harriman (USA), Sir Edwin Plowden (Britain), and Jean Monnet (France), the acknowledged 'Father' of any united Europe that might be created, to examine and report on the problem of reconciling collective defence requirements with the political and economic capabilities of each member state. A big opportunity was lost, however, when we failed to give the TCC a decisive role in attempting to pool within the Alliance research, development, standardization, and joint production of armaments. We did obtain a regular annual review of collective defence needs and national performances which was as important to the coalition as it was occasionally irritating to governments. This annual survey with its praise and blame and its recommendations, had, of course, no binding effect on member governments. These remained masters of their own policies and appropriations, but the surveys were bound to influence their planning for, and participation in, the common defence.

The TCC made the first of these reports to the Council meeting at Lisbon in February 1952. That meeting remains vivid in my memory for a variety of reasons, of which an unimportant one was my arrival. As Chairman of the Council, I was given military honours at the airport and listened to a Portuguese Army band play 'O Canada' in a manner so stirring that it almost sounded like 'La Marseillaise.' This was not the way it was done at home for political meetings or football games. After musical honours, I was escorted in style to a VIP suite purported to be in one of the most exclusive luxury hotels in Europe. When I signed the guest book on leaving, I noticed that a well-known American humourist had written opposite his name, under Remarks; 'This is a most aristocratic hotel. Even the flies on the wall have very blue blood and are extremely well bred.'

In later years NATO did discuss economic and financial policies, especially in their relation to defence spending and security. From time to time it would look into the possibility of co-ordination of its policies in the General Agreement on Tariffs and Trade (GATT) and in the specialized agencies at the United Nations, thus increasing its sense of Atlantic community. The Council also considered increasing freedom of movement of persons and goods within the Alliance countries, or of acting together in planning and giving aid to developing countries. Members could put the case in NATO for co-operation in removing barriers to trade and, in particular, the folly of raising barriers against one another. But it was felt that there were other and more effective international agencies for action in these fields on the world level, either the United Nations Economic and Social Council (ECOSOC) or GATT, and on the regional level, OEEC. In fact, no 'frank' exchanges on each other's economic policies took place.

Article 2 remained virtually a dead letter for substantive action in economic matters. It may have been that this Article was both too broad and not broad enough for its purposes; that each of us had economic relations with some Atlantic countries, not NATO members, that were more important than our relations with certain countries which were members. The reality is that the spirit to implement the economic aspects of Article 2 was *never* there and that an economic basis for the realization of its larger political goal was never created.

And, perhaps, it simply took me too long to realize this. Certainly, if 1948 and 1949 were victorious years for the Atlanticists, the 1950s belonged to the European unionists as was clearly shown by the creation of the European Common Market with the Treaty of Rome in March 1957.

As the possibilities of action for economic co-operation under Article 2 diminished, criticism of NATO as simply a military alliance, dominated by the United States, grew in our House of Commons, especially by the socialist CCF. We tried to meet this criticism by supporting initiatives for social and cultural co-operation, but this did not amount to very much. More important, we pressed for political consultation and co-operation in and through the Council – especially after the Lisbon meeting of February 1952, when the three ministerial bodies created in September 1949 were replaced by a single Council which Defence, Finance, and Supply Ministers could attend, if they so wished, together with the Foreign Ministers. The Council was now in permanent session with officials representing their governments between ministerial meetings. More was achieved here.

The Korean War underlined the necessity for political consultation and co-operation with the smaller members of the North Atlantic Alliance, including Canada. The Alliance was becoming subject to strains over US policies in the Far East. It was further strained over the diplomatic moves and manners of the new United States Secretary of State, Foster Dulles, when he took office in January 1953. I was one of those who thought doubts and differences should be frankly aired in the North Atlantic Council, if they were not to result later in public disagreement. As I had reported after the Council meeting in May 1950: 'there was, as usual, a general reluctance, not shared by the Canadian representative [myself], to express any misgivings felt as to proposals put forward by the US representative.' I believed that genuine consultation and frank exchanges of views, not for recrimination but to bring about maximum co-ordination of foreign policies, were essential functions of the Alliance.

In my first speech as a politician in September 1948, I had laid down the principle which I never ceased to advocate as essential to our coalition: '*If obligations and resources are to be shared, it is obvious that some sort of constitutional machinery must be established under which each participating country will have a fair share in determining the policies of all which affect all.* Otherwise, without their consent, the policy of one or two, or three may increase the risks and obligations of all.'

In the North Atlantic Council, we had an adequate mechanism for full consultation. As in the area of economic co-operation, however, more important than the machinery was the will to use it, to ensure that no North Atlantic government should make a decision on an important issue of direct concern to other members without previous consultation with them or without taking their views into consideration. Consultation must mean more than announcement of a decision already determined.

I recognized, of course, that exceptions had to be made for situations of crisis or emergency where immediate decisions had to be taken. Even in the normal conduct of foreign policy, there are inescapable difficulties on conducting continuous and useful consultation between members of a coalition, especially when they vary greatly in size, power, and responsibility. For one thing, there is the need for secrecy in regard to contemplated policies and plans. It is difficult enough, and it is becoming even more difficult, to maintain secrecy within a single government. This difficulty is even greater if a dozen other governments must be kept informed. There is also a natural reluctance, after having gone through all the processes of consultation required for a national decision, to go through this delaying process again with one's allies, especially when this may require that the whole matter be reopened within your own government. This is particularly true of the United States where the processes of consultation and discussion within the Executive Branch and between it and Congress are complex, time-consuming, and exhausting. When I once suggested to Dean Acheson that the other members of the Alliance should have been consulted before a certain American decision was made final, since it was of great importance to them, he exploded: 'If you think, after the agonies of consultation we have gone through here to get agreement on this matter, that we are going to start all over again with our NATO allies, especially with you moralistic, interfering Canadians, then you're crazy.'

Perhaps a story of an encounter I once had with Foster Dulles will explain something of what Acheson had in mind. We were flying from Washington one afternoon in March 1956 to join our chiefs, President Eisenhower and Prime Minister St Laurent, and the President of Mexico, at White Sulphur Springs for an informal exchange of views on North American matters. Dulles offered me a lift in the government plane that was taking him, so that we could have a preliminary talk before the dinner that evening. It was a small plane and I found myself strapped in with the Secretary on a seat behind the pilot. It was certainly the closest contact I had had with him, closer than was comfort-able. He began to talk about the state of the world and if my few responses lacked some of their usual clarity and wisdom it was because I was fully preoccupied with trying not to be air-sick. I was certainly in no position to yield to that constitutional weakness, so I let him do the talking. However, he made one observation which I could not allow to pass unchallenged. It was about consultation: 'You Canadians [he almost sneered] are always complaining that we never consult you about our policies. "Ike" as you know, is a great golfer and, who knows, he may want us to play a few holes together on this visit. If we do and the score is all square on the 18th green, I'll wager that you will inter-vene just as I am about to make the deciding putt to demand that I consult you about it first.' My reply, I thought, was much to the point: 'If I did, Foster, it would be merely to tell you that you were using a No 9 iron.'

The central difficulty in respect of consultation within a coalition stemmed, as I have indicated, from the basic reluctance of the great powers to have their freedom of action limited by a formal commitment requiring international consultation with all the others before national decisions could be made. I had no difficulty in appreciating this diffi-culty, but I was determined to do my best to ensure that in our own coalition collective security was based on collective decisions collec-tively determined except in situations of real emergency. I knew that the conversion of that principle into practice was not going to be easy.

The United States, with its power and resources, was bound to have a dominant position in the North Atlantic Alliance. For this reason the other members wished to ensure that US policy did not become Alliance policy without their agreement, and that collective security was not replaced by the insecurity that comes from commitments without ap-proval or, sometimes, without even knowledge. Consultation and the exchange of information alone must not be deliberately misinterpreted by the Big One or the Big Three as providing that approval, or authoriz-ing any one member to speak for the Alliance as a whole. Each member country had its own responsibilities as a sovereign state and these could not be delegated except by its own express decision.

For these reasons and others the position of a smaller country in a coalition, under the leadership of a super-power with world-wide in-terests and responsibilities, is never easy. The fact remains, however, that progress was made in NATO over the years in developing prac-tices and procedures for wide consultation between all the members beyond anything ever before achieved in a coalition of free, democratic states. Our failure to do more under Article 2 should not obscure this fact.

Worried about Alliance matters, I visited some European countries in July 1951. I was to discover that I was far from alone in my preoccupations. A diary I kept at the time makes this clear.

Monday, July 2, 1951 (London)
'At lunch today at the High Commissioner's, Mr Wilgress and I had an interesting talk with Spofford [Deputy United States Representative on the North Atlantic Council and Chairman of the Council Deputies] and Achilles on NATO matters. Spofford seemed to be reasonably satisfied at the way the deputies were working, but expressed the hope, which had been repeated to me from more than one quarter, that representation of certain governments might be on a higher level to enable decisions to be taken more quickly and to give deputies greater authority. He certainly feels, however, that Canadian representation is not open to any such criticism, and considers Mr Wilgress to be one of the more effective colleagues.

'We discussed the date and place of the next Council meeting. Spofford feels that we should get into the habit of having regular meetings of the Council two or three times a year, even when there are no vital decisions to be taken. This will accomplish two things: it would develop the habit of consultation, and it will remove the impression which is now created by infrequent irregular meetings that big, dramatic decisions must be made every time such a meeting is held.

'We then discussed growing NATO concentration on the military aspects of the Alliance as exemplified by the proposals to admit Turkey and Greece. Mr Wilgress and I deplored the fact that this concentration would endanger the "Article 2" idea of the Pact, the development of a North Atlantic community. We agreed that this idea should not be lost, but should be stressed. It was not, however, easy to see how this could be done when defence was the immediate and urgent problem. On the non-military side, there seemed to be developing a confusion of machinery – OEEC, Council of Europe, all of which increased the temptation to restrict NATO to military matters.

'I threw out very tentatively the idea of a complete over-haul, or at least a complete re-examination of all the machinery for European co-operation, economic, social and military; to see whether it would be possible, as a result of such a re-examination, to separate the military and the non-military aspects of NATO, and to include in any agency which would deal only with the former, any country which wished to join and make its contribution to and accept the obligations of military collective action. This, of course, would be a return to the "Article 51 Protocol" idea of collective defence. I emphasized to Spofford that I was merely thinking aloud, and that I appreciated that there would be very real difficulties at this stage in any such re-examination. For one thing, it might mean going to our respective legislatures with new proposals. However, the problem certainly was there, and the Turkish-Greek application for NATO membership underlined it ...

Monday, July 2, 1951 (The Hague)
'I had dinner at the Embassy with Dupuy [our Ambassador] and Stikker [the Dutch Foreign Minister] ...

'We then discussed the question of the admission of Turkey and Greece to NATO. Stikker certainly shares the doubts of some of the rest of us in regard to the wisdom of this. He thought that it might fatally weaken the idea of the North Atlantic Pact as the basis for social, political and economic development. I concurred in this, and threw out the same idea that I had tried on Spofford about a North Atlantic political association, separate from the military coalition, and which might include in its membership all the OEEC countries except Turkey and Greece, as well as the United States and Canada. Stikker was intrigued by the idea of a "bifurcated" NATO, but agreed with me when I said there would be very great difficulty at this time in bringing it about. We both felt, however, that it was something that should be looked into ...

Tuesday and Wednesday, July 3 and 4, 1951 (Oslo)
'I flew from The Hague to Oslo where I had dinner on the 3rd and luncheon on the 4th with Lange [Norway's Foreign Minister]. Also on the evening of the 4th, when we were dining with Michael Wright at the British Embassy, Lange phoned around 10 o'clock to say he would like to have another chat before we left Oslo the next morning.

'These talks were useful as Lange is one of the best and wisest of Europeans whom I have met ...

'... The most important immediate concern was defence, and Turkey could add considerable strength to the military coalition. Therefore, we should have to be very careful not to rebuff or discourage her. Lange was as interested as Stikker in the idea of segregating political and military questions under NATO. He would go a long way to include Sweden in any political grouping. We had an interesting exchange of views on the development of the real North Atlantic community which would include Sweden and Switzerland, but exclude the Mediterranean

countries. Norwegian interest in this matter is, of course, obvious, because of their special Scandinavian relationship. It was anomalous for
them (and I added that it would be for us, too) to accept permanently a
situation under which Turkey and Greece had a closer formal association with them than Sweden ...

'Lange was good enough to say some very kind things about Canada's
influence in NATO and UN questions. He was especially happy that
we were on such frank and friendly terms with the United States and
that we could influence Washington in a way that other countries could
not. He did not disguise his worries about some aspects of United
States tactics in European matters. At the same time, he was a strong
supporter of the closest possible United States association with Europe,
and he agreed that any worries about tactics which we may have were
small in comparison with the great results already achieved by the
strong and courageous leadership already given by the United States
to the free world against the danger of communist aggression ...

Saturday, July 14, 1951 (Copenhagen)
'We arrived at Copenhagen about 4 o'clock and I went immediately to
the Foreign Office where I had arranged to meet Mr Kraft, the Foreign
Secretary, and the Secretary-General, Mr Svenningfen ...

'He [Kraft] expressed the same worry that I had heard from others
about certain NATO developments, more particularly the accession of
Turkey and Greece, where his point of view is the same as that of the
Norwegians. We had a good deal of discussion of this, and agreed that
if any satisfactory alternative to full membership is possible we should
seize it, but we both felt that getting US agreement on anything short
of full membership would be very difficult now.

'Kraft was also interested in the problem of co-operation with the
United States in regard to bases, mentioning this subject because he felt
that Canada and Denmark were in somewhat the same position in regard to it. He expressed confidence in US policy in regard to bases in
Greenland, but was worried lest we be pushed too fast and too far in
this matter, about which public opinion in his country was somewhat
sensitive. I outlined to him the Canadian position in regard to co-operation with the United States on bases for mutual defence on Canadian
territory; how we were ironing out the various problems; how we tried
to impress on the United States the need to respect Canadian opinion,
while we, on our side, had to respect the responsibility that the United
States had accepted in regard to the general defence against Russian
communism.

'Kraft also outlined to me what Denmark was trying to do in regard to rearmament. He emphasized, as others had done previously, that their economic resources were small, that Denmark especially was dependent on maintaining export trade if anything like the present standard of living was to be maintained. Incidentally, that standard of living to a casual visitor seems remarkably high. Kraft finally pointed out that he and his government had to be pretty careful in their handling of controversial international matters because they were governing without a majority in the Legislature.

'They [the Danes] pin their faith on the growing strength of the North Atlantic coalition, and on the hope that this strength will be used by the United States wisely, and without unnecessary provocation. On the last point, however, they, like others, have some natural worries.'

I wound up my talks in London (climaxed would be a better word) with an hour with Mr Churchill, then Leader of the Opposition but soon to be Prime Minister again, in his office in the House of Commons. I described this meeting in a letter to Mr St Laurent:

'He was in great form and, I thought, more vigorous than when I saw him last, a year ago. Possibly, it was one of his good days, because he had all his old verve and twinkling humour. He even offered me one of his cigars!

'He began by asking me to tell him something about North American affairs, and then proceeded to talk to me almost steadily for the duration of my visit. He was interesting about Franco Spain and recent developments there. He felt we would be making a great mistake if we intervened in any way in purely bilateral military and security discussions between Spain and the United States. He admitted that this was not the time to provoke controversies by trying to get Spain into the North Atlantic Council or, indeed, collectively to have security talks with her. But if the Americans were willing to take steps on their own, which could only be advantageous to us all from the security point of view, the least we could do was not to interfere with or criticize their efforts. I think that this makes sense.

'Incidentally, I was talking to Patrick Gordon-Walker [the Secretary of State for Commonwealth Relations] shortly afterwards, and he agreed with this point of view, which is, I suspect, more than some of his colleagues would do.

'Churchill said that he himself was not even opposed to Franco politically, as many others are, because he had reason to know that although

Franco had deceived us during the war, he had also deceived the Nazis. In fact, as Churchill put it, he had double-crossed everybody impartially in order to keep Spain out of the conflict.

'Churchill also mentioned North Atlantic developments, including Turkey and Greece, and is quite obviously interested in the North Atlantic solely as a military organization. From that point of view he was emphatic that anything that can be done to strengthen it, and especially to encourage the United States to get stronger and keep whole-heartedly committed to the defence of Western Europe, should be supported. He said that not only at the present time, but in the next year or two, Western Europe, without American help, would be a very easy victim for any Russian invader, and that we should never forget that fact. All this sounds very prosaic, but I can assure you that the way he put it to me was far from prosaic. In fact, at times he was quite brilliant and honoured me by talking to me as if I was a favourite audience, worthy of choice epigrams!

'Mr Churchill tried hard, of course, not to be too critical of the Labour Government in my presence, but he did not entirely succeed. When I mentioned, for instance, that I hoped that Spain would not be sprung on us at a North Atlantic Council meeting as Germany had been a year ago, he at once retorted that when he was Prime Minister he had no difficulty in maintaining such close touch with Washington that he knew in advance what they were going to do. There seems to be something wrong now, he added. He also rather amused me by suggesting that whereas he had been able to keep the soldiers in check here by tempering their military advice with political wisdom, the Socialist Service Ministers were completely in the pockets of the Service Chiefs and were afraid to reject any advice given to them. He thought that this was too bad because a Minister in these days should be just as tough with the senior soldiers as with the junior politicians. Every piece of military advice, he said, must have a political content and he felt that a good many of the soldiers were not capable of supplying that content. This was an interesting doctrine, coming from him, and no doubt is based on his own experiences during the war. I think, though, that he might find it a little more difficult to apply at the present.

'As he was showing me out, he met his next caller, the Spanish Ambassador, the Duke de Primo de Rivera and, taking his cigar from his mouth, introduced me proudly to him as "the Canadian High Commissioner, Mr Lester Pearson, who is over here from Ottawa"! In spite of what I said at the beginning of this letter, I think Mr Churchill must be getting older.'

My tour showed that, apart from Winston Churchill, all the Western European leaders I consulted were torn between relief at the security the North Atlantic Alliance, under United States leadership, was giving to Western Europe in the face of the Soviet threat of aggression, and anxiety over some aspects of United States policy which might commit them as members of the Alliance to courses and consequences they did not desire. For this reason they strongly supported the greatest possible political consultation between the North Atlantic countries through the Council, and all hoped that the Alliance would not become too exclusively military.

The next meeting of the Council was held in Ottawa in September 1951. To my satisfaction and surprise, an item was put on the agenda by the United States, but on Dirk Stikker's initiative, to consider the 'practical development of the Atlantic community as a major objective of the NATO countries.' In response, my department produced a policy paper on 'Western Europe and the North Atlantic Community,' which stated that the ultimate goal of co-operation in NATO should be 'a political Commonwealth of the Atlantic.'

I agreed with this principle as an 'ultimate' objective, but I was even more conscious now than earlier of the difficulties in achieving it. I also agreed that it might be wise to reduce some of the rhetoric about implementing Article 2 and stress its value as a rule of conduct and as a guide for national policies rather than as a commitment to collective action and to the machinery necessary for that purpose. I also felt that any discussion on the development of the Atlantic community, consideration of which the United States now proposed, would have to include current moves toward a united Europe and the place of Germany in that unity.

My own view was that Canada should support in every practicable way the unification of Western Europe. I could think of no more important step in removing the major cause of the great wars of the last hundred years than to end the feud, and the fears, between Gaul and Teuton, which had killed one hundred thousand Canadians in this century. I saw no reason why European integration and the closer cohesion of an Atlantic community need be mutually exclusive. I saw every reason why West Germany, and one day perhaps a united Germany, should be a part of both.

I went further. I believed that, if and when Britain decided that neither its Commonwealth ties nor its cherished special relationship with the United States should prevent it from crossing the channel politically in peacetime, before it was again driven across militarily by war, Canada should support that decision. I did not change my mind later when this meant that Britain would become a member of the European Common Market which, I knew, would cause some trading problems for us. Britain, as part of a united Western Europe, would give new and essential strength and stability to the whole continent. This, I thought, outweighed any immediate disadvantages and dislocations that might ensue for Canada. I was assuming, however, that a stronger and more united Western Europe would remain part of an Atlantic coalition, taking a greater share of responsibility for the defence and development of that coalition.

The United States-Dutch proposal for the practical development of the Atlantic community was discussed at a restricted meeting of the Council on the morning of 19 September 1951. As a result, a small step forward was made. A committee was set up to study and report on the proposal and, more specifically, to examine the possibility of the co-ordination of and frequent consultation on foreign policy, as well as of closer economic, financial, and social co-operation, without duplicating the work of existing bodies. This committee consisted of Belgium, Canada, Italy, the Netherlands, and Norway, with the Chairman of the Council Deputies, Spofford, as an *ex-officio* member. I had been asking for a NATO study of the possibilities of action under Article 2. I got it. For my pains I was appointed to preside over the Committee of Five and Canadian officials did most of the work.

We soon found out, as we had feared we would, that the attitude of our most powerful members made the prospects for any broad advance under Article 2 negligible. Thus the report of our committee to the Lisbon meeting of the Council in February 1952 was in very general terms. After all, there was not much point in making specific recommendations that would be rejected by the Big Three and, as a consequence, would merely emphasize the division within the Alliance. We excused ourselves by stating that a committee which represented only five of the treaty's members, and excluded the United States, Britain, and France, was not an effective agency for recommending a programme of specific action likely to get unanimous acceptance. The Ministers at Lisbon simply asked the Permanent Representatives on the Council to take over our work and to continue the examination of these matters.

ॐ

More important in terms of the work of the Alliance, the Lisbon meeting created the post of Secretary General. To fill it, the Council chose

Lord Ismay, a bluff, John Bull type of Englishman, wise and broad-minded, with a genius for making friends and getting on with people, whatever their nationality, race, or station. There could have been no better choice to take charge of the Secretariat during its vital formative period.

The circumstances of Lord Ismay's appointment were interesting. The British felt that the first Secretary General should be British, as the first Supreme Allied Commander Europe had been American. They said that they would be glad to support me – I was, at least, 'Commonwealth British.' I had also been approached by other delegations, including the American, to accept the post. It was a most attractive prospect and, personally, I would have been happy to become Secretary General. I felt, however, that to resign as Canada's Secretary of State for External Affairs would have been a poor way of showing my appreciation for all that Prime Minister St Laurent had done for me and for the confidence he had shown in me. So I indicated that I was not available for NATO.

The first choice of Britain for the post was not Lord Ismay but their Ambassador in Washington, Sir Oliver Franks, who had an enviable record in diplomacy and in public service via a professorship of moral philosophy. I knew and greatly admired Franks, and warmly approved his nomination as did my colleagues in the Alliance. I doubted, however, whether he would accept, and found that my doubts were justified. As Chairman of the Council that year I was charged with the duty of offering him the position and persuading him to take it. My intentions were of the best, my arguments were, I thought, strong, but my tactics were unfortunate. 'Phone him now,' said Eden and Acheson one morning after the Council had agreed. I did. It was 10 AM in Lisbon. We forgot it was 4 AM in Washington. I got the Ambassador out of a sound sleep and, though normally a very mild and courteous person, he was naturally irritated by the interruption of his slumbers and unimpressed by my reason for it. However, he at least agreed to consider the offer, no doubt in order to get back to bed. Knowing Oliver Franks, I am comforted by the certainty that my bad timing was not entirely responsible for his subsequent rejection of the offer. I doubt whether that rejection disturbed Churchill, who would not be inclined in principle to prefer a professor to a general, certainly not a general so close to him as 'Pug' Ismay, his personal Chief of Staff in World War II.

Initially, Lord Ismay's position was quite difficult, a reflection, no doubt, of the Council's general lack of authority. In fact, 'Pug' (who became a valued friend) told me at a dinner party in New York in

March 1953 that he had had more authority as a first subaltern in the British army than as Secretary General of NATO. Nevertheless, by the time he resigned after four years in office, NATO's civil organization had been well established – largely through his efforts.

After Ismay announced his resignation in December 1956, Paul-Henri Spaak, once again Belgian Foreign Minister, came to see me at the Council meeting in Paris to tell me that his colleagues wished me to succeed Ismay. I asked him if he was available. He was, but wanted me to know that, if I would take the post, he would put my name forward. This time I was not even tempted. Another Canadian election was in the offing and Mr St Laurent, we knew, would find the going difficult. Our party fortunes, after twenty years of office, were, to say the least, not in the ascendant. This was no time to abandon Canadian politics. Furthermore, Spaak was qualified in every way for the post and it was appropriate that it should go to a European, especially since the headquarters were now in Paris, at the Palais de Chaillot.

ॐ

The purely military aspects of the Alliance have proved generally somewhat more complex than the organizational. Again the 1952 Lisbon meeting provides the example. It was a particularly difficult meeting in respect of defence planning, upon which Britain and the United States found themselves in some strong disagreement. One evening, I needed every power of persuasion and conciliation I possessed to pacify Dean Acheson and Anthony Eden, then British Foreign Secretary, in a vigorous, post-prandial verbal battle. Acheson had the best of it. He was a master of the brilliant, biting phrase, but Eden's assumption of Oxonian, Foreign Office superiority never faltered. Their rapport became more amiable as they got to know each other better. The military force goals set and accepted at Lisbon were quite unrealistic. The level to be reached by the end of 1952 was fifty divisions of land forces, increasing to ninety-six divisions by the end of 1954. Of these, twenty-five divisions were to be ready on the Central European front at all times. The actual force level reached on the Central European front by 1957, however, was sixteen to eighteen divisions, and these were not backed by the required reserve strength.

There was real difficulty over the appointment of the senior naval commander. In December 1951, during a talk I had at Chequers with Winston Churchill, he told me that he would be attending the upcoming Lisbon meeting since it would be a very important one and since he was at the time Minister of Defence as well as Prime Minister. Indeed, with his tongue in his cheek pressing against a cigar, he flattered me (we had reached the brandy stage in our luncheon) by remarking that he would be 'proud to sit at my feet as Chairman.' That would have been a memorable, if somewhat awesome, experience for me. If he had actually turned up, my feet would never have been the same again.

More important, Mr Churchill asserted that in the NATO command structure, which the Americans were building up and which he thought was too unwieldy, there was one point on which he was adamant. A British not an American admiral should be Supreme Allied Commander Atlantic (SACLANT). Britannia must command, even if she could no longer rule, that sea. This did not happen. An American admiral was appointed. There was much displeasure in London, only partially mitigated by agreement that an Eastern Atlantic Command, under SACLANT, should be created whose commander would be British.

After Lisbon, the defence organization was improved, and its activities were enlarged with the increase of the armed forces under its control. But the basic structure was now established. Commanders were, naturally, never satisfied with the strength of the North Atlantic Treaty forces which they continually compared unfavourably to the larger forces of the Soviet bloc countries. This comparison, however, lost much of its impact as nuclear weapons became more and more decisive both for deterrence and destruction.

A 'balance of terror' was really achieved after the development of the hydrogen bomb, with a destructive capacity hundreds of times greater than even atomic weapons. Winston Churchill provided one of the most interesting appreciations I have ever heard on the implications of thermonuclear weapons at a Commonwealth Prime Ministers' Conference early in 1955, as I recorded in my diary on 2 February:

'This morning the "old gentleman" had his chance to discuss the world and the H-Bomb, and he made the most of it.

'I happened to sit right across the table from him and it is a fascinating pastime to watch him; his cherubic "baby" face, at times gleeful, at times petulant, at times impish and at times sombre and dramatic, but never in repose. He also fiddles around with his hearing aid, his pencil, his inevitable cigar, like a curious and eager small boy. He seems to keep up a prodding interest in whatever Norman Brook [Secretary to the British Cabinet], who sits beside him, is doing; or he busies himself with ordering the window to be opened, or something else to be done. He often peers at me over his glasses as if he is wondering what I may be up to. Everything he does is dramatized and is full of life.

'He really let himself go on the H-Bomb – the shattering implications of which, on our society, he has fully grasped. His sweeping imagination and range of mind has sensed that this discovery has made all the old concepts of strategy and defence as out of date as the spear or the Macedonian phalanx. He is horrified and comforted at the same time; by the immensity of the bomb, and by its value as a deterrent against Russia. He finds solace in the fact that the Moscow men are cold-blooded realists who know what power means and don't wish to be destroyed. So he thinks the bomb may mean the destruction of war, not of humanity. As he puts it in concluding his statement, "It was an ironic fact that we had reached a stage where safety might well be the child of terror and life the twin of annihilation." '

But in February 1952, at the time of the Lisbon meeting, the testing by the United States of the first hydrogen device (which event was for some reason code-named 'Mike') was still eight months away.

The publication of the force totals agreed on at Lisbon and the continuing insistence of SACEUR that more must be done, together with the failure to implement Article 2, led to vigorous criticism by some members in our Parliament, as I have already mentioned, that the North Atlantic Alliance had now become merely a military alliance, dominated by the Pentagon, for pursuing the Cold War. Naturally I had to defend the policy of the government and myself against these attacks. I answered part of the criticism on the radio programme 'The Nation's Business' on 11 March 1952:

To designate the growing strength of our North Atlantic coalition, as it is expressed in present NATO military programmes, which, even when they are completed, will, in the face of Russian might, be barely adequate for defence; to designate this defence build-up as "irresponsible and disastrous," as the CCF have now done, is I think itself irresponsible. If such an attitude becomes prevalent it might well be also disastrous.

It would be foolish – and worse – to slacken in our determination now to carry out the policy of collective defence which is beginning to make an impression inside the Kremlin walls. It would also, I admit, be foolish to push that policy to such a point that it would dangerously weaken our social and economic structure. We have to reconcile these two things – military security and economic health – and that is what we are trying to do in NATO.

More specifically on Article 2, I replied to my CCF critics in the House on 1 April 1952:

Mr Speaker, I suggest that notwithstanding what has been said by the Honourable Member of the CCF group ... we are building up those habits of co-operation and consultation ... I believe that Canada, far from being condemned for doing nothing under the article, has done as much or more than any other particular country to achieve its implementation by developing economic and political co-operation, and by building up the Atlantic community; but I would remind Honourable Members that no one country can achieve implementation of NATO policy and that it must be done by common agreement. If we look at Article 2, I think we will find that, unlike certain other articles in the Treaty, it does not provide specifically for any special NATO machinery; nor does it necessarily entail joint programmes of action among member nations, althought that might, of course, develop. It is a rule of conduct which member nations undertake to follow in their internal and external policies generally, and not merely in their policies vis-à-vis one another ...

We are not so concerned in NATO with talking about some grandiose Atlantic structure ... as we are in laying foundations on which to build the future.

This was the best case I could make but it did not satisfy our critics; or, indeed, completely satisfy me.

To the force totals of the Alliance accepted at Lisbon, Canada was expected to make an appropriate contribution. If we had not done so, we would have had little or no influence in the foreign policy discussions at the Council. Having regard to the fact that we were the only overseas member of the Alliance apart from the USA (and, of course, Iceland, which had no armed forces) and since our NATO defence contingents had to be maintained across the ocean, I felt that we were carrying our fair share of the burden on land, sea, and in the air. Our contribution, moreover, included substantial aid, much stimulated by the Korean War, in providing equipment and training facilities to some of the smaller NATO countries. Our NATO forces (a brigade group, an air division, and a number of destroyers) may not have been large, but they were highly trained and fully professional.

During 1953 one matter came up which should be mentioned. On Friday, 13 March, a telegram was received by Brooke Claxton, our Minister of National Defence, from our NATO air representative which indicated that General Norstad, Deputy (Air) at SHAPE, might want to move Canadian F-86 squadrons from their bases in France to

the frontiers of West Germany, or even into the air corridor to West
Berlin, as protection against MIG attacks. There had been two such
attacks, one against a US fighter plane on the Czech border and one
against a British bomber in the north. Feeling was high, especially in
the press, and it was felt that some protective measures should be
taken. As the RCAF had the only F-86s in Europe, they would obviously be considered for such a move. The situation, however, was
not an easy one from our point of view, because we did not wish to
become involved in any move arising out of occupation policy or,
indeed, to become involved in any retaliatory incidents. Nevertheless,
our forces in Europe were part of the NATO forces, and had to accept
duties as such. Claxton was all for instructing Air Marshall Campbell,
Air Officer Commanding, Canadian Air Division, Europe, to tell Norstad that he had better find some other aircraft for these purposes. I
was anxious that we should take no such negative attitude, but merely
point out some of the considerations involved and wait to see if a
formal request would be made. The situation was made more difficult
by the fact that secret information which came to our knowledge made
it quite clear that the British bomber was well off its course and a good
many miles into communist territory when it was attacked by the
MIGs. Before returning to New York from Ottawa I had a talk with
the PM and he agreed that we should proceed very cautiously in this
matter and hope that public opinion would die down and no dramatic
retaliatory protective action would be required. It seemed pretty clear,
by the end of the week, that these two incidents did not signify any
new pattern of aggression by Malenkov, the Soviet Premier succeeding
Stalin, but rather a nervousness and jumpiness on the part of the
Russian air force, which expressed itself in its normal brutal way. If
this were true, then it would obviously be unwise to fan the flames by
moving the F-86s to patrol the border, especially as Malenkov was
talking so peacefully in Moscow. Apparently these considerations
prevailed in Washington and London, because nothing further was
heard of the possibility of moving RCAF jets to border areas.

The difficulty of co-ordinating policy through NATO in defence
matters, when decision-making power rested in the hands of one
member, was most clearly shown in nuclear matters. I remember a
discussion with Mr Dulles in Paris in December 1954. Tactical nuclear
weapons were then just appearing in the armoury for the defence of
Western Europe. The questions that concerned us in the North Atlantic
Council involved their employment and control. Following my talk
with the United States Secretary of State, I made the following note:

'I spent an hour this morning, Sunday, December 19th, with Mr Dulles at the US Embassy.

'He seemed happy about the results of the North Atlantic Council meeting, and felt that the formula which we had worked out in regard to military planning for the use of NATO atomic tactical weapons was a good one, and that the unanimity revealed on this matter at the Council was encouraging, especially in view of the unfortunate and tendentious press speculations which had preceded our meeting.

'Mr Dulles was worried, however, about the possibility of subsequent discussion in the Council as to how the governments would exercise their right of decision in regard to the use of atomic weapons if an emergency developed. He felt, and I agreed with him, that any such discussion would likely not be helpful and might be dangerous. It simply was not possible to work out in advance an agreement between fifteen nations on a subject of this kind which would cover every situation. There were, for instance, constitutional difficulties in Washington (and, I added, in Ottawa) which would prevent governments delegating powers in such a vital matter. But these could not be discussed without giving a potential aggressor aid and comfort. Dulles spoke of the trouble they had had in the Senate when the NATO pact was up for ratification in regard to the effect of this pact on the President's and Congress's sole right to declare war. He admitted that there might be some understanding reached with the powers principally concerned, notably the United Kingdom, France and Canada, as to the procedure which should be followed for making quick and necessary decisions if an emergency developed. He thought, however, that any such arrangements should be kept very secret and that NATO Council discussion of these matters, let alone public discussion, should be discouraged. I told him that I was inclined to agree because it was practically impossible to reconcile constitutional positions with practical necessities in a case of this kind; that, in any event, developments would determine decisions and probably in a way which could not now be foreseen.

'I said that there were two things, however, that we should do; first, by continuous consultation keep our policies in alignment, especially if the political situation should deteriorate, and secondly, agree, if possible, on "alert" procedures so that the military would know what had to be done in an emergency.

'I then went on to explain to Mr Dulles some new problems that had arisen for Canada in respect of the NATO collective defence effort; problems which arose, as we had pointed out in a statement to the

Council, over the increasing importance attached to northern defence, particularly through the setting up of early warning systems. We were anxious to emphasize that this was an important part of NATO defence, because without such effective early warning arrangements the retaliatory power of the United States might be destroyed and, in present circumstances, this would be as fatal for Europe as for America. Canada was anxious to play a full part in these northern defence developments, especially in respect of those which were on Canadian territory. This might result eventually in reducing somewhat our air defence contribution in Europe and the transfer of some of our squadrons back to Canada to back up the early warning systems. I told him that this was not a matter of immediate necessity or for early decision, and that we would in any event, I assumed, wish to maintain some forces in Europe as an evidence of solidarity in the defence of that area. Nevertheless, the problem for us existed and was becoming more difficult as our resources would not permit an increase of our defence activities in Canada and a maintenance of those activities in Europe on the present scale.'

As I saw it, with the threat of nuclear bombs (and later missiles), defence of the North American Arctic became as much a part of the Alliance's responsibility as the defence of Europe. The treaty was, after all, more than European and I believed that the North American sector should be considered an integral part of the North Atlantic defence structure. Any continental command should be an Alliance responsibility. It seemed to me, for example, that Norwegian contingents should operate in our Arctic just as Canadian forces occasionally took part in exercises in Norway. Canada's contribution to Arctic defence, therefore, should be accepted on the same basis as her contribution to overseas defence.

Later developments showed that there would have been great political advantages for us in such arrangements. But nothing effective could be done. The Americans would have none of this concept which, they thought, would interfere with their own control. Our own service people also, I suspect, preferred bilateral dealings and arrangements with Washington. Canadians had become accustomed to serving overseas in Europe; the idea that even token European contingents might share the responsibility of our continental defence was a novelty unworthy of serious consideration. Thus, the Canada-United States regional group was merely a formal part of the North Atlantic Treaty defence structure.

ℐ

The NATO Council meeting in Ottawa in September 1951, which had created the Committee of Five, agreed to admit Greece and Turkey to the Alliance and a Protocol of Accession was signed in London on 21 October 1951. It was ironic that this decision should have been taken in Ottawa because, in earlier private discussions, I had opposed bringing in these two Eastern Mediterranean countries since I believed that this made nonsense of the North Atlantic character of our association, diminished our credibility as the foundation for an Atlantic community, and gave greater validity to the criticism that we were purely and simply a military alliance. It would also be hard to convince the Canadian people that we should have closer ties with, say, Turkey, because she was a member of the Alliance, than with Ireland or Sweden who were not.

My attitude was not in any way a reflection on the importance of, or a lack of respect for, Greece and Turkey. Those friendly countries were indeed in a vulnerable position vis-à-vis the Soviet Union and its Eastern European Communist allies. They were as much entitled to collective security arrangements under Article 51 of the Charter as any other country and were in greater need of them than most. I judged, however, that this could best be done by a Mediterranean pact, but Washington insisted for strategic reasons on full treaty membership for Greece and Turkey. My own position was weakened, of course, by the fact that Italy, a Mediterranean country, was already in the Alliance.

Even more important was the difficult and sensitive question of the Federal Republic of Germany's accession to the North Atlantic Treaty. As early as September 1950, at the third Council meeting in New York, Dean Acheson, without any preliminary warning, introduced the question of German participation which, he said, must be brought about 'in some form.' The Korean War had increased our fears of Soviet military aggression; a contribution by West Germany to NATO forces and its acceptance of NATO responsibilities was held to be essential. France, Belgium, the Netherlands, Denmark, and Norway, however, had vivid memories of Nazi aggression and occupation and feared a recrudescence of German militarism and power. They were not going to be rushed into a solution of the problem by Washington. Therefore, at the Brussels Council meeting in December 1950, while West Germany's participation was approved in principle, the United

States, British, and French delegates were asked to examine and report on how this might best be brought about.

It was considered that the best solution, from all points of view, would be for the European Defence Community, then under consideration, to include the Federal Republic of Germany. The fact that there would thus be no separate German defence forces should allay any fears that might be created by German membership. In May 1951, therefore, a formula was approved for German association with NATO through its accession to the Brussels Pact and membership in the European Defence Community.

That community, however, failed to materialize. The initiative and impetus for it had come, ironically (in view of later developments), from the French. I recall a talk I had in December 1951 with President Auriol, who became quite emotional in asserting that there could be no question of Germany's admission to the North Atlantic Treaty without a European Defence Community in which German forces would form part of a European army. He feared, however, that if Britain did not also become part of the community, agreement might be impossible.

In London shortly afterwards I reported President Auriol's views to Anthony Eden. He considered it quite unfair that the French, or anyone else, saddle the British with responsibility for any such failure when the Europeans' inability to reach agreement was largely because the 'Pleven Plan' for an integrated European army, a French proposal, was neither clear nor realistic. Eden also claimed, and this surprised me, that only a few days before General Eisenhower (SACEUR) and Hervé Alphand, French Deputy on the North Atlantic Council, had advised him not to make any move toward British participation in the proposed European army, because this would require alteration in the proposed basis of that army and thereby postpone its acceptance even further.

All I could do at that time was to urge Eden at least to do something to remove the impression that Britain was not really in favour of any form of European Defence Community. He agreed that this should be done. Mr Churchill and he were to be in Paris shortly and they would make positive and sympathetic noises about the desirability in principle of European defence unity and try to remove the impression that Britain was remaining aloof because of her desire to maintain special and separate relations with the Commonwealth and the United States.

Winston Churchill, it was true, had made his famous speech calling for a united states of Europe at the University of Zürich in 1946. But he did not have anything like the 'Pleven Plan' in mind at all. I know this because when I saw Churchill at Chequers, two days after my meeting with Eden, he told me that the proper way to bring European armies together was to maintain their national identity and tie them together as a 'bunch of sticks,' bound together by common interest in their own salvation, rather than to mix them all up as 'wood-pulp.' Britain, he insisted, would fight *with* European forces, but not *in* them. Thus, Britain was unwilling to join the kind of European army now proposed by the French; or to lose herself in Europe. Indeed, he found it difficult to understand how the French, with their strong national and military traditions, were willing to allow their army to become absorbed in any such European force. Nevertheless, Britain was very sympathetic, Churchill assured me, to the idea of European unity. British association with any practicable moves to this end would be close and continuous, but not necessarily organic. In short, Churchill spoke like an Anglo-Saxon de Gaulle, in favour of a *union des patries*.

The next day, at a dinner which he gave for me, Eden returned to the subject of the European Defence Community. While he still felt that they could not join the EDC, he agreed that Britain should have participated actively in the discussions of the French plan from the beginning and tried to work out a better one. If the present plan were accepted by the European countries, Britain should see what they could do, short of joining, to make it work. If it were *not* accepted, then the British should join the Europeans in seeking an alternative plan for closer European defence co-operation, which would be based on close integration of national forces, but with a looser form of international control. Whatever happened, however, and this was what worried me most (it also worried Eden and the Foreign Office), the failure of these European plans should not result in Germany and the United States working out their own arrangements for defence co-operation in a way which would anger and frighten the French and unnecessarily provoke the Soviets.

If I spend so much time on the European Defence Community, with which Canada did not become directly involved, it is because, first, I believed that the failure of the negotiations in 1951 would be a serious, though not a fatal, setback in the move toward Western European unity, so important for peace and security in the future; and, second, because it had a direct bearing on the organization of a strong NATO integrated force for collective defence, with West German participation, and with a solid political structure to support it. This would reduce the danger of the separation of the continent from North America,

with separate and special United States-German defence arrangements. Indeed, I recall meeting the senior officers of my department
one afternoon in January 1953 to discuss the possibility of a Canadian initiative of some kind which would pull NATO out of its present
doldrums; whether we could save the EDC by enlarging it into a NATO
defence community with American and Canadian as well as British
participation. We decided, however, that any such move on our part
at that time would certainly be premature since there was still hope
that EDC and NATO would be in a better position as soon as the new
American administration got going.

The French, however, who had first sponsored the European Defence Community, rejected it on 29 August 1954 by the vote of their
Assembly after Mendès-France became Prime Minister. A meeting of
the Foreign Ministers of West Germany, France, Italy, and Benelux
(the proposed members of the EDC), plus those of Britain, the United
States, and Canada was summoned for 28 September 1954 in London
to find a new solution for the problem of German accession to the
North Atlantic Treaty.

I was in New York at the time attending the UN General Assembly.
The situation seemed to require an exercise of that instant diplomacy
made possible by air travel. This is a practice not to be recommended,
except in a real emergency. The growing tendency to fly a few thousand miles and then go straight to a conference room with a tired body
and mind, where you are expected to talk clearly, argue convincingly,
and be courteous and genial to all, is to be deprecated. It can severely
impair the results of any international meeting. There should be a
self-imposed rule which requires every negotiator to have at least
twenty-four hours of complete rest after a long flight before he goes
to work, especially if he has passed through a number of time zones
in travel. There is, however, a kind of travel disease which affects some
politicians, officials, and diplomats. The virus is a feeling of indispensa-
bility, born of vanity, which compels one to leave a meeting, rush to
an airport, fly through the night, hurry to another meeting, fly back
home or to another continent for a conference. All this feverish activity
creates a sensation of achievement, of importance, and of power. It
can also make for sloppy, half-finished work. The responsible Minister feels that he *must* be present because he *can* be present. He can
be here, there and everywhere, and nowhere long enough: 'We must
come to some conclusion within the next half-hour when my plane
leaves to take me to the Pitcairn Islands where I must see the Prime
Minister on a very important matter tomorrow morning.' One result

of all this is that we increasingly confuse motion with progress and agitation with achievement. In today's feverish and impatient world, the man who wishes to take time to consider before deciding is often urged: 'Don't just stand there, *do* something.' This advice might often, with advantage, be replaced by: 'Don't do anything, just stand there – and think.' Nonetheless, I was willing to make a speech at the United Nations on a Thursday afternoon, and after the night flight, begin discussing the European defence situation with my colleagues in London on Friday morning.

My notes for 25 September 1954, the day I arrived in London from New York, read:

'I found Eden relaxed and cheerful, moderately optimistic about the Conference. He thinks Canada can play quite an important part with the French (he is certainly worried about Mendès-France) and with the Americans (Dulles is not his soul mate) in helping to solve our problems.

'I gave him my view that it was most important (1) to make Mendès-France feel that he was among friends who sympathized with his difficulties and (2) to keep the Atlantic aspect of our problem always in mind; for no exclusively European solution would do.'

Then, on the following Monday:

'Dinner given for Mendès-France; we got along fine. He is a tough, volatile little man who doesn't waste time on social graces, or on small talk! His views on the Conference, given after dinner, depressed us more and more as the evening went on. He talked about conditions which must be acceptable to the French Parliament before Germany could even be considered for membership in NATO: settlement of the Saar, control of all arms production, etc. Eden began to get more and more impatient and finally told him very frankly that insistence on these views would mean the failure of the Conference; the withdrawal of the United States from the Atlantic Alliance; a policy of peripheral strategy in Washington; Germany would be the favourite friend, etc., etc. I tried to back up Eden in this, especially in insisting on the disastrous effect of the failure of the Conference on United States policy.

'Mendès-France didn't seem much impressed by our worries or our arguments and kept returning to his own parliamentary difficulties, which we must help him overcome! He has a single track mind on this problem; also determination and tenacity.'

I soon found that the other Alliance Foreign Ministers were worried about the possible failure of the conference, and impatient with the attitude and the manners of Mendès-France. I was urged, since as a Canadian I was not directly involved, to be an 'honest broker' in the search for agreement. I could only counsel patience and the avoidance of doing or saying anything that would isolate Mendès-France. At the conference, my interventions were designed to prevent the impasse which seemed to be developing by putting forward various suggestions for discussion, even for rejection. We needed time. As it happened, the conference, though once or twice seeming to be on the verge of disaster, eventually managed to work out the broad lines of an agreement associating West Germany with NATO on the only basis (I expressed strongly my own views to the conference on this) which she could accept – equality and non-discrimination.

The conference resumed in Paris in October, with the rest of the North Atlantic Treaty members now present, and two Protocols were agreed and signed there on the 23rd. One, which did not concern Canada directly, provided for the accession of Italy and the German Federal Republic to the Brussels Treaty and for accompanying arrangements concerning the control of armed forces and armaments. The other, which I did sign, was a Protocol to the North Atlantic Treaty which provided for the admission of Germany to NATO as a member of the Brussels group, now called 'Western European Union.' It provided also for the termination of the allied occupation regime in the Federal Republic and for a German defence contribution to NATO. These meetings, so important and so difficult, ended any hope for a European Defence Community at this time. But they brought Germany into NATO and in Ottawa we considered this to be essential.

I remember that at the Commonwealth Prime Ministers' Conference in 1955, in the course of a clear, comprehensive, and even dramatic analysis of developments leading up to the Paris agreements, Anthony Eden was good enough to say I had played some part in all this. He was at his best and most impressive. Churchill, puffing at one of those out-size cigars he was always pressing his companions to smoke, was obviously quite pleased with the performance of his protégé. Eden's star was very much in the ascendent; he was no longer the heir apparent – he was the heir. Sir Winston was himself very impressive on Germany. He recognized that the Paris agreements contained an element of risk, but asserted that it was part of statesmanship 'to forgive and forget, and if you can't forgive, forget. Fear from the past must not determine the pattern of the future.'

The Protocol admitting West Germany became effective on 5 May

1955. The Warsaw Pact was signed on 14 May 1955. There was, however, a difference between the two. NATO was a voluntary coalition of free countries under a treaty freely negotiated and approved, with one exception, by the democratically elected members of their legislatures. As a coalition it negotiated for the inclusion of Bonn in its membership. The Warsaw Pact was imposed, without any real negotiation, by the government of the USSR on her communist satellite states, where it was accepted without any reference to the popular will. NATO operated on the basis of free discussion and decision by its members. Its leader, the United States, could not, without great difficulty, impose its will on the other members. The opposite was the case with the Warsaw Pact where the will and the policy of the USSR prevailed without question. It is well to remember this.

At another Council meeting in December 1955, Article 2 found its way once again on to the agenda (no one could say we did not talk enough about it). This time the Italians were the sponsors and Lord Ismay made a plea that we broaden our discussions on foreign and defence matters to include the economic policies of member states. A resolution was passed reaffirming that closer co-operation between members of the Alliance, as envisaged in Article 2, was a very good thing and that the permanent Council should examine once again how this could best be brought about. Naturally, I supported the resolution, though I was sceptical that anything would happen, particularly since neither Dulles nor Harold Macmillan, who was briefly British Foreign Secretary, had intervened in the discussion. I was right.

I had long since become cynical about pronouncements on Article 2. When NATO questions came up in the House of Commons, I took refuge in the increasing importance of the Council as a mechanism for political consultation. As I said on 31 March 1954: 'In the meeting of the NATO Council which will take place in a few weeks ... we have only one item on the agenda, an exchange of views on the international political situation ... The fact that we can meet and talk about these things regularly, frankly and fully does, I think, help to bring about the closer political integration, if I may use that word, which we had in mind when we signed the NATO Agreement.' I repeated this encouraging assessment in the Commons on 20 January 1955. My Deputy Minister, now Jules Léger, with no responsibility to answer criticism in Parliament, was not impressed by my encouraging analysis, or even by my assurance to M.J. Coldwell in the House of Commons Committee on External Affairs on 24 May 1955 that Paul-Henri Spaak had told me after the last Council meeting: 'Our discussions were ... becoming more and more like Cabinet discussions in a Commonwealth of Atlantic powers.'

By 1956, in fact, I was losing hope that NATO would evolve beyond an alliance for defence; and even there I was beginning to have doubts about its future. An improvement in relations with the USSR was beginning to lessen the common fears which were the cement that held us together. Interest in and support for the Alliance was dropping in some of the member countries. This was worrying. I was asked by some of my North Atlantic Council colleagues in March 1956 to raise once again the whole question of closer co-operation within NATO and was told that, if I did, it would get a more serious and searching consideration than before. I agreed to do so. On 20 April I received a comprehensive memorandum from my Department with suggestions for making some real progress in spite of the discouraging experiences of the past. This memorandum, while opposing any new NATO machinery, recommended 'the enhancement of the authority of the Council so that its voice can be heard and its influence recognized, accompanied by an improvement in the structure of its committees and working groups where the views of governments are examined and, if possible, reconciled.'

When the Council met on 4 May 1956, there appeared a renewed impetus to re-examine non-military co-operation; fresh and serious thinking seemed to have been given to the problem. Even Mr Dulles spoke openly and earnestly about the necessity to do something really constructive to develop the non-military responsibilities and opportunities of NATO, 'which,' he said, 'had reached a critical moment of its life.'

I kept my fingers crossed. My caution was justified; when the US Secretary of State later spoke at the Council meeting – which, of course, was private – he seemed less concerned about non-military co-operation than in ensuring that any strengthening in this area should not be at the expense of the collective military effort. His only proposal to strengthen the solidarity of the Alliance was to appoint a committee of three ministers 'to advise the Council on the ways and means to improve and extend NATO co-operation into non-military fields and to develop greater unity within the Atlantic Community.' Dulles pledged, once again, the full and earnest co-operation of the United States to this study.

The basic question to be answered now went beyond methods and plans for co-operation. It was whether the Alliance could successfully adapt itself to a changing political environment in which the likelihood of imminent military aggression had diminished, and whether something other than fear could ensure close and effective co-ordination of policies between member governments. To find the answer, we had now our Committee of Three. It was immediately, and inevitably, handicapped by being dubbed 'The Three Wise Men.' There were moments when I thought that it might more appropriately be called 'The Three Stooges.' The 'Three' consisted of my friend, Halvard Lange of Norway, Dr Gaetano Martino, Foreign Minister of Italy, and myself. We were very fortunate in having a small but first-class staff of experts (I was given the task of securing them) headed by a very able American diplomat, Lincoln Gordon. The work of this committee, along with the Hungarian and Suez crises at the UN and the parliamentary situation in Ottawa, made this year, 1956, the busiest and most exciting of my ministerial decade.

Before leaving for Paris to attend the first meeting of 'The Three,' I went to Washington to get at least the preliminary views of Foster Dulles and of Senator George, a highly respected veteran Democrat from Georgia whom President Eisenhower had made his special representative in charge of relations with our committee. We met for several hours on 12 June, along with senior officials of the State Department. I asked for their views on the questions which we were to consider. These formed the substance of the United States answers to the questionnaire which we were soon to send to member governments. The questions included:

1   If NATO was being formed today would the present grouping of states be the most satisfactory for (a) collective defence and (b) non-military co-operation?

2   What kind of organization would best reflect a sense of Atlantic community as a basis for co-operation, NATO or OEEC? Or would it be wise to seek a new kind of organization for this purpose?

3   How can European integration be brought about so that it will strengthen rather than weaken Atlantic ties?

4   What do we really mean by 'political consultation'? What is its extent and purpose; should it be carried on through the permanent members of the Council or through ministers? Is it merely to exchange information; or to co-ordinate foreign policies and seek agreement on a common policy? Should consultation extend to problems outside the NATO area? What role should Parliamentarians play in consultation? Is a strong NATO Parliamentary Association desirable?

5   What should be the relationship between NATO and the UN; between NATO and OEEC, EURATOM, the Economic Commission for Europe, and other functional and regional agencies?
6   Can NATO deal effectively with the problem of closer economic collaboration between its members?
7   Should NATO concern itself with colonial problems; with economic aid to developing countries?

In dealing with these points Dulles was cautious and not very encouraging, even though he kept emphasizing their importance. He was particularly careful about the obligation to consult or even to exchange information on matters of only general concern to the NATO members. On matters of direct concern falling within the NATO area, he agreed that better procedures should be worked out; but since ministerial meetings were likely to be infrequent, short, and discursive, he thought the best course would be to strengthen the permanent machinery. He also emphasized once again the difficulty of the United States in reconciling effective allied consultation with the necessity for quick decisions in an emergency. He assured me that in respect of consultation, the United States 'would be willing to go as far as any other country *with comparable responsibilities* ... even further.' The fact that no other member had such responsibilities made the assurance of doubtful importance.

As for economic matters, while there was no sense in trying to make NATO an operating agency in this field, Dulles thought that there might be more consultation in the Council on economic policies, or at least on those that bore directly on foreign policy, such as the economic integration of Europe. He thought that NATO should keep out of the business of aid to developing countries, and he was non-committal about greater parliamentary association within NATO. All in all, his observations were not a very cheerful prelude to the work of the committee.

The Canadian reply to the questionnaire was more positive. This was perhaps not surprising, since I had a lot to do with the drafting of our reply, a reply to myself as one of the Three. For example, the Canadian government had this to say:

Member governments:
1   Should accept the responsibility of informing the NATO Council of any political development in any area which may affect significantly relations among member governments or between NATO countries and the Soviet bloc.
2   Should recognize the right to raise any subject of common concern to NATO for discussion.

3 Should endeavour not to make political declarations significantly affecting the Alliance or other members without prior consultation through the Council.

4 Should seek to develop their national policies in the light of the interests and views of other NATO governments as expressed in consultations.

5 Should not adopt firm policies on matters of concern to the whole Alliance without advance consultation.

Commitment to consult, once again, should not prejudice the need for prompt action in real emergencies, or lead to action constituting interference in the domestic affairs of any member government.

On economic questions we were more cautious in our reply, having learned from experience that earlier ideas on this aspect of Article 2 simply could not be realized. We approved the discussion of economic matters in the North Atlantic Council but opposed taking over any of the functions of existing international economic agencies. We also agreed that NATO should not become an agency for formulating or carrying out trade or aid policies on behalf of its members. We came out strongly for the greater use of national North Atlantic parliamentary associations, including meetings with the North Atlantic Council.

Finally, we made certain proposals for strengthening the organization of the Alliance. There should be greater ministerial attendance at Council meetings; and the Secretary General should become the permanent Chairman of all Council meetings.

Our committee worked diligently. We went over the replies with each government individually. We then discussed among ourselves and with our experts what should go into our report. I was given a special responsibility for working with the Secretariat in drafting that report. Our draft was gone over carefully by the committee on 14 November in New York. I was then at the UN and deeply involved in the problems of the Suez and Hungarian crises.

By this time experience had confirmed beyond any doubt that the North Atlantic coalition, in spite of ringing public speeches and declarations by governments, could develop its non-military potential only as far as the United States and, to a lesser degree, Britain and France, were prepared to go. Middle and smaller powers can rarely lay down policies which greater powers will adopt unless it is clearly in their own interests to do so. They can, however, influence the policy of their more powerful friends if their proposals are sound in principle and their diplomacy in advocating them is skilful and determined. We kept this very much in mind in preparing our report. We did not venture so far beyond what we knew to be the views of the Big Three as to risk swift and impatient rejection, but we did not hesitate to make proposals for change based on principles which the Three had endorsed in public statements. These they were bound to consider, even if the consideration led to no positive results.

The essence of our report appeared in this paragraph of the Introduction: 'North Atlantic political and economic co-operation, however, let alone unity, will not be brought about in a day or by a declaration, but by creating over the years and through a whole series of national acts and policies, the habits and traditions and precedents for such co-operation and unity. The process will be a slow and gradual one at best; slower than we might wish. We can be satisfied if it is steady and sure.' We hoped that our recommendations would facilitate this process. I do not propose to give them in any detail. They included most of the points contained in the Canadian reply to the questionnaire, already outlined. They were designed primarily to bring about a more fruitful political co-operation, in which consultation was to become 'an integral part of national policy.' This meant, we emphasized: '... the discussion of problems collectively in the early stages of policy formation and before national positions become fixed. At best this will result in collective decisions on matters of common interest affecting the Alliance. At the least it will ensure that no action is taken by one member without a knowledge of the views of the others.'

We were also concerned to make the organization more effective in carrying out its existing functions, particularly by strengthening the position of the Council and of the Secretary General. I believed that the permanent members of the Council should have a political connection with their governments which would enhance their authority and that of the Council. The United States agreed with this in principle, and its representatives on the Council were usually men not only of ability but of political influence. The British, however, strongly objected to this concept and insisted that the Council, apart from its ministerial meetings, should be strictly a body of diplomatic representatives. Even though the quality of the representation was high (certainly we sent our very best from Ottawa), I always regretted that the idea of political membership was rejected. It would have given consultation in NATO a greater influence on the policy of member governments.

Other recommendations of the 'Three' dealt with the peaceful settlement of disputes between members and with measures for greater co-operation in scientific, technical, cultural, and information fields. On economic matters, it was clear beyond any doubt that NATO neither could, nor should, duplicate the work of other international economic agencies. We therefore simply recommended more consultation, especially on matters of direct interest to the Alliance, to ensure maximum co-ordination of economic policies.

We had begun our work in June. Our report, comprehensive and carefully researched, was completed by December. That it was ready for consideration by the Council at its December meeting was a triumph, particularly for our secretariat and experts. The report was approved by the Council on 16 December. The members said many agreeable things about our work and then, as expected, instructed the Permanent Council and the Secretary General to determine what the governments thought about the proposals. Their thoughts were neither startling nor likely to form a consensus for action.

Political development within the Alliance did not prove to be a sufficient foundation for the growth of an Atlantic community. What growth there was in this field was Western European, rather than Atlantic. While the Council and its committees grew in effectiveness and authority as an agency for political consultation and diplomatic co-ordination, its main purpose remained the development and operation of a defence system for Western Europe. Our firm commitment to collective action against an aggressor was the main factor in removing the greatest temptation to aggression, the hope and expectation of easy victory.

5

THE NEW COMMONWEALTH

We have moved in my own lifetime from an Empire without sunset, which God had made mighty and was implored to make mightier yet, to today's mini-United Nations of equal sovereign states. I was present at that significant Commonwealth Conference in 1949 which initiated the new Commonwealth by the inclusion of India as a republic. There followed the grant of independence by Britain to one dependency after another, in Africa, Asia, the Pacific, the Caribbean, the Mediterranean. The old, small club of prosperous, mainly Anglo-Saxon members has grown to over thirty, all but six of them non-white, undeveloped industrially, and often economically poor and weak. Their representatives, who used to need for a meeting place only a small Cabinet room in 10 Downing Street, can now scarcely be accommodated in the largest of the conference rooms in Marlborough House.

On 12 November 1948 Mr Nehru stated his hope that a republican India would be able to stay in the Commonwealth. With Ireland about to leave we were the more anxious that India stay in – if some formula could be found. Mr Attlee discussed Nehru's proposals with representatives of Australia, New Zealand, and Canada in London on 11 December, and reported to Nehru that there would have to be some link with the Crown. A common citizenship, which Nehru had suggested, was not enough, if indeed it was practicable. It was decided that a Commonwealth Prime Ministers conference should be held in April 1949 to deal with this difficult and complex problem.

Mr St Laurent, now the Canadian Prime Minister, was getting ready for the 1949 election, however, and felt he should not go to London. Although I was the junior member of the Cabinet, he asked me to take his place. Given the constitutional nature of the conference, I suppose this was quite natural, though it may have disturbed some of my colleagues who liked dining off gold plate at Buckingham Palace. I found it an intensely interesting conference not only because I was the Canadian representative, but because Canada, as the first overseas Dominion, was the senior member of the Commonwealth. This meant that, in representing Canada, I was the senior spokesman.

Before the April conference Mr St Laurent wrote to various Prime Ministers, and to Mr Nehru in particular, expressing strongly the hope that India could be kept in the Commonwealth, even as a republic. His message to Nehru, however, while friendly and sympathetic, admitted that he found some difficulty in visualizing 'the continued existence of the Commonwealth relationship without some link with the Crown.' At the same time, with Cabinet approval, he instructed me to do everything possible to keep India in the association.

I arrived in London before the conference opened to have preliminary discussions with British and Dominion representatives on the problem which confronted us: could a republic remain in the Commonwealth; and if so, on what terms? On this basic point I saw my good friend, Sir Norman Brook, Secretary to the British Cabinet, before seeing Mr Attlee and Mr Nehru. (It was always my practice to talk to the officials before seeing the ministers.) I kept a record of our conversation:

'I had lunch today [Tuesday, 19 April] with Sir Norman Brook, who brought me up to date on the thinking here in regard to the Indian problem ... There has apparently been a strengthening of the feeling in certain quarters that India must be kept in the Commonwealth, even as a Republic. They have given up the idea of two types of membership in the Commonwealth, and rightly so, but feel that, while Nehru is not willing to accept the Crown as the source of allegiance, he may be willing to accept the Crown as, to use Sir Norman Brook's phrase, "Head of the Commonwealth." I told him that I did not like this phrase much, as the word "Head" might be misinterpreted but I thought that the idea was a good one and adequate as a basis for Indian membership. There may however, be some difficulty with other Dominions who wish to go further in keeping the Crown as the link through common allegiance, and also with South Africa. If this idea is carried out, there may have to be some kind of declaration of continuing membership emerge from this meeting, and also some alteration in the King's title. Norman Brook said in regard to the latter, that they have in mind something like, "George VI, of Canada (United Kingdom, Australia, etc. as the case may be), the other Monarchies (Nations) (Realms) of the Commonwealth, King, Defender of the Faith, Head of the Commonwealth." This of course is awkward, but something like this may be worked out.

'Brook also discussed with me the procedure for the forthcoming meetings. It is the intention to have bilateral discussions between Mr Attlee and the Dominion Ministers and between the Dominion Ministers themselves before having a general meeting. This is a good idea in order to keep things from becoming too large and too formal. Apparently Attlee took up the idea I expressed to Brook in Ottawa that there were usually too many UK Ministers at these Commonwealth meetings as a result of which the room tended to become divided between the UK and the rest on a basis of more or less numerical equality. Attlee had decided that only three UK Ministers should attend, but he was having real difficulty in choosing his two colleagues as five or six wished to come and three or four insisted. They had hoped that only two from each Dominion should be present, but here again, the Australian High Commissioner was vehement in his determination to attend so there may have to be three from each Dominion. This Constitutional business is the kind of problem that cannot be solved at meetings of thirty or forty people with formal speeches, etc.'

The next morning, I saw Mr Attleee at 10 Downing Street and we went over the procedure for the forthcoming meeting, discussing ways and means to overcome some of the difficulties that might occur. Most of the ground I had already traversed with Brook. Attlee was reasonably optimistic, taking practically the same line in regard to India as ourselves. I thought that he had gained a great deal of authority since becoming Prime Minister and that he would make a good chairman of our meeting.

That afternoon I left for St John's College, Oxford, where I dined with the Fellows. It was like old times, and I was relieved to find that nothing had changed at St John's, or indeed was ever likely to change. I spent the night in my old room and it was as uncomfortable as ever. I was treated just as I used to be treated. In other words, no towel, no hot water, no comfort! Food and drink were of course far better than could be obtained in London, and the dons did full justice to it.

On Thursday, 21 April, we had our first meeting at 10 Downing Street. It took the form of a pre-luncheon sherry party to establish the social basis on which to rest our political work. It was a very friendly and informal affair; afterwards, we motored to Buckingham Palace for luncheon with the Royal Family, all of whom, except Prince Charles, were present. As it was Princess Elizabeth's birthday, it was a nice combination of gold-plate royal formality and friendly family atmosphere. The Royal Family were well briefed for the occasion. For example, each of them commiserated with me on a recent decision which had prohibited the use of dollars by Britain for the purchase of Canadian wheat. So far as I was concerned, however, Queen Mary stole the show. It was quite startling to see her begin the smoking at lunch by putting her cigarette in a long holder which she proceeded to tip at a rakish angle.

Afterwards we went into the grand drawing-room and were photographed in various poses and groups. It was a relief to note that even the Buckingham Palace press photographer was as irreverent and tyrannical as members of his craft invariably are. He pushed the Royal Family around like ordinary beings. When one group seemed too stiff, he tried to make us unbend by announcing that we were not a very handsome looking crowd, and if we talked and smiled this might minimize our defects and make a better picture. The King gave out quite a guffaw at this sally, at which moment the photographer snapped his camera.

That afternoon I called on some of the other representatives at the conference. First, on Dr Malan, the steady, stolid Boer Prime Minister, who was, I thought, a nice old boy, though tough enough when he wanted to be. He was also reasonably optimistic on the success of our meeting and I judged would not be so difficult as some people feared. I had tea with him and his wife, and then at five o'clock called on Pandit Nehru with whom, in the interests of the Commonwealth, I consumed another cup of tea. We had a good talk, and I got the impression that he would do his part to make this Commonwealth conference a success by accepting the King in some form as the symbol of our association. He showed a very cultivated and subtle mind – not the sort of person one could get to know easily on first meeting.

The first formal meeting of the conference was Friday, 22 April, at which Mr Nehru stated that India had decided to become a republic but wished to remain in the Commonwealth. He suggested that India's association with the Commonwealth as a republic might be based on:
1 Commonwealth citizenship;

2 A declaration of India's continuing membership;

3 The continued acceptance by India of the status of the King as the symbol of the free association of the Commonwealth countries.

That evening I dined with Tommy Lascelles, the King's secretary. I thought it would be wise to pass on the sentiments of the morning's meeting and get the reaction of the Palace. I told him that there was every likelihood that India would accept recognition of the King as a symbol of the association and Head of the Commonwealth and that the rest of us were willing to accept India as a republic in the Commonwealth on this basis. Lascelles thought that this was a very wise and important solution and that the King would be pleased. He said that they had been looking into the question of inclusion of a republic in an association of monarchies and found that this had been done in the Holy Roman Empire for Danzig and Lübeck. The Palace was obviously not going to put any obstacle in the way of solution.

Early next morning, 23 April, a draft declaration was circulated to us by Mr Attlee. In fact, it consisted of two declarations, one by India which wished to remain in the Commonwealth, recognizing the King as outlined previously, and another by the rest of us saying that we were going to retain the Crown on the old basis. This was an unfortunate idea since the two declarations would really have underlined the division between two types of membership in the Commonwealth.

Later in the morning I called on the Prime Minister of Pakistan. We both agreed that there should be only one declaration. He was worried about the effect on Pakistan of the admission of a republic and believed that public opinion in his country would demand the same treatment. I tried to persuade him not to take any precipitate action on this point. At the same time, I agreed that Pakistan was entitled to have every assurance from our meeting that, if she became a republic, she could do so on exactly the same terms as India. Liaquat Ali Khan seemed an easier person to talk to than Nehru, franker and more straightforward. The strong feeling of hostility between Pakistan and India was discouraging. He and Sir Zafrullah Khan were bitter about what they called the unfriendly attitude of India towards them, not only on Kashmir, but on trade and economic matters. I tried to convey the impression of sympathetic neutrality.

I got the other side of the case when I called on Sir Girja Bajpai, Secretary General of the Indian Foreign Ministry. He was also worried about the double declaration and gave me a very confidential paper of his own, a sort of Balfour Report on the new Commonwealth of Republics and Monarchies. It was very well done, but I gathered that he had not been able to persuade his own Prime Minister to put it forward. I thought we might be able to use it in connection with a draft we were preparing to put forward at the next meeting, if the situation seemed to require it.

Later that afternoon I had tea with Princess Elizabeth, the Duke of Edinburgh, and Prince Charles, who was brought in after tea and displayed to Joseph Chifley, the Australian Prime Minister, and myself. I recorded in my diary: 'I hope that relations, not at the moment too good between Australia and Canada, were not further disturbed by the fact that I was able to make the baby laugh while Chifley was not successful. Possibly I tried harder! The Princess and her husband and child are a charming family group, and would be, irrespective of their station. She is a sweet and good-natured person, obviously conditioned to her job by long years of training, and very sincere in her desire to do well what she is destined to do. He seems to be a high-spirited lad, intelligent and attractive, but will no doubt settle down to the business of royalty.'

At 2:30 on Monday, 25 April, we met again at 10 Downing Street and discussed the documents circulated on Saturday by Mr Attlee. I said at once that the two statements suggested, one by India and one by the rest of us, would be unsatisfactory and we should try to combine them in one draft. Australia, supported by New Zealand, threw the whole emphasis on the desire of the rest of us to retain our allegiance to the King, and played down the Indian development as a single exception to the general rule that the Commonwealth could include only monarchies. This was of course unsatisfactory to Pakistan and Ceylon who insisted very vigorously, and in strong language, that they could not subscribe to any declaration which seemed to put them in a less free position than India. The difficulty of course was that Australia and New Zealand, and indeed ourselves, were anxious that our declaration should not give the impression that we were all about to become republics. On the other hand, Pakistan and Ceylon insisted that any attempt to give India prior and exclusive consideration would be repugnant to public opinion in their countries. In supporting this view, they emphasized that they were quite happy with the existing constitutional position but, if it were changed for India, it might have to be changed for their countries. I was in a rather easy position as this was a battle that could be left to other delegations who took extreme views on one side or the other and my efforts could be devoted to finding compromises between the extremes. Attlee and Sir Stafford Cripps, the Chancellor of the Exchequer, were in the same situation.

There were of course other points of difference. Dr Malan did not like the expression 'symbol of our association and Head of the Commonwealth.' He thought that this might be interpreted in South Africa as a move towards a centralized empire. I was inclined to agree with him and suggested a form of words to get over this difficulty, 'The King as symbol of our association and *as such* Head of the Commonwealth.' The Indians did not like this for some reason so subtle as to be almost metaphysical and proposed for 'as such' to substitute 'thus.' We also had quite a long discussion on whether the word 'British' should appear before 'Commonwealth.' Our Anzac friends were of course insistent on this and South Africa, India, Pakistan, and Ceylon were on the other side. This was another fight which I found we could skip, but I did suggest that we could use the words 'British Commonwealth of Nations' to refer to the present situation and 'Commonwealth of Nations' when referring to the new state of affairs. At first this did not get much support but, as it happened, was finally adopted.

At the end of the afternoon, we were all tired and intellectually dishevelled, but the gap had been narrowed and the atmosphere was friendlier. Mr Attlee asked Sir Stafford Cripps, Sir Norman Brook, and Sir Percivale Liesching, of the British delegation, to work out a revised single draft, and invited me to join them. He later approved our new draft which was then submitted to the conference. The other delegates had been attending a cocktail party while we were drafting, which was helpful. It was given a first reading at 9:00 that night and, with some minor changes, including 'as such' instead of 'thus' before 'Head of the Commonwealth,' was adopted the next day. Australia, New Zealand, Pakistan, and Ceylon were not too happy about the wording – for different reasons – while Dr Malan still rather disapproved of 'Head,' though he agreed that the addition of the words 'as such' helped. The inclusion of the words 'the basis of whose membership is not changed,' which emphasized their own desire to retain the monarchy, was also helpful. No one was going to be able to accuse us of losing the battle for want of a nail!

We had a final business meeting at 9:45 PM on 26 April when we agreed on the procedure to be followed the next day in reporting our declaration to the King. There was some suggestion that we should give him collective advice on the matter, but I demurred as it seemed that constitutionally we could not do so. Instead, we agreed to call on him collectively and to have Mr Attlee read the declaration on our behalf. We then gave final approval to our document and closed our business session in an atmosphere of great good humour and goodwill.

The next morning, we met at 10:30 to put the finishing touches to our work and to begin a discussion of the King's title, which was now to be changed by removing the word 'Ireland.' We also wanted the phrase 'Dominions beyond the seas' taken out, and in its place a title which would mention all the countries by name, or a different title for the different countries. For example, for Canada it would be 'George the Sixth, King of Canada,' for the United Kingdom 'George the Sixth, King of Great Britain and Northern Ireland,' and so on. It soon became obvious that it was impossible to get any agreement on this. The New Zealand Prime Minister, Peter Fraser, and Chifley said they were not going to touch their titles and we could do what we liked with ours. I said that we would certainly change ours as indicated at the earliest opportunity as we did not like 'Dominions,' especially Dominions with a small 'd.' I was attacked on this, and it was pointed out to me that Dominions in the King's title had a capital 'D.' I found out, to my chagrin, that I was wrong. We had a good deal of chat also about whether we should keep or reject 'by the Grace of God' and 'Defender of the Faith.' Nobody seemed to be quite certain what faith the King was now supposed to be defending, and it was generally felt that while this phrase may have been satisfactory in the early days of the reign of Henry VIII, it was somewhat anomalous in 1949. No decisions, however, were taken, and we agreed to consider the matter further.

Peter Fraser then began to throw more fat into the fire by asking the meeting in general and Nehru in particular to define what each meant by Commonwealth co-operation. Peter had been muttering for some days that he was determined to thrash out this matter, and he certainly did so. Nehru, who was put on the spot, made a brilliant reply, arguing that there could be no co-operation except for constructive and peaceful purposes, and that it was not enough to build up a Commonwealth defence bloc and hope to check communism in that way. I have seldom listened to a more impressive dialectical statement. Nehru certainly displayed a magnificent mind.

At 12 o'clock we left Downing Street for the palace where in one of the large rooms we paraded before the King and Attlee read our declaration. The King read a few well chosen words in reply, in which incidentally he mentioned the 'British' Commonwealth of Nations and hinted that he hoped that there would not be too many more republics in the Commonwealth. However, he gave our work his blessing and seemed genuinely happy about what we had done. Afterwards, we all joined him in a glass of sherry and some informal conversation. Nehru and Dr Malan left together in one car. I hoped that there might be some symbolic significance in this, because it was obvious even then that, unless those two Prime Ministers and their countries got along better together, the King was going to be head of a somewhat disunited and disrupted Commonwealth.

So far as I was concerned, my part was easy to play. Once we had decided in Ottawa to support the inclusion of a republican India in the Commonwealth and once India accepted the Crown as the symbol of that association, all I had to do was help with suggestions to meet the difficulties raised by Pakistan, South Africa, and the 'down under' countries. In the actual drafting of the final document, I was lucky enough to be able to work with Cripps, Brook, and Liesching during the hour and a half in which the real job was done. Finally, no delegate had as advisers two people who knew more about the problem or how best to seek a solution than John Kearney and Bert MacKay.

So began the new 'Commonwealth of Nations': British Empire to British Commonwealth to Commonwealth; Emperor to King to Head. This was one of the most important landmarks in the history of the Commonwealth. It was the critical moment in her postwar development. Had we been unable to solve the problem of India's admission as a republic, we would not have the Commonwealth we have today with all the new members from Asia and Africa. Because of the solution we found, however, which seemed very sensible at the time, we did break an institutional bond within the Commonwealth, the Monarchy. This meant that only self-interest would hold the new Commonwealth together. The bond of sentiment between the new members of the Commonwealth and the old was bound to diminish, sustained as it had been by the common educational, legal, and even political backgrounds of many of the leaders; by shared experiences as students at Oxford, Cambridge, the London School of Economics, or Sandhurst, or even as political prisoners in one of His Majesty's gaols; or by a dedication to common constitutional, philosophical, or political traditions. All these bonds continue to weaken, as new conditions arise and as new leaders take over, leaders who have a different outlook in a different world and to whom parliamentary institutions and western traditions and values may have no appeal or even little positive meaning. Thus, in making this change, which was inevitable and worthwhile at the time, the critics would say that we sowed the seeds of the Commonwealth's eventual disintegration. There was no alternative. Had we not made the change, disintegration would have taken place much sooner.

I fully believe, however, that there are sound, practical reasons for continuing our association quite apart from sentiment. I could not imagine anything more valuable than an association based on the old British Commonwealth which would permit members from the emerging continents of Africa and Asia to share with Britain, Australia, New Zealand, and ourselves a multilateral, multiracial association. I thought that this might be a very useful piece of international machinery, as indeed it has turned out to be, because it is different from any other kind of international structure. We were not oblivious to enlightened self-interest as an important bond in 1949. Indeed, in the next year the Colombo Plan was initiated.

ॐ

On 2 January 1950 I set off from Ottawa on one of the longest trips I ever made. I was to attend the Colombo Conference of Commonwealth Foreign Ministers. Since Ceylon, that lush and lovely island where 'every prospect pleases,' is almost exactly on the other side of the globe from Canada, I decided to take the opportunity afforded by the conference to travel around the world.

The most important part of these travels was, of course, the conference. There we considered and took the first tentative steps toward creating the scheme that would extend aid to South and Southeast Asia and, although I was not sure how great our contribution could be, I was favourably inclined to the idea. As I told the assembly of Foreign Ministers at the meeting of 9 January, Canadian foreign policy was greatly influenced by consciousness of two dangers: the 'aggressive imperialism' of the USSR and the increase of communism through the inability of countries to deal with their own economic and social problems. To counter the first danger, Canada had welcomed the North Atlantic Pact. I went on to point out, however, that the best defence against communism as opposed to Russian imperialism was a domestic policy of sound economic development. Since there was little value in preaching the virtues of the democratic way of life to starving people, we would be prepared to play our part in any practical scheme for promoting world stability and peace.

The British delegation was under the direction of a very great man, representative not only of a new Commonwealth but a new Britain, Ernie Bevin. I had met the British Foreign Secretary in London at the Commonwealth meeting in 1949, but I did not get to know him until the conference in Ceylon. It is impossible to forget him in those discussions. He had his own inimitable way of expressing his thoughts in his own inimitable English. Behind him in a row would be three or four Foreign Office officials, the perfect flowers of British diplomacy, who alternated between intense pride in their chief because they loved him for the way he stood up for his country, and intense anxiety as to how he was going to pronounce the words they had written for him.

Although the British did not arrive with any settled tactical intentions, they hoped that in the course of the conference action could be initiated which would make it easier for the United States later to participate in some kind of economic assistance plan for Asia. Thus, in the Foreign Ministers' meetings, Bevin picked up and turned to account suggestions made by Spender of Australia and (in a somewhat different form) by Jayewardene of Ceylon at an early stage in the conference that the Commonwealth should extend economic assistance to the underdeveloped countries of South and Southeast Asia. This would have the result not only of strengthening the economies of the recipient countries and so of helping them to combat the spread of communism, but also of supplying the sterling area as a whole with a flow of dollars which might be expected to continue after the end of the European Recovery Programme. It would provide a framework in which attempts to scale down the sterling accumulations, or at least severely restrict drawings on them, would have a greater chance of success.

When on 12 January the Australian, New Zealand, and Ceylonese delegations presented their joint memorandum which was the basis of the Colombo Plan, my only reservation was that the recommendations, which I believed were of great importance, should be scrutinized by the delegations' economic advisers so that any ambiguities of phrasing might be avoided. I was particularly anxious that the wording not be misleading about the part to be played by the US or in arousing expectations of immediate results that could not be realized.

A telegram which I sent to Arnold Heeney, my Under-Secretary in Ottawa, at the conclusion of the conference described briefly the various stages by which it was intended that the circle of economic co-operation centred on South and Southeast Asia be progressively widened:

As a first step, the Australian Government would extend invitations to all other Commonwealth Governments to participate in the new Consultative Committee, the establishment of which has been recommended in the Conference resolution. Although we, like other Commonwealth Governments, would receive an invitation, it would cause no surprise to any of the Governments more directly concerned if we were to decline on the grounds that we have heavy commitments in other areas. My provisional view is that our proper course would be to suggest that we be represented on the Consultative Committee by an observer. The United Kingdom would almost certainly accept an invitation at this first stage. But Bevin made it clear in the Conference that the financial assistance which the United Kingdom could contribute would be severely limited because of the substantial financial contributions which it has made, and is currently making, in this area.

In the first instance, then, the Consultative Committee would be a purely Commonwealth body. It would include Australia, New Zealand, India, Pakistan, Ceylon, and the United Kingdom. This nuclear group of countries would hold its first meeting in Canberra and would examine the possibilities of self-help and mutual aid. As the next step, invitations would be issued to other countries in the area, i.e. Burma, Malaya, Indonesia, Indo-China and Thailand.

When such an expanded committee had become a reality, the hope is that the United States would agree to collaborate and to underwrite the initiative with new financial aid. If this hope were fulfilled and United States dollars were granted in some form to India, for example, it should be possible to curtail much more rigorously India's drawings on its accumulated balances, even if the Indian Government still could not be induced to agree to partial cancellation.

The manœuvre which is developing is still vague and shadowy, as you will see; and there are many possible contingencies which could falsify the cautious hopes which are entertained for it here. But it is a promising move, I think, and deserves at least our sympathy.

Following my return from Colombo, the questions of Canadian participation in the Consultative Committee and of the form of that participation came up for active consideration. It was decided that we would participate and that we would be represented by a Minister. Since I was already committed to attend a meeting of the North Atlantic Council in London at the time of the Australian meeting, the Minister of Fisheries, R.W. Mayhew, who had attended the Colombo Conference with me, was appointed our representative.

On 10 March 1950 the Cabinet formally ratified the Colombo resolution and agreed that Canada would accept full membership on the committee and attend the first meeting. A memorandum of instructions was prepared and given to Mayhew, based on the presupposition that the meeting was merely a beginning and would be followed by the appointment of a working group which would explore particular avenues for development. In the area of financial assistance the delegation was told to

carefully avoid at this stage committing the Canadian Government in any way, either directly or by inference, to extending financial assistance to the countries of South and South-East Asia. It should be stressed that the Canadian Government cannot even consider this question until the basic elements of the problem have been carefully examined, until the possibilities of self-help, maximum utilization of local resources, and mutual aid among the under-developed countries themselves have been thoroughly explored and until procedures have been suggested to ensure that whatever external financial aid may be available will be put to effective use. The Canadian delegation should discourage any tendency to elaborate programmes designed to establish the overall need for outside assistance in terms of large balance of payments gaps on the example of the Marshall Plan.

The Delegation should resist any attempts that may be made to oversimplify the problem of raising the standard of living in these countries by expressing it in exclusively financial terms without regard to the social conditions which stand in the way of increasing agricultural and other production. They should also look with scepticism at overly grandiose schemes of development. Ordinary handpumps may be more suited to some regions than vast irrigation works; and ploughs may be more needed than tractors.

Under the heading 'Technical Assistance,' the delegation was authorized to indicate that Canada would co-operate in 'any well-conceived' plan and would be willing to receive students for training in Canada. Although we would prefer that this be done under the auspices of the United Nations, we would be prepared to consider 'additional proposals if it were felt that more help was needed than could be had through the UN.' In general, however, 'The Delegation should urge on the Committee the importance of making full use of the resources of the United Nations and its specialized agencies in the field of technical assistance, and the necessity of not duplicating their efforts.' Any special Commonwealth effort should be designed to supplement existing UN programmes.

Before the meetings got under way, we made it clear to Spender that, while we considered it desirable that the Commonwealth governments take the initiative in exploring ways to promote development in South and Southeast Asia, we did not want to see the United Nations aid and development programmes bypassed. We also stipulated that we did not want to see participation in the plan limited to the Commonwealth. I was particularly anxious to see US aid extended to Asia.

The meetings in Australia created what Mayhew described as a 'crisis in Commonwealth relations.' Spender, with a characteristic lack of tact, brought great pressure on the other delegates to bring a concrete scheme into existence immediately. In view of the reservations which I had made at Colombo, however, Spender acknowledged that Canada was exempt from the charges of bad faith that he had levelled at the others, particularly the British.

Faced with this turn-about, Mayhew reported back to Ottawa. Brooke Claxton, who was Acting Secretary of State for External Affairs while I was in London, placed the matter before the Cabinet, pointing out at the same time that it was not yet known whether Britain would accept the plan. Since the British were the key to the success or failure of the scheme, at least in its initial stages, the Cabinet decided to follow whatever course they adopted. The British did decide to participate and by the time I returned to Canada, therefore, we were full partners in the Colombo Plan.

By the end of 1950, the next round of meetings had taken place and the report of the Colombo Plan had been published. This report was most favourably received in Canada both by the press and public. Also, by the end of the year, Britain and Australia had announced their full commitment to the plan and their proposed contributions over the next six years of £300 million and £25 million respectively. The United States, meanwhile, informed the Commonwealth countries that it supported the aims of the plan and, although not yet making any financial commitment, asked to be associated with the Consultative Committee.

Since no definite decision had yet been taken on the extent of Canadian participation, I wrote to the Prime Minister on 29 December 1950 urging that Cabinet make a decision by 15 January on the extent of Canadian support, and suggesting $25 million a year for six years, with a firm commitment for only the first year. On 5 January 1951 Cabinet, while welcoming the US into the Consultative Committee and agreeing to Canada's representation at the next meeting, again deferred the question of the form and amount of the Canadian contribution. Just over a month later, however, Cabinet approved my recommendation committing Canada to a contribution of $25 million in 1951–2. At the same time, I was authorized to enter into discussions with India on the desirability of sending $10–15 million worth of wheat to India as part of the Canadian contribution.

Many factors contributed to the original Canadian caution concerning the Colombo Plan. For one thing, as I have already said, I did not want to see the UN undercut in its aid programmes. I was also convinced that effective assistance to Asia could be realized only with the support of the massive wealth and resources of the United States. In addition, given the balance-of-payments problems of the time, the fact that Canada was the only non-sterling country at Colombo also tended to make us hesitant.

Canadian involvement in foreign aid was a gradual development. Caution was in keeping with a realistic appraisal of our position in the community of nations and of the commitments we had already undertaken. As a result, we were always careful not to assume the leadership in international schemes if there was not at least a reasonable chance of getting the support needed to see them through. This desire to stay out of the vanguard was not so much a matter of whether our reputation would suffer if a scheme failed as whether there was a contribution for us to make to it within the limit of our resources.

Later, when I became Prime Minister, there was a new interest and commitment to foreign aid, especially during the period 1963–5. Paul Martin, as Secretary of State for External Affairs, in November 1963 proposed the acceptance of the principle of a phased expansion of the Canadian aid effort and almost doubling of budgetary and non-budgetary items of the Canadian aid programme over the two-year period. I supported him in this; the Cabinet adopted the recommendations and authorized him to announce the programme for 1964–5 in the House of Commons. There were a number of factors which contributed to this decision. In the first place, there were strong humanitarian considerations – which need not be spelled out, but should not be obscured. Second, our aid programmes were an integral part of our foreign policy and, in recent years, the level of our aid, relative to that of other major donors, had declined sharply. This had to be corrected. Third, an increased aid programme would indirectly stimulate the Canadian economy. While this was not the main object of our aid programme, it was, nevertheless, important. Canada, as a trading nation, could expect to benefit in the long term from the enlarged world trading patterns which would accompany the economic expansion of the less developed countries which our aid programme was designed to help.

ॐ

I should now retrace my steps and talk about the round-the-world trip I made in connection with the Colombo Conference. In the course of my travels, I had an opportunity to visit many places and to gain a clearer understanding of the problems facing men in these other climes. The trip began when I left Ottawa at 6 PM on 2 January 1950, reaching the Azores the next morning, after a stop at Gander, Newfoundland.

After stops at Gibraltar and Malta, we flew to Fayid airfield in the Suez Canal Zone, since we were unable to reach Hubaniyeh owing to dust storms on the Arabian desert. We spent the evening there with the British Army Commander in the Middle East, Sir John Crocker, who gave me an interesting account of the difficulties he had with the Egyptian government because of their sensitivity to anything seeming to constitute British interference with Egypt's sovereignty. Here we got a hint of later troubles. Sir John Crocker wondered aloud how long the British would be able to stay in the Canal Zone. He had just returned from Palestine where he visited Jerusalem, and took a very dark view of the aggressive designs of the State of Israel on neighbouring Arab territories.

From Fayid we flew to Karachi, and the next morning took off for Colombo where we were welcomed by the Prime Minister; here we spent the next two weeks. During our stay at Colombo I had several informal discussions with the Prime Minister, other members of his Cabinet, and a few leading citizens. I learned something of the state of affairs on that island paradise where man, if not 'vile,' at least shared the unrest that seemed endemic throughout the world.

Sentiment for Britain in Ceylon was still strong and British influence was clearly much greater than in Pakistan or India. I noted in my diary, however, that this would probably decrease and 'time may confirm the statement that whereas the Portuguese left music and language in Ceylon, the Dutch Roman law and domestic cleanliness, the British left only cricket.' Ceylon was a rich island, but I could see that here, as elsewhere, the pressure of population on resources was explosive; the average income, though higher than in other eastern countries, was only a few dollars a year and life expectancy was only fifty years as against seventy in New Zealand. Economic difficulties arose from the over-population, the concentration of wealth in a few hands, and the almost complete dependence of the island on exports of tea, coconut, and rubber. These facts had led me at the conference to urge the need for social reform as well as foreign aid.

Of Ceylon and the Ceylonese I wrote at the time: 'The Government is now in the hands of a few native families and the great mass of the people seem to have little influence. There is a strong Communist movement which has captured 21 seats out of the 92 in the legislature, but it has itself spilt into three groups – Stalinists, Leninists and Trotskyists, which seems to me to be characteristic of this island. It is hard to imagine the people of Ceylon, "lotus eaters," Nehru called them, developing enough energy and drive either for forced economic development or for violent revolution. I have a feeling, however, that there may be trouble before long because of economic difficulties, and the narrow basis of government support. Another real difficulty is the strong feeling of the Hindu element of the population for India and the consequent Ceylonese fear of Indian penetration. Wherever Nehru appeared in the streets of Colombo thousands of the local citizens, not all of them Hindus, gave him the kind of ovation which is usually reserved for a prophet or a conqueror. It may have made his Ceylon hosts somewhat uneasy.'

At the conclusion of the conference we flew back to Karachi, where we spent two days. I was impressed by the drive, energy, and disorder in this essentially frontier city. The Pakistanis were literally attempting to construct the capital of a new state on the foundations of a frontier desert town and were displaying a fanatical zeal in the process. Their achievements in two years had been notable. However, Pakistan was obviously facing very great difficulties in its determination to build up a modern state. The division of the country into two parts, separated by 1300 miles and by a country which all Pakistanis seem to fear, as well as the influx of millions of refugees and the absence of any extensive industrial development, all presented almost insuperable difficulties which the Pakistani leaders were attempting to meet with determination and a spirit of ardent patriotism. Pakistan to them was a religion as much as a state, with India the threat to both. It would be twenty years until their bold experiment failed.

During our visit I had discussions with the Governor General, a roly-poly little Muslim from East Bengal, who seemed at the time more interested in his hobby of collecting poultry than in the problems of his country. I saw the Prime Minister, Liaquat Ali Khan, twice, the Minister of Finance, the British and American representatives, and various Pakistani officials. They were all intensely preoccupied with their task of establishing Pakistan as a balanced industrial state in the face of the great difficulties which they recognized. These difficulties arose largely from the fact that the division of the sub-continent was, economically, artificial. Pakistan was a producer of raw materials without industries, while India had industries without enough food and raw materials. Obviously, from an economic point of view, this was a senseless partition. To this major difficulty there had been added the problems arising out of the millions of refugees from India, which made Karachi one of the most uncomfortable cities in the world.

I wrote at the time: 'The Prime Minister is an able man, as is his Minister of Finance. They seem to me to be practical, hard-headed persons; anxious to strengthen the association with Canada and other members of the Commonwealth, but even more anxious that this association should be of help to them, economically, and in their political difficulties with India. The bitterness of feeling in Pakistan toward India is intense, and it is depressing to realize that these two nations have begun their existence in an atmosphere of mutual fear, distrust and ill-will; something which usually is the product of long historical development. This feeling centres on the Kashmir dispute, which is regarded in Pakistan and in India with an emotional intensity which can hardly be exaggerated. Liaquat said quite calmly to me that the acquisition of Kashmir was a matter of life or death for them and that they would "go down fighting" rather than lose this province to India. Behind Kashmir is the more fundamental fear of Indian aggression, economic and political, a feeling expressed by Firaz Khan Noon when he said they would prefer to be swallowed up by Russia than by India. The Pakistanis feel that they have done everything possible to solve the Kashmir dispute by peaceful means, have accepted all the United Nations proposals for this purpose, but that in the face of India's intransigent attitude they can make no further concessions. Talks I had in Karachi certainly gave me the Pakistan side of this case (previously I had heard more of the Indian side) and I left feeling that it was hopeless, and indeed unjustifiable, to ask them to make any further concessions. [Philip] Noel-Baker [British Secretary of State for Commonwealth Relations] who was in Karachi when we were there, attempted to strengthen this feeling by begging us to back Pakistan to the limit. He argued that if we pressed India hard she would yield. He has certainly taken a very strong anti-India stand on this matter and is, I think, not doing much to help settle things by his activities.'

When I met with the Minister of Finance he talked to me about economic relations between Canada and Pakistan (when he could get off Kashmir), and was disappointed that he had not heard from our Minister of Finance, Mr Abbott, about a proposal which he made to him in London the previous summer regarding long-term credits in Canada. He also hoped that we could help Pakistan with technical assistance in their industrial transformation, and that we could interest Canadians to start factories in his country.

Incidental activities in Karachi included a tea with the Karachi Chamber of Commerce, in which I once again beat the drum of increased multilateral trade before a bearded assembly of Muslim worthies. It was a difficult occasion, this Chamber of Commerce meeting, because I was speaking to them in the garden of a hotel which ran alongside the busiest thoroughfare of Karachi. I therefore had a good deal of competition from trams, trucks, shouting Muslims, ox carts, and camel bells.

Of Pakistani hospitality I wrote: 'The Pakistan authorities did everything they could to make us welcome in Karachi and they seemed genuinely glad to see us. The Governor General, with whom we were to have stayed but couldn't because Government House was being re-decorated for a visit from the Shah of Persia, gave us a very colourful and impressive garden party, while everywhere we went we were given a friendly and hospitable welcome. We were put up in the Government Guest House where I distinguished myself at breakfast the first morning by asking for bacon and eggs! This faux pas was only exceeded by my determination on my arrival at the airport to shake hands with a gentleman who boarded the plane first and who I thought was probably the vanguard of the welcoming party from the government, but who turned out to be a disinfecting functionary who wanted to spray me and the plane!'

We left Karachi on Sunday, 22 January, and reached New Delhi a few hours later where we were welcomed at the airport by our High Commissioner, Warwick Chipman, representatives of the government of India, as well as the customary, as it became, guard of honour. Our three-day visit to New Delhi coincided with the last three days of the old era, because the republic was proclaimed the day after we left, though not for this reason.

It was a very moving moment in world history. I was able to contemplate and ruminate and brood over it at a state dinner anticipating the event, since the lady on my left was the Queen of Nepal, who did not know or speak any language that I knew anything about, and the lady on my right was Queen of some other Himalayan country, familiar no doubt with many tongues, but with none familiar to me.

We stayed at Government House, the former vice-regal palace, Lutyens' glory, a tremendous and grandiose establishment meant, no doubt, to glorify imperial rule. There we were given a suite which made up in space what it lacked in comfort. The gardens of this place were among the most beautiful in the world, and were at their best. That this palace should be occupied by a Governor General such as Rajagopalachari, a gnome-like man who looked and dressed like Gandhi, was one among the many anomalies in India. He seemed gentle, very wise, and detached. He was philosophic, almost nostalgic, about the past, and somewhat doubtful about India's future prospects.

During our stay at New Delhi Mr Nehru, who was preoccupied with many other matters, was especially kind to us and I had several talks with him on a variety of matters, including, of course, Kashmir, which we had covered pretty thoroughly in Colombo. He was stiffer on this issue than previously, largely because of a note which Bajpai, Secretary

General of the Indian Foreign Office, had received in New York from the Americans and which aroused a violent reaction in New Delhi. It seemed quite clear to me that Noel-Baker's thesis, that all that was required was to push Nehru and he would yield on the matter, was dangerously incorrect. My conclusion on this point was strengthened by a talk I had with the British High Commissioner, Sir Archibald Nye, who impressed me as one of the most intelligent representatives I had met on our trip. Nye did not think that much progress could be made at the UN regarding Kashmir. I reported these conclusions to Ottawa and suggested that we should extricate ourselves from any special responsibility we might have incurred because of General McNaughton's presidency of the Security Council in December 1949. At that time, the members of the Council had asked him, as President rather than as Canadian delegate, to mediate between India and Pakistan. General McNaughton prepared a plan which had been, in effect, rejected by India. My visit to New Delhi confirmed my feeling that there was not much hope now for a solution through the Security Council, and little possibility that any resolution of that Council would be acceptable to or make any impression on the Indian government.

I also discussed Kashmir with other Indian Cabinet Ministers, more particularly with Deputy Prime Minister Patel who, contrary to what I had been told, seemed even more rigid on the subject than Nehru himself. Patel, I should say, was a very tough, hard-headed person. The general line that I took with him and the others was that whatever may be the rights and wrongs of this case, it was tragic beyond words that the strength and prestige of India (to say nothing of Pakistan) should be sapped by their inability to settle this dispute; India had much to contribute to Asia, but her ability to contribute anything would be seriously prejudiced if she could not settle her difficulties with her nearest neighbour, difficulties poisoning every aspect of the life of the two countries from which only the Communists could benefit. Patel and the others all admitted this, but then took refuge in the moral strength, as they put it, of their case, and the wickedness of the policy of Pakistan. Even the Minister of Health, a saintly lady who had been Gandhi's secretary for fifteen years, stressed the morality of the Indian case and the inability of the government to do anything in the face of Pakistan obstinacy. In short, all the arguments I heard in Karachi were repeated in reverse in Delhi. It was all very depressing and baffling and fraught with danger to peace. It still is today.

Incidentally, the Minister of Health gave us one of the most interesting days of our entire trip when she took us on a tour of some village communities outside Delhi and showed us what they were trying to do in the face of terrific odds to improve life as it has been lived for centuries by 95 per cent of the Indian population. I got much closer to India in these villages than in the vice-regal palace in New Delhi and formed a deeper understanding of the tremendous obstacles to be overcome before the people of India could be given a better standard of material living.

My general conclusion, if one can make any general conclusion on the basis of a visit of this kind, was that the Indians were going to have a very difficult time indeed in overcoming the problems before them. As Nehru put it to me one afternoon, in the old days they could tell the people when things went wrong that it was due to faulty British administration; but now their people had achieved freedom without the immediate material improvement which they had naturally, though unreasonably, expected to follow freedom. The communists were, of course, exploiting these and other grievances and would be able to create serious difficulties if economic conditions deteriorated. Deterioration had taken place in Bengal because of the economic war with Pakistan, with resulting unemployment in the jute mills. The men we met in India, and I think I met all the Cabinet Ministers, were realistic about these difficulties and I thought were approaching them in an intelligent and energetic way. However, I thought it not unlikely that India would go through a period of confusion and possible distress before acquiring political and economic stability. A country which, having just won its freedom, was now spending over 60 per cent of its budget on defence was not constructing a very solid foundation for the future. But it remained true in India, as in all the other new Asian states, that the politically conscious part of the population would rather suffer any kind of distress and disturbance as a free state than admit any form of imperial or outside control. They were all extremely sensitive on this matter. It appeared to me to be almost a pathological condition, perhaps best personified in Nehru, who loathed and abhorred colonialism in any form in any part of the world. There were a great many in Asia who would, in fact, have preferred communism to colonialism, if they had to make a choice.

I had a chance to become better acquainted with Pandit Nehru in 1955 when I went to India again, after my visit to Russia (which is described in Chapter 9). He was one of the most subtle and difficult men to understand whom I had ever met, an extraordinary combination of a Hindu mystic, who had become almost a Hindu god, and an Eton-Oxbridge type of Englishman. At times it seemed almost as if the Englishman predominated. I remember sitting beside him at a garden party in a beautiful setting under the moonlight, with lights in the trees and haunting Indian music. Just before some dancing was due to begin, the performers rushed over and fell down before him; Nehru's comment was, 'Isn't that ridiculous.' Later, as we chatted, he said something that really shocked me. He was talking about Gandhi and his relationship with him, what a great actor Gandhi was, how clever he was with the British, how he cultivated this simple mystic character because this would appeal to them. 'You know,' he said, 'he really was an awful old hypocrite.' What a strange thing for him to say of a man the people considered a prophet almost divine! There were times when I was tempted to think: 'This is really not a very nice man, rather second-rate.' But when he began to talk about his philosophy of life or his philosophy of politics, I realized I was in the presence of someone truly great.

To return to 1950. We left India for Burma on 25 January and spent the evening at Rangoon, dining with the Foreign Minister and some of his colleagues. Rangoon, with two or three civil wars raging, presented a very gloomy picture of confusion, almost of chaos. The Burmese hierarchy seemed childishly optimistic about the situation. I had the strong impression that the country was down at the heel, that there was a real danger of complete collapse. The atmosphere of Rangoon was almost that of a town behind a front line, indeed the front line of rebellion was only thirty or forty miles away. When we left our hotel to dine with the Foreign Minister we had truckloads of soldiers with tommy guns before and behind; when we turned into his driveway we were challenged and escorted past a strong point, picked up by a searchlight, challenged again at barbed wire entanglements, before eventually reaching his front door. Yet the Burmese leaders seemed to think that everything was improving and that they would have civil disturbance under control very shortly. The British Ambassador, Sir Reginald Bowker, with whom I had a talk before dinner, felt that such optimism was quite unjustified. He expressed impatience at the inability of the government to come to terms with the Karen rebels, a strong and vigorous element in the population, who had not been well treated by the government. Rangoon was a gloomy place and we were glad to leave it next morning, reaching Singapore that evening, where we stayed with the Commissioner General, Malcolm MacDonald, at his Johore mansion, Bukit Serene.

Colonial Singapore was a pleasant change from independent Rangoon – alive, bustling, clean, well ordered, and moving ahead, politically, to independence by stages. There were troubles, of course, and the bandits – nearly all Chinese with communist leaders – were still a problem. But Malaya had a future, I felt, if it could work out a satisfactory arrangement for a federal independent state with the various races co-operating. It would be a mistake, I thought, to hurry this process – as long as the goal was accepted without reservation. At Colombo, when we were talking of Malaya, the representative of Pakistan urged caution in the steps being taken toward freedom. 'We don't want another Burma,' he said. Coming from a Pakistani, this was interesting.

Malcolm MacDonald was doing a fine job there in bringing the various races together and in breaking down barriers between them and the British. The night of our arrival he had a men's dinner for us, where the guests included Chinese, Malays, Indians, as well as British officials and businessmen. It was all free and easy with good, frank talk. The Chinese guests complained to Spender, who was also present, in no uncertain terms about race discrimination in Australia, but without bitterness or a sense of inferiority. They gave me the impression, which I received on many other occasions, that the old forms of racial and social discrimination were now definitely 'out.' The Europeans, not the Asians, were now on the defensive.

At dinner, we also talked about trade and the Malayan economic picture; the desire of the local guests was to keep the price of commodities such as wheat down and products such as rubber up. I demurred. These people, like the Ceylonese, are very vulnerable, since their prosperity, indeed their very existence, depends on what others pay for their exports, especially rubber. They naturally interpreted North America's fine words about raising the standard of living in Asia in terms of our willingness to pay a good price for these exports.

After MacDonald's dinner, I had a very good discussion with Spender, the Australian Foreign Minister, a lively, intelligent, and self-confident man. He had just come from Pakistan and, not having been exposed to Kashmir as long as I had, was shocked and distressed by the bitterness of feeling he had found and the real danger of an explosion. He wondered what we could do about it. So did I.

After a brief visit to Hong Kong, we arrived in Tokyo on 29 January where, for the first time since leaving Gander, we lived on Canadian soil as the guests of the Herbert Normans of the Canadian Liaison Mission. The purpose of my visit to Japan was two meetings with General Douglas MacArthur, Supreme Commander of Allied Forces in the Pacific, of which I shall write more later. From Tokyo we carried on to Wake Island, Honolulu, San Francisco, and Ottawa. I was glad to be home.

6

AT THE UNITED NATIONS

Support for the United Nations was a major element in Canada's foreign policy. This remained true despite the early disappointment of our high hopes for international co-operation. Although its progress in the area of security was slow, the United Nations did become an essential agency for general international co-operation. There was no reason to abandon hope that it could one day become more effective for maintaining peace. In this policy we had strong parliamentary and popular support, though I felt that this support was at times less of a call to action than a prayerful and undemanding expression of our idealism and our hopes, a kind of satisfying ritual like the automatic repetition of the Lord's Prayer.

The early breakdown between the Big Powers in the United Nations, on whose co-operation so much of the Charter was based, made the position of Middle Powers such as Canada more important than it would otherwise have been, especially in situations where the Security Council could not function. Middle Powers were likely to have the sense of responsibility that comes from the knowledge that they were strong enough to contribute to carrying out decisions made, but were without the world-wide interests and responsibilities that could affect and confuse these decisions. They stood between the increasing number of small states which had little power and the great states which had too much.

Canada was one of the most active of these Middle Powers. For example, in 1955 we succeeded, largely through the work of Paul

Martin as Chairman of our delegation to the General Assembly that year, in leading the efforts which resulted in the admission to the United Nations of the first new members in five years. This was the so-called 'package deal,' which broke a deadlock caused by the general hostility between the United States and the Soviet Union and brought sixteen countries, pro-Western, communist, and neutral, into the UN. Earlier, to overcome the veto power of the Permanent Members of the Security Council, we had supported the 'Uniting for Peace Resolution' which enabled the General Assembly (where the veto did not operate) to deal with a threat to peace and security when the Council could not act. We also believed that there was no better way to give practical evidence of our faith in collective action to strengthen security than in the organization of peace forces under the UN to carry out UN decisions. Our own defence forces could be put to no more effective or constructive use.

Thus, peace-keeping became a major political interest for us during the early years of the United Nations. In this field we took initiatives, gave support to those of other members, and backed up our words by deeds whenever we were called on. This was an important and a practical activity for us because of our economic and military capability. In doing this, however, we did not advocate impracticable collective measures or those beyond the resources of the UN. Indeed, we often warned against this. Nor did we take on commitments beyond our own resources. But when the UN takes decisions which are right and are enforceable, then it should have forces available to implement those decisions; and we ought to be able to contribute to them.

This work of organizing and strengthening the peace was more than an official concern of mine. I was deeply involved personally and considered it a great privilege to be in a position where I could make some contribution to what I felt to be the most important aspect of national as well as of international policy (in this case the two were indivisible) – the removal of 'the scourge of war.' When the hopes and idealism of San Francisco diminished, we entered into those bitter times of futile, acrimonious debate and verbal warfare that came to be called the Cold War. This only emphasized, however, the need for greater and more sustained effort, based on a deeper understanding of the difficulties in the way.

Vishinsky of the Soviet Union was the most gifted, energetic, articulate, and unscrupulous of the communist polemicists at the UN. He would stop at nothing in the flow of his bitter oratorical assault. Sometimes it seemed that nothing would stop the flow; he carried on for hours, without pause. Yet, off duty he was a cultivated, amusing, and agreeable person, and he could impress you as such, unless you recalled his conduct during the Moscow purges. He flattered me one day by stating that he listened to my speeches at the UN with particular care as I was usually more frank than 'the others.' Once I was seated beside him at a dinner after he had spoken for four or five hours during that day, consigning to the nether regions all of us from the West, sparing neither our characters nor our capacity. But he was all smiles, and lively with engaging conversation about literature and life. I suggested that he must be exhausted after talking so vehemently most of the day. 'Not at all,' he replied, smiling. 'It is only diversions that are exhausting and I am too old to have any.' Personally, I prefer my 'villains' to be more easily recognized when off duty.

In our concern with the work of the UN in the field of peace and security, we did not ignore our responsibilities in humanitarian, social, and economic matters. We were active in these fields as we were also in legal, administrative, and budgetary questions. In short, constructive and concrete support for the United Nations and its specialized agencies was a central part of our foreign policy during those years. I think it can be said without exaggeration that this brought us a respected and influential position in the world organization.

One of the reasons for our prominence over some of the other Middle Powers at the UN was our relatively important activity at the San Francisco founding conference, and in the organizational work before and after that conference. Another was our close relationship with the two most important Western members of the UN, Britain and the United States, and with other Commonwealth countries. It was, in the circumstances of that time, quite natural that we should have had a position of some importance at the United Nations, and that we should so often be asked to become members of committees, even to take on their chairmanship, and to supply personnel for UN operations of all kinds. We did not seek any prominent or special role at the UN in those early years. But the role often sought us. Certainly, we did not back away from responsibilities reasonable for a country in our position in the circumstances that then existed. Nor did we over-emphasize our importance in discharging them.

As a result of Canada's active policy toward the United Nations, I was privileged to be elected President of the General Assembly in 1952. I shall have more to say of the work of the presidency later in reference to the search for an end to the Korean War and will touch on it only briefly here. I was elected by a large majority with only the Soviet bloc voting against me. The Arab states abstained in consequence of my attitude in the Palestine debate (see Chapter 10).

My jubilation, however, was to be short-lived. Following the election, I was led to my place in the chair at the top of the rostrum. There were the usual introductory and congratulatory speeches; then the Assembly got down to business. Early in the debate, the inevitable point-of-order was raised and it appeared we would descend into the usual interminable wrangle that plagued Assembly meetings. I had already determined that if elected President of the Assembly, I would try to bring to an end the practice of debating points-of-order for hours on end. Faced with my first point-of-order, I listened to the speaker and allowed one or two others to speak to the point. Then, waving aside the list of others who wished to enter the discussion, I gave my ruling. There was a loud protest (I was later told by the experts that it was not a very good ruling). My ruling was immediately challenged. Although my position was sustained on that occasion, there were others when my quick decisions were reversed.

I made my point, however. We had far fewer points-of-order than previously. Although the debates went more smoothly, there still remained the ordeal of sitting there hour after hour (sometimes well on into the early hours of the next morning) listening to debates. Only once or twice did I manage to escape. I am an inveterate doodler, so I would take refuge in doodling while pretending to make notes of the speaker's brilliant intervention. I tried to keep in mind, however, the occasion a couple of years before when Charles Ritchie of our delegation went into the delegates' lounge for a drink, and there watched the proceedings of the Assembly on closed-circuit television. Quickly he sent a messenger with the note: 'The camera is on your hands. Stick to geometric patterns.' I had not realized that they were using telescopic lenses!

During my presidency of the Assembly, I was also a candidate for another important UN job, the office of Secretary General. On 11 September 1952 Trygve Lie informed me on a personal and confidential basis that he would soon be submitting his resignation as Secretary General. In 1945 I had been a candidate for the position with the support of the British and Americans. But that in itself had apparently been reason enough for the Russians to reject my name. They doubtless thought that Trygve Lie would be more amenable to their policies. As time passed they found out, however, that he was neither a tool to be manipulated nor a weak man to be intimidated. In return, the Russians added greatly to the tremendous pressure of his duties and made life impossible for him. On 10 November 1952 he addressed his letter of resignation to me, in my capacity as President of the General Assembly, and asked me to place the question of the appointment of a successor on the agenda of the Assembly.

Lie had already indicated to me his own choice of a successor. He wanted to see me appointed. The Secretary General was not alone in his view and, soon after the announcement of the resignation, a 'draft Pearson' campaign was in full swing. I was greatly moved by this, and would not have been able to refuse a summons to be Secretary General.

Feeling as I did, I decided on my return to Ottawa from my presidential duties in New York for the Christmas recess in 1952 to take the matter up with the Prime Minister. To this end I drafted a personal letter to Mr St Laurent on 29 December 1952, outlining the developments and my own feelings about them:

'I have been meaning to write you for some time concerning a development at the recent United Nations Assembly which is of great significance for the world organization, and may have some special significance for myself. I am referring to the notice of resignation given by the Secretary General, Mr Lie, last November. I am not myself certain that this notice will result in Mr Lie's actual departure. It may be that if agreement on a successor is impossible, Mr Lie will be persuaded to remain for a further and longer term of office. There are some cynical people who even suggest that he had this in mind in raising the issue, and that the impossibility of agreement on a successor will make it possible for him to lay down his own conditions for a renewed contract. He may have had this in the back of his mind, but I think myself that he was also sincere in announcing his intention to resign. The two things are not necessarily incompatible.

'So far as Mr Lie's successor is concerned, there have been as yet none of the discussions between the permanent members of the Council which are essential if a nomination is to emerge from the Security Council. However, if Mr Lie persists in his resignation, steps will soon have to be taken which will either result in agreement on a successor, or prove that no such agreement is possible. The Russians are so anxious to get rid of Lie that it is possible that they may accept almost anyone to succeed him if they are pressed hard enough by the British and the Americans. Before this happens, however, they are bound to put forward a number of candidates who will not be acceptable to Washington or London or Paris, even though some of them may not provoke a veto. Among these candidates, the names most frequently mentioned are Romulo (Philippines), Entezam (Iran), Nervo (Mexico), and myself. Certainly the Russians would never agree to me unless agreement on any other candidate is impossible, in which case they *might* accept me as the last alternative to the re-appointment of the present Secretary General.

'Though the contingency, therefore, is a remote one, I think I should let you know that if my name did come from the Security Council for recommendation to the Assembly, as the only person on whom they could agree, I would not, I think, be able to refuse the nomination. As I see it, the situation is not the same as that which arose over the NATO Secretary Generalship where there was no possibility of a deadlock on candidates, and where the Organization had such a close and direct relationship to us that the position of a Canadian as Secretary General might be misunderstood in our country and complicate Canadian policy to NATO.

'I mention this matter now, not because I think I am likely to be confronted with the problem it involves, but because I feel that I should tell you in advance how I would be disposed to act in case such a development occurred. I would, of course, take no final action without consulting you.'

As it turned out, I did not send this letter to the Prime Minister. Shortly after I drafted it, an opportunity arose to discuss the matter with him personally.

With the beginning of the new year the question of the appointment of a Secretary General became more pressing and began to occupy more and more of the time of the delegates to the Assembly. Essentially, the positions adopted by the USA and the USSR and the relationship of these two powers to each other in the days ahead would determine the appointment. Although my own future was intrinsically bound up in the outcome of the discussions then going on, I was careful not to become involved in any campaign for the position. I did, however, arrange with some key Canadian representatives abroad to be kept informed of developments and shifts in the thinking of the various delegates. In particular, I asked David Johnson, our Permanent Representative at the United Nations, Hume Wrong in Washington, and Norman Robertson in London to pass on to me the information they picked up from that most volatile and most fallible of information channels – the diplomatic grapevine. The following letter which I received from David Johnson early in January 1953 is illustrative not only of the attitude towards my candidacy, but also of the workings of the international diplomatic grapevine and of the faultiness of its information.

'In the course of the last few days we have received information from two sources about possible successors to Mr Lie as Secretary General.

'Epstein of the Secretariat reported to us a conversation he had had with Raphael of the Israeli Delegation. Raphael, as a result of conversations with members of the Soviet Delegation, received the impression that the Soviets would not oppose your appointment as Secretary General. According to Raphael, however, the Soviet members added the qualification "provided Mr Pearson is not promoted by the Americans." This according to Raphael, would make it difficult for the Soviet Government to agree to your nomination.

'Fowler of the United Kingdom Delegation told [Jim] George [of our Delegation] yesterday that the United Kingdom, French and United States Governments have been considering possible candidates to succeed Mr Lie as Secretary General. Mr Eden had suggested that when the Security Council meets to consider this question the three Western Governments should propose three names, any one of which they would be prepared to accept as Secretary General: Mr Pearson, Mr Stikker [of The Netherlands], and Mr Boheman [of Sweden]. If the Soviet Government turned down all three persons then Mr Eden would recommend that the Western Powers stand by Mr Lie and ask him to continue to serve.

'According to Fowler, Mr Entezam's name had been proposed by the French Government but actively discouraged by the United Kingdom Government. Hence Fowler now thought that the French would not press for Entezam. As for General Romulo, the United States Government would support him if his name came up but neither the United Kingdom nor French Governments would be able to do so.

'I have not been actively soliciting information about this question. I have contented myself with recording information volunteered by other persons. I should be very grateful if you would let me know if you wish me to play a more active role.'

At no time before the actual balloting did the Russians clearly indicate their position with regard to my nomination. As a result of this, for a period of some two months I received a stream of contradictory reports from various sources. One such report, not unlike that cited above, caused me to record in my diary for 5 February 1953: 'I received today a letter from New York which indicates that the Russians might be willing to accept my nomination as Secretary General. This is, to say the least, disturbing. I have been taking a very high-minded attitude in the matter, to the effect that if duty called I would serve, but frankly I didn't think that duty would call. The situation seems to be that they are so anxious to get rid of Lie that the Russians would accept me if the British and the Americans insisted on it.'

I thought it better at this time to have another chat with Mr St Laurent about the possibility of my leaving his Cabinet to go to the UN. The next day I took an opportunity to talk to him. Afterwards I wrote in my diary: 'After the session I dropped in to see the Prime Minister and told him about my dilemma regarding the Secretary Generalship. I said that if I were nominated by the Security Council, I would accept it, but if they merely put two or three names to the Assembly, and one of them was mine, I would withdraw. He seemed quite disturbed about the possibility of my departure, especially on the eve of the election, but agreed that I would really have no alternative if I were, in fact, the only nominee. He is about the kindest and most understanding man I have ever met, and the most selfless. He said that some people might think that I was running out before an election, but far more would think that if I turned down the job, I was running out on the United Nations.'

We went on to discuss a possible successor to me in External Affairs. Then the Prime Minister hinted at another job offer that might soon be coming my way: 'He surprised me by telling me that Doug Abbott [Minister of Finance] had definitely made up his mind to retire from politics after the next election. His position would be the same as the Prime Minister's; they would see one additional session through and both would leave. He hinted that this would, of course, mean that I would have practically no opposition for the leadership.' This was not the first time it had been suggested that I might expect to succeed to the leadership of the Liberal party. Mackenzie King had mentioned this possibility in 1947, and there was some talk in the early 1950s of Mr St Laurent's early retirement in which my name, with others, was mentioned as a possible successor. I remember one conversation on this subject with that great Canadian journalist and dear friend Bruce Hutchison in October 1950. Bruce raised the question of Mr St Laurent's early retirement and the possibility of my succeeding him. I emphasized to him how important it was that Mr St Laurent lead us in the next election campaign. In that time of grave international danger and general rearmament, with war a few months old in Korea and the haunting fear that World War III might not be far off, I felt it necessary to have our selfless and well-loved leader at the helm of the ship of state. Personally, I was appalled at the very thought of taking on the premiership, and I told Hutchison so. But, as with the secretary generalship, if drafted I would have accepted the responsibility.

As it was, I did not have to worry about tackling either job for some time to come, and I never had to worry about the secretary generalship. Despite the rumours I was hearing that the Russians would support my candidature in the end, there was other, more concrete evidence to the contrary. In the middle of all the gossip, Vishinsky went out of his way to launch an attack on me in his speech before the First Committee on 2 March 1953. I remember talking to Trygve Lie after that meeting. He was highly amused and rather pleased that, as he put it, I was placed in his class by the Russians. With regard to Vishinsky's speech I noted in my diary: '... all this means is that Vishinsky is just trying to remove the impression that they will accept my nomination automatically. There never was any intention of them doing this as I know the Russians well enough to realize that they will bargain hard on this issue. If so, I may be the eventual winner by being relieved of the nomination.'

Another diary entry I made for the period 8 to 19 March 1953 tells the rest of the story of my candidacy:

'Now for the Secretary Generalship. The situation was crystallizing in so far as nominees were concerned. Three names were now to be put forward – the Pole by the Russians, merely a bargaining move; Romulo by the Americans; and mine by the Danes, aided and abetted by the British. On Tuesday, [Henry Cabot] Lodge [the American Representative] had a discussion with Dulles about the matter after which he told me that they had decided to nominate Romulo, but that this did not mean that they would not support me. He gave me to understand that as a tactical matter, and to avoid trouble with the Philippines, they had to support Romulo at the beginning, but that they did not expect him to get enough votes, and that they would then swing to me. I told Lodge that it was quite all right with me whatever they did or did not do. However, the American position caused a good deal of surprise around the UN where it was interpreted variously as an indication Dulles would not have me, or alternatively, that the Americans were anxious to have me and were clever enough to realize that the only way the Russians would agree with this would be to divorce my own position entirely from that of Washington. Therefore, they were nominating someone else for tactical purposes. Meanwhile, Romulo was scurrying about trying to get support and Jebb was trying to bully everybody into supporting me. This seemed to be a good time to leave New York, so when the Security Council met on Friday I was in Ottawa. It was about 6:00 o'clock when the telephone message came from New York that the meeting had been held, that the Russians had begged for a postponement of the vote, that Jebb had insisted on voting immediately, and had been supported by the majority of the Security Council. Therefore, the three candidates were voted on in turn. Romulo got only 5 votes, and I got 9. The Russians, however, vetoed me. There was much discussion of these tactics over the week-end, both in New York and in Ottawa, and also over the reasons why the US formally had proposed Romulo. The general opinion was that Jebb ... had practically forced the Russians to veto me; that if he had given them more time and agreed that the vote should not have been taken until the next week, they might have abstained.

'When I returned to New York on Monday I saw Jebb. He was somewhat disappointed and even inclined to admit that maybe his tactics had not been right. His idea was to force the vote so that Romulo would be disposed of and that my own strong position would be made clear. He felt that a Russian veto at this stage would not necessarily be final, but other people think that the Russians having vetoed me will not now change their position, even though originally, as a last resort, they might have been willing to abstain. This is Trygve Lie's position. He phoned me to congratulate me on joining him as an object of a Russian veto and indicated, with some satisfaction I thought, that because of bad tactics there was little chance now of me getting the job. In fact, he seemed to me to rather relish the prospect of now being begged to stay on.

'I had another talk with Jebb on Tuesday and I suggested to him that whatever might be the result, the matter must now be brought quickly to a head or the UN will look ridiculous. I suggested, therefore, that the five permanent members should do their best to get together, or at least agree to disagree, before another meeting of the Security Council; that all possible candidates should be put forward and disposed of one way or another before Monday, March 23; and that when it became clear that no one either had the necessary 7 votes, or if they did would be vetoed, then the Russians be told that Lie would have to stay on. That could bring matters to a head. Jebb thinks that these tactics might result in a Russian reconsideration of my name, but Lodge thinks that, on the contrary, the Russians now will not worry too much about Lie staying on as they are glad to have this particular grievance.

'On Wednesday at Mrs Reid's dinner, I went further and suggested that Jebb should invite Lodge and Gromyko [Deputy Soviet Foreign Minister] to dinner informally and very secretly so that the three of them could thrash the matter out. Incidentally, this would also give Lodge a chance to meet a Russian for the first time, and other things than the election of a Secretary General might come out of such a meeting. Jebb was quite willing to do this and somewhat to my surprise, Lodge was equally willing. This may be an important development. Meanwhile, the five permanent members met for some hours on Wednesday to see if they could make any progress toward agreement on an SG. All that happened was that 6 or 7 new names were put forward, none of whom is likely to pass the test of Security Council election. After this meeting, the way was cleared for the full Security Council to meet on Thursday afternoon. This went on for 3 or 4 hours, the only result of which being that Madame Pandit was put forward formally by the Russians and rejected. Zorin [another Deputy Soviet Foreign Minister] spent hours trying to avoid any kind of a vote and to stall for time. It may be that the Russians are waiting for instructions which Vishinsky, who is on his way back, will be bringing from Moscow, or it may be that they are merely dragging out and exploiting a situation which may divide their enemies and gain some propaganda advantage for themselves by putting forward Madame Pandit and Sir Benegal Rau [both of India], and indicating that other Asians would be agreeable to them. They are obviously making a play for Asian support, and equally obviously trying to force the Americans and the British to reject Asians. Jebb is helping in this propaganda by standing firm on the line, Pearson or nobody ... In fact, some of my friends among the Americans are hinting that I am being very badly served by my "campaign manager," who seems to be doing his best, in trying to get me elected, to prevent it. As, however, I am not interested in a campaign, I can't very well do anything about my campaign manager!'

When Vishinsky returned to the UN from the Soviet Union, he let it be known that they were not going to change their minds over Pearson for Secretary General. The Five continued meeting and talking, and recessing. They were talking now of Entezam or Nervo – but I thought the Soviets were just wearing the others down, hoping, perhaps, to stall until Vishinsky took the chairmanship of the Security Council. To all intents and purposes I was now out of the race, though my name continued to be bandied about as a possible candidate. Then, early in April, a compromise candidate was found in the person of Dag Hammarskjöld of Sweden. As President of the Assembly, it fell on me both to inform Hammarskjöld of his appointment and to induct him into his new office. He was a very great human being in terms of compassion and insight and moral quality. The years of his secretary generalship until his tragic death in 1961 were difficult years for the UN. Against tremendous odds, he patiently pursued those ideals of peace and reconciliation, which are the cornerstone of the United Nations dream. For myself, the following extract from a letter to a friend on 8 April 1953 is perhaps the best summary of my feelings: 'Thank you for your kind letter of April 1. I am not really distressed about a Scandinavian for the second time ousting me from the Secretary Generalship, with, in both cases, the kind co-operation of the Soviet Union. It would have been a challenging job and in many ways I would have enjoyed it, but I am enjoying very much my present work so why worry about the fire when you are so comfortable in the frying pan.'

☞

In large measure this story reflects Canada's position in the world at the time. We would never have gained the good international position which was ours during these years, nor would we have secured the strong public support in Canada which alone made our policies possible, if we had become, or seemed to be, an echo of another's voice, especially that of the United States. Our membership in the Atlantic group, of which the US was the leader (it, alone, in those years had the strength, resources, and the will to give that leadership), did not prevent us speaking with our own voice or making our own decisions at the UN. These decisions were influenced, but not determined, by our friends. We were the satellite of no one. When we had to differ with Washington, or London, or Paris, we did so, if always reluctantly and only after consultation had failed to produce agreement.

When Mr St Laurent was the responsible Minister he was the framer and strong supporter of our UN policy. He believed in it. Mr King felt differently. He became more and more worried about the UN, its activities, and interventions. Indeed, before he left office he had reverted to the fears of the thirties about international commitments, though he continued to preach the proper sermons about peace and international co-operation. However, as he was on the verge of retirement from political life, he does not seem to have done more than complain about the UN and the activism of External Affairs at New York. His diary expressed his anxieties: 'I believed,' he confided to himself and for posterity, in 1948, in writing about some remarks he had made in Cabinet, 'the United Nations would get Canada into no end of trouble before very long, that we would be drawn into situations ... that our own people would not wish to be drawn into and we would find out only when it was too late where we had landed our country.' He added, '... I could see that every member of the Cabinet was strongly with me.' He was wrong in this, though I know that some of his Cabinet colleagues certainly shared his views. Those who did not, however, and we in External Affairs certainly did not, were given no alternate policies to propose. Isolation was admittedly impossible; but to sit in a back seat at the UN, acquiescent or critical, but in either case silent, was certainly not a policy.

While we actively supported the United Nations, we had no illusions about its weaknesses, especially about the growing tendency to substitute propaganda for constructive debate and action. Here the communist bloc were the main, but not the only, culprits. We were also increasingly worried about the tendency of the Assembly to be stampeded into impracticable resolutions passed by a majority which did not include those powers essential to their implementation. This tendency increased as the membership expanded far beyond the original signatories of the Charter, giving small and economically weak states a dominant voting position in the Assembly. And this development had to be reckoned with in our policies on peace-keeping. The general principles, however, which underlay our policy of support for the United Nations remained, even if their application changed, and rightly so, with changing conditions.

A review of Canada's foreign policy made during the winter of 1967–8 by Norman Robertson at the request of the Secretary of State for External Affairs, Mr Paul Martin, and myself gives an excellent analysis of our UN policy in a section entitled 'Canada and the United Nations.' It summarizes my views better than I could myself:

Broadly speaking, as regards all other members of the United Nations, Canada's firm support for the Organization has served to strengthen bilateral relations, particularly with the emerging nations and others with which we had not established diplomatic relations. The give and take of United Nations debate, the intensive consultations behind the scenes, the opportunities for personal contacts at all levels of representation, have provided a unique facility for international consideration of the widest range of subject matter. Even though the subjects may not always be intrinsically significant, in the course of debates and consultations it has often been necessary to explain in quite some detail national policies and attitudes. This is one of the hidden dividends of the United Nations which has continued to be valuable even at times of solid political impasse. Canadian delegations have always engaged very actively in the processes of consultation in pursuing their effort to make the United Nations system work. While some other middle powers, from time to time, may have resented or envied Canada's prominent role, by and large it has been the object of respect and admiration, especially from the lesser powers. This reputation at the United Nations (including the specialized agencies) has been based on a number of factors which would include: significant political leadership in the Assembly, usually at times of crisis; our close relations with Great Powers; our prompt and practical response to economic and social programmes and humanitarian appeals; our understanding of the rights and interests of the smaller powers, sometimes at the risk of differing with powerful friends; our inclination and ability to work for compromise solutions; our lack of global commitments or interests.

Mr Robertson then made these wise observations, which take me beyond the period I am writing about, but they are worth quoting here:

Nevertheless, we should not be under any illusion that this reputation, forged during the early years of the United Nations, remains intact. The spotlight has shifted to new issues and new members and Canada has not found it easy to adapt to the new situations. It is harder for us now to seem to act objectively on most issues. The differences between states are wider than they were, except possibly at the top, and as the balance of opinion and voting is weighted on the side of the "have-nots" there is less room for bargaining. It should be noted as well that Canada benefitted from the virtual paralysis of the Security Council in the fifties and the consequent emphasis on the role of the Assembly. As the latter in turn is confronted by its incapacity to take action in the face of new problems, despite the wide support given to many of its resolutions, attention is once more being paid to the Security Council and to the prospects of agreement between its permanent members.

The hopes we once had for and the expectations once aroused by the United Nations are, therefore, far different now in view of its present character and capabilities. Nevertheless, I still think that the work of the United Nations provides ground for a reasoned faith in its future. In any event, there is no other agency or organization for discussion and action on a global basis. Such machinery is indispensable in this age of interdependence. If our present world organization disappeared, we would soon have to form another one. It is foolish and short-sighted for governments not to recognize this and give stronger support to what we now possess.

7

KOREA:
RESPONSE TO AGGRESSION

The Korean War was the most important international situation with which I was concerned as Canadian Secretary of State for External Affairs during the first half of the fifties. If collective security was exhibited in its political aspect by the establishment of NATO, it was demonstrated in an active, although imperfect, form in Korea. The Korean dispute began before 1950, of course, through the inability of the United States and the USSR to reach agreement on its unification. From 1910 to 1945 Korea had been under Japanese rule; at the end of World War II it was divided; the USSR occupying the northern half of the peninsula and the USA the southern half. In the early postwar period, no terms could be agreed on for a general election to cover the whole of the peninsula largely because of Russian insistence that none of what they called the anti-democratic groups should be allowed to participate in any general election. They were determined, according to the United States government (and there is some evidence to support this), to rig any election so that it would result in a communist victory. Nevertheless, the United Nations General Assembly on 14 November 1947 decided to set up the United Nations Temporary Commission on Korea (UNTCOK) to supervise free elections.

Although our major involvement in Korea came during the Korean War, there did develop a serious crisis within the Canadian Cabinet over the United Nations attempt to unify Korea through the commission. While Mackenzie King was in London in November 1947, Mr

St Laurent and Mr Ilsley, the Minister of Justice, agreed that Canada would serve on UNTCOK. Mr King, however, had begun to revert to his isolationist instincts. When he returned from London and heard about our involvement in the Korean Commission, he became most annoyed and told Mr St Laurent that Canada must resign from the commission. St Laurent and Ilsley stood firm. They had accepted the responsibility on behalf of Canada and were unwilling to have anything to do with our withdrawal.

Mackenzie King took up the matter with Ray Atherton, United States Ambassador to Canada, and eventually received a letter from Robert Lovett, the US Acting Secretary of State, on instructions from the President, which put the case, as the Americans saw it, for our participation in the Korean Commission. On receipt of this, the Prime Minister called Mr St Laurent and me into his office before the Cabinet meeting on 30 December 1947. I wrote the following notes after the meeting:

'Mr King read the United States communication to us. It certainly did not have, on the Prime Minister, the effect the Americans had hoped for. Mr King felt that its arguments were fallacious and its tone unpleasing. He said that if he had had any doubts before about the rightness of the case against Canadian participation in the work of this Commission, those doubts were removed by this communication. It merely confirmed his view that the Commission itself was completely useless, could do nothing to bring about a solution of the Korean problem and, on the other hand, could very definitely cause trouble between the USA and the USSR. He felt that the United States had proposed the establishment of this Commission for the purpose of relieving it of its responsibilities in Korea, and he was determined that Canada should not be a party to any such tactics. He was particularly incensed over the inclusion of Canada with countries like El Salvador and the Philippines. He was convinced that Canada would be expected to take the lead in the work of the Commission and thereby get into most of the trouble. So long as he was Prime Minister no Canadian would be appointed to this Commission. He had tried to make this clear to Atherton Saturday night, and he was even more fixed in his resolve now.

'Mr King appreciated that Mr Ilsley and Mr St Laurent did not feel as he did in this matter; that they felt responsible for Canada's membership on the Committee and that we should discharge that responsibility. However, Mr King added, he was convinced that the rest of his

Cabinet colleagues were behind him; that all parties in the House would support him, and that the country also would be on his side in this matter. It was a case of keeping Canada out of trouble and not allowing it to be used as the cat's paw of United States policy. If, however, the Cabinet did not support him, he did not wish to force any resignations, because he himself would resign. In any event, he would be resigning in the summer and it might be just as well if it took place now. Certainly, if there was any difficulty over this issue in the Cabinet, that would be his decision. If he had to take this decision, he would explain the whole matter to the House of Commons and to the country. He was willing to accept this responsibility, and no one could persuade him otherwise. He did not blame Mr St Laurent or the Delegation to the recent Assembly for Canada's election to membership on the Commission because he realized that we had been pushed on it by the United States. Furthermore, we did not know, indeed he did not know himself at that time, how grave and dangerous was the international situation. It was particularly in the light of the discussions he had had in London that he was convinced that Canada should adopt the most cautious and non-committal policy possible in United Nations matters. The United Nations, after all, had no force to back up its decisions and, if care was not exercised, it would become a mischievous and dangerous agency. The Russians would use it for propaganda just as long as it suited their purposes, and would then withdraw and proclaim to the world that they had been driven out by the Americans. Indeed, they might be able to make a very plausible case for this. The Americans, on the other hand, were showing signs of using the United Nations as the agency of their foreign policy, just as the French did in the old days of the League of Nations.

'Mr St Laurent said that it would be catastrophic if the Government broke up on this issue, and he was convinced that some way could be found to save the situation. He did not share the Prime Minister's fears about the Commission, though he realized that there was cause for uneasiness in recent developments. However, he agreed that the Korean Commission was not likely to be a very valuable piece of international machinery. So far as Canada's membership on it was concerned, he accepted full responsibility. If he had been aware of the importance which the Prime Minister attached to this matter, he would have taken steps to see that we were not elected. He alone was to blame in the matter, if any blame were attached to it. He wondered, however, whether it would not be possible, even at this late date, to explain the situation to the United States, so that they might realize the uselessness of sending a Commission to Korea without assurances of Russian co-operation. He suggested, therefore, that I should go to Washington to see President Truman and General Marshall on the matter, also Trygve Lie in New York. Mr King agreed with this, but added that I should tell the President and the Secretary of State how strongly he felt [and] that the note which they had addressed to him had done nothing to change his views. If I could do something along the lines indicated by Mr St Laurent, it would be most helpful, but there must be no misunderstanding about his own position. I could tell the President that the Prime Minister would resign rather than agree to any Canadian serving on this Commission.

'I said that I would, of course, carry out any instructions I was given, but that I felt this was a mission which would be more effectively performed by a Cabinet Minister. Neither Mr King nor Mr St Laurent agreed. They felt that I should do this job. They also agreed that, until I returned and reported, the matter need not be discussed in the Cabinet.

'Mr St Laurent suggested that I might be able to persuade the United Nations Secretary General to call a meeting of the Commission at Lake Success [the temporary headquarters of the United Nations a few miles outside New York], when they would realize the impossibility of carrying out their mandate in Korea and thereby return that mandate to the Interim Committee of the Assembly, without going to Korea at all. I asked if this meant that I was to represent Canada at such a meeting of the Korean Commission for the purpose of advancing this argument. Mr King said no; that in no circumstances would a Canadian attend a meeting of the Korean Commission at Lake Success or anywhere else; that what I might do was to try to persuade Mr Lie to call a meeting of the Commission so that he could point out to them that it would be useless for them to go to Korea. However, if the Commission went, they would go without a Canadian.

'I have never seen Mr King more worked up or impassioned than he was on this occasion. He was very deeply stirred and very emphatic in his language.'

Mr King and Mr St Laurent then went off to attend the Cabinet meeting. Later in the day, however, I had another interview with the Prime Minister. Again I kept a record of the meeting:

'I told him that I could understand his anxiety about certain developments in United States foreign policy that were possibly unwise and provocative. I felt, however, that the reality of the situation at the moment was not concerned with our membership or non-membership on a Korean Commission, but the hardening of the position between the USA on the one side and the USSR on the other, which would eventually lead to conflict. I added that, if I were to see the President, I felt that I would be in a much stronger position as his emissary if I were to convey to Mr Truman our worries on the whole situation, more particularly in regard to certain difficulties and possibly dangers which were developing in Canadian-American relations. The United States insistence that we should serve on the Korean Commission was only one, and I thought not the most important, of these. There were other danger spots, such as the United States tendency to ignore our rights in the Arctic; the United States tendency to take it for granted that we would back them in all their United Nations proposals, irrespective of the wisdom or the unwisdom of those proposals; the United States tendency to put pressure on us when our international economic policies did not coincide with theirs. Mr King agreed that it might be useful to broaden the basis of my discussions with the President and the others in Washington. He emphasized, once again, that just as he had been misunderstood and misjudged when he had refused to declare, before 1939, that come what may, Canada would be with Britain in any war against the Nazis, so he might be misunderstood and misjudged (though he did not think so) if he insisted now that we should not automatically support the United States in all of its proposals. The justification of his previous policy of caution had been the entry of Canada into the war as a united nation. He was, at this time, as determined to follow the same policy and he would not be deterred from it. If this meant that we would have to play a subordinate role in the United Nations, we would do so. He would even face the possibility of withdrawal from the United Nations if it were used to commit Canada to too many things which did not concern her directly. I mentioned to Mr King that the situation was, I thought, different from that of 1938–9. At that time, many people in Canada thought that we could remain aloof from the approaching struggle, and that our participation arose, in part, through our membership in the Commonwealth. Now the pressures were all from Washington, not from London, and it would be extremely difficult for us to isolate ourselves from United States policies because of continental considerations. On the other hand, as the enemy this time would be Russian Communism, feeling in Canada would be united in opposition to that enemy. Mr King agreed, but this did not alter his determination to adopt a cautious attitude. He would do what he could, and he would speak out frankly on the matter, to prevent Canada being dragged along dangerous paths by Washington.'

So on New Year's Day 1948 I was off to Washington. That trip was one of the most difficult assignments I had ever been given. When I arrived in Washington and informed Hume Wrong, our Ambassador, of the problem, he was completely bewildered by all the excitement and inclined, at least at first, to be somewhat amused at the idea of a Cabinet crisis over Korea – this was two and a half years before the Korean War. Wrong warned me that I could expect a pretty cold reception from Bob Lovett when I met with him the next morning. He was right. When the Ambassador and I arrived at the State Department, we found Mr Lovett flanked by an impressive array of senior officials and inclined to be rather stiff and formal. To break the ice I suggested we delay the meeting until I could send for a third secretary from the Embassy to even the sides.

Although I personally thought the US position was both understandable and reasonable, I explained Mr King's position as frankly and fully as I could. Later that morning, although he could see no point in my meeting with the President, Mr Lovett accompanied me to see Mr Truman. Since we were both concerned lest the press discover my presence and the split between the two countries, we entered the White House by the back door. I had also decided, if I was discovered, to throw the press off the track by telling them that I had come to see the President about Korea; that would have sounded so fantastic they would have assumed I was joking and that I really was there to talk about dollars or fuel oil.

In spite of my lack of sympathy with the Prime Minister's position, I was careful to give the President no reason to believe that Mr King would change his mind. I told Mr Truman about the Canadian uneasiness at being pushed into a position at the head of the procession in a country so far away as Korea, where the USSR and the USA could not themselves get along. To this the President replied: 'Don't worry, you won't get into any trouble over there, and if you do we are behind you.' If I had reported that comment to Mr King, which was, of course, merely a casual observation, our Prime Minister would have considered that his worst fears had been realized. Throughout the interview, Mr Truman kept emphasizing to me that Canada was the most respectable member on the Commission. I noted later in my diary, 'That was exactly what worried Mr King.'

All in all, the conversation with President Truman was amiable and somewhat aimless. I tried twice to persuade the President to phone the Prime Minister but to no avail. Later that day, Jack Hickerson, Director for European Affairs in the State Department, practically admitted to me that Mr Truman did not know very much about the Korean business and that the State Department were afraid that Mr King might overwhelm him on the telephone. Instead, it was agreed that the President would write a personal letter to the Prime Minister.

After giving the State Department some hints on the most effective approach for the President to take in drafting the letter to Mr King, I left that night for New York where I was to attend the meeting of the Interim Committee of the Assembly and also the first meeting of the Security Council with Canada as a member. The fact that Canada was to be on the Security Council loomed large in these discussions on UNTCOK. I had told Mr Lovett that the close relationship between our two countries made it desirable for us to maintain an independent position on the Security Council. On the other hand, he had expressed to me concern about the Canadian attitude on the Council if we were as afraid of commitments as we appeared to be in this matter.

I reported from New York by telegram to Mr King and Mr St Laurent on my Washington visit. On receipt of my telegram Mr King telephoned me at my hotel and we talked for more than half an hour – or rather, he talked and I listened. He did not think much of the State Department arguments, and said that he was more determined than ever to follow the course he had laid down. He seemed disappointed that the President had not been able to help him more, and asked me if I had told Mr Truman that the Cabinet might split up on this issue. I said that I had not; that I did not think it was proper for a Canadian official to emphasize our political difficulties to the President of the United States. I added that I might have been able to say more if I had been having an informal chat with the President, but that with Mr Lovett present at a formal appointment, I could not really go further than I had. Mr King agreed. This was a depressing telephone conversation and left me more worried than ever about the outcome of the whole business.

The next day, after he had received the President's letter, Mr King again telephoned me, calling me away from the Security Council initiation ceremony. He told me that he thought Mr Truman's arguments were very unimpressive, and his position remained unchanged. He also instructed me to come back to Ottawa to talk to him about the whole business. That sounded ominous.

On the way back to Ottawa that night I had time to consider the affair and try to reach some understanding of what exactly the Prime Minister was after. I made note of the three possible explanations that occurred to me:

'1 He has been so thoroughly frightened in London about the approach of war that his mind has fallen back into its accustomed pre-1939 pattern of isolation and suspicion of commitments. In this case, it is the United States, rather than the United Kingdom, which is the villain, and trying to lure Canada into foreign adventures.

2 He has manufactured this crisis in order to establish his supremacy over the two strong members of his Cabinet, Mr St Laurent and Mr Ilsley, even at the risk of their resignation which, in fact, he may be manœuvring. This explanation becomes intelligible only if Mr King has picked his own successor, and it is not to be Mr St Laurent, or has decided to continue in office himself.

3 He may be merely attempting to re-establish a position in the Cabinet which has been slipping, as the day comes for his retirement, though he does not intend to carry this attitude to a point where it really will break up the government.'

On my return to Ottawa, the issue came to a head. I had no sooner reached my office than the Prime Minister telephoned and read to me a stiff and uncompromising reply which he intended sending to President Truman. It was quite clear to me that, if it were sent, either he or Mr St Laurent and Mr Ilsley would resign. I suggested to him that he might wish to have this reply considered by the Cabinet before it went, but he felt that it was a personal reply to a personal letter, and did not require Cabinet consideration. I then mentioned to him that, if this reply laid down government policy, it would require a telegram to the United Nations stating that we would not take up our place on the Korean Commission; that this telegram would have to be made public, and the controversy within the Cabinet would be exposed. Mr King said he was quite willing to take the responsibility for this, and that it was up to the Department of External Affairs to send the message. I then said that, if the Secretary of State for External Affairs were to send the message, presumably he should have a look at the draft reply to Mr Truman. Mr King agreed to this, and said that the reply should be held up until Mr St Laurent had seen it.

He sent his draft letter to me and I immediately took it to Mr St Laurent, who informed me that if the Prime Minister sent this letter he would resign. He was quite calm about it, but quite firm. He said he had no objection to the telegram in question going to Trygve Lie, but it would not go over his signature because he would not be Secretary of State for External Affairs. He had been head of the delegation which accepted Canada's membership on the Korean Commission, and a refusal to confirm that was a repudiation of his action and that of Mr Ilsley. They both, therefore, would resign, though he, Mr St Laurent, would do it as quietly and non-controversially as possible.

In an effort to avert the crisis, I persuaded Mr St Laurent to take advantage of the opportunity available and explain his position to the Prime Minister who, I felt, did not realize the position Mr St Laurent had reached. After some persuasion, the Minister agreed to telephone Mr King, who invited him to dine that evening. I knew this would be the critical occasion which would resolve or precipitate the crisis.

I also discussed with Mr St Laurent my own position if he failed to persuade the Prime Minister to alter his course, and should resign. My record of this part of the conversation reads: 'We had some talk about the duty of a civil servant in a break-up of this kind. Mr St Laurent thought that it did not really concern me as an official. I said that I felt I should either resign or ask for an appointment abroad; that I really could not carry on in the Department when policies with which I did not agree were being laid down by the Prime Minister, against the wishes of the Secretary of State for External Affairs. Mr St Laurent said that he would come round to the house to see me after his dinner with the Prime Minister.' Of his visit later that evening I wrote: 'At ten o'clock the door bell rang and I let him in. He was looking very happy, and I knew everything must have been worked out all right. What had happened was this. The Prime Minister and the Minister, in the mellow mood that a good dinner and bright fire sometimes induces, had talked over the whole question and had agreed on a compromise, by which a Canadian member could be appointed to the Commission, though he would withdraw from its work if it became apparent that Russian co-operation was not forthcoming. In other words, our member was to have nothing to do with elections for South Korea only. This is not an unreasonable stipulation and one that can be defended. There is no doubt that the compromise represents a very definite withdrawal by the Prime Minister from his earlier position, and in that respect is a victory for Mr St Laurent. He has certainly established his position vis-à-vis the Prime Minister and, having established it, is now anxious to meet Mr King as far as possible on the general question of caution and conservatism in regard to our United Nations commitments.'

Mr King phoned me the next morning to say that he was very satisfied with the way things had worked out, and that he was revising his letter to the President accordingly. When I saw Mr. King's new letter, I thought:

'This letter may do some good, as it will show the Americans that we are not going to be pushed around by them on Security Council matters. The more depressing implication of the business is that the Prime Minister is going to watch with suspicious attention every detail of our activity on that council, with the result that we may find ourselves filling too often the role of inglorious abstainers. However, it is only for a few months, as Mr King seems to have made it clear in his talk with Mr St Laurent that he will persist in his determination to retire this Summer.

'With the Prime Minister's permission, I sent a telegram at once to the Secretary General of the United Nations, appointing Patterson [Counsellor of our Embassy in China] to the Commission, and drafted a telegram of instructions for him which the Prime Minister approved, and which brought this whole strange business to an end.

'The aftermath will become apparent in our work on the Security Council. I am glad that it is [General] McNaughton and not I who is to be responsible for representing Canada on that body for the next six months.'

Soon after UNTCOK began its work in Seoul, it became obvious that the Russians would not co-operate and would not allow the commission to operate in their zone of Korea. We believed that this effectively ended the commission's mandate to supervise free elections for the unification of the country, and that nothing more should be done. Elections in the South alone would only freeze the division of the country. However, the United States wanted elections and when the question was raised at the Temporary Committee of the General Assembly, they succeeded in getting a vote of 31 to 2 with 11 abstentions in favour of elections 'in such parts of Korea as are accessible to the Commission.' Canada was one of the two countries opposing the resolution, which I described as 'unwise' in my speech against it. Nonetheless, we could not stop the Americans on the course they had chosen.

On 28 February, while Dr Patterson was absent in Japan, UNTCOK decided that elections should be held in the American zone before 10 May. This decision was taken in spite of the fact that Dr Patterson had left his telephone number in Japan with the principal secretary of the commission and asked that he be called, should any important matter arise.

Even so we allowed Dr Patterson to co-operate in the observation of the elections, having first made it clear that, in our view, any government based on them would be a creation of the occupying military authorities (the United States) and not of the United Nations. Following the elections, which UNTCOK reported unanimously as being 'a valid expression of the free will of the electorate in those parts of Korea which were accessible to the Commission,' a government of the 'Republic of Korea' was set up under Syngman Rhee. Two and a half months later the Russians established a 'People's Democratic Republic' in the north. The stage was being set for the Korean War.

ᙡ

I had little further to do with Korea until the hostilities broke out on 25 June 1950. When that happened I was caught completely off-guard by the North Korean aggression and by the United States response to it. At almost the exact time on 26 June when President Truman was deciding that the United States would be giving air and sea support to the South Koreans, I was talking to some press people in Ottawa and telling them, off the record, that I did not expect a US military response to the invasion.

In part, my surprise was occasioned by a visit I had paid to General Douglas MacArthur in late January and early February, 1950. I was on the last lap of the round-the-world trip which I made that year in connection with the Colombo Conference of Commonwealth Foreign Ministers. I stopped off in Tokyo for four or five days mainly to see General MacArthur, then Supreme Commander for the Allied Powers (SCAP) in Japan. In some ways the General was the most arresting and magnetic personality that I have ever been exposed to. A fascinating man to talk with, he had a great deal of knowledge and a great sweeping sense of history; he spoke with extreme clarity and a sense of drama. Although I did not think too highly of some of his subsequent actions or ideas, there is no doubt that, in Japan after the war, he was the right man in the right place.

MacArthur was the most imperial, proconsular figure I have ever seen. He carried it all off with great élan and great impressiveness. Indeed, he had got to the point, so I was told, where the Japanese practically treated him like the Mikado himself. They would even bow when he passed by. I recall a luncheon he gave for my wife and me. There was more ceremony than I have ever encountered in Buckingham Palace or in the Vatican. Mrs MacArthur was already there with all the aides in attendance. As we waited we started to get fifteen-second bulletins: the General has left his office; the General is on the way; the General will be here shortly. We were lined up. There was a hush. The doors were thrown open and there was General of the Army and Field Marshal of the Philippines Douglas MacArthur. I felt that I ought to fall down and worship; but I do not very readily fall down and worship in that kind of ceremony.

It was, nonetheless, most interesting to meet with him and to get his views on the situation in Japan. In turn, I told him about the Colombo Conference, though the honours were not even, as his sermon was a much longer one than mine, and repeated. Herbert Norman, the head of our Liaison Mission in Tokyo, who was with me, said, however, that MacArthur listened to me longer than he had to anyone else whom he had seen with the General, and that I was to be congratulated!

During the course of our conversation he spoke mainly of Japan. I noted in my diary: 'He is absolutely convinced that the Japanese have seen the error of their ways and are now convinced democrats, and that the conversion is permanent. It is hard to be as confident in this matter as he is, but he speaks with great conviction on the subject. At the same time, he feels that we should not seek to embroil the Japanese in the cold war against communism but that we should strive to convert Japan into a Pacific "Switzerland" whose neutrality would be guaranteed by everyone. He seems to think that even the Russians might be prevailed on to support this. At the same time, he gave his case away, I thought, by adding that, of course, Japan would be quite willing to give the United States certain defence rights on her islands. If she ever did, she would not, of course, be a Switzerland and the Russians could not be expected to respect her neutrality. The General treats Japan and her problems with a paternal solicitude, and obviously feels he is much better able to deal with "his people" than those in authority in Washington, for whose judgment on far eastern affairs he showed scant respect. In fact, he talked very frankly about what seemed to him to be the weaknesses of the State Department and the Pentagon in their handling of Japanese and Pacific matters.'

In the course of our conversation the General gave me his strategic appreciation. On this I wrote:

'He was not alarmist about the spread of communism on the mainland and surprised me by stating that with a chain of island bases in the Pacific from which American air power could be brought to bear on the continent, the United States had little to fear. In this strategical chain he did not seem to include Formosa, which also surprised me. He did worry, however, about the lack of understanding in the United States of what was required and the lack of interest in Pacific strategic problems generally by the Chiefs of Staff, who concentrated too much of their attention on Europe. For this reason he said that he welcomed the visit of the Chiefs of Staff which was to begin the next day, though he made it quite clear that it would be the Chiefs who would be educated, not SCAP!

'As to a Japanese peace treaty, here again he surprised me by taking a view which we had been led to believe was not held in Washington, namely, that the western powers should seize the initiative which they had lost to Russia and press ahead for a Japanese peace conference. This conference should, if possible, include the Russians and the Chinese, but if that could not be done, then the other countries concerned should make a peace settlement with Japan. He kept repeating, however, that it was folly to have lost the initiative in this matter to the Russians and that the sooner a peace arrangement with Japan was made, even if the Russians and the Chinese were not included, the better it would be. He did not think that such a partial arrangement would weaken the strategic and legal position of the United States at all. Even Herbert Norman was surprised at the frank and emphatic way in which he talked to me on this subject.'

As he made these remarks, I remember that he went to a great map of the Pacific on the wall of his office. He was pointing out to me the line of defence where, if there was any threat of aggression, the United States would have to say 'thus far and no farther.' I have never forgotten that his line did not include Korea. I remarked on this and he said: 'No, it would be very difficult, it would be embarrassing, it would be disappointing, it would be worrying if an enemy took Korea; but it is not vital to our security.' This was not too many months before Korea did become vital.

When the North Korean invasion came, then, I was caught by surprise, not only by the aggression but, what is more to the point, by the United States reaction. I had no doubts, however, on what the Canadian position should be. We had to keep the US action within the framework of the UN. In this endeavour, circumstances were on our side. Some six months before, the Soviet delegate, Yakov Malik, had walked out of the Security Council because Russia could not get Communist China seated in place of Nationalist China. They were still boycotting the Security Council when the Korean attack took place, and thus not able to use their veto. The United States had already taken military action to help South Korea and was, therefore, able to get a resolution passed in the Council on 27 June declaring that there had been a breach of the peace and requesting that assistance be given to the South. There was no doubt that the North Koreans had been well prepared for this attack while the South Koreans were not. A United Nations Unified Command was created ten days later making the action, in theory at least, a United Nations operation. I considered this to be a very important event; the first time in history, so far as I know, an assembly of the nations had formally condemned and voted against an aggressor and, unlike the League of Nations in 1935 and 1936, had followed through. I felt at the time very excited about this historical precedent. I have always felt since that, however it worked out in practice, it was a most valuable precedent for the future of the United Nations.

After the resolution condemning the North as aggressors was approved, we were at once under pressure from the United States, which was organizing this collective security operation, to announce the form of Canadian participation. This was not an easy problem. The Security Council resolution of 27 June had been passed and had been accepted even by uncommitted countries (the Indian delegate, who had abstained since he was without instructions, later said he would have supported the resolution if his instructions had arrived on time). We felt that we should participate as a member of the United Nations but we wanted to be absolutely certain that this would be a United Nations and not a United States operation. Further, we hoped that our participation need not be extensive.

We agreed first to send destroyers to Korean waters, and then to airlift supplies and arms to the South Koreans. There was some hope at the time that this would be enough. It soon became clear (with the House of Commons reflecting opinion in the country) that we were not doing enough. The issue quickly resolved itself into the question of whether or not we should contribute ground forces to the military effort in Korea. There was considerable division within the Cabinet on this and, although I was in New York a good deal of the time, I kept in very close touch with Prime Minister St Laurent on what we ought to do. Nonetheless, it was uncertain for some time whether the Prime Minister would agree that Canada should become an active combatant.

Mr Mackenzie King died on 22 July 1950, and the Cabinet went to Toronto in a special train for the funeral. On the way back to Ottawa the Cabinet at last got down to the business of Korea. For almost the

entire trip we argued about what we should do. I was anxious that
Canada should assume a full responsibility by sending an expedition-
ary force. There were, however, members of the Cabinet, as there were
throughout my time as Secretary of State for External Affairs, who did
not support a forward foreign policy. They asked: 'What would Mr
King do?' and replied, 'He wouldn't be getting involved.' It was during
that train ride that Mr St Laurent first expressed his support for an
active Canadian involvement in Korea. At a series of Cabinet meetings
following our return to Ottawa, the final decision to send a force was
taken. I might add that there was no difficulty at all in raising the men
for our volunteer brigade.

Between our return from Toronto and the Cabinet's final decision to
contribute ground forces, however, the Secretary to the Cabinet, Norman Robertson, and I went on a secret visit to Washington and New
York for talks with the US Secretary of State and the UN Secretary
General. Mr Acheson and Mr George Perkins, Assistant Secretary of
State for European Affairs, had dinner and spent the evening with us
at the Canadian Embassy on Saturday, 29 July. As always, our Ambassador, Hume Wrong, was most helpful. That he was able to arrange
these talks not only at short notice, but at a time when the top people
in the State Department were so busy, was convincing evidence of the
special position which he and Canada held with Mr Acheson and his
associates in Washington. The discussion that evening went on for
three or four hours. Mr Acheson could not have been more frank or
forthcoming. He seemed in very good condition, cool, calm, but determined. He was, I thought, in better shape, physically and mentally,
than when I had seen him last, that May at the North Atlantic Council
meeting in London.

I outlined briefly to Mr Acheson the purpose of our very private and
somewhat sudden visit to Washington. I said that we were anxious to
get his views on three questions, each of which was related to the
others:

'First, we wanted to have his appreciation of the general international
picture as illuminated and affected by Korean developments; more
particularly, what were United States plans and policies for dealing
with it. Where did the United States Government think that we were
going, and what were the prospects ahead?

'Then we were interested to get his more specific views on Korean
developments; their relation to Far Eastern questions generally, more
particularly to Formosa.

'Finally, we were concerned with the United Nations aspect of the above developments; what the policy of members of the United Nations, like Canada, should be in these circumstances, particularly in regard to active assistance to operations in Korea.'

Mr Acheson responded with an exhaustive and impressive analysis of the whole position as it appeared to him and to the American government. He emphasized at the beginning that the Korean situation could be understood and intelligently dealt with only as a phase, and not, in the long run, the most important phase, of the general conflict between the free and the communist worlds. Strategically, as they had pointed out more than once, Korea was not an important sector in that conflict, and the decision to meet the challenge represented by the aggression on that sector had been purely political, made by the President as such. When this aggression occurred, the President and his advisers, without delay and without hesitation, agreed that this challenge must be met by the free peoples; that they must call a halt to communist aggressive tactics. He admitted that this decision must have been a surprise to some – including people in Washington. Certainly, if there had been a general aggressive move, they would not have acted so quickly in Korea. But in the circumstances he felt that they were right to act quickly and through the United Nations. We agreed.

In my memorandum of our conversation, I noted:

'Mr Acheson emphasized, and more than once, that the most significant deduction to be made from the Korean attack was the necessity for strengthening as rapidly as possible the forces of the free world to meet aggression elsewhere and to act as an effective deterrent against a general attack. To Mr Acheson the fighting in Korea was only an incident – though politically an incident of great and immediate importance – in a very dangerous international situation. This incident had underlined the danger of that situation and in doing so had made it politically possible for the United States to secure congressional and public support for a quick and great increase in defence expenditures; for further assistance to those of its friends who are willing to make a similar increased effort; for the imposition of needed controls, higher taxes, the diversion of manpower to the armed forces and defence industries, etc. This will amount to a partial mobilization and will prepare the way for a rapid and complete mobilization in the event of war. The naked aggression of the communists against Korea has made this possible, and for that reason, according to Mr Acheson, the USSR has made a great and stupid mistake in permitting, and possibly encouraging, this aggression. That mistake was made even clearer when it is realized that the aggression took place in a part of the world where the United States had, if not sufficient power, at least some power which could be brought to bear at once against the aggressor. This was done possibly to Moscow's surprise – and done through the United Nations. Though the United States forces, which consisted mostly of youngsters who had no experience of war, and were insufficiently trained and equipped, had taken bad beatings from North Korean troops which were well equipped and battle hardened ... nevertheless, their sacrifices had roused the American people to the point that not only would the battle in Korea be won, but they would organize themselves for the real struggle ahead against Russian communism, in a way which would not have previously been possible.

'Korea was not that struggle, but it made possible quick action to prevent that struggle. Furthermore, to Mr Acheson, Korea was now the touchstone of our determination to meet the challenge elsewhere, whatever form it takes. If the United States had to do all the fighting in Korea, there was a real danger that public opinion in the United States would favour preparing in isolation for the larger conflict ahead and writing its allies off. This danger would be increased if there were no parallel efforts made by others to re-arm for defence along the lines that the United States was now following. He himself was intensely concerned, as the President was, that the struggle ahead should not be one of the United States vs the communist world. The American people could be convinced of this if we all acted together on the Korean front as members of the United Nations, and if we worked together to strengthen our defences generally. Mr Acheson is deeply sincere on this point. He and his government are convinced that steadily but, he hopes, unprovocatively, with others of the United Nations, but alone if necessary, the American people will now put themselves in a position to have freedom from the menace of international communism. If all the free democracies could co-operate to these ends, then it will be infinitely easier for each of them to achieve the common peace-preserving objective, through defensive strength or, at the worst, the sure defeat of aggression.'

For these reasons Mr Acheson made a very eloquent plea to us for an effective and co-ordinated United Nations effort in Korea; for a United Nations effort, led by the members of the North Atlantic Pact, to increase our defensive strength on land, in the air, and on the sea. So far as Korea was concerned, he was emphatic that even single battalions would be not only politically valuable but effective help in present circumstances.

My memorandum on our meeting continued:

'In answer to our questions, he said that he did not feel that the danger of diverting too much strength to Korea was a very great one. Six or seven Divisions would be all that would be required and these Divisions could not, in any event, save the free world if the general war began. However, their successful use in Korea would make that general war less likely and would make a co-ordinated international effort for further rearmament far more acceptable to public opinion than if the United States withdrew from Korea, were defeated there, or won there alone. Furthermore, according to Mr Acheson, victory in Korea, achieved not merely by the United States but by the United Nations, would have more than a heartening effect among the democracies; it would make a very strong impression in Moscow.

'I asked Mr Acheson what would happen if the communists initiated other attacks during the Korean operation. He said that if these attacks resulted in a general war, Korea would, of course, be a mere sideshow, and forces there would have to be withdrawn as soon as possible. The free countries would have to do what they could to defend themselves from Russia while American air power was brought to bear on Russian cities and industries. However, they would all be in a much better position, he hoped, in a year to deal with this contingency. (Sir Oliver Franks, the British Ambassador, to whom I talked the next day, gave us to believe that this opinion had also been given to him by General Bradley, Chairman of the Joint Chiefs of Staff; that involvement in Korea would not seriously affect the outcome of operations elsewhere in the present circumstances.)

'If, however, there were an aggression elsewhere of a similar nature to that committed in Korea, that is through communist satellites, then Mr Acheson thought the United Nations should meet the challenge in the same way that it had met it in Korea. However, in this case the United States might not be able to take the lead that it had in Korea. Others might have to bear the initial burden of United Nations intervention in places like Iran, though naturally the United States would do what it could to help, as it expects others to in Korea.

'I mentioned to him that there seemed to be a conflict in the position which had been taken by the United States in Korea and the strategic plan for a country like Denmark. He said there was no conflict here.

If Denmark were attacked by the USSR, even though we could not defend her directly at present, we would be obligated to bring what power we had to bear on Russia itself. That would mean World War Three. Korea does not necessarily mean that, and therefore does not have to be abandoned ...

'So far as the policy of other United Nations countries was concerned, Mr Acheson felt that the main thing was for the free democracies to work together to strengthen their defences and their war economies immediately. For that purpose the United States had been making some strong statements at the North Atlantic Deputies meeting which is taking place in London. At the same time he emphasized again the tremendous importance of contributions to the Korean operations from United Nations countries, especially from those who, like Canada, have prestige and influence and command respect. Everything possible must be done to emphasize the United Nations character of the operations there; that a United Nations force is now in being and that the United States Army is only part of that force, though the biggest part. For this purpose there must be ground forces from other countries and he strongly hoped that Canada could join others in offering such forces. A Canadian detachment of trained men would be of great immediate help and of even greater political value. Later, Canadian volunteers might be able to join with other forces in a special United Nations Division to serve with United States Divisions in Korea. He recognized, however, that the burden in Korea would have to be borne on the ground largely by the United States, and that, while aid should be proffered as soon as possible, this should be regarded more as part of the general process of building up Western strength than as the provision of succour to hard-pressed United States troops.'

I told Mr Acheson that we were giving earnest consideration in Ottawa to these matters but that we did not like to be needled about them from Washington. He said that he understood our position in this matter and would certainly not be a party to any such pressure directed either at Ottawa or elsewhere. He pointed out that United States public opinion was in a very emotional state and that, while it was that very emotionalism which made action in Washington easier, it might also lead to irritating mistakes in its impact on other countries.

During the evening Mr Acheson made some interesting comments on certain personages whose names had come up in the course of our discussions. He was full of admiration at the leadership which Mr Truman was giving to his country. He criticized severely Nehru, both in respect of his mediation efforts and in respect of his general policies. He was obviously not impressed by Nehru's wisdom and sincerity. I, of course, thought Acheson mistaken here. He referred to Trygve Lie as an honest man but one without too much common sense. Personally, I thought that Mr Lie had handled himself extremely well in difficult circumstances during the preceding two or three months. For Mr Menzies, the Australian Prime Minister, who was in Washington while we were there, Acheson had great admiration.

The general impression I got of that evening's discussion was that Mr Acheson and the administration were resolved that the United States would give firm leadership to the move to organize the United Nations for defence against Russian communism. He seemed deeply conscious of the menace of communist aggression and willing to stand or fall on his policy of action for defence against it. There was no doubt in my mind that he was inspired by the highest motives. There was no trace of warlike excitement or boastful imperialism in his attitude, but a sober and realistic determination to press along the path which he thought was the only one that could lead to peace.

Two days later, on 30 July, Norman Robertson and I were in New York where we met with Trygve Lie over lunch. Mr Robertson made a record of our meeting from which the following is taken:

'In the course of a frank and wide-ranging conversation, Mr Lie made it clear that, in his view, there was no hope of peace being preserved unless the North Korean aggression could be contained and thrown back. He had hoped, longer than most people, that some accommodation between East and West could be found through the United Nations. He had been severely criticized for his visit to Moscow in an effort to find some common ground on which the Soviet Union could co-operate with the Western countries for the preservation of peace. He now felt that the invasion of South Korea had been the real Soviet answer to his plea for co-operation inside the United Nations. It was the touchstone by which Soviet assurances of "peace-loving intentions" would henceforth have to be judged. It was obvious that the experience of this last month had greatly shaken the Secretary General, and he now talked about the problem of preserving peace in terms that one might have expected from a signatory of the North Atlantic Pact rather than from the Secretary General of the United Nations. He felt that Soviet aggression could only be contained by adequate forces in the hands of the free nations, and repeatedly spoke of the necessity of them all building up their armed forces as a matter of the highest urgency, "otherwise, in 10 or 15 years we would all be slaves" ...

'He hoped it would be possible to build up United Nations forces primarily for help in the liberation of Korea, but which could be used in resisting aggression wherever it might break out. The present circumstances might well fix a pattern for the organization of an international United Nations police force, whose existence could help to prevent future breaches of the peace ...

'In the course of conversation, Mr Lie referred to the criticisms which he had received for appealing, on his own motion, to member states to provide ground troops for Korea. We said that our Government had been surprised and embarrassed by this action, which we did not think should have been taken without adequate consultation with the countries concerned. Whereupon, the Secretary General gave us a full and explicit account of the events which had led up to his taking this action, and about which he had been very worried at the time. He said that, on the evening of Thursday, the 13th of July, he had received Senator Austin, the United States member of the Security Council, accompanied by other senior members of the United States delegation to the United Nations, who had read to him an oral communication from the United States Government requesting him, as Secretary General, to communicate an urgent request to other members of the United Nations to provide troops, particularly ground troops, for Korea. It was put to him that the matter was one of the highest gravity and urgency, and that effective Congressional and political support of the action which the United States Government was taking in support of the United Nations would be put in jeopardy if United States military action in opposing aggression appeared to be isolated and unsupported by other members of the United Nations. If there were any weakening or compromising of the United States position, the whole position of the United Nations itself would be endangered. He asked if he could transmit this message to other members of the United Nations at the request of the United States Government, but, at their urging that the appeal would be more effective if it came from him as Secretary General, he agreed not to make reference in his communication to the fact that he had been asked to take this action by the Government of the United States. At the same time, he was given to understand that the United States delegation at Lake Success would inform the other members of the Security Council of the initiative they had taken with the Secretary General and would also advise the other national delegations to the United Nations. Simultaneously, American diplomatic representatives, accredited to other states members of the United Nations, would be informed of the action taken and of the reasons why the United States attached such importance to it being done in this way, and at this time. In the event,

Lie went ahead with his share of the arrangement, but, for some un-explained reason, the United States delegation did not take any of the complementary actions which he had understood they would take. He had taken a good deal of bruising over the whole business but, in the circumstances, though tempted to issue an explanatory and self-excul-patory statement, he had decided not to do so and was prepared to carry on, taking full responsibility for what, in any case, had been a difficult and critical decision ...

'One interesting thing that the Secretary General told us was about his part in the separation of Henry Wallace [US Vice-President from 1940 to 1944 and Progressive party presidential candidate in 1948] from his Communist and fellow-traveller supporters over the Korean issue. Wallace's public statement supporting United Nations and Uni-ted States action in Korea, which had come as such a shock to the Amer-ican Communist Party, had followed on two long sessions with Trygve Lie, in which the latter had taken him over all the evidence. He was quite happy about having helped to straighten Wallace out on the issue, but did not feel confident that there would be no backsliding. He observed that in his rather wide experience, Wallace was the "woolliest minded" politician he had ever met.'

When I returned to Ottawa, I reported on these talks to the Prime Minister. On 3 August I sent the following memorandum to Mr St Laurent urging a Cabinet decision on sending troops to Korea:

I have been trying to clear my own mind on this problem, in the light of our discussions yesterday. My view then was that we should call Parliament for September, to consider three main questions. I still feel that way.

The three main questions are:

1 The strengthening of our defences and the economic and financial steps that may have to be taken as a consequence of our own and American re-armament. What is happening across the border cannot fail to have strong impact here. I think we should at once begin to examine these matters so that a concrete programme to deal with them can be laid before Parliament. If this programme does not require any legislative action at this time, should we not put Parliament in possession of the facts as we see them, and the plans and intentions of the government for dealing with them?

2 We should report, I think, to Parliament on North Atlantic developments; especially the plans to increase speedily and greatly the strength of the alli-ance. We will certainly be asked to join the United States in assisting the European members – by supplies and equipment – to bring about that in-crease. This will involve extra expenditures by us. Equipment for a Nether-

lands Division from our reserve stocks is one way we could help. So far, we have not, I think, considered this project – or any other like it – in Defence Committee or in Cabinet.

3 Then there is the question of further assistance to United Nations forces in Korea. Even if the decision were to do nothing more, I think the reasons for that decision should be explained to Parliament.

I feel strongly, however, that this would be the wrong decision, and personally I would have great difficulty in reconciling it with my views on the menace which faces us, on the expression of that menace in Korea, and the necessity of defeating it there by United Nations action.

At the same time, I appreciate the difficulties and, indeed, the objections to an offer of land forces to the United Nations for Korea which could not be justified by the actual situation; strategic and political; domestic and international.

By 7 August the Cabinet had decided to support the position I had taken, and work began on recruiting a Canadian brigade for Korea.

We wanted it to remain as a Canadian brigade under Canadian officers. The best way to achieve this was to unite our brigade with the forces of the other participating Commonwealth countries in a Commonwealth Division. Mr King certainly would not have been happy. He had always worried about British Commonwealth forces under centralized control. In Korea, however, we had as much trouble with the Americans in keeping our forces together as we ever had earlier with the British.

In the spring of 1952, for example, very severe riots broke out in the American-run prison camp on Koje Island. The climax came when the prisoners took the camp commander hostage, and, in order to secure his release, his deputy signed a statement that the prisoners were being maltreated. It was a fantastic propaganda coup for the communists.

In an effort to distribute responsibility for the camps more widely, General Mark Clark, who had just replaced General Ridgway as UN Commander, ordered detachments from other UN contingents, including a company of Canadians, to the camp. We did not want to be thus associated with the recent events on Koje, nor did we want the principle of the unity of our forces violated. Short of a major confrontation, however, we could not countermand the order. But we did protest publicly. I stated in the House on 26 May that 'the Canadian Government ... views with concern the dispatch of a Company ... to Koje Island without prior consultation with the Canadian Government, and hopes that it may be possible to re-unite this Company with the rest of the Canadian brigade as soon as possible.' In less than two months, when order had been restored on Koje Island, the company was returned to the Canadian brigade.

☞

The real Korean crisis, and it was a crisis, came in September 1950 after General MacArthur, by a stroke of military genius, reversed the initial defeat and retreat of the UN forces by landing troops at Inchon, cutting off the North Koreans, and driving them into headlong rout. I have learned since that this was one of the most touch-and-go military operations in history. It worked, but it was most hazardous. We were, however, much elated as the UN forces under MacArthur's command pressed on in pursuit of the North Koreans.

On 27 September 1950, in speaking to the UN General Assembly, I had enunciated a series of specific principles which should govern the UN decisions on Korea now that a victory had virtually been won. I said:

As hostilities draw to a close in Korea, and the Assembly takes up its new responsibilities there, it seems to our delegation that certain specific principles should govern its decisions and that we should embody these principles at once in an Assembly resolution.

In the first place, the general objective as we see it of the United Nations in Korea should be to fulfil now the purposes which have repeatedly been stated at previous Assemblies – a united Korea, a free Korea, a Korea which the Korean people themselves govern without interference from outside. This should be achieved by United Nations action and not through decisions reached by certain of its members.

Secondly, the United Nations must assist the people of Korea to establish peace and order throughout their territory as the firm foundation for democratic institutions and free self-government. It is our hope that people of Northern Korea, having been forced into a perilous and disastrous venture by their Communist rulers, will now themselves repudiate these rulers and co-operate with the United Nations in bringing to Korea the peace and unity which its people desire. This is the time for the aggressors to cease fire, to admit defeat. If they do, it may not be necessary for United Nations forces in Korean territory to advance far beyond their present positions. The United Nations must, however, leave its forces free to do whatever is practicable to make certain that the Communist aggressors of North Korea are not permitted to re-establish some new base in the peninsula from which they could sally forth again upon a peaceful people.

Third, the Korean people – once peace has been restored – must be assured that no nation will exploit the present situation in Korea for its own particular advantage. This of course means a Korea without foreign bases and free of foreign military domination; it means a Korea which will be responsible for its own defence within the framework of our collective security system. Above all, it means a Korea which will not be divided and disturbed by subversive Communist elements directed from outside Korea.

The fourth principle should be that nothing shall be done in the establishment of a united, free Korea which carries any menace to Korea's neighbours. There have been comments in the press and elsewhere about the role which the Korean peninsula has played in invasions of the Asiatic mainland. Nothing must be done in Korea, as indeed nothing will be done, which holds the least suggestion that any member of the United Nations has any purpose whatever in Korea, other than to establish that country under the full sovereignty of its own people. Korea does not menace any of its neighbours, though in recent years it has had reason to fear the menace of at least one of those neighbours.

My fifth principle is that the free governments of Asia should take a major share of the responsibility for advising the Korean people upon methods of government which they should adopt and procedures which they should follow in establishing these methods of government. The countries of Asia and of the Western Pacific have made an outstanding contribution to the work of the United Nations. I think we should now make sure that we gain full advantage of the judgment of these states in charting a course for the future in Korea in the difficult days ahead.

My hope that hostilities in Korea were coming to a close was, to say the least, premature. Behind the scenes at the United Nations we were already discussing whether the United Nations forces (the United States forces largely) should go beyond the 38th parallel which divided the two Koreas. We took the view in our delegation, the view of the Canadian government, that the United Nations had discharged its obligations when the aggressor was driven back behind the line dividing the two Koreas, and that we should be very cautious in extending our mandate to include a march into northern territory. The Americans and one or two others (the Turks I remember especially), said in effect: 'This would be to throw away our victory.' By 'victory' they meant the punishment of the aggressor and assurance that aggression would not recur. 'We have him now at our mercy, we must go beyond the 38th parallel and destroy him.' I had long and, at times, very frank discussions with the United States delegates in New York about this, and Hume Wrong, acting on my instructions, talked with Dean Acheson, Dean Rusk (Assistant Secretary of State for Far Eastern Affairs), and Philip Jessup (US representative to the General Assembly), along the same lines. I told them, in effect, that I could not accept their reasoning and that I had my instructions to press for a halt.

When it became obvious that the Americans would not stop at the 38th parallel, I tried to persuade them that we might at least try out the inevitable Canadian compromise on this problem. I suggested that if they insisted on the UN troops crossing the border, we should first give the North Koreans a period of grace, three or four days, by saying: 'If you don't cease fire and begin to negotiate an armistice with us within a certain length of time, we will be forced to follow through and destroy your capacity for aggression.' I also urged that if we had to cross the 38th parallel we should then stop at the very narrow point in the north between the 39th and 40th parallels known as the northern neck of Korea. That seemed a reasonable place to halt as it was not so close to the Chinese border as to make the Chinese decide that their territory was threatened. The Americans agreed that this was not an unreasonable – indeed that it was a wise – course. As I understood it, after a meeting in the Waldorf Towers, this course had been agreed on and proposals to this end would be put forward at a meeting of the Assembly the following morning. When the meeting opened, to my amazement and disgust, the United States representative got up and, in effect, asked support for an immediate pursuit of the North Koreans beyond the 38th parallel and for their destruction – for a follow through to the Chinese boundary, if necessary, to destroy the aggressor.

The first Canadian peace initiative had failed. Although I spent the rest of that Saturday, 7 October 1950, watching the World Series with the Governor General who was in New York, my embarrassment and my anger at the Americans was in no way lessened. I had worked out the arrangements for approaching the North Koreans with Senator Austin, the head of the US delegation. After he had reversed his stand on the matter, I was informed that he had been instructed to see me to explain what had happened. My anger was not diminished when, rather than coming himself to see me, and in private, he sent a subordinate, John Ross, to talk to me on the floor of the Assembly. As I noted at the time: '[Ross] added to my surprise and annoyance by saying that he understood that I wished to see Senator Austin about something connected with the Korean resolution. I told him that I did not want to see Senator Austin about anything, but I understood that he wished to see me in an attempt to explain why the United States had withdrawn from the arrangements previously agreed on. I told Ross that it was now too late to do anything in any event, and that we were surprised and disturbed by the whole business.'

Just how 'disturbed' I was at the United States action is perhaps best demonstrated in the following two paragraphs from my telegraphed report to Ottawa on 9 October:

The whole episode is a disheartening one, both as an indication of the confusion and division in United States counsels at the Assembly and, more important, of their impatience with any line of policy than that which seems to be dictated by General MacArthur and the immediate military situation in Korea. What I find most worrying is the inability of certain people in Washington to realize that it is not enough to occupy North Korea; that it is more important to remove, if possible, the impression in Asian minds, especially in Indian minds, that the policies and designs of the United States in this whole Korean question are not above suspicion. Apparently in Washington they feel that it is more important not to interfere with the military timetable than to make every possible move to bring fighting to an end in a way which would command the approval of Asian members of the United Nations.

I feel that we will have to keep this weakness, as I construe it, of the United States Government in mind in our consideration of the problem of Canadian association with the relief and rehabilitation work in Korea (Acheson said they would like us to supply the Director of this work), and of making available Canadian forces for police duties in Korea. If everything in Korea is to be determined by the United States military authorities, and if the Korean Commission, which is now not likely to be a strong one in any event, becomes a tool of those authorities, then the less responsibility we have for subsequent developments in Korea, the better.

Later that Saturday afternoon I spoke to Hume Wrong on the phone and asked him to pass on word of my displeasure to the State Department. As a result of Wrong's protests, Dean Acheson called me on 9 October to apologize. I sent a telegram to Ottawa the next day.

Mr Acheson phoned me yesterday morning from Washington to express personally his very great regret at the mix-up which occurred Saturday, and to assure me that he knew nothing about the change of plans which took place. He asked me to accept his word that there was nothing deliberate in the change, but it was the result of an unfortunate mix-up. He himself had thought that everything had been arranged and that the President would make the statement in question which he, Mr Acheson, felt might do some good and of which he approved. It appears, however, that someone else in Washington heard of this development and without consulting the State Department managed to get instructions to Austin to persuade the President to forgo the statement. We shall probably never find out exactly who was responsible for the mix-up, but I am satisfied that Acheson and the senior officers in the State Department were not, and that they were genuinely apologetic and embarrassed by the whole incident. I told Acheson that so far as I was concerned, the matter was ended and I, of course, accepted without reservation his own good faith and regrets. My own feeling now is that the intervention by the unknown American source was inspired by the desire to prevent anybody minimizing the effect of General Mac-Arthur's pronouncement to the North Koreans [calling on them to surrender unconditionally], which has been given great publicity here. It was also due no doubt to Entezam's [President of the Assembly] anxiety not to tangle with the Russians on the issue of whether he had or had not the right to make such a statement.

Acheson's apology, however, did nothing to ease the situation in Korea. We had tried to ensure that the United States resolution would be interpreted in such a way that the UN forces would not go too near the Yalu River, the frontier between North Korea and Manchuria, lest the Chinese intervene. We had received word that the Indian Ambassador in Peking had been told that if the UN forces went to the Yalu then China would intervene directly. General MacArthur assured us, however, that we had nothing to worry about from the Chinese. He felt they were just bluffing. 'Don't worry about them,' he argued. 'They have no capacity. And if we really let our aircraft loose on them and we blow up the bridges on the Yalu, they couldn't get across anyway. So we're going ahead.' I remember that I was pretty frightened about this. My judgment was that the Chinese were not bluffing. If the Americans went to the Yalu River and destroyed the bridges and the power stations, my view was that the Chinese had enough military capacity to do a lot of damage.

In fact Chinese troops had secretly moved into Korea around the middle of October – possibly to protect the hydro-electric installations on the Yalu which provided power for Manchuria. Later that month and early in November there were a few short, sharp engagements between the Chinese and the American and South Korean forces. General MacArthur announced on 5 November that the Chinese had appeared on the battlefield. Then, two days later, the Chinese broke off all contact.

On 6 November I spoke to Hume Wrong and then sent a telegram to him giving my view of the situation.

In this message I should like to confirm and expand the misgivings I expressed to you over the telephone this morning concerning MacArthur's communiqué on Chinese intervention in Korea.

You will recall that we were given the very definite impression, both here and in Washington, that when the United Nations forces were approaching the Chinese border, the United States would follow a very prudent and unprovocative course of action and that they were considering leaving a strip of no man's land between their forward positions and the border, so that the Government in Peking would have no excuse for committing their forces in North Korea. The events of the last week or so, obscure though they are in many respects, nevertheless seem clear enough to suggest that this policy of prudence has gone by the board. MacArthur appears to be regarding his assignment from a limited military point of view (except when he talks to the press) and apparently was determined to rout out the North Koreans from their final redoubts, even if that involved sending United States forces as far as the Yalu River. He may have been encouraged in this view by what seemed to be, until the last few days, the collapse of opposition in North Korea. They must surely be aware now in the State Department of the extremely serious risks of a war with China, and realize that their earlier confidence on this score doesn't seem to be justified.

The motives and intentions of the Peking Government are, of course, difficult to decipher. One likely reason, however, for their intervention is that they are afraid that the hydro-electric installations on the Yalu may be destroyed and that they have ordered their troops to cross the Korean frontier in order to protect them. If that is the case, an assurance from the United States authorities that these installations would not be damaged might produce a more moderate attitude in Peking. Such an assurance might conceivably be conveyed through the good offices of the Indians, though their present attitude of 'we told you so' and also current developments in Tibet may make them reluctant to intervene. I realize, of course, that there are other possible interpretations of the Chinese intervention. But I feel strongly that nothing should be left undone which might help to remove the danger of conflict with China which could benefit no one but the Soviet Union.

In a matter of this gravity, it seems to me odd that MacArthur, when speaking specifically as the United Nations commander, should comment on the Chinese position in the terms that he did and in the form of a communiqué to the press rather than in the form of a report to the United Nations. You will by now, I imagine, have expressed my surprise at this procedure to the State Department.

Following my telegram to Hume Wrong, a memorandum outlining the main considerations of Canadian policy was prepared which I authorized for transmission to our major posts. This was a clear statement of our position and is, I think, valuable in showing our thinking at that time, November 1950:

'The purpose of the resistance to the aggression of North Korea was to demonstrate that aggression does not pay. Aggression will, however, pay most substantial dividends to the Cominform bloc if it leads to a war between the United States and China. The interest of the Western democratic powers is to limit hostilities in the Korean area and to have hostilities come to an end as quickly as possible in order that stability may be restored and foreign troops withdrawn. It would also seem to be in the interest of the Chinese to limit hostilities in order that they may get ahead with the job of reconstructing China. The only country whose interest would be served by an extension of hostilities in the Korean area is the Soviet Union.

'When the Western democratic powers are as weak on land as they are today, they must play for time in which to get stronger. The main front is Western Europe and we must resist efforts of the Soviet Union to get us committed to a theatre of secondary importance.

'If a war with China should break out, it is of the utmost importance that public opinion throughout the world, not only in North America but in Western Europe and in the democratic states of Asia, should be convinced that the United States and its partners have done everything they possibly could to avoid war. The record must clearly show this. It must now, for example, show that decisions were arrived at in haste and that the Chinese, either as witnesses, or defendants, or parties at interest, were not given their day in court.

'In dealing with the Chinese we must take full account of the possibility that their suspicions of the intent of the United States to encircle them have been genuinely aroused because, for example, of actions in Formosa, General MacArthur's statements, and the refusal to admit them to the United Nations. The increased influence of violently anti-Chinese Communist elements in the Republican party which may be expected as the result of the recent elections will not help to allay these suspicions.'

I felt an advance to the Yalu was a wrong and a risky move. But who was I to put my judgment against the experts of the United States? On 24 November General MacArthur launched his 'end the war campaign' which he promised would have the boys 'home for Christmas.' He pushed toward the frontier, and a major military disaster followed – the Chinese 'volunteers' counter-attacked, repulsed the UN forces, and very nearly won the war before a more or less stable front could be established. For once General MacArthur was not making an overstatement when he notified the United Nations on 28 November that 'we face an entirely new war.'

8

KOREA:
THE SEARCH FOR PEACE

Just as we were deeply concerned lest the war spread beyond the borders of Korea, so we were also concerned lest the war spread in its weaponry. From time to time there had been some talk from General MacArthur about using atomic bombs against the enemy. Our worries on this score were only reinforced at the end of November 1950 by statements made by President Truman during a press conference which implied that MacArthur had the authority to use these weapons if he so decided. Even though the White House quickly 'interpreted' the President's statement by assurances that the bomb could not be used without explicit presidential authorization, this incident really made us shudder. While Chinese retaliation against MacArthur's advance to the Yalu was not so bad as it might have been – it was bad enough – one more atomic bomb dropped by the United States anywhere in Asia would have had disastrous political consequences. I felt very strongly that whatever might be the military result of dropping an atomic bomb, whatever its tactical value, it would be a political disaster which would haunt the Western world for a long time.

In a speech to the Federal-Provincial Conference in Ottawa on 4 December I took the opportunity to express these fears publicly. In reviewing the whole question of the Korean War, I said:

There is some discussion going on at present whether the atom bomb should or should not be used against the aggressors in Korea. One consideration in this matter – an important one – must be the effect of such use on the relations of the Western world with Asia. The military, and others, may argue that the atomic bomb is just another weapon. But, in the minds of ordinary people everywhere in the world, it is far more than that, and its use has acquired an immensely greater significance than any other aspect of war ...

It would be hard to exaggerate the psychological and political consequences of the employment of the bomb, or the threat of its employment, in the present critical situation. The strategic use of the bomb against Chinese cities might conceivably reverse the course of military events in Korea now, but at the cost, possibly, of destroying the cohesion and unity of purpose of the Atlantic community. Certainly its use for a second time against an Asian people would dangerously weaken the links that remain between the Western world and the peoples of the East ...

Before a decision of such immense and awful consequence, for all of us, is taken, there should surely be consultation through the UN, particularly with the governments principally concerned. One of those would be the Canadian government, which has from the beginning been a partner in the tri-partite development of atomic energy ...

From this time on the main Canadian objective was to bring the hostilities in Korea to an end. On 2 December 1950 the Canadian government circulated a memorandum to friendly governments stating: 'Every opportunity for discussion of the issues with Communist China should be explored. Once the military situation has been stabilized, a cease-fire might be attainable. This might be followed by the creation of a demilitarized zone. In these conditions, a *modus vivendi* might be sought by negotiation. In this connection, consideration might have to be given to the other related aspects of the Chinese problem, such as Formosa and Chinese representation in the United Nations.'

My first major opportunity to assist in the search for peace or at least a cease-fire came in December 1950. Nasrollah Entezam of Iran, as President of the General Assembly, had been authorized to set up a Cease-Fire Committee. When he invited me to join him and Sir Benegal Rau of the Indian delegation on the three-man committee, I was happy to serve, although I was not sanguine about its success. I kept a full diary on the work of the committee which is too detailed to include here, but is printed at the back of the book as Appendix 1. I need not repeat the whole story of our activities here. Suffice it to say that in our first series of meetings from 15 to 19 December 1950, we failed not only to find any solution but also even to meet with the delegation of Communist Chinese, under the leadership of General Wu Hsui-chuan, who had been invited to New York by the Security Council to discuss Taiwan. We did, however, send a telegram giving what assurance we could to Peking that, if a cease-fire were arranged, it would be followed immediately by negotiations on outstanding Far

Eastern questions. I felt that we had made it a little more difficult for the Chinese to launch a major offensive in Korea. We had also made it more difficult for the United States to demand more decisive UN action against the Chinese – at least until we had a chance to meet again in New York in January.

I returned to Ottawa after the meeting of the Cease-Fire Committee for Christmas 1950. That Christmas season was marked by a brief glimmer of hope that the war could soon be brought to an end. Following my return to Ottawa, I emphasized to several of our posts and to United States Embassy officials my hope that the United Nations would continue as long as possible in its wise and careful course of not naming China an aggressor. While emphasizing this, I was happy to find out that the United States' attitude to our cease-fire work was becoming more constructive and more flexible. On 22 December I received word through Don Bliss of the United States Embassy that the US wanted a cessation of hostilities and were now willing to associate themselves with a positive assurance to the Chinese that, in the negotiations following a cease-fire, other than strictly Korean matters would be discussed. I told Bliss how happy I was to hear this and how important it was to have the United States attitude communicated clearly, forcibly and quickly to Peking.

I felt that the new United States position was extremely valuable and that it would be tragic if it were rudely rebuffed by the Chinese. Although the United States would be making their own approach to Peking, I decided to urge the Indian government to do what they could to get a favourable Chinese response. The reply from the Indians was disappointing. Bajpai, the Secretary General of the Indian Foreign Office, thought the US statement insufficient and ambiguous and suggested that I attempt to get a more direct and precise assurance from them. Although I decided to go along with that suggestion, I also decided to try to make it clear to the Indians that the United States had made a major step forward. I therefore wired the following message to Warwick Chipman, our High Commissioner in New Delhi:

I hope that they appreciate at New Delhi, and will emphasize at Peking, that the United States has already made important concessions but that concessions on these matters cannot all be made by the United Nations or the United States, and that so far Peking has done nothing to bridge the gap which exists between the two positions. I hope also they realize that a renewal of Chinese military action in Korea, which may have taken place even before you receive this, will automatically end, at least for the time being, all United Nations efforts to bring about a cease-fire and a negotiated settlement. It will also inevitably result in formal charges of Chinese Communist aggression which the majority of United Nations members will be forced on the evidence to support, and in full awareness of all the tragic consequences which will inevitably follow. To prevent such a development, I hope that the Americans may go somewhat further in assurance to Peking than they have gone. That is why I sent this morning's message to Washington. It is equally if not more important that the Chinese should do something other than insult the United Nations and attack United Nations forces.

I hope therefore that as a result of India's wise and timely intervention the Peking authorities will understand this and give us some hope that a peaceful solution of these problems *can* be achieved.

On 26 December in a telegram to Hume Wrong I stated that:

... if the United States could be somewhat more specific in describing the subjects which, among others, could be included in post-cease-fire discussions, it would be more difficult for the Chinese to refuse this offer, assuming of course, that Formosa and recognition were to be mentioned. Rusk has told you that they cannot do this and I appreciate the difficulties, but some of these might be overcome if Tibet and Indo-China were also mentioned ... I don't think myself that the United States would have anything to lose by going a little further in their assurances regarding post-cease-fire talks. At best, it might make such talks possible. At worst, it might smoke out and expose the hypocrisy of the Chinese position.

There is no doubt that we cannot get the Chinese to isolate Korea from other Far Eastern issues, especially Formosa. Personally, I doubt whether we should expect them to. If that is true, shouldn't we go further even than we have gone in linking up general Far Eastern discussion with a cease-fire? As long as we continue to insist, as we must do, that *nothing* can be done until a cease-fire arrangement has actually been made effective, I don't think that this course of action can justifiably be attacked as yielding to blackmail or 'appeasement.' But we will certainly have to act quickly if we act at all.

The US, however, refused to be more specific and the Chinese failed to respond to the new overtures. Thus, the brief glimmer of hope surrounding Christmas 1950 went out.

On 2 January 1951 I returned to New York and the Cease-Fire Committee, no progress having been made. Again the interested reader can refer to my diary in the Appendix for the details of that month's activities. The main point which emerged was that the Cease-Fire Committee managed to produce and secure general agreement to a statement of principles which could form the basis for an end to hostilities. These were sent to Peking and received a rather ambiguous response. The American reaction was to proceed at once to a resolution of the Assembly declaring China to be an aggressor. I felt, however, that the

Chinese response was sufficiently ambiguous to warrant further investigation. I discussed this with the Prime Minister while back in Ottawa in mid-January and he agreed. On 18 January therefore, Mr St Laurent wired Mr Nehru asking him to have the Indian Ambassador in Peking approach Chou En-lai, the Chinese Foreign Minister, to find out whether their call for the withdrawal of all foreign troops included the withdrawal of so-called Chinese 'volunteers' in the North Korean army; whether their insistence on negotiations preceding a cease-fire meant full negotiations of the political issues or merely the negotiations for the cease-fire itself; and whether they were insisting on UN recognition prior to negotiations or as a necessary result of negotiations.

With this telegram off to Nehru, I returned to New York where discussions were proceeding on an American draft resolution naming China an aggressor. While these discussions were going on I received, through Sir Benegal Rau, the Chinese reply to Mr St Laurent's enquiries.

Their response indicated that we had been right in making our approach. The relevant part of the reply read:

1 If the principle that all foreign troops should be withdrawn from Korea has been accepted and is being put into practice, the Central People's Government of People's Republic of China will assume the responsibility to advise the Chinese volunteers to return to China.

2 Regarding the conclusion of the war in Korea and the peaceful settlement of the Korean problem, we think that we can proceed in two steps. First – a cease-fire for a limited time-period can be agreed upon in the first meeting of the seven-nation conference and put into effect so that the negotiations may proceed further. Second step – in order that the war in Korea may be concluded completely and peace in East Asia may be ensured. All the conditions for the conclusion of the war must be discussed in connection with the political problems in order to reach agreement upon the following. The steps and measures for the withdrawal of all foreign troops from Korea; the proposals to the Korean people on the steps and measures to effect the settlement of the internal affairs of Korea by the Korean people themselves; the withdrawal of the United States armed forces from Taiwan and the Taiwan Straits in accordance with Cairo Declaration [of 1 December 1943, issued by Roosevelt, Churchill, and Chiang Kai-shek which stated that Taiwan 'shall be restored' to China and that 'in due course Korea shall become free and independent'] and Potsdam Declaration [of 26 July 1945, in which Truman, Churchill, and Stalin declared that 'the terms of the Cairo declaration shall be carried out']; and other problems concerning the Far East.

3 The definite affirmation of the legitimate status of the People's Republic of China in the United Nations must be ensured.

Nonetheless, we got into a great deal of trouble with the Americans who felt that we were dealing behind their backs. As a result, our approaches came to nothing and we were faced with great American pressure to support their resolution of condemnation. We succumbed to that pressure, although I made it clear to the Assembly that we did not think the course was the wisest.

In supporting the American resolution we had been forced to abstain on an Asian resolution supported by India. When I returned to Ottawa, therefore, I was most anxious to bridge the gap between Canada and India resulting from our voting in opposition to each other on the two resolutions. To this end, Mr St Laurent agreed to send the following message to Mr Nehru:

However harmful you may feel the United States resolution in its final form to have been, I am sure you would consider that our influence, together with that of other delegations, had improved it very substantially.

Our joint efforts have, of course, been subject to a great deal of misinterpretation in both the United States and China. It is, I suppose, inevitable that such efforts as ours should be misunderstood, and I am not therefore surprised that Chou En-lai, as reported by Mr Panikkar [Indian Ambassador in Peking], should have said that Canada had altered its position because of United States pressure, and that under this pressure we were trying to trap the Chinese and appease America. I am sure that your representative in Peking will do whatever is possible to correct that misinterpretation of our position.

The great question before us now is, of course, whether or not adoption of the United States resolution will put an end to all possibility of a peaceful settlement of Far Eastern questions within the foreseeable future. The Chinese have, as your representative has reported, said that this would be the case, and it may well be that their prophecy will turn out to be correct on this as on previous occasions. It should be pointed out, of course, that the Chinese People's Government on their part do not hesitate to condemn in violent terms the United States, acting as an agent of the United Nations, for aggression in Korea, and nevertheless expect that country and the rest of us to enter into negotiations around the council table. I hope Chou En-lai can be made aware of this inconsistency. We have not hesitated on our part to press for negotiations with the Peking régime in spite of the language used by them in their reference to United Nations action in Korea. If they now take the position that a United Nations resolution condemning them puts an end finally to all hope of settlement, it will seem to confirm the view of many that there was from the beginning no hope of success in such negotiations and that the Chinese régime has been insincere in discussing their possibility.

In the long run, however, it seems to me that the attitude adopted on both sides will be determined by the realities of the material situation in the Far East generally and in Korea in particular. Though it may be extremely difficult to make any progress in the near future, I nevertheless hope that before long a further chance of negotiated settlement may emerge. With this in mind, I think we should hold firm to the view that the statement of principles which we enunciated and which was accepted by the Political Committee provides an adequate basis for a peaceful settlement.

With the passage of the condemnatory resolution our hopes for an early cease-fire vanished. Our chief interest now was to prevent the war from spreading beyond the Korean border. We thus had to bring our influence to bear on the United States and therefore had to gain an intimate knowledge of United States thinking. To this end I sent the following formal despatch to Hume Wrong on 9 February 1951:

'In view of the rapid drift in United States policy toward an irrevocable break with the Chinese Communists and of the danger of the United States adopting a policy of assisting the Chinese resistance movement on the mainland and of further rearming Chiang Kai-shek, I think you should seek an early opportunity to discuss with the United States Government, at a high level, the long term objectives of their Far Eastern policy, in which we must inevitably be involved.

'Since Mr Acheson and other officials of the United States Government may feel that we may have been giving them too much gratuitous advice lately on United States policy in the Far East, I do not think that at this stage we need to make suggestions to them on what their policy should be. You should instead do your best to draw them out. What follows in this despatch is material which I hope will be of use to you in doing this.

'There may be some lessons to be drawn between our present position in relation to China and the situation which existed in 1939 when the Soviet Union attacked Finland. At that time it was plain that the Soviet attack was an outrageous betrayal of all the principles which underlay the international community and one had to define the Soviet action in those terms. Yet, it would have been disastrous if we had come into conflict with the Soviet Union over Finland, particularly when it was clear that the Soviet-German alliance was of the most opportunistic nature and that unless any precipitate action on our side had prevented it, these two powers were bound to fall out, thereby bringing Russian manpower to bear against Germany. The parallel obviously should not be pressed too far, especially since Sino-Soviet relations today are undoubtedly closer and more stable than Soviet-

German relations in 1939–41. Nevertheless, the principle of keeping an eye on the main danger still holds good and any hostile action which we launch against China would only have the effect of strengthening the grip of the Communist régime upon the people on the one hand and increasing its dependence on the Soviet Government on the other ...

'We think it is now a fitting time to review the events leading up to the vote of January 30 and to frame a policy for the next stage. The main burden of responsibility for framing a constructive policy for that stage rests on the United States. It is therefore essential for us to know as precisely as we can what present United States objectives are as regards the Far East in general and China in particular.

'The Canadian Government and people have, as you know, been deeply concerned during the past seven months over some aspects of United States Far Eastern policy. If a policy is coherent and logical, even if one disagrees with it, it may still command respect but some aspects of recent United States policy have seemed to us erratic and confused. At times it has been difficult for the Canadian Government to discover exactly what the current United States policy is. There have been occasions when, within a comparatively brief period, we have been given or have noted in the press statements by persons claiming to speak on behalf of the United States Government which have been conflicting or indeed contradictory. Dean Rusk has been wise and restrained but his expositions of United States policy have not always been consistent with public or private expositions by officers of equal or higher rank in the Administration, such as Hickerson, Gross or Austin. MacArthur's statements have, of course, added to the confusion.

'This, plus outbursts of impatience and tactlessness, and the absence of any clear-cut sense of direction, both in the forming and carrying out of current United States policy, have, as you know, caused some differences between the United States and their Western allies. These differences are, however, even wider with certain Eastern governments, especially India ...

'An alternative policy would have been to explore the possibilities of negotiation. The United States, however, not only pushed through the Assembly a resolution condemning China as an aggressor, but also gave the impression during the debate at Lake Success and even more in Washington that they were anxious to seize on the first Chinese reply to the statement of principles of January 17 as an excuse for withdrawing from their own commitment to these principles. One could only deduce from this that the United States had no real desire to enter into negotiations with China at that time.

'We ourselves remained convinced throughout that negotiations with China should be our objective and condemnation voted only as a last resort. Nevertheless, in view of our recent experience at Lake Success we are not now prepared to lend our support to any plan for negotiations unless we are certain that the United States intends to work for their success. That is one reason why I did not accept the invitation to serve on the Good Offices Committee. It seems to me that it would be better to abandon for the immediate future all plans for negotiation than to enter into negotiations which are clearly foredoomed to failure ... I doubt if the Good Offices Committee, tied up as it is with the resolution of condemnation, can do very much at this stage, though it may be very useful later.

'It is important that we know what objectives the United States would seek in any negotiations. Would the United States subscribe to the following or would they suggest others:

1 Localization of the war in Korea and, if possible, its liquidation;
2 Prevention or postponement of Chinese Communist attacks on Indonesia, Malaya, Hong Kong, Burma, etc.;
3 As a corollary of the above, the retention of the access to areas of raw materials vital both to the West and to non-Communist Asian countries;
4 Agreement that our objective in the Far East is the defeat of aggression and not the use of the United Nations to overthrow Communist Governments;
5 Elimination of the danger of our being drawn into a lengthy and perhaps indecisive military struggle with Chinese Communism when we have accepted the axiom that Western Europe should be the principle area of our defensive effort;
6 The desirability of doing everything possible to drive a wedge between Communist China and the USSR; as a step towards this end, the opening up of China to our diplomatic and economic influences; and
7 Finally, and following from the above, stabilizing the Far East.

'Even the partial achievement of these objectives would tend to strengthen friendly relations between the West and the non-Communist East which recent United States tactics have strained. The United States Administration must be aware that their recent policy has noticeably dismayed and vexed some of our potential friends in non-Communist Asia ...

'We are, we hope, under no illusions about Mr Nehru and Indian policy. We do not look upon the present Indian leadership as being the heir to all the Wisdom of the East, nor do we view all Indian proposals as realistic, as we showed by abstaining on the Asian resolution. At the same time, we believe that in the present circumstances we can hope for no more sympathetic or helpful administration in that country, which is still in a formative condition.

'We consider that in the present lull in the diplomatic front it is up to the United States Government, following the vote of January 30, to indicate to countries such as Canada what they envisage as the next step and particularly whether they can hold out any positive hopes that negotiations with China will bear fruit.

'... we would appreciate a State Department assessement on ... the extent of Soviet influence on China, particularly on the conduct of the Korean aggression, and more generally, whether the Soviet Union is exercising a restraining hand upon Chinese Communist expansionist ambitions or pressing China forward. The answer to this, it seems to us, depends in large part on a calculation of the extent of the risks of a general war this year which the Soviet Union is prepared to run.

'We are not blind to the powerful position which the Chinese would enjoy at a conference table as a result of their vast armies, their strategic location in regard to Korea and Indo-China and their backing by the military might of the Soviet Union. It seems to us, however, that the United States and Communist China through a realistic appraisal of both their own and others' strength could cautiously enter a wary and tortuous process of disengagement on both sides from the fixed positions in which each party has entrenched itself. If this process can only be commenced and followed up, even with all the disappointments and problems it would involve, we consider that it offers the only hope for a lessening of tensions and in the long run a comparative stabilization of the Far East. The chances of success of such negotiations, we realize, are slender. Chief among the difficulties, of course, are the fanatic marxist obsessions of Chinese Communist leaders and the excitable state of public opinion in the United States. Nevertheless, it is the task of diplomacy to pursue patiently and doggedly what appears to be the only sensible course.

'During your discussions with the United States Government at a high level on the long term objectives of their policy in the Far East, I should be grateful if you would take advantage of any opportunity which presents itself to make clear that, while we have over the past seven months differed from the United States on their Far Eastern policy, and while we continue to have apprehensions about the drift of their policy in the Far East, the Canadian Government and people are fully conscious of the great debt of gratitude which they owe to the United States, and particularly to Mr Truman and Mr Acheson, for the way in which they have, during the past seven months, rallied the whole of the free world to defend its common liberties against the increasing danger of Soviet aggression. Three years ago when the Communists seized Czechoslovakia, the United States and its fellow-members of the North Atlantic Community embarked on a process of strengthening their armed forces and their unity. Looking back at this period of the last three years, it is clear that up to the time of the attack on Korea last summer none of us in the North Atlantic Community was moving fast enough. The result, I am afraid, was that, instead of the gap between our strength and the Soviet strength narrowing, it was in fact widening and the inevitable result would have been disaster. This suicidal policy has been reversed because of United States leadership under Mr Truman and Mr Acheson, and latterly General Marshall. The United States has with courage and imagination seized the opportunity which was presented by the developments in Korea to double and later to quadruple its defence effort and has carried its North Atlantic allies with it. The result is that for the first time since the end of hostilities there is good reason for believing that time is on our side and that if we continue with our present defence policies and pursue a patient, restrained and firm diplomacy, we may succeed in averting war and finally in reaching a tolerable *modus vivendi* with the Soviet Union.'

On receipt of this despatch Hume Wrong met with Dean Rusk. Some of what Rusk had to say was rather startling. As a result Wrong reported back to me in a personal letter which he himself brought to Ottawa:

'This letter and its enclosure are a partial reply to your despatch number Y650 of February 9th asking me to seek information on the objectives of the Far Eastern policy of the United States. The enclosure is my note of a long discussion on February 14th on this subject with Mr Dean Rusk. I had originally intended to follow up a talk with Mr Rusk by seeking an early interview with Mr Acheson, but I now feel it better to postpone seeing him until I have had an opportunity of talking over with you the results of my meeting with Mr Rusk ...

'I think that you will agree that Mr Rusk's explanation gives a more coherent account of the policy towards China than anything that we have previously received. It also throws a good deal of light on the reasons why the tactics of the United States representatives have been at times disingenuous and inconsistent. Mr Rusk states that the belief or hope that the attitude of the Peking Government may be changed by some kind of upheaval within the régime is based on very secret intelligence. A public avowal of their aim would tend to prevent its fulfilment, and they are not in a position to give their reasons even in strictest secrecy to more than a very few trusted people ...

'While it is a relief for us to secure a rational explanation such as that given by Mr Rusk, we are inevitably at a disadvantage in assessing its possibility of success, since this could only be determined by access to the secret intelligence which is determining US thinking or by the availability of other good intelligence sources inside China. We must, in short, take what we are told either with scepticism or as providing a real chance of success. Furthermore, we are not in a position to give even the slightest public indication of what the present aim of the United States in Peking is.

'In your despatch you emphasize the objectives to be sought in any Far Eastern negotiations. I think from what Mr Rusk has told me and from my discussions with others here that the United States would endorse the objectives ... and would agree that they can only be attained through eventual negotiations with the Peking Government. They would, however, in my judgment take the position that unless there were changes in that régime a negotiation aimed to achieve these objectives would not only be fruitless but would solidify the Moscow-Peking axis; they are therefore looking for time in the hope that internal pressures in Peking will before long reach a bursting point. If the present pattern of fighting in Korea can be maintained, with hugely disproportionate Chinese losses, this should in their view hasten the desired development inside the Chinese Communist Party.

'The outcome they hope for seems to be neither the evolution of Mao Tse-tung into a Chinese Tito nor the transformation of the Chinese Communists into agrarian reformers. It appears to be rather the overthrow or submergence of the leaders whose first loyalty seems to be rather to Moscow than to the Chinese revolution, and their replacement by others who would be Communists still but with a definite nationalist slant. I did not get as far as this in my talk with Mr Rusk, so that this is my own deduction.'

The record of the conversation which he enclosed with his report was certainly a fascinating and highly sensitive document. It said in part:

'Our discussion then turned to the longer term purposes of United States policy towards the Peking Government, and this was the most interesting part of our talk. I started it by saying that it seemed to me that the difficulties in working out an agreed policy between the United States, the United Kingdom, Canada and other free countries centred around the answer to a question which might be framed as: "Is the United States reconciled to the continued existence of the Peking Government for some time or is its aim to overthrow the Peking Government?" Mr Rusk agreed that this was the central issue, and remarked that there had been very little discussion of it between the governments concerned. He went on to give me some very secret information on what was guiding the policy of the United States.

'The United States, he said, considers the existence of the Peking régime disadvantageous to the Western world and does not intend to do anything which would have the effect of consolidating its authority in China. He did not believe that Peking could be wooed away from Moscow by making concessions now on the issues on which the Peking Government was demanding the adoption of their views, such as the handing over of Formosa and seating in the UN. The United States, in short, wished the existing régime in Peking to fall but they did not intend to undertake any overt commitment to bring it down. They could, however, do something to confuse and impede its activities.

'He went on to tell me some of the reasons which led them to believe that such a policy might succeed – reasons which he asked me not to put on paper. These led to the view that the present régime was not nearly as monolithic as it might appear. There are factions inside the régime which are much disturbed about the relations with Moscow.

'... In Peking the pro-Moscow elements in the Communist Party are now on top, but there is a strong nationalist element. It would probably take some time before the balance could change, and one could not guess in advance what would be effective in changing the balance ...

'The current appreciation in the State Department of the extent of Soviet influence on China is that it is now very great and that Moscow therefore is playing a controlling part in Chinese actions in Korea. China, however, is the weakest part of the whole Communist sphere and the area most likely to break off from Soviet domination. Concessions to current Chinese demands would strengthen the position of the elements in Peking who are most subservient to Moscow ...'

On 23 February, after Wrong returned to Washington, he had another talk with Dean Rusk. Later that day he wrote to me:

'Mr Rusk suggested that I have a talk with him this afternoon after one of the meetings of Ambassadors at the State Department, and I therefore took the opportunity of going over with him some of the matters which arose during our discussions in Ottawa this week, especially with reference to your consideration of my report of my talk with Mr Rusk on February 14th which I handed to you in Ottawa on Monday morning.

'I sought to lead him into developing further the evidence in the possession of the United States Government about the balance of forces inside the Peking Government. I was not very successful in this, and although he repeated the general observations which he had made at our previous talk he did not amplify them significantly. He pointed out, however, that public reports were coming in today from Peking about internal difficulties in China. He would not go so far as to say that he had a "reasonable hope" that the nationalist elements would supersede or get control of the pro-Moscow forces within a few months, although he thought that there was enough chance of this taking place to warrant some waiting on events. He added that the position should be rather clearer in a month or so.

'He agreed when I said that his explanation of the basis of US policy seemed to show that the differences with the British in particular were over means rather than ends. The withdrawal of recognition from Chiang Kai-shek, for example, would in his judgment be acclaimed inside China as a considerable victory for those now in power and therefore would strengthen their hold. I told him that some thought had been given in Ottawa to a Canadian withdrawal of recognition but that I judged from my discussions there that consideration of this step would be deferred for some weeks ...

'I then asked about their attitude in the event of a Chinese move into Indo-China. He told me that there were some Chinese already in Indo-China although the French had not publicly admitted this. Chinese had been killed in action and a few prisoners had been taken. If the intervention became really strong he thought it would be impossible for the French to defend Tonkin although they might be able to hold out in the strong redoubt of Haiphong for a considerable period. There was no possibility of the United States providing ground forces and it was doubtful whether air strikes from carriers could do sufficient damage. He believed it unlikely that the French would bring the issues before the United Nations, as they would be unsure of the votes. He left me with the impression that the United States would not take the initiative in such a case and also that they had not got very far in their consideration of various courses of action.

'He went on to say that their estimate of Chinese military capabilities was that if they went all out they were strong enough in time to deal with Indo-China, Korea and Hong Kong. They took the possible threat to Hong Kong more seriously than the British. He showed me a telegram just received from their man there passing on reports of substantial Chinese troop movements to the Hong Kong region. Their conclusion from their current intelligence is that intervention in Hong Kong and in Indo-China, or in one or the other of them, is more likely than an attack on Formosa.

'He remarked that an attack on Hong Kong would bring to an end the current differences on policy between the British and the Americans, which would be to Chinese disadvantage. He thought, however, that inside China it might well solidify the supporters of the Peking régime and ease the present strains and stresses. They might think that this would make an attack worthwhile ...

'PS. They are puzzled about the absence of Russian equipment among the Chinese forces in Korea. Apparently none has been identified with the Chinese. Rusk said that the explanation might be that the Russians were only providing equipment on a barter or payment basis which the Chinese were unable to meet. From documents taken last year in Pyongyang [North Korean capital] they had found that there had been no free delivery of Russian equipment to North Korea ...'

ॐ

Throughout this period, as I have already indicated, we were concerned about the leadership of General MacArthur. As long as he was in charge of the United Nations forces it would be difficult to bring the war to an end. He was all for fighting it out. 'The only result of war,' he used to say, 'is victory. There is no other object in war but victory.' I always thought myself that the object of war is peace; whether you obtain peace or not depends on the kind of victory you win. He did not make any qualifications. He wanted to fight through, if necessary bomb the Chinese, not merely the Yalu bridges, but the Chinese industrial establishments in Manchuria. Fortunately, he was not allowed to do that. Mr Truman showed a very wise sense of restraint. He kept his nerve, but he also got into a good deal of trouble with General MacArthur and vice versa.

As the winter of 1950–1 drew to a close, I became more and more worried about MacArthur's continuing command of the UN forces. In February 1951 I let Washington know that I was concerned about statements which suggested that the State Department was not sure whether MacArthur could be kept under control. By early April control of the General became a crucial affair. MacArthur had been making public statements urging a UN return north of the 38th parallel, and also urging the bombing of Manchuria.

On 31 March, while speaking to the Canadian Bar Association in Toronto, with MacArthur in mind, I said that one of the two main dangers to the unity of the free world arose '... when those who have been charged by the United Nations with military responsibility make controversial pronouncements which go far beyond that responsibility, and create confusion, disquiet and even discord. It seems to me to be as unwise, indeed as dangerous, for the generals to intervene in international policy matters as it would be for the diplomats to try and lay down military strategy. This is a case, I think, where the specialist should stick to his specialty. Otherwise, wholehearted co-operation between friends which is so essential is hindered.'

When I received word from British sources that General MacArthur was contemplating a landing on mainland China from Formosa, my fears were greatly heightened.

About a week later, on 10 April, I was addressing the Empire and Canadian Clubs, again in Toronto. My speech that night created much controversy. Little notice was taken of those parts dealing with Canadian policy in the cold war, the UN, and collective security. The last part, however, which touched on our relations with the United States, got a great deal of attention in Canada, the United States, and in Europe. I had said: 'The days of relatively easy and automatic political relations with our neighbour are, I think, over. They are over because, on our side, we are more important in the continental and international scheme of things, and we loom more largely now as an important element in United States and in free world plans for defence and development. They are over also because the United States is now the dominating world power on the side of freedom. Our preoccupation is no longer *whether* the United States will discharge her international responsibilities, but how she will do it and whether the rest of us will be involved.' It was not so much my speech which caused the controversy as the fact that it was delivered on the same day as President Truman relieved General MacArthur of his command.

I wrote a personal letter to Hume Wrong a few days later:

'It is, I think, important that our friends in Washington, and elsewhere in the United States, understand the anxiety and hesitation with which the majority of people in Canada watch the development of United States policy, especially in regard to the Far East. There is no use deceiving ourselves about this or deceiving them. The deep-seated, though often unconsciously felt, origin of this is, I suppose, our feeling of dependence on the United States and frustration over the fact that we can't escape this no matter how hard we might try. The immediate cause, however, is found in recent United States attitudes and policies, which seem to many Canadians to be based on the acceptance of inevitable wars not so much against an aggressor as against communism itself.

'You know, as well as I do, that we have a fundamentally friendly feeling toward Americans, and that we really are anxious, on the official and other levels, to support them in the leadership which they are giving in the struggle against Russian communist imperialism. I have not made any statements in the last six months without emphasizing that fact; indeed, I have gone further and said, both in the House of Commons and outside, that there will be times when, in the interests of the unity which is so necessary we may have to abandon our own views in favour of those held by the United States. But we feel that Americans also should modify some of their own partisan views in the interest of their *national* unity in foreign policy, which is just as important as a united front internationally. The MacArthur outburst is an example of what I mean. Our worries are, in fact, not so much over the actual policies which are being followed in Washington, though in their Far Eastern manifestations they have aroused considerable anxiety up here, as in the atmosphere of excitement, controversy, instability and emotion in which policy is formulated, attacked and altered, and formulated again. What so many of us fear is that public opinion in the United States, and especially in Congress (the focus of so many of our fears) will make any consistent and stable line impossible, and that there will be times in the future when we will have to do what we avoided doing in recent months, namely, take our own line even at the risk of weakening that unity, which it is our first objective to preserve. It is because I feel that this may, at times, be unavoidable in the months ahead that I thought our own people should be given some indication of its possibility. I do not think that anyone is serving the cause of Canada-American relations at this time by continuing the pleasant platitudes which are normally so agreeable, and conveying, thereby, the impression that everything is going to be easy and smooth when this may not prove to be the case.

'At the time I made my Toronto statement, I was filled with anxiety that any moment General MacArthur might authorize some action in the Far East, such as an air bombardment of Chinese cities, which would have required us to dissociate ourselves formally from the decision taken. Telegram 876 of April 3 from London shows that we had a real reason for such fears. If, for instance, the Formosan operation, mentioned in the telegram, had been carried out and a Canadian ship asked to participate, that would have faced us with a very difficult problem. Either we would have had to remove the ship from the operation and precipitate a political crisis, or we would have had to allow the ship to participate in carrying out a policy which we would not have approved.

'The immediate difficulty of MacArthur has been removed, or has it? The general feeling in Parliament at this news was one of relief, coupled with dismay at the apparently sudden, rough way it was done and the wild outburst of unbridled controversy, exploited for political purposes, which has followed it. The events of the next two or three weeks will show whether moderate, wise and healthy influences on American opinion will prevail over hysteria, prejudice and immaturity. I think the President is going to win out on this issue, but if he doesn't, and if the forces which are backing MacArthur prevail, there will be stronger expressions used up here about American policy than have been even contemplated previously. The President's broadcast the other night was good, I thought. It put the problems of both MacArthur and his policy and the dangers from both in the proper perspective. It represented the kind of thing that we can really back, and I hope effectively. If that policy wins out, there won't be much to fear. If the other policy wins out, then we really will be up against some difficult decisions in our relations with Washington.

'You may be interested to know that I have received a lot of correspondence from the States in the last couple of weeks, practically all hostile, and some of it quite abusive. There is nothing very significant in this. More significant is that I have been receiving some very friendly letters and messages from all over Canada. In this episode, I am more worried about extravagant praise from Canada than abusive criticism from Americans, because it shows how easy it would be to work up a

strong anti-American feeling in this country at this time. The danger
is obvious, and that is one reason why, having now said my piece, I
will lapse back into the traditional Canadian-American speech pattern
unless specific events and developments make that impossible, when I
shall do my best to say nothing – in public! I hope that you agree with
this, and I would be very glad to get your views on all these matters.

'We are now, as you know, making an exhaustive study of outstanding Canadian-American problems, of which there are many. These
problems, some of them difficult enough to solve, and which are far
more important to us, naturally, than they are to the Americans, make
it all the more important that the general atmosphere and general relationship between the two countries should be good.'

With General Ridgway now in command of UN and US forces, and
with a fairly stable front established slightly north of the 38th parallel,
the door was opened to negotiations for an armistice. These got underway during the summer of 1951 between representatives of the military
commands, but were to prove long and protracted. Canada was not a
part of the negotiating team and, although we were kept informed, we
had little diplomatic responsibility. The only exception was in the autumn of 1951 when we insisted on modifying the US draft of a warning
declaration to be issued in the event of an armistice. The operative
sentences of the declaration first proposed by the US were stronger than
we liked. Only after it had been revised to read as follows were we prepared to accept it: 'We affirm, in the interests of world peace, that if
there is a renewal of the armed attack, challenging again the principles
of the United Nations, we should again be united and prompt to resist.
The consequences of such a breach of armistice would be so grave that,
in all probability, it would not be possible to confine hostilities within
the frontiers of Korea.' The purpose of this declaration was to make it
possible for General Ridgway to make more concessions to meet Communist reluctance to agree to adequate conditions for supervising an
armistice. General Ridgway, it was argued, would feel free to accept
greater risks if he knew that the enemy would be warned that a breach
of faith would have serious consequences.

The armistice negotiations proceeded slowly, the question of prisoners of war looming larger on the horizon as time went by. Although
we were still not directly involved, I continued to keep myself well-
informed of what was happening by, for example, talking with Dean
Acheson when the opportunity arose, as in April 1952. From time to
time I intervened to make specific points. For example, I urged careful

consideration of two proposals made by Chou En-lai in July 1952 on the POW question. Similarly, in May, I had our representatives in Washington and London raise questions on information we had received that USAF planes were pursuing enemy planes into Manchuria. My next major involvement in Korea did not come, however, until the autumn and winter of 1952 when the General Assembly again took up the question of Korea. I have spoken earlier of the honour that was bestowed upon me in 1952 when I was elected President of the United Nations General Assembly. My main task as President was to help find a solution to the Korean conflict.

℃

My efforts began when Canada co-sponsored a United States resolution (the '21-power resolution') which called on the Chinese and North Koreans to 'agree to an armistice which recognizes the rights of all prisoners of war ... to be repatriated and avoids the use of force in their repatriation.' The Indians could not support this resolution since they were sure it would be unacceptable to the other side. I therefore took it upon myself to mediate between the Americans and the Indians, between Dean Acheson and Krishna Menon. Menon was a very clever man with a great capacity for constructive action and an almost equal capacity for mischief. The result was a very difficult negotiation between Corporal Pearson and General Acheson. Indeed, I have never in my life worked so hard on any negotiation as I did to get a resolution acceptable to India and her uncommitted Asian friends and satisfactory to the United States.

In his memoirs, *Present at the Creation*, Dean Acheson refers to a Canadian conspiracy with the Indians; to my joining Krishna Menon's cabal and becoming enmeshed in an illusory proposal which he said amounted to an about-face. He complains of my 'sophistries' and lack of candour, and suggests that we were unnecessarily negative and obstructionist. He also implies that when he went to Ottawa one weekend and saw Mr St Laurent, the whole thing was cleared up at once. This is a travesty of the facts. It is, however, a good example of how different an account of a single event can be, as told by one participant and another. Fortunately, I kept a summary of the confidential discussions which I had with the various delegates. Again I will not impose my diary upon the general reader but will include it as Appendix 2 to this book for those who may wish to know the details.

Krishna Menon of the Indian delegation was the first delegate to approach me when I arrived in New York in the fall of 1952 and from then on I worked to reconcile the American and the Indian points of view and to seek a resolution by the Assembly which could form the basis of a solution to the prisoner of war problem – more and more the block against achieving an armistice. Eventually we succeeded in this and when we went home from New York for Christmas 1952 the Indian resolution, after a long and stormy passage, was a matter of record at the United Nations, together with the Chinese and North Korean rejections of the resolution.

Only time and a variation on the armistice theme were now needed to bring about a settlement. But this is to speak with the advantage of hindsight. At the time, no one could know this; although I was convinced that the Indian resolution was a major step forward, the whole Korean question still required close scrutiny.

During the month of January 1953, the presidency of the US passed from Harry Truman to Dwight Eisenhower and John Foster Dulles replaced Dean Acheson as Secretary of State. I was anxious to meet with Dulles at an early date. When the opportunity came in mid-February, I flew down to Washington. My first impression of the new Secretary of State was favourable. Of our lunch and good three hour talk on Sunday, 15 February 1953, I wrote in my diary: 'He seemed relaxed and rested and was very friendly and frank. It is too bad that the superficial impression he makes in negotiation is that of a cold and rather unsympathetic person. Dulles is not an easy man to exchange banter with, and I would never be on the same terms with him as I was with Dean Acheson, but we shall get along all right. There is no doubt that he himself is very worried about the problem of conducting a foreign policy – he admitted this – in the present American set-up of irresponsible and inquisitive Congressmen, talkative and ambitious Generals, and a sensational press.'

I spoke in the House of Commons a couple of days later and was able to reassure them about the new administration in the following words:

I feel reasonably assured that there is no intention on the part of the Administration in Washington to do anything that is rash, provocative or adventurous, and that on their part they have no desire to extend the war to the continent of Asia.

I also feel that, like their predecessors in Washington, they appreciate the necessity and the desirability of consultation before decisions are taken in Washington which affect the other members of the United Nations who, whether or not they are committed formally by those decisions, cannot escape the consequences of them. Mr Dulles, the Secretary of State, made a broadcast the other night ... in which he said: '... in order to win and hold the confidence of those whom we need as friends and allies, we must at all times play the part of a nation which is fully aware of the grave responsibility which it carries.'

I am sure that when the Secretary of State uttered those words he was sincere in his own determination to do his best to carry them out. I am reinforced in that feeling by my visit to Washington.

Throughout 1953 I was back and forward between New York and Ottawa. It was at this time that I was a leading contender for the position of Secretary General of the UN (I have spoken of that in an earlier chapter). Although there was little activity concerning Korea, I had other responsibilities as President of the Assembly. The following extracts from my diary describe some of these.

February 27, 1953 (Friday)
'... much against my will, I attended a reception given by the Dominican Permanent Delegate to his Dictator, Trujillo. This was a duty, but certainly no pleasure, especially as the Generalissimo did not arrive to receive his guests until 30 or 40 minutes after our own arrival. The poor Dominican Representative and his wife were in the last stages of embarrassment, equalled only by the irritation of Lodge, Trygve Lie and myself and others. As soon as Trujillo arrived, we shook hands with him and I led the procession out, though we were begged to stay and fraternize with the great little man! ...

March 3, 1953 (Tuesday)
'... Spoke at Town Hall this afternoon on the bases of Canada's foreign policy, and was followed by Bill Mackintosh [Vice-Chancellor and Principal of Queen's University], in a brilliant performance. Afterwards there were questions from the afternoon audience, a movie on Canada, and then a dinner attended by 30 or 40 tycoons, where we were given more questions. It is the beginning of a series of lectures and radio performances to stimulate interest in this country in Canada and things Canadian. High time too!

March 4, 1953 (Wednesday)
'We flew to Washington this afternoon on a private plane with the Edens and Butlers [Chancellor of the Exchequer] who had arrived by the *Queen Elizabeth*. There was a regular invasion and every seat on the plane was filled with officials, stenographers, etc. The British certainly

take their international meetings seriously, especially when they are in Washington.

'I sneaked out of the plane at the Washington airport without becoming involved in the welcoming group. We are staying at the Embassy where the Wrongs gave the Edens and Butlers a dinner tonight, the only other guests being the Makins [the British Ambassador] and the Towers [the Governor of the Bank of Canada] who are here from Ottawa. It was a pleasant and very informal occasion. I sat beside the new Mrs Eden, and found her diffident and not too easy to talk to. [Later, as I got to know her, I found her easier to talk to.] Anthony, however, was very relaxed and friendly and delighted at the fact that the President had sent for him and that they had had an hour's talk largely devoted to the Middle East. He thinks that at last the two governments are seeing eye to eye regarding the problems of this area. They didn't expect to accomplish very much in the economic and financial talks but hoped to lay the basis for future progress. One of their difficulties, which they experienced, indeed, at the first meeting, was the fact that practically every senior American they were talking to is new ...

'Much telephoning to New York all evening about Stalin's illness and imminent death. I took an hour off and drafted a message as President of the Assembly when the news of the death is given out. It was a tricky document and I certainly didn't want to say too much, and yet, in my UN position, I couldn't say too little.

March 5, 1953 (Thursday)
'We flew back this morning ... The UN is, of course, agog with gossip about Moscow developments.

'David Johnson [our Permanent Representative to the UN] gave a cocktail party this evening during the course of which the news of Stalin's death arrived. I gave out my statement, which I had re-written again during the afternoon. The one from the White House yesterday on his illness was certainly an unusual one, and the one given out this evening very cold and formal.

March 6, 1953 (Friday)
'Quite an emotional scene at the First Committee this morning when the Chairman called for a moment's silence, and Vishinsky delivered his eulogy of his great "leader and teacher." They tell me he almost broke down. He also insulted Lie by refusing to shake his hand, and the latter, who came up to see me shortly afterwards, is now deter-

mined to issue a blast against the Russians when he talks about personnel policy. I thought we had talked him out of this. Lie is determined to have this matter discussed before the Secretary Generalship
is brought before the Security Council. The British are equally determined on the other course. I suggested to Lie that he get the British
and Americans together on this as any course would suit me. Andy
Cordier [Lie's Executive Assistant] told me very confidentially this
afternoon that Lie was so furious at the Russian insult this morning
that he has decided to withdraw his resignation. It seems a strange way
to react, and I suspect he will change his mind tomorrow.

'At the end of the First Committee meeting this morning I sent for
the delegates of the USSR, Byelorussia and the Ukraine to convey to
them personally, as President of the Assembly, my sympathy on the
death of Stalin. Vishinsky had gone and was replaced by a junior, but
Baranovsky and Kiselev turned up. I said a few sympathetic words
and Baranovsky made rather an emotional reply. A strange performance!'

For the rest of 1953 I continued back and forth between Ottawa
and New York. During the spring and early summer the negotiations
for a Korean settlement at Panmunjom continued until finally successful. But as it became obvious that a solution to the POW problem
would be found, Syngman Rhee, the President of the southern
Republic of Korea, became determined to scuttle the arrangements if
at all possible. The Canadian aim was to repel the aggression, his was
to have a unified Korea under his rule. Rhee's government was just as
dictatorial as the one in the North, just as totalitarian. Indeed, it was
more so in some ways, based as it was on Rhee's strong personal appeal
as leader in exile for many years.

In an eleventh hour attempt to scuttle the armistice negotiations,
Rhee, through his Provost Marshal-in-Chief, engineered a massive
co-ordinated break-out of northern prisoners of war. Over 25,000
'non-repatriables,' Communist prisoners who did not wish to return
home, walked away from their South Korean guarded compounds on
18 June 1953. As Secretary of State for External Affairs of Canada, I
spoke out against this. After a political meeting in Orono, Ontario,
that night, I told the press: 'We are under no obligation to support or
participate in any operation brought on by the Government of the
Republic of South Korea, and not by a decision of the United Nations.
From this it follows that we must condemn the last-minute action
ordered by the Government of the Republic of Korea which might

prejudice an armistice agreement which, in turn, we hoped would be the first step for bringing about peace and unification of that unhappy land.'

About a week later, I wrote to Syngman Rhee in my capacity of President of the UN:

As President of the General Assembly of the United Nations I have been shocked to hear of the unilateral action which you have sanctioned in bringing about the release of non-repatriable North Korean prisoners from the United Nations prisoner-of-war camps in Korea.

I take this occasion to recall the decisive action taken by the United Nations when aggression was initiated in June 1950, and the satisfaction which you expressed in the response of the United Nations to the urgent appeals made by you for military and other assistance. That collaboration, aimed at the repelling of aggression and the restoration of your country to a condition of peace and economic well-being, has been marked by three years of effective effort on the part of Members of the United Nations, and of your Government and people, under the direction of the United Nations Command. In view of what this collaboration has meant to your people it is most regrettable that you have taken action which threatens the results already achieved and the prospect of a peaceful solution of remaining problems.

This release of North Korean prisoners from United Nations prisoner-of-war camps in Korea is particularly shocking in view of the progress made by the armistice negotiators in Panmunjom, which has resulted in the acceptance of principles laid down in the United Nations General Assembly's resolution of 3 December 1952, endorsed by 54 Member Nations. The acceptance of the principles underlying this resolution, especially that of no forcible repatriation of prisoners, which has been the basis of your position as well as that of the United Nations, has been obtained only after two years of patient and persistent negotiation by the United Nations Command.

The action taken with your consent, in releasing the North Korean prisoners, violates the agreement reached by the two sides on June 8, 1953, embodying these principles, and it occurs at a time when hostilities are about to cease, and when the question of the unification of Korea and related Korean problems can be dealt with by a political conference involving the parties concerned.

In July 1950, as a means of assuring necessary military solidarity with the United Nations effort in repelling aggression, you undertook to place the land, sea and air forces of the Republic of Korea under the 'command authority' of the United Nations Command. Your action referred to above violates that undertaking.

As President of the General Assembly of the United Nations, I feel it my duty to bring to your attention the gravity of this situation. I hope and trust that you will cooperate with the United Nations Command in its continuing and determined efforts to obtain an early and honourable armistice.

I should like to take this occasion to express, as President of the United Nations General Assembly, my profound sympathy for the sufferings of the people of Korea during the past three years, and my admiration for the valiant efforts of the ROK Army in its cooperation with the forces of the United Nations. It is my earnest hope that this cooperation will continue, not only in the immediate task of obtaining the armistice but in assuring that the armistice is thereafter faithfully observed, in order that we may jointly proceed toward our common objective of the unification of Korea by peaceful means. If this cooperation were ended, it would be the Korean people who would suffer first and suffer most.

As events proved, Rhee's efforts were in vain. On 27 July 1953 the following telegram was received by the Department of National Defence in Ottawa: 'For the CGS from Allard Cease Fire will become effective 2200 hours Monday 27 Jul 53.' The war in Korea was over.

The subsequent arrangements for a political settlement provided for in the armistice bogged down, however, both before and during the 1954 Geneva Conference. It is, indeed, only in recent times that the possibility of a lasting political solution in Korea seems likely.

As retiring President, I told the opening session of the eighth Assembly of the UN: 'From the Korean experience we have, I hope, learned some lessons. One is that collective action against aggression can work, even when that action is incomplete, in organization, support and participation. Korea, then, has been a vindication of the principle of collective action, but even more, it has shown what could be done if all members of the United Nations were willing, collectively, to pay the price to make such action effective.'

9

A VISIT TO MR KHRUSHCHEV

In 1955 I went to Russia – the first time a Canadian foreign minister (or any NATO foreign minister) had visited the Soviet Union. There had, however, by this time developed a slight warming of relations between the East and the West.

The invitation for my visit to the USSR was in the first instance probably as strange as any ever received. To celebrate the tenth anniversary of the signing of the UN Charter, a special meeting was held in San Francisco, the city of its birth, and I attended as the Canadian delegate. It was a ceremonial occasion – a return to the place where we began our career with such high, illusory hopes. There was a succession of emotional speeches about the United Nations, full of praise but not all praise. As I was coming out of one of the afternoon meetings, I was met in the hall by the Soviet Foreign Minister, Molotov, who was surrounded by the usual four or five colleagues. They encircled me. I wondered what I had done. Molotov said: 'Do you mind coming in here?' and led me into a sort of tunnel. I thought, 'I am for it now.' He explained that he did not want to talk to me in public, then very formally and with a little bow invited me to pay an official visit to the Soviet Union in the autumn or as soon as I could get there. This was really quite a surprise, but I told him that I would let him know. When I returned to Ottawa a few days later I spoke to Mr St Laurent who agreed that I should accept the invitation. So, on 30 September, after clearing up some last-minute difficulties, we left Ottawa with a good deal of fanfare.

The first stop was London, where I had no sooner met with Norman Robertson, our High Commissioner there, and checked into the Dorchester, than I had to be off to Chequers to meet Anthony Eden, now Prime Minister, in order to have a private talk with him before we were joined by Richard Casey of Australia. I found Eden unhappy about the violent reaction in New York and Washington to the recent news of communist arms deals with Nasser. He told me that he was thinking of making a personal appeal to Bulganin not to start an arms race between Egypt and Israel. He showed me the draft of his letter to this end which he wanted the Americans to support, and he asked me if I would back it up in any talks I had with Bulganin or Khrushchev. I told him that I would do so only if the United States supported his initiative and he promised to let me know of this before I reached Moscow. However, nothing came of this. Of the luncheon itself I noted at the time: 'Pleasant luncheon, but no significant talk. Casey full of ideas about Soviet policy, psychological warfare, etc. Eden recovering from a cold, but relaxed and in good form. Wants to come to Canada next year – could I arrange an invitation to open the Toronto Exhibition?'

The next day, after talking about many things with Norman Robertson, we flew to Paris where my wife and I spent a quiet evening with our son Geoffrey and his family who were now posted to the Canadian Embassy there. This gave us a chance to become better acquainted with a young lady who was, to us, the most important person in all Paris – Miss Hilary Pearson, our one-year-old grand-daughter.

While in Paris, Charles Ritchie (our Ambassador to Germany) brought Herbert Blankenhorn (the German Ambassador to NATO) to fill me in on Chancellor Adenauer's recent visit to Russia. My diary recalls of this interview: 'He, Blankenhorn, gave us a most entertaining account of the Adenauer visit to the Russian bears. He thinks Bulganin has far more authority than many believe, but that Khrushchev is the real power – a primitive brute – but childishly naive in many little things; like his desire to please socially. Adenauer, according to Blankenhorn, was the master of the proceedings at all times during the recent visit to Moscow. I wonder. Molotov of no importance – called by Khrushchev "merely a file clerk," or, even worse, "just a diplomat." '

On 4 October we left Paris for Berlin. Of our arrival in that beaten and bruised city, that monument, even today, to the wastefulness of war, I wrote in my diary:

'Greeted at Tempelhof by the Keiths (of the Canadian Mission in Berlin), Berlin's Chief of Protocol, Dr Klein, and the Soviet Ambassador, Pushkin, a solid, square man. No one had expected him in West Berlin! We were motored at once to the Town Hall where I was welcomed by the Burgomaster, Dr Suhr, signed the "Golden Book," listened to a speech of welcome, replied in kind, drank coffee with the Burgomaster and some civic leaders, and drove to our hotel, the Kempinski, a new one rising like so many buildings from Berlin ruins. Dined with our delegation, had a chat with the Canadian press men who are travelling with us; listened to the American forces radio during which I learned that Brooklyn won the World Series! Then to bed.

'Great changes in Berlin since I was last here. The city is on the way to reconstruction, or at least the Western Zones. The communist part is far behind. It is dramatic here, where the two worlds meet, and the contrast is encouraging for our world.'

The next morning, having taken on a Russian pilot and navigator, we were off again – this time for Moscow and another world.

We flew over Frankfurt-on-Oder, which seemed still to be a dead city, and then as we reached the Polish border a continuous layer of clouds hid the land. I thought, 'communist security arrangements, no doubt.' Thirty minutes later the cloud curtain lifted and the vast land of Russia – rivers, forests, collective farms, villages, and an occasional town or city spread out below us as we got nearer Moscow. We flew over the city and then landed at the airfield, Vnukova, about seventeen miles beyond. It was a rather nerve-tingling moment as our shiny big plane, Canadian flag flying, drew up to a stop in front of the Soviet dignitaries, headed by Mr Molotov, and all the diplomatic chiefs who were there to welcome us.

From the airport we were driven to the government guest 'mansion' where we were to stay, unfortunately, instead of at the Embassy. It was a spacious, but somewhat gloomy nineteenth-century mansion furnished according to the taste of that age, but modernized, no doubt, with microphones. We knew perfectly well, of course, that anything we said would be taken down. That might have happened at the Embassy too but it would not have been quite as simple there. One incident in particular emphasized this aspect of life in Russia.

One night my wife and I went to a magnificent, lavishly staged opera. It was, as I recall, a performance of Glinka's 'A Life for the Czar' under its new Russian title, 'Ivan Susanin.' Despite the superb bass soloist and the excellent performance, I was too tired to enjoy it and I decided to leave my wife with the official party and slip home alone after the second act. I went down the stairs from the box, found my car and told the driver, who looked a little surprised, 'home.' When I got to the guest house, unexpected, and rang the bell, they were very startled to see me alone there. I went into my room, an enormous sort of Victorian bedroom, and the man inside was even more startled because he was fooling around in the walls changing the tape or something. Since we knew that what we said in this room and the breakfast room was being recorded, we had great fun in saying things that would mystify our hosts – for instance, 'You know, that fellow Dulles, if he sticks his snoot into our Canadian affairs again, we'll just, etc., etc.' We wondered what the security department of the Russian government would make of this. They might think those Canadians were a little more independent than they had supposed.

We had hardly unpacked at our Victorian mansion when the festivities began. First, at 5:30 PM, a courtesy call on Mr Molotov at the Foreign Office, and then a drink at the Embassy to meet everybody there. Next to the Bolshoi Theatre in state for the ballet, 'Don Quixote.' Molotov, Zorin, and a few others ushered us into what was once the Royal Box and to our amazement the spotlight was thrown on us and we got a standing ovation for a couple of minutes. I wrote in my diary, 'I felt like the Czar – most embarrassing. Ottawa's "Little Elgin" was never like this!'

The next day, 6 October, accompanied by Watkins (our Ambassador to the USSR), Holmes, Ignatieff, and Crépault (from the Department of External Affairs in Ottawa), I went off to the Foreign Office for the first of my talks with Molotov. After an exchange of pleasantries and a short discussion of arrangements for my visit – which were not yet definite since Bulganin and Khrushchev were in the Crimea – we got down to business. I asked Molotov what he thought of the international picture, with particular reference to the forthcoming Geneva Disarmament Conference and the work of the UN Assembly. He spoke for twenty or thirty minutes but told me little. I recorded afterwards:

'He plays his diplomatic cards very close to his chest. So he merely repeated the Soviet line about how international tension had now eased, things were better at the UN, the Disarmament Sub-Committee was making progress, and there must be "positive" results at Geneva. We mustn't get impatient, however, if all problems were not solved at once. Germany, he agreed, was the big difficulty and there could be no solution here until there was a system of European security with all states in. I countered by telling him that there could be no security in Europe as long as Germany was divided into hostile parts, with a part in each camp.

'I gave him the Canadian view on the work of the Disarmament Sub-Committee, and on the danger to the UN through forcing "domestic" questions on the agenda. Then I brought up Indochina. He was cautious and non-committal, thought there must be elections in Vietnam and that the [International Control] Commission [of which we were a member] could help there. He would not be drawn on Laos, but wanted to know how we felt about Korea and China. I in turn was "cautious and non-committal," but let him know that while we did not agree with all of US policy on China, especially regarding the off-shore islands, we were not going to get into any unnecessary difficulties with our American friends over this problem, and that there were many on the North American continent who still felt Communist China to be a dangerous aggressive force, and a threat to peace. However, I added we were having a new look at Peking and public opinion in Canada was moving toward a recognition of the facts of the situation.'

So it seemed at the time, but events showed the difficulty in recognizing the Communist government in China. It was not until 1970 that we finally achieved that goal. Afterwards I summed up the meeting: 'Molotov was complimentary about Canada's part in international affairs and did his very best to be friendly. But we didn't really get very far. There is little possibility of a down-to-earth, frank talk with him; and anyway he matters less and less in the hierarchy here. Bulganin and Khrushchev are the boys.'

At an official lunch at the Spiridonovka Palace that day I sat beside Malenkov (who became Premier after Stalin's death but had by now been demoted to Deputy Premier) and found him a witty, intelligent, and interesting personality. I thought he was worth a dozen Molotovs as a person, but that his survival value might not be as high. That day, however, he certainly showed no signs of uncertainty or timidity as to his position. At the lunch Molotov proposed several flattering toasts to Canada, and to me personally, and I had to think of some in response. 'Peace with security,' 'peace with justice' were my standby phrases.

That afternoon we held a reception at the Canadian Embassy – a big crowd and a journalistic free-for-all. It was the custom in Moscow to use social occasions for every kind of journalistic and diplomatic activity – no holds barred and nothing off the record. So when six members of the Politbureau all turned up, together with all the diplomats, high-ranking Soviet civil and military people, the excitement was great. Also, in accordance with custom, the top Communists were shepherded into a separate room where we toasted and talked, with journalists surging forward and scribbling, radio microphones being pushed forward, diplomats edging in to catch what was said. Much *was* said – but I tried to keep it on a bantering note, with quick and good humoured responses from the Soviet people, especially Kaganovitch and Malenkov. It was a frightfully difficult operation, however – quite nerve-wracking – in the press-and-pressure atmosphere that prevailed. Your jokes or those of the Russians' might seem very unfunny, or worse, when they appeared later in newspapers 5000 miles away. Innocuous toasts might take on terrific significance as reported by correspondents in Moscow who were hungry for news, and some of them not too scrupulous on how they got or made it.

After the great men had gone, in a body and with their guards, just as they arrived – a sort of flying wedge of buddies – the press kept pushing me about unmercifully to explain what I said, to add to it, or subtract from it, or interpret it, while all the time I wanted to talk to last night's prima ballerina who was there.

It was a strange party and left me done in – quite incapable of appreciating the truly marvellous Obratsov puppet show which we attended afterwards. The Russians loved it, but shared their attention between the puppets, our Mountie's scarlet magnificence, and Mrs Pearson's smart clothes. There seemed to be no smart women in Moscow, but many who did very heavy work and looked the part.

In the course of that first day we had also managed a tour of the Kremlin. The halls, churches, treasures (historic and revolutionary) were all very interesting – there were some amazing things to see – but far more interesting for me was the holiday atmosphere that prevailed inside those once grim and mysterious walls. It was just as easy for the public to enter the Kremlin as the Parliament Buildings in Ottawa, and thousands did each day. They wandered around as ordinary sightseers, which must have been a startling change from the days of Stalin.

The following morning we began our trade talks with Kabanov; Mitchell Sharp (then Associate Deputy Minister of Trade and Commerce), Watkins, and Ignatieff were with me. We got the discussions off to a good start but it was evident that they were going to make us pay a high price if we wanted to sign them up for a large wheat deal. 'Most favoured nation,' of course, did not mean much to them economically, while they asked us some embarrassing things about our 'strategic list.' I insisted on calling it our 'list of shortages,' but they were not fooled. These chaps did not allow their friendly toasting off duty to interfere with tough negotiation. Nor did we.

That afternoon Sharp continued the talks while I visited the Agricultural Exhibition, walking for miles around the buildings. The director, I remember, was a delightful person, a cerealist who loved roses and music. Later, I was driven to a state farm, for a quick packed-full-of-facts tour by a wonderful old horny-handed farmer type who was very reserved at first, but loosened up, and by the end was a great friend of everybody. The farm itself was run on the lines of a large agricultural factory, with 700 operatives.

Then in the evening we caught the 'Red Arrow' for Leningrad. The pullman, which we had to ourselves, was railway magnificence of a 1911 vintage. The Czar must have used it! Before disembarking from the ancient magnificence the next morning, we were offered for breakfast steaks, chicken, eggs, caviar, seven kinds of hors d'œuvres, and sundry other foods when all we wanted was toast, coffee, and marmalade.

Leningrad is a lovely city, beautifully planned with fine buildings. But in 1955 it was very down-at-heel, as well it might have been after its ordeals during the war. It was like a tired, ravaged, but very beautiful lady who had not been able to afford make-up for years! They were, however, very proud of their past, those Leningraders, and seemed a much livelier people than the Muscovites of whom they were jealous. We saw all the points of interest, historic and revolutionary, and our guide, or rather our very nice and intelligent interpreter, Tanya, of whom we had become very fond (even though she was undoubtedly a secret agent from the MVD), made Leningrad live for us.

After lunch, we spent two hours in the Hermitage. I will not even attempt to describe that fabulous place, with its literally priceless treasures. It is, I think, the most magnificent museum in the world. In one great gallery full of pictures of Czarist grandees, George Ignatieff, who had been born in St Petersburg, found a full-size portrait of his ancestor, General Kutuzov, in a hall dedicated to the 'first fatherland war,' Kutuzov having led the Russian forces against the Grande Armée of Napoleon.

Then we motored out to Peterhof (the summer palace of Peter the Great), past the wrecked area on the outskirts where the Germans were held for three years. The suffering and privations of the people at that time must have been terrible, but they took an immense pride in their resistance. I mentioned their war courage and sufferings of course on every occasion that I had to say 'a few words' (and there were several). Peterhof was also an amazing place, but even more amazing was that the communists had expended so much energy and resources on restoring it.

That night, the Leningrad Soviet gave me a dinner. Fifteen courses and more than fifteen toasts, two or three by me. It was a most agreeable evening, the dinner very well done, waiters in dinner suits (over there only waiters and musicians dressed), and all served in a very lovely room in the Town Hall, which was once the Marinsky Palace. It seemed that practically every big house in Leningrad was once a palace of a czar or grand duke, while every big house in Moscow apparently belonged to a sugar or textile millionaire, or a mistress of one. After dinner artists from the Leningrad opera sang for us, and then all our hosts escorted us to the station for our return to Moscow. They would not leave until the train pulled out, so we invited them into our Czarist car reception room where we tossed off more toasts. It was a very pleasant ending to an interesting day, but one which left us just about exhausted.

Exchanging notes, we found that our hosts had been not only friendly, but very frank, and had not hesitated to broach controversial subjects – above all, their fear based on their horror of war from experience, that the Americans had aggressive designs on Holy Russia. There is no doubt that this fear on the part of the men we talked to here – not high political communists, but administrators, artists, engineers, scientists, technicians – was perfectly genuine.

I pondered, however, whether the tough, top political personages were not using it, and indeed fomenting it for their own purposes; or had that gone with the Stalin era, which had now been replaced by something better? Incidentally, even then nobody ever seemed to mention Stalin. Lenin, Marx – yes; but Stalin – no. I wondered, 'Is he being allowed to slide back into history as merely a personage, and not a communist god?' The answer was yes, but perhaps only for a while.

Sunday, 9 October, was almost a day of rest – and high time. I was interested in looking out of the train window during the last hour of the trip. It was very early but people were already in the fields; the villages were very busy, and the stations were thronged with peasants and villagers, laden with parcels and bags, waiting to go into Moscow. The amount of building going on in the outskirts – and this was also true of Leningrad – was tremendous, with great blocks of apartments rising out of the flat fields. The bottom floors seemed to be occupied before the top ones were completed. A whole new city was growing up around Moscow University.

That morning I worked at the Embassy drafting a communiqué. This was a tricky business but Molotov wanted it. I talked to Mitchell Sharp about the trade talks which he had continued on the Saturday. The Russians were pressing us hard to sign some kind of agreement and had even submitted a draft. There were a few jokers in it, however, so we sent it to Ottawa for study. They had to be satisfied with a reference to the trade talks in the communiqué and an expression of hope that concrete results would soon be achieved. You did not, or you could not, sign an agreement of that kind, especially with the Russians, without a good deal of care and consideration.

At 6 PM on Sunday I left for the Moscow Baptist church. The service there was in some ways the most interesting experience I had in Moscow. The church was an old, dingy building which our MVD escort understandably had difficulty in finding. I am sure they had never been there before. I was ushered in through the back and led to a seat behind the minister. The church was absolutely packed, every inch taken by people – all standing, shoulder to shoulder – mostly the rough, weary, but somehow serene faces of old women, but many younger persons too, especially in the choir of sixty or seventy fine voices. As the minister introduced me, George Ignatieff asked me if I knew what he was saying. 'No,' I said. 'Well', explained George, 'He's introducing you and saying what a great honour it is to have the Canadian Foreign Minister and that you will take the sermon.' I retorted, 'You'd better tell him that I won't be taking the sermon.' 'No, no,' he said, 'You've got to say something. He's telling them what a great man you are and a peace-loving man. So you better get up and say something in English. It will be translated.'

So I got up and preached on the beatitude 'Blessed are the peacemakers.' It seemed to be a safe text for the occasion and one of the verses which I remembered. I said a few words about how we must all live together in peace and amity. When I had finished, the choir, to my amazement, started to sing in Russian. The words were strange to me but the tune was unmistakable and brought back old Methodist memories: 'Rescue the Perishing.' I was not sure what the significance of that was.

The next day was one of our busiest. I kept the following diary of its activities:

'I conferred with Molotov at the Kremlin at 10:00 – mostly about the communiqué. This was a difficult operation as he wanted to put a lot of their pet phrases in and we wanted them kept out. So we sent our draft, with his suggestions, to Zorin, Chuvakhin [the Soviet Ambassador to Canada], John Holmes and George Ignatieff to work on during the afternoon.

'The luncheon at the Embassy that day was a great success socially, gastronomically and conversationally. Molotov, Kaganovitch (certainly an engaging old pirate) and Malenkov were the ranking guests. We had room only for 22, and with 13 Russians, 6 of our party, and 2 of our journalists (chosen by lot) there was room only for Watkins from the Embassy. I was particularly anxious to get the journalists there and they were very pleased, especially as it was the first time, we were told, that Molotov and the others had ever lunched with press men in Moscow.

'The conversation, thanks to Malenkov and Kaganovitch, was very frank and argumentative, but friendly. I did my best to disabuse them of some of their ideas about Americans in general and Mr Dulles in particular; also about socialism vs capitalism, etc., etc. It was the frankest talk we have had, but I doubt if anybody convinced anybody of anything very much. I gained, however, a better idea of the mental processes of those gentlemen, and a considerable respect for their toughness and ability, though doubts remained about their policies and motives.

'After luncheon I was taken to the Ministry of Culture and, to my horror, greeted with brandy and a toast. I felt like saying that it was most "uncultured" to ask me to drink any more toasts at 3:30 PM when the luncheon, and its toasts, had finished only at 3:00.

'We talked for an hour, rather aimlessly but amiably, about friendly cultural relations – ballet dancers vs hockey players – and then (Kaganovitch had insisted on this at lunch) I was taken to Kaganovitch's pride and joy of creation – the Metro. I had hoped to be the first Westerner to leave Moscow without seeing the Metro but it was not to be! The director met us at one station and, riding in front, or inside a crowded coach, or between coaches, we visited 4 stations. They were magnificent – no doubt of that – and the President of a Los Angeles Chamber of Commerce could not have done a better job of expressing pride in them.

'After an exit from the 4th station we drove to the Mausoleum where I was given a private showing of Lenin ... and Stalin, who looked more as if he had once lived. Then I paid my respects to the ashes of my old UN antagonist, Vishinsky, in the Kremlin wall ...

'We then left for the Spiridonovka Palace where Molotov was to give us a reception. It was the counterpart of the one at our Embassy.

The Politbureau were there, the press and the diplomats. We eventually got sorted out, so that (in this egalitarian society) the élite got to their separate room for toasts, food and conversation. The élite were a mixed bag – the very top Soviet brass, *all* of the Canadians, including our Mountie Corporal, some Ambassadors, all, apparently, of the Western Press representatives, and a few artists and intellectuals, no doubt for John Watkins' benefit. Something new was added, however, by a few US congressmen, who seemed to be enjoying immensely this particular form of co-existence.

'We toasted and talked, while the press and diplomats scribbled and listened. The place of honour seems to have been behind the table (where the food and drink was) and Molotov summoned to that summit, Hayter [the British Ambassador], Menon [not Krishna, but the Indian Ambassador], and the Yugoslav. Also, with a gentle reminder from me, our prima ballerina friend, who seemed thrilled at being among the politicos. She told me that her only chance of realizing her dream of dancing in Europe and America was by a "political" decision and this party, she thought, might bring it about! However, I wasn't able to talk long with her because Pervukhin (a fast rising star in the Soviet firmament) took her over.

'Kaganovitch asked me what I liked best about the Soviet Union, whereupon Malenkov, with a twinkle, asked me what I liked least. I dodged both questions, whereupon Kaganovitch said that at least you have learned that we are not devils with horns sprouting from our heads.

'I left the reception about 8:00 and then had a press conference at the Embassy. The Canadians were particularly anxious to hear about the trade talks. Mitchell Sharp had made great progress while we were in Leningrad. The Russians are willing to give us a firm order for 300-500,000 tons of wheat a year for 3 to 5 years, and are not now asking anything impossible in return. They are willing to continue the talks in Ottawa.

'I was to have gone to the ballet afterwards to see the great Ulanova, but had to stay behind to work on the communiqué. Mrs P, however, made it, though she has had a terrible cold for 2 or 3 days and spent yesterday and most of today in bed.

'The communiqué has been difficult. The Russians want to put far more into it than we can agree to and make it sound just right for Soviet propaganda. We are on guard against this, however, and when we take a strong stand, they are not unreasonable.

'George Ignatieff and John Holmes were working with Zorin and

Chuvakhin all evening, and about midnight showed me the agreed draft. It seems all right except in one or two places where I cannot accept their text, and told George to tell them so in no uncertain terms.

'I slept not at all tonight – cold coming on, too much tension and excitement. In any event, we had to get up at 6:00 to go to the airport and fly to the Crimea where, at some mysterious spot, we are to see Bulganin and Khrushchev.'

On this last evening in Moscow, however, a truck load of presents was sent to our Embassy for members of our party. I received an enormous oil painting and a magnificent double-barrelled shotgun made by the famous Tula iron workers; Mrs Pearson a fur jacket and an oriental rug, together with sundry smaller mementos. All this was most embarrassing. However, we had an oil painting of our own and a large silver box for Molotov, so our retaliation, if not massive, was not too inadequate.

Of the next day, Tuesday, 11 October 1955, I wrote in my diary, 'what a day – what a day.' We arrived at the airport in cold gray rain (the first break in perfect weather) at 7.15 in the morning. Molotov and the greeters were all there and, believe it or not, the heads of all the diplomatic missions. They had been instructed by the Dean of the Diplomatic Corps to be present, which must have made him singularly unpopular. The only one missing was the US Chargé d'Affaires, but a serious diplomatic incident was avoided when he came rushing up just as I was getting into the plane. A final broadcast and much leave-taking and I was off.

Our first stop was Stalingrad, where I paid my tribute to the immortal bravery of Stalingrad in war, and its energy and determination in reconstruction in peace. At one point in our tour our hosts arranged for me to lay a wreath to the victims of Stalingrad. Our car was stopped at a square and I got out. As we approached the monument George Ignatieff grabbed me by the arm and said, 'This is the wrong place. This monument is to the victims of the White Terror of 1918–19!' Ignatieff then told our Russian guides that they had obviously made a mistake. They did not put up any argument even though it would hardly have been a mistake from the point of view of their propaganda had they photographed me laying the wreath there. Instead, however, we placed it on a hill where over 36,000 had perished during World War II.

We then continued our two-hour tour of the city, with the Mayor explaining the details of the battle and progress in the recovery. For communities like Leningrad and Stalingrad the war was not over. It was not hard to believe them when they kept emphasizing that because they knew so much of the horrors of war, they had a passionate desire for peace and a deep fear that war might begin again. Characteristically, the reconstruction from the most awful ruins of war that ever existed had begun with a public square, theatres, schools, and public buildings. Houses were left until the last. This can be done in a totalitarian society and from their point of view it was only common sense to proceed from the collective to the individual. No democratic government that operated in that way would last long.

Then we flew on into the Crimea, learning en route that we were to land at Sebastopol. This was a surprise as that important naval base was supposed to be strictly out of bounds to foreign officials and visitors. However, they made an exception for us, though it was probably as much to impress us with their military might as to bring us nearer to our destination. As usual, we were met by the Mayor at the airport, which was merely a field with a steel matting for a runway. He insisted that we do an hour's tour of the city. He was particularly anxious to show us the 'great, historic' panorama of the siege of the city during the Crimean war – no doubt to take our minds off all the jets we had seen at the airport and the warships in the harbour. Sebastopol had been almost as completely destroyed in the war as Stalingrad, but an even better job of rebuilding had been done. It was, I think, the most attractive and up-to-date Russian city that we saw.

The drive to the ministerial dacha near Yalta, which we now learned was our destination, took us over the fields of Balaclava, stopping at the site of the Charge of the Light Brigade. Then we got to the exciting mountainous coast, with its hairpin turns and sheer drops of a thousand feet or so. The coastline is covered with magnificent country houses and palaces of Czarist days, now sanitoria and rest homes, to which have been added new ones constructed since the revolution. The scenery was very beautiful – rugged, grand, and green, worthy of comparison with the Corniche or the Californian coast, while the country seemed richer, the houses more like ours, the fields better kept, and the people brighter and smarter than up north.

Our destination turned out to be an elaborate mansion right on the sea, with rocky patches and lush gardens all around. Proletarian luxury de luxe. I was met at the door by a pleasant lady doctor who had heard I had a bad cold (which was true) and a laryngitic throat (which was also true). She brought me pills and a gargle; my voice, which had almost disappeared, began to return. I was certainly to need it later.

At eight o'clock we drove down the road for half a mile until we came to Khrushchev's holiday retreat, the fabulous Yusupof Palace, where he and Bulganin (who had flown over from Sochi in Georgia) were to entertain the four of us, Ignatieff, Crépault, Watkins, and me. They met us at the door – the squat, tough-looking Ukrainian peasant, very baggy trousers, a waddling walk, a mobile face with signs of a sense of humour, and no social graces, obviously, of any kind. Bulganin, quite the opposite, well dressed, courtly manners, and aristocratic appearance. He looked quite at home in a palace like this. Khrushchev did not, but was obviously very much at home.

Khrushchev lived up to his reputation for brutal frankness by opening up at once on the iniquity of NATO. We talked very frankly around the table for a couple of hours. I reported our conversation to Ottawa in the following terms:

'The two hours' talk which I had with Khrushchev and Bulganin on the last night of my visit was undoubtedly the most interesting both on account of the two Soviet personalities involved and the frankness with which Khrushchev in particular put forward the Soviet attitude to such important matters as NATO and the security of Europe. I am having this summary report despatched by Ignatieff at the first opportunity on his way back to Ottawa.

'Khrushchev, who is as blunt and volatile as only a Ukrainian peasant turned one of the most powerful figures in the world can be, came straight to the point before we even sat down. With a CBC microphone pushed in front of him (this was permitted for the first few minutes of our visit along with photographers and a few journalists), he asked me why Canada does not leave NATO, which he described as an aggressive alliance and a direct threat to Russia and to peace. I replied that I had talked myself hoarse (I had indeed almost lost my voice at that time) trying to convince people in Moscow that NATO was purely defensive and had no aggressive intent whatever. I added for good measure that I had also been trying to convince them that the Americans were fine people, good neighbours with no thought of attacking anybody. Khrushchev also said that he hoped I was convinced by my visit that there was no economic or food crisis in the Soviet Union. It was typical of wishful thinking in the West who were looking in vain for Soviet weaknesses. I said that I doubted any such reports of crisis and that my own experience would suggest there was lots of food!

'After this characteristic outburst and after we had taken our places around a table I tried to direct the discussion into more orderly channels by referring to my talks in Moscow and the communiqué. Khrushchev said that he had been kept informed and regarded the communiqué as acceptable though disappointingly vague and non-committal. From their point of view perhaps they cannot expect more at this stage in Canada-Soviet relations, he added somewhat revealingly.

'This gave me an opening to say that Canada is increasingly conscious of the fact of being between two powerful neighbours; with the United States we are on very friendly terms of good neighbourhood and we hope to be on better terms with the Soviet Union also. Khrushchev replied that Russia never had conflict with Canada and that he could not foresee any conflict arising. He did not neglect to point out, however, we were on the air route to United States cities if war was ever forced on them. In that tragic contingency he reminded me they also had buttons which could be pushed with devastating effect.

'In reply to my remark that Canada cannot feel comfortable unless Soviet-United States relations are also satisfactory, Khrushchev agreed adding that he saw no special grounds for concern at present; things would work out all right he thought. People like McCarthy [US Senator Joseph McCarthy] who flourished on the line that the Soviet Union wanted war had been discredited. I emphasized that no right thinking people in the United States and especially the President even considered any aggressive attack on anybody; that much of the news from the United States reaching Europe and the USSR was misleading as to United States intentions and United States feelings. The sensational was shouted too much which distorted the picture so far as the United States was concerned. One of the advantages of visits was the opportunity to dispel misapprehensions and remove misunderstanding and distortions.

'Khrushchev then brought up the alleged Carpenter statement again saying that he (who was described as "the Chief of the Air Staff in Canada") had said that the USSR should be made to understand that they could be "utterly destroyed" and that the Soviet military set-up was "20 years behind the times." I reacted strongly to this by saying that Carpenter was not Chief of Air Staff but a subordinate officer and that if it was found that he had made such irresponsible statements he would no doubt be appropriately dealt with. I went on to say that what disturbed me more was that such an inaccurate and misleading report should have reached the Soviet leaders. In Canada it could be denied by responsible persons in our free press while in the USSR it was accepted without question or any opportunity of correction.

'Khrushchev said that the Soviet leaders were not concerned by the implied threat in the statement but by the suggestion that the Soviet Union's military establishment was out of date. This kind of talk might encourage aggressors.

'I then turned the conversation to the Geneva conference and the German problem. Khrushchev said that the Soviet Government had no illusions about the prospects of the forthcoming foreign ministers' meeting at Geneva. He agreed with me, however, when I said that even if much did not come out of this meeting it was only the beginning of what I hoped would be a continuous search for solutions to problems at such meetings. The main stumbling block Khrushchev said would be Germany and the approach to the solution of this problem agreed between the three Western powers. This was definitely not acceptable to the Soviet Union. They could not agree to having the NATO military organization of the West which Khrushchev said again was directed against the USSR further strengthened by the addition of 17 million Germans from the Democratic Republic: "better have 2/3 of Germany against us than the whole of it. We cannot be so stupid as to agree to strengthening the organization which is directed against us."

'This gave me the chance to say that I might be willing to agree that the Soviet Union was justified in its fear of Germany if NATO were not a purely defensive organization. I was about to explain why NATO should be so regarded when Khrushchev broke in with the remark, "you should let us into NATO – we have been knocking at the door two years." I replied that if the world situation were such as to permit entry of the USSR into NATO it would also presumably permit proper functioning of the United Nations in the security field; that NATO was resorted to by the Western powers because the United Nations was not given a chance to do work intended for it ... I also pointed out that if the Soviets were in NATO they would have to accept an integrated defence system and unified command. If they were prepared to accept that why not make the United Nations security system work?

'This seemed unfamiliar ground for Khrushchev who returned to the charge against NATO with the remark that the Soviets could afford to wait for the breakup of NATO owing to over-spending on armaments by inter-allied disagreements. I countered this with the argument that without NATO the Soviets might be worse off with the United States "going it alone" and Germany free-wheeling in the centre of Europe without the cautious and restraining influence of countries like the United Kingdom, Belgium, France and Canada.

'I left Khrushchev in no doubt that while we consider NATO a purely defensive arrangement it is an essential element in our defence and foreign policy and would remain so until international confidence reached a point where United Nations itself could effectively guarantee international security.

'I asked Khrushchev if he would clarify the Soviet attitude to the German problem. His reply could not have been more categorical: "so long as the Paris agreements exist and Germany remains in NATO we shall do everything possible to prevent the re-unification of Germany." I asked him whether he was aware that it was the intention that a united Germany as a sovereign state would not be forced into NATO but would be free to choose whether to be in NATO or remain neutral? Khrushchev answered that this was the first time he had heard of it. While I was replying that he ought to look into this possibility Khrushchev got some prompting from Bulganin and returned to the charge with the statement that the USSR had suggested a general security system which would include the United States and Canada as well as the USSR and European states.

'Referring to the United Kingdom proposals put forward by Sir Anthony Eden at the "summit" meeting for a security guarantee Khrushchev said that so long as the Paris agreements and NATO remained in effect a guarantee by the Western powers would be regarded as humiliating for the USSR and unacceptable. In reply to my question – why they would not regard membership in NATO involving mutual guarantees as equally humiliating Khrushchev said that Soviet membership in NATO would put them on a footing of complete equality with the other powers in the matter of security and they would not then have to depend upon the favours or goodwill of the four powers envisaged in the United Kingdom proposals. Getting quite excited at this point Khrushchev said that the USSR would prefer to "exist by ourselves and impose co-existence on others." "After all," he said, "we have to co-exist, don't we, or else fly away to Mars?"

'Then more soberly Khrushchev (after prompting from Bulganin) said that the Soviet Union does not reject the Eden proposals completely. If they could be altered, for instance, to include not four other powers but say 8 or 10 they might be made acceptable. Khrushchev's idea for the composition of such a group which might undertake mutual guarantees included: the United States, France, the United Kingdom, both Germanys, the USSR, Poland, Czechoslovakia, Belgium, Denmark (and then added "even Canada").

'If the obstacle to agreement to such an approach were the two Germanys perhaps it would be better to keep them both out of the mutual guarantee arrangement, he said, but at the same time restrict their armaments. They would be indirectly associated with the guarantee arrangement through their association respectively with NATO and the Warsaw pact. To my question whether it would not be better to let a united free Germany decide by free choice how best to provide for its security, Khrushchev abruptly said, "We want either both Germanys in the European security system or else neither." As to re-unification, he said the USSR could wait – "Why the hurry?" he said.

'Khrushchev said that the approach to European security which he had outlined could open the way to a solution. So long as the Western powers insisted on trying to negotiate from positions of strength there could be no chance of agreement. Russians, he said, do not like to negotiate with a "knife in their backs." To my rejoinder that the Western powers sought only defensive strength adequate to deter aggression, Khrushchev bluntly said that the policy of the Western powers was plainly designed "to impose solutions" on the USSR which the USSR would not tolerate. I rejected this view.

'Getting again quite excited at this point, Khrushchev said that Russians knew better than any other people what war means (he mentioned that he had lost a son) – only the Germans had comparable experience. If NATO starts a war, he said, the alliance would fall apart since most of its members would not be willing to fight. He returned to this theme of NATO falling apart a number of times either in the context of defence costs or because of unwillingness to fight. At one point he said that the war if it occurred would inevitably involve Germany and the allies might as well face up to the fact that the Germans will not fight having had enough of war.

'I replied that no one wanted war in the nuclear age and the West would never be the first to start a war, to which Khrushchev replied, "We shall never fire the first shot but we shall be in at the finish." To my answer that under present circumstances any world war would be infinitely worse than the last Khrushchev agreed but added "this time Canada would not be geographically secure"...

'Khrushchev dismissed the current disarmament discussion in the United Nations as just a "talking shop" – if they were serious why had the other powers not replied to the Soviet proposals of May 10? he said. I reminded him that we had reacted but the difference had been the introduction of political conditions by the Soviets relating to security.

'In conclusion Khrushchev, now in a more mellow mood, said that what the world needs is "time and patience." "The Soviet Union," he said, "could afford to be patient" – "our system is solid, our economy developing." Western leaders, however, have to accord, he said, "civil rights to communism" and not react to it "like a bull to a red rag." "If you don't like it," he said, "you don't have to join it." In reply I said that it was not the Soviet system that we reacted to but to the parties who boast that their loyalty is for their "socialist fatherland" rather than for their own, but that was our own problem. Khrushchev agreed. When I pressed the matter of outside assistance to local communist parties, Khrushchev laughed it off with "what – a dollar a day? We haven't the dollars for that." What they also wanted, Khrushchev said, was foreign trade with the West and business contacts; there could be peaceful competition between different systems. The talk ended with my thanking the Soviet leaders for this opportunity of talking frankly with them and telling them that it was our desire to have friendly working relations with them to which my visit, I hoped, had contributed. Both Bulganin and Khrushchev hoped that this would not be the last such visit from Canada.'

Some time after 10 PM Khrushchev suggested that we eat, and we followed him down the hall to a great dining room. He carefully pointed out to us *three* bathrooms off the dining room, the significance of which, at least in his mind, became apparent later during the 'vodka' part of the evening. After sitting down to a table groaning with every kind of Russian food and drink, Khrushchev asked if we minded if the family joined us for dinner, as 'they are hungry too.' We thought this was fine, so he waddled away, returning with Mrs Khrushchev, who turned out to be a plainly dressed, sturdy peasant type, with a strong, weather-beaten, but not unpleasant face. Their daughter had tired of waiting for dinner and had gone to the cinema.

Khrushchev was intensely interested in Ignatieff, 'the Count,' as he kept calling him, in tones which were half way between insult and respect. Mrs Khrushchev, who sat next to him, was all respect. It soon became apparent that Khrushchev was determined, ably seconded by Bulganin, to put us all 'under the table.' He and Bulganin proposed toast after toast in 'pepper vodka' and they kept eagle eyes on us, especially on George and Ray Crépault (the 'wily French boy,' as they called him) to make sure that it was 'bottoms up' each time. Someone said we drank eighteen toasts, but I wouldn't know. I do remember we even drank to the Canadian wheat surplus. 'Drink up like a Russian,' Khrushchev kept warning George. The conversation and the toasts were pretty general and Khrushchev did most of the talking, though Bulganin did not hesitate to pull him up once or twice. Once Bulganin proposed a toast to our Prime Minister, with whom he knew, so he said, I was on very close and friendly terms. This gave him a cue to emphasize that he and 'Nikita' were on the same terms, had worked together as the closest of friends for years, and would continue to do so and with their colleagues. This was not the first time that it had been strongly suggested to me that the government was a 'collective' or a 'group' one, the inference being that there was no Stalin and hence no Stalinism. That may have been true, but I wondered how long it would remain so. In fact, collective leadership lasted two more years. In 1957 Khrushchev banished Molotov to Outer Mongolia as Ambassador, put Malenkov in charge of a power station, and let Kaganovitch look after industry in the Urals. A year later Bulganin was ousted and Khrushchev became Premier as well as Leader of the Communist party.

We also toasted President Eisenhower's recovery from his illness and both Bulganin and Khrushchev said, and it sounded genuine, how much they had been impressed by him at Geneva, and that he was a good and 'peace-loving' man. Khrushchev even went further and said that he had established good personal relations with Mr Dulles whom, to his surprise, he had found to be a man he could talk to.

As for the Americans in general, Khrushchev said they talked too much, boasted too much, and had no realization of what war and sacrifice and fighting meant. That, he thought, was the great danger. I told him that this did not apply to Canadians so far as sacrifice in war was concerned; that twice we had gone to war, though we had not been directly attacked and were remote from the actual conflict. We knew all about the human sacrifice of war and that was the sacrifice that counted the most. Khrushchev, who seemed to be moved by this, averred that the Canadians were a fine fighting race, hoped and felt that there would never be conflict between Canada and the Soviet Union, but reminded me again that next time, if there ever was one, we would certainly not be remote geographically from the conflict.

As the evening went on, the atmosphere became mellower and mellower. John Watkins, however, looked less and less happy, and the rest of us also found the going pretty tough, except the two Russians, Watkins' friend 'Aloysha' and Chuvakhin, who were not pressed to drink anything, and Troyanovsky, who couldn't possibly drink *and* translate. The latter he did magnificently and, according to our own two Russian speakers, fairly and accurately.

If Khrushchev had had his way, we would have been there, in one way or another, all night, but Bulganin finally assisted us in breaking up the party. About 12:30 the four Canadians marched straightly, heads up, with fixed determination and without any assistance, to our car, after a very spirited leave taking. We left our two Russian hosts in worse condition than we were, and we felt that we had not done too badly, either socially or diplomatically. I would like to think that we had earned medals that night for conviviality beyond the line of duty! But 'once in a lifetime' only!

The sky was blue, the sun clear and bright, the prospect fair on the morning of 12 October. The four Canadians were not quite so fair or bright. After sunning ourselves for an hour the next morning we left by motor for a 148 kilometre drive to the airport. George was our hero because right after returning from the party the night before he had phoned Moscow, got Bob Dunn, our Press Officer, on the wire, and passed on through him to the Canadian journalists some information I thought they should have. That was a *tour de force* at that hour and after that dinner.

Half the drive was along the Black Sea coast, with the roads, the curves, and the cliffs even more spectacular and, in view of the night before, far more disturbing than they had been the previous afternoon. It really was a very trying experience, as we screeched around the bends. At one point I stopped the car on the pretence of looking at the view. Then, about five miles down the road, we stopped to see a monument to Marshal Kutusov. 'At this very point,' said Chuvakhin with pride, 'the Marshal lost an eye defeating the Turks.' My sour reply was that you had better raise a monument to me some miles back at that place where I lost my stomach! On we went through Yalta and Simferopol to Sochi, the 'off-limits' military air station where Churchill and Roosevelt landed for the Yalta Conference and where no Westerner had landed since. If the Prime Minister and President had to ride over those mountain curves to Yalta, as we did that morning, no wonder they were easy vicims for Stalin at the conference.

At Sochi our Canadian plane with the Moscow section of the party was waiting. We said many good-byes to the remaining Russians, and to poor John Watkins who had really suffered agonies on the motor trip, and then took flight into the fairer, clearer atmosphere of less official hospitality and more freedom.

FROM PALESTINE TO SUEZ

Formally and without warning on 2 April 1947, Britain referred to the United Nations the question of its mandate in Palestine, saying, in effect, 'Here it is. We can't deal with it. We have tried and we have failed. You take it on.' This threw everybody into a tailspin. Before World War II, there had been no Canadian policy on Palestine or on the Arab-Jewish difficulties under the British mandate. Mr King had merely stated once or twice that he supported, in theory, the British pledge in the 1917 Balfour Declaration to establish a national home for the Jews. But in his view there was no need to do more about a purely British problem, even when this problem was made tragically more serious by Nazi persecution. Then came the war and the massacre of the Jews, and the postwar question of what was to be done with those who survived and were now displaced persons. In Canada we remained cautious.

Now the British government decided that it could no longer discharge its responsibilities in Palestine and at a special session of the General Assembly called on 28 April 1947 to deal with the Palestine question, Canada became involved. Circumstances threw me into the midst of that involvement as a Canadian delegate to the Assembly and as chairman of the Assembly's Political Committee. There could have been no more complicated or difficult political and diplomatic problem, or a problem where passions between the contending parties could have been deeper or more bitter. To hold the balance between them risked incurring the enmity of both.

It was my first experience with this kind of crisis and I was deeply concerned that if we failed there would be bloodshed and chaos. I must admit that I became emotionally involved in a very special way because we were dealing with the Holy Land – the land of my Sunday School lessons. At one stage of my life I knew far more about the geography of Palestine than I did about the geography of Canada. I could tell you all the towns from Dan to Beer-sheba but certainly not all from Victoria to Halifax. I think that in the back of my mind I felt I was concerning myself with something close to my early life and religious background. Although this was only an ancillary factor, it made the dispute much more real in my mind than, for instance, Korea. I do not recall ever getting very worked up about Korea when I went to Sunday School.

With the British government determined to avoid special responsibility or initiative, the question of how the United Nations Assembly should handle the matter was the first problem to be faced. To this end, a United Nations Special Committee on Palestine (UNSCOP) was immediately set up to examine and report on the whole problem. This committee consisted of the representatives of eleven states, including a highly respected Canadian, Mr Justice Ivan Rand, who made invaluable contributions to its work. Great Britain, the Arab States and the Jewish Agency (which had been established under the British mandate to co-operate in looking after Jewish interests in Palestine) were excluded.

Later in the summer, UNSCOP submitted majority and minority reports. The former, which Justice Rand signed and strongly supported, recommended the partition of Palestine into an Arab and a Jewish state, with economic union and freedom of transit between them; and a demilitarized Jerusalem, under a United Nations governor responsible to the Trusteeship Council. The minority report recommended a federal state for Palestine.

When the regular General Assembly met in September, it appointed an ad hoc committee of all its members, under the chairmanship of the redoubtable Australian External Affairs Minister, Dr Evatt, to consider the two UNSCOP reports, the original British submission, and a proposal from Iraq and Saudi Arabia for an independent, unitary Palestine state. In turn, this full committee set up two sub-committees: the first, of which I became chairman, to draw up a detailed plan based on the principle of partition; the second, to draw up a detailed plan for the recognition of Palestine as a single unitary state.

The recommendations of the second sub-committee were rejected by the full committee. Those of the first sub-committee, however, were approved by the majority of the committee, including Canada, on 25 November. They provided for the withdrawal of British troops and the end of the mandate not later than 1 August 1948. Palestine would then be partitioned into Jewish and Arab states, and Jerusalem put under UN control, along the lines recommended by UNSCOP. The vote in the full Assembly on 29 November 1947 was 33 in favour, 13 against, and 10 abstentions. Canada voted 'for,' along with Australia, New Zealand, South Africa, Belgium, Brazil, France, the Netherlands, Norway, Sweden, the USSR, the USA, and others. We were in strong company. Britain abstained, while the Arab and Moslem states voted 'against.'

The Canadian government did not support partition without a great deal of heart-searching and careful consideration; and only after we were convinced that there was no possibility of an agreement between Britain, the USA, and the USSR which might make possible any other solution. The British government had made it depressingly clear that they would not support or help to enforce any settlement of the Palestine question which was not agreed to by Arabs and Jews. By this time we knew there was no hope of any such agreement. No practicable alternative to partition was put forward which had any chance of adoption. This alone offered a settlement in which the USA and the USSR could co-operate, thereby preventing, at least for the time being, direct intervention in the area by Moscow or Washington on opposite sides.

Partition was certainly no ideal solution but it seemed, certainly to me, the best that could possibly be achieved, the only solution that might bring peace and order to Palestine, with some recognition of the just claims of both sides. Provision was made for a Jewish state in Palestine, a 'national home,' something which I felt was a *sine qua non* of any settlement. Its boundaries, however, were restricted to include only those areas where Jews were in a majority. On their part, the Palestinian Arabs were also to have their own state, where they would be in the majority. Jerusalem was to be brought under international control. To bring a measure of viability to the area there was to be economic union and a free flow of population between the parts.

It is true that the Arabs threatened armed resistance to partition, a threat soon carried out. But rejection of partition at the UN would have resulted in even more violence and bloodshed. It would also have placed an even greater strain on Anglo-American relations and an increased danger of exploitation of the situation by the USSR.

As for the political settlement, that is yet to come. With all the advantage of hindsight and the knowledge that the Holy Land is still torn with strife and hatred between Arab and Jew, I still think that this was the best of all the solutions offered, even though events have long since overtaken it. If it failed to bring peace and reconciliation between the Jewish and Arab states in Palestine, this must be attributed to shifting policies of the Big Powers as much as to the intractable nature of the problem, and to their inability to work together, inside and outside the Security Council, in search of a good solution.

To pass a resolution for a partition plan was one thing. To put it into effect was something else, even though a Palestine Commission had been set up for that specific purpose. The Arabs violently rejected the UN plan, and fighting broke out in December. The British refused to take any further responsibility for law and order not directly related to their withdrawal. A settlement was now a matter, they claimed, for the United Nations Security Council. Faced with this situation, the United States government began to reverse its support for partition. The resolution, it now claimed, was only a recommendation which the UN was not under any obligation to enforce unless and until a second decision was taken to put Palestine under a UN mandate. We became anxious about the collapse of the partition plan in the welter of Jewish-Arab fighting, and in the widening breach between London and Washington.

As for our Prime Minister, Mr King, his position was firm. He was opposed to any UN attempt to impose partition on Palestine or to try to keep order there. His diary makes this clear: 'I do not think for one moment that our House of Commons would vote to send troops from this country into Palestine,' and 'If we were not prepared to send troops, we should not support any measure which would logically place us in the position where we would have no escape from so doing.' To Mr King, 'Ready, Aye, Ready' was as objectionable now in sharing in a United Nations peace-keeping operation as it had been in 1922 on a request from London for military backing against the Turks. Had he lived until 1956, he might have believed that the Chanak incident had been revived to plague him.

The Security Council failed to produce any solution, and a new Special Session of the Assembly was called. It opened on 20 April and began earnest if somewhat confused efforts to end the fighting and to set up some kind of provisional régime, pending a permanent agreed settlement which we still hoped for in spite of the collapse of partition. However, on 14 May the Jewish Provisional Government formally proclaimed the State of Israel within the very limited frontiers, it should be noted, approved by the UN Resolution of 29 November 1947.

Sixteen minutes after the declaration, the US, followed shortly afterwards by the USSR, recognized the new country and the next day introduced a resolution in the Security Council to initiate enforcement action under the UN Charter to stop the war now begun between Israel and its Arab neighbours.

Canadian recognition was slower in coming. When Israel applied at once for UN membership, Canada abstained. On 17 May Britain informed us that, unlike the United States, they saw no reason for recognizing, even *de facto*, the Republic of Israel. Mr King agreed and on 18 May the Cabinet decided 'that it would not be desirable for Canada to reach any hasty decision in the matter of recognition.' My reaction was contained in a telegram I sent to Norman Robertson, our High Commissioner in London, on 18 May:

So far as I am concerned, my own impatience with the attitude and policy of both the United Kingdom and the United States toward Palestine has not been diminished by the developments of the last week. The legal argument of the United Kingdom that there is no difference between Arabs invading Palestine and Jews who may be attempting to set up a state within a United Nations resolution, does not impress me very favourably, though no doubt it is explained by strategy and oil. On the other hand, the United States' revolving-door policy, each push determined to a large extent by domestic political considerations and culminating in the sorry recognition episode of last Saturday, inspires no confidence and warrants little support.

During May, the UN, through Count Bernadotte of Sweden, the mediator it had appointed, worked to bring about a cease-fire and a truce as a prelude to a settlement. The Security Council, pressed hard by the USSR, also considered action to impose a truce if mediation failed. This happily was not necessary since Arabs and Jews accepted a truce which went into effect on 11 June.

The mediator then met with the two sides on the Island of Rhodes and made proposals for a settlement based on a Federation of Jewish and Arab states. This was rejected by both and the fighting began again. Then, on 15 July, the Security Council, on the recommendation of Count Bernadotte, ordered an immediate cease-fire under the threat of sanctions. This was accepted by both sides and another truce began. Count Bernadotte was continuing his mediatory efforts with courage and perseverance when he was murdered on 17 September. His assistant, Ralph Bunche, succeeded him and carried on the work magnificently. This did not surprise me because I knew Bunche to be a man of exceptional character and wisdom, strength and patience. He faced a desperate situation. Fighting was again in progress, and not until 13 January 1949 were negotiations resumed at Rhodes by Bunche. As a result of his superlative diplomacy, a cease-fire was formally agreed. But no armistice agreement could be reached. Thus, by the end of January 1949, there was an uneasy truce through deadlock and exhaustion.

During these months, there was little that Canada could do at the United Nations. We had been prominent in the partition debates, often at the very centre of things. When partition failed, however, there was no particular role that Canada need or should play, except privately to help remove difficulties and differences between Washington and London, and these occurred frequently.

There was, however, now a State of Israel whose formal recognition continued to be a problem for Canada. We moved carefully. By November 1948, however, the government agreed that the situation had developed to the point where some measure of *de facto* recognition should be considered. In my speech to the First Committee of the Assembly on 22 November, I spoke in favour of this limited recognition which was given in Ottawa on 24 December with no demur from London. This was followed by *de jure* recognition when we voted for the admission of Israel to the United Nations on 11 May 1949.

I have never wavered in my view that a solution to the problem was impossible without the recognition of a Jewish state in some form in Palestine. To me this was always the core of the matter. This conviction did not add to my popularity with Arab delegates, some of whom did not hesitate to tell me at the time what they thought of my views and of the policy of my government.

By the summer of 1949, the armistice ending the first Arab-Israeli war was in effect, with a United Nations Truce Supervision Organization in place. In 1954 a Canadian, Major-General E.L.M. 'Tommy' Burns, became its Chief of Staff. A tripartite agreement in 1950 between Britain, the United States, and France guaranteed the armistice boundaries and pledged co-operation to maintain peace in the area. But peace demands more than a cease-fire and armistice; and there was no peace, since there was no progress toward a political settlement. Everyone pledged everything possible to reach a settlement; but the gap of suspicion and fear between the two sides widened and conflicting objectives seemed to become less and less reconcilable. It was now the firm and unqualified policy of the Arab states to refuse recognition to any state of Israel, with the more violent Arab spokesmen vowing that they would not rest until the Jews were driven into the sea.

I heard some pretty wild speeches at the United Nations during the Cold War by Mr Vishinsky and others, but nothing to equal the venom and the fury of the Arabs. I do not mean that sort of synthetic fury often found in Vishinsky's speeches – there was an air of unreality about many of the debates when he used to sound off. There was nothing unreal about the Arabs. This was genuine; this was sincere; this was from the very depths of their being. And one of the things that made this rather different from other disputes at the UN was that Jewish feeling was equally deep and sincere. This was no diplomatic conflict; it was a life and death confrontation between two peoples. It still is.

As the situation deteriorated, to Israel's disadvantage so she thought, the new state became more and more determined to establish, maintain, and defend her boundaries and to ensure her survival – dig in, organize, develop, arm. If there were armed incursions by Palestine guerrillas (the fedayeen) – and these increased markedly after David Ben-Gurion returned to power in 1955 – the Israelis at once retaliated on the principle of 'ten teeth for a tooth,' especially as neither the United Nations nor the Great Powers were able to do anything effective to establish security. By 1956 violence had become endemic on the armistice borders, with military incursions by the Arabs and immediate and violent reaction by the Jews. It is of some interest, in the light of subsequent events, that when the British Foreign Secretary, Selwyn Lloyd, was in Ottawa in the spring of 1956, he suggested that it might be necessary to put some kind of UN force into the area to keep the lid from blowing off. The idea was not novel and had received a considerable circulation over the years as a talking point. Only in acceptance would it become unique.

A vital development in the events which followed was the expulsion of King Farouk from Egypt in 1952. A corrupt and weak regime, headed by a selfish and slothful monarch, was thrown out by the army and shortly afterwards replaced by a government under the leadership of the charismatic, energetic, and patriotic Colonel Nasser, first as Prime Minister and, after 1956, as President. He and his colleagues were determined to pursue in every possible way the conflict with Israel. They were passionately dedicated to wiping out the humiliation of Egypt's reverses from the Jews in the war of 1947–8. Not unrelated to this was Nasser's equal determination to make Egypt strong and independent, free of foreign (in effect British) control which he believed had thwarted the growth of a strong national state.

To this end, the British military base in the Canal Zone had to be eliminated. A treaty signed in 1936 to end the military occupation of Egypt had given the British the right to maintain a base in order to defend the Suez Canal, but without infringing Egyptian sovereignty. This treaty was to expire in 1956. The United States government, which tended to view this complex question as a contest between imperialism and nationalism, urged an agreement on London; and this was achieved, after difficult negotiations, in 1954. The last British troops left the Canal Zone in June 1956. As is often the case, the agreement, while removing one source of possible conflict, at the same time created new misunderstandings over the circumstances surrounding its negotiation.

The British, and more particularly Sir Anthony Eden, felt that a main argument in favour of British withdrawal was the prospect of developing good and friendly relations with the Nasser government. Nasser, on his side, thought that acceptance of certain British conditions in negotiating the agreement would lead to greater economic and arms assistance from Washington. Finally, the Americans hoped that the agreement would open the Suez Canal to Israeli shipping – which, of course, it did not. Thus new seeds of suspicion and conflict were sown.

If, after the agreement, the British and Americans hoped to establish friendly co-operation with Nasser for collective defence and for countering Soviet pressures and designs on the Arab world, they were soon disenchanted. Israel, a democratic state – an outpost, if you will, of the West in the Middle East – was increasingly dependent on Western help. The Arab states on their part turned more and more to Moscow for military and diplomatic support. The developing line-up was ominous for peace.

The USSR, originally one of the strongest supporters of the formation of Israel, became increasingly anxious for her own purposes to side with the Arabs. Britain and France were particularly disturbed by the prospect of Soviet penetration into the Middle East since they depended largely on that part of the world for their supplies of oil (as did the great US oil companies for their profits); and especially since much of Western Europe's oil was shipped through the Suez Canal. While Britain, the United States, and France tried to keep a balance in arms shipments to both sides (in default of any general and agreed embargo on or control of arms to the area), in 1955 Czechoslovakia, with, of course, Moscow's knowledge and approval, agreed to supply arms to Egypt.

Even Canada became involved in a small way in the arms traffic to the Middle East. We had sold some anti-aircraft and anti-tank guns to

Israel, as 'defensive' equipment, and were not criticized, as it was agreed by the great majority in the House of Commons that an embargo on all arms shipments to either side would be unfair to Israel. But when, in 1955, we sold fifteen Harvard trainer planes to Egypt, the Conservative Opposition in the House of Commons vigorously attacked the government for helping an anti-British dictator. One or two went so far in absurdity as to worry about the fighting value of these old and slow planes if someone were to arm them with machine guns. My reply to this argument in the House, that you could put a machine gun on a bicycle but that did not make it a tank, was not so convincing to the Opposition as I had hoped. They had found a good stick with which to beat the government, while getting Jewish and anti-Communist support.

In November 1955 I had the opportunity to spend a few days in Cairo on my way home from a Colombo conference. The Egyptian Foreign Minister, Fawzi Bey, was a personal friend from early UN meetings, in spite of our differences over Middle East policies. At the previous Assembly, he had invited me to come to Cairo and meet Colonel Nasser. I welcomed this opportunity, and spent a most interesting hour with him on 10 November. I went away much impressed by his sincerity, even though he spoke very differently in public to Egyptian crowds. I reported accordingly that we should not write Nasser off as a rabble-rouser and mischief-maker, and that perhaps everything would turn out for the best – though, of course, it did not. I reported our frank discussions to Mr St Laurent:

'I spent an hour with Colonel Nasser last night (7.00–8.00), having previously discussed international matters, especially North Africa and Israel, with the Foreign Minister for twenty minutes. Nothing very significant developed in the talk with Mahmoud Fawzi, who was as friendly and courteous as ever. He said how very glad he was that I was in Cairo, gave me a personality sketch of his Prime Minister (a plain, blunt, but very sincere and honest soldier-patriot), and underlined the seriousness of the deterioration of relations between Israel and the Arab States, in the face, as he put it, of the aggressive military attitude and strength of the former. He thought, however, that the very seriousness of the situation might assist in finding a solution, if the United States and the United Kingdom showed understanding and wisdom, and if Israel did not force all-out war.

'I found Colonel Nasser quite as impressive and attractive a personality as I had been told he was. He is certainly plain and blunt in words, but friendly and modest in manner. He gives an impression of sincerity and strength, without any trace of arrogance or self-assertion. He said, of course, that he was a man of peace, "as every decent soldier is," and that his great ambition was to work for Egypt's social progress and economic development. But national security came first and, there-fore, because of Israel's aggressive attitude, he had had to divert re-sources, meant for peaceful development, to defence. If he had not done so, public opinion would have forced him to. I merely said that it was a tragedy for Egypt, as it would have been for any country, that this was felt to be necessary.

'The Prime Minister then went into the history, in detail, of the recent controversial arms transactions. He said that it was necessitated by the aggressive attitude and the boasted military superiority of Is-rael, with all the resources of Zionism, especially United States Zion-ism, behind it.

'He had warned Washington and London that he could not remain passive in these circumstances, that he would prefer to get arms from them, but that if this were not possible, he would secure them from behind the "Iron Curtain." He claimed that the United Kingdom and, particularly, the United States (who always put the interests of Israel ahead of the Arab States, because of Jewish power and wealth and influence there), thought that he was "bluffing." Their surprise and violent reaction when the transaction was announced, therefore, was more because their "bluff" was called, than because they had not had any knowledge of such a possibility.

'I ventured to give Colonel Nasser my own view that the United States and United Kingdom were far less prejudiced in favour of Israel than he thought, and that I was sure that they tried to follow an im-partial policy in these matters. We knew from our own experience in Canada that Israeli requests for arms which would add to their present level of offensive strength were turned down in the three capitals, in spite of great pressure exercised on their behalf. That pressure would now be much greater and more difficult to resist. But where would an arms race get us? Egypt felt herself threatened and weak – therefore she strengthened her armaments for security. No one could object to that in principle, but the result was that Israel would then feel insecure (especially because of the refusal of the Arab States to recognize her existence), and in her turn would get more arms. Then Egypt had to catch up again. Where would it all end?

'Colonel Nasser agreed that it was a very unfortunate and even dan-gerous development, but what could Egypt do?

'This gave me an opportunity to ask whether the Arab States would recognize the existence of a State of Israel on any terms. He said that they would. I said that then it becomes a problem of political negotiation to agree on terms. Such agreement would give them far more security than communist arms.

'I asked him about the Dulles proposals of August [for a general settlement in the Middle East under which, if the armistice lines were accepted as frontiers, the United States promised to guarantee them by treaty] which, I said, my government thought wise and sensible and would support as the basis for a solution. He said that they were too general, but he agreed that the points mentioned by Dulles were those that had to be settled: first of all, boundaries, where there would have to be important changes, and secondly, refugees. Nasser insisted that the Arab refugees would not agree to be settled in any place except Palestine. They had tried unsuccessfully to persuade some to settle in Egypt. He also stated that Arabs were still fleeing from Israel because of the unjust and discriminatory treatment they received there. When I expressed some scepticism about this, he insisted that Arabs in Israel were "second-class" citizens only.

'I asked the Prime Minister about the possibilities of practical co-operation between Israel and the Arab States, particularly in such a project as the Johnston Irrigation Scheme [a plan to use the water of the Jordan River for the benefit of Israel, Jordan and Egypt]. Colonel Nasser said that this was a good project and would benefit the Arab States, but that no Arab would believe, in the present circumstances of fear and hatred, that it was not designed to favour Israel. He felt that the Johnston proposals could not be implemented until the political situation was better.

'Colonel Nasser more than once mentioned Israel's aggressive military actions, breaches of the truce, etc., and claimed that Egyptian forces had shown great patience and discipline. He said that he was having increased difficulty in holding back the army in the face of these provocations.

'I told Colonel Nasser that while there were extremists in Israel, as in all countries, there were also moderate men there doing their best to avoid extreme courses and working for a fair and agreed settlement. I thought that Mr Sharett [the previous Prime Minister] was one of these, and Colonel Nasser agreed. He blamed Mr Ben-Gurion, however, for much of Israel's new aggressiveness and for trying to force a solution on the basis of recognition of the present boundaries.

'Colonel Nasser was interested in my trip to Russia [which I described in Chapter 9] and this gave me a chance not only to mention Russia's power and expansive strength, but the danger of encouraging her in the old Russian designs against the Mediterranean and the Middle East. These designs, which were historic, could mean no good for Egypt, especially when Russian imperialism could use international communism to stir up trouble and further its ends. I said that I thought that these designs were very much in Moscow's minds when they offered military and diplomatic assistance to Egypt and the other Arab States; that "he who supped with the devil," etc.

'Colonel Nasser said that these considerations were very much in his mind, but he thought that they could avoid the dangers I had mentioned. In any event, what was the alternative? I repeated, "an agreed political solution," and I assured him that every nation which desired peace would be glad to assist in bringing it about.

'I confess that my talk did not give me any reason for undue optimism that a solution would be found in the immediate future.'

Colonel Nasser's policies had become increasingly irritating to the Western powers. He was hostile to the Baghdad Pact, which was pushed by Dulles in his passion for surrounding the communist bloc with a ring of mini-NATOs. Nasser considered this pact a threat to his ambitions to unify and lead all the Arab states, especially because of the inclusion of Iraq in the new arrangement. He was also determined to escape involvement in the Cold War and consequently had no desire to adhere to a Western-oriented treaty and become a pawn, as he felt the case would be, on the Western side. He was getting help from the Soviet bloc, and, if he played his cards skilfully enough, he hoped to get at least equal assistance from the Western side, particularly from that champion of nationalism against imperialism, John Foster Dulles. It did not work out that way.

An interesting aspect of Cold War politics may be found in the following memorandum on the sales of Canadian arms to Israel that I wrote for Mr St Laurent on 10 May 1956:

'Mr Dulles discussed with me in Paris the question of arms shipments to the Middle East. He knew that we were faced with a request for 24 F-86 jet interceptors from Israel and he wished, very frankly and confidentially, to explain to me the policy of his government on these requests, as it might help us in the decision we would have to make.

'The United States had decided to release shortly some miscellaneous military supplies for Israel, but not, at least at this time, aircraft. They realized that while Israel could probably defend herself at the present time against attack from her Arab neighbours, the balance of military strength was moving against her because of arms, especially jet aircraft, sent from the Soviet bloc to Egypt. This growing imbalance, especially in the air, was a danger to peace, first, because it might strengthen the position of the extremists in Israel who felt that the only hope for survival was a preventive war waged while Israel was strong enough to defeat her neighbours; and, secondly, it would later encourage extremists on the Arab side determined to destroy Israel. Mr Dulles thought that it was, therefore, important from the point of view of maintaining peace, and also for psychological reasons, to permit some military supplies to reach Israel, especially jet interceptors.

'The American government was not releasing these aircraft primarily because of their anxiety not to be identified conclusively with the Israeli side and not to participate in an arms race, which would not be so much between Israel and Egypt as between the Soviet Union and the United States. These considerations did not apply, at least to the same extent, to other countries. Mr Dulles hoped, therefore, that their inconsistency in refusing to supply Israel with the equipment which they hoped other countries would be able to supply would be understood.

'He then gave me some very confidential information about American policy, which was known to only a very few people in Washington, and to no one else except, I think, the British Foreign Minister. He was giving me this information because he felt it had a bearing on the Israeli request for Canadian jet interceptors. While the United States would not at this time ship F-86s to Israel, they did intend to have 2 or 3 squadrons of them available at air bases close to Israel under United States control, so that they could reach Israel within an hour or two if that country became the victim of aggression. However, it would not help Israel very much to have 50 or 60 F-86s land at Tel Aviv if there were not Israeli pilots trained to fly them. For this reason F-86s from Canada at this time could be particularly important to Israel; she could train pilots in their use who would be, therefore, ready to man the additional machines, if and when they were sent.

'I told Mr Dulles that requests of this kind from Israel were a very serious problem for Canada which was not any more anxious than the United States to become identified with one side or the other in this quarrel, but was anxious to assist in preserving the peace. We realized that for this purpose some additional armed strength for Israel might be advisable, but we were even more conscious of the need to reach a political settlement which would stop the arms race and give both

Israel and her neighbours some guarantee of security. For that purpose, the three major powers should act quickly and effectively, through the United Nations, and bring the Soviet Union into consultation with them from the beginning. This was an idea which I subsequently repeated at the NATO Council. I told Mr Dulles that the talks which the British had had with Bulganin and Khrushchev in London gave them at least some reason to believe that the Russians were becoming more worried about the possibility of serious trouble in the Middle East, and that they *might* now co-operate with the other three powers to avoid it. Sir Anthony Eden told me that he received the firm impression from his talks with the Russian leaders that they did not realize the extent to which they were playing with fire in their present Middle Eastern policy; he thought he may have sent them back to Moscow in a more chastened and even in a co-operative mood on this issue.

'Mr Dulles agreed that the major objective now should be to press on for a political settlement through the United Nations, though the bitterness of feeling between the two sides in the Middle East made a settlement extremely difficult to bring about. Meanwhile, he emphasized that if we found it possible to send at least half the order of 24 F-86s to Israel at this time, it would be an important and constructive move; since the MIGs and jet bombers were going to the other side, he did not think that the Arab states could seriously complain.'

In spite of Mr Dulles' urging we did not act immediately on his suggestion.

Dulles had begun to think of Egypt as a threat to his policy of containment of Soviet Russia, rather than as a people struggling to be free from British imperialism. The matter came to a head over the issue of help to build the Aswan high dam, the core of Colonel Nasser's great design for the economic development of his country and the improved welfare of its people.

When the Egyptian leader first began in 1955 to negotiate with the United States, Britain, and the World Bank for financial assistance to build the Aswan Dam, the results were not encouraging. However, after the Soviets announced their willingness to consider aid for the project if the Western powers refused, Washington made a rather hasty and somewhat dramatic offer to help finance the dam. Britain joined in the offer, and negotiations for a loan also began in January 1956 with the World Bank. Specific offers were made by the two governments and the bank and on 17 July 1956 Egypt announced formally its decision to accept them. Dulles, however, had become worried about Congressional reactions, and was angered by Nasser's recognition of Red China earlier in May. He was also increasingly disturbed by the friendly relations developing between the USSR, its satellites, and Egypt, and with their economic and military assistance. On 19 July the US therefore announced its withdrawal from the whole Aswan project. This was done by Dulles, not only suddenly, but in terms and in a manner bound to produce an angry reaction in Cairo, by casting doubts on Egypt's good faith and on her ability to follow through with the project.

The Foreign Office followed the next day with a statement that British participation in the Aswan Dam project was not 'feasible in present circumstances.' The World Bank then announced that in consequence of US and British withdrawal, its proposal for a loan of $200,000,000 automatically expired. The Soviet Foreign Minister on 22 July responded that while his government did not regard the dam as the most urgent of Egypt's projects, they would give 'favourable and friendly consideration' to any request for economic aid which Egypt might make.

Nasser's reaction was quick. He turned at once to his friends in Moscow, and on 24 July made a furious verbal assault on the Americans, his famous 'let them choke with rage' speech. He did more than orate. Two days later he took over the Suez Canal. In his speech in Alexandria on 26 July, President Nasser announced that the Egyptian government had nationalized the Suez Canal Company, frozen its assets in Egypt, and would use the canal tolls to underwrite the construction of the Aswan High Dam. Nasser's decree, however, did contain the promise of compensation: 'Stockholders and holders of founder shares shall be compensated for the ordinary or founder shares they own in accordance with the value of the shares shown in the closing quotations of the Paris Stock Exchange on the day preceding the effective date of the present law.' Nationalization of the canal was the beginning of all that followed. The reaction was strong and immediate, especially in London where Nasser's action aroused a great deal of anger in government circles, particularly on the part of the British Prime Minister who was quite unprepared for this turn of events. Britain sent a note to the Egyptian government on 27 July protesting against the nationalization. In the House of Commons, Sir Anthony Eden promised that his government would act with 'firmness and care' and in Cabinet appears to have defined 'firmness' as military action, if necessary.

That same day, I issued a brief statement to the press in Ottawa expressing Canadian concern at the threat to what was recognized as an international waterway, although the Canadian government had no participation in the Suez Canal Company. I also stated that there appeared to have been no technical violation of the Constantinople Convention of 1888 so long as the Egyptians did not interfere with shipping through the canal. Egyptian violations of the Convention against Israeli shipping had been condoned in the past, and the British government would find it difficult to make these violations a basis for action against Egypt. There had, of course, been a unilateral breach of the Suez Canal Company's concession, but our initial concern with regard to Nasser's action was more with the operation than with the ownership of the canal.

What worried us still more in Ottawa was the threat to the peace implicit in a message from Eden to Prime Minister St Laurent. We had hoped, to use the words of our High Commissioner in London, Norman Robertson, that Britain would not be too quick to 'gather too many spears to its own bosom.' At two meetings of the Commonwealth High Commissioners in London on 27 July, Mr Robertson had urged caution upon the British. I telegraphed him the next day:

Quite apart from the legal and technical aspects of the Egyptian action we are aware that it has broad implications of a potentially explosive character. We believe that you have adopted a prudent line in urging upon the United Kingdom the wisdom of proceeding in a manner designed to obtain the greatest amount of international support.

The Prime Minister today received a message from Sir Anthony Eden stating the necessity of taking a firm stand and of endeavouring to get a permanent arrangement to put the Canal under proper international control. We have also been asked by the United Kingdom authorities to take action in regard to the Suez Canal Co's assets. We have stated to Earnscliffe [the British High Commission in Ottawa] that we will examine this matter but that our initial reaction is to doubt its practicability in this country.

I am deeply concerned at the implications of some parts of Eden's message; especially as I doubt very much whether he will receive strong support from Washington in the firm line which he proposes to follow. A talk which I have just had with the United States Ambassador here strengthens these doubts. Surely the UK Government will not do anything which would commit them to strong action against Egypt until they know that the US will back them.

I am also worried as to the meaning to be given Eden's words, 'We believe that we should seize this opportunity of putting the Canal under proper international control and permanent arrangement.' Surely with the Russians dissenting and supporting Egypt, the UK do not think that this can be done, as they profess to hope, 'by political pressure' alone. There remains force – which they visualize as a last resort. But is it not clear that to be effective enough force would have to be used to destroy the Nasser Government and take over Egypt? Any effort to use force, in fact, would in all likelihood result in an appeal by Egypt to the UN. That would be bringing the UN into the matter with a vengeance, and by the wrong party.

I'm glad that you have stressed the importance of bringing the UN into the question. This may not be practicable but it certainly shouldn't be dismissed without the most careful consideration. It might well be argued that if an international dispute is of such a character that force is envisaged, it is also one that should be brought before the UN in order to try to avoid the use of such force.

These observations, which are sent to you in haste, may all seem pretty negative, but at the moment I am less worried about being negative than about being rashly positive.

Increasingly, we would become concerned over the widening gap in policy between Britain and France on the one side, and the United States on the other – always a nightmare to Canadians.

The first retaliatory action against Egypt came on 28 July when Britain froze the assets of the Suez Canal Company and placed all Egyptian sterling accounts under controls. France took similar action and the United States placed the assets of the Canal Company and the Egyptian government under a temporary licensing procedure.

Between 29 July and 2 August tripartite talks between representatives of France, Britain, and the United States were held in London. All agreed that Egypt's action threatened the freedom and security of the canal and 'that steps should be taken to establish operating arrangements under an international system designed to assure the continuity of operation of the canal, as guaranteed by the Convention of 29 October 1888, consistently with legitimate Egyptian interests.' Apparently, Britain and France in the talks reserved the 'right to use force,' although it is not clear what language they used on this point with the United States.

The tripartite talks ended with the announcement of a further meeting in London, to which were to be invited the eight parties to the Constantinople Convention and sixteen other states 'largely concerned in the use of the canal either through ownership of tonnage or pattern of trade.' Of these countries only Egypt and Greece refused invitations, and a conference of twenty-two states sat from 16 to 23 August. Canada was not invited, because we were not one of the important users of the canal and had not the same stake as other countries. We had not expected an invitation, but we were kept informed of conference developments.

We were certainly never given any secret information on Anglo-French military plans. The Suez question was mentioned briefly at a private session of the NATO Council on 31 July, where we expressed the hope that the governments most directly concerned would, in due course, provide their NATO allies with information. I have in Chapter 4 referred to the effects of these developments on my work as one of the NATO 'Three Wise Men.'

We were aware, of course, that military plans were being worked out by the British in collaboration with the French. It is quite normal to prepare for contingencies. We were not surprised, then, when the British Admiralty announced on 31 July that certain naval movements had been ordered, nor when the War Office followed with an announcement that precautionary military measures had been taken. The other public announcements were of the same order. On 2 August further naval movements of aircraft carriers and troop ships were announced, and a limited number of reservists were recalled. The French announced that their Mediterranean Fleet was assembling. Between 4 and 11 August, the British War Office announced that soldiers due for discharge would be temporarily retained and that merchant ships were still being requisitioned for emergency transport of troops and equipment. Wives and children of British citizens were evacuated from the Canal Zone.

On 3 August I instructed Robertson to take any suitable opportunity to impress upon British officials the desirability of having the Suez question considered by the NATO Council before the London Conference. What we had in mind was to seek out some area of common agreement among the NATO members who were to participate in the conference (France, Italy, the Netherlands, Turkey, Britain, Denmark, West Germany, Norway, Portugal, and the United States) and, at the same time, to underline the strategic importance of the Suez Canal to NATO. To that end, an advance text of a tripartite resolution proposed for circulation among the delegates to the London Conference was placed before a restricted meeting of the NATO Council on 6 August. It turned out to be a relatively meaningless exercise in political consultation. The Commonwealth Relations Office, through Sir Saville Garner, offered this initial explanation to Norman Robertson on 7 August: Britain was satisfied that, in view of India's key role in the dispute and Mr Nehru's opposition towards military pacts, to involve NATO directly would antagonize and alienate the Indian Prime Minister. This danger outweighed the advantages of fuller NATO consultation!

On 6 August Mr Diefenbaker had asked me in the House of Com-

mons whether our official stand followed that of Britain and France, or
that of the United States. My reply conveyed our hopes rather than
our fears:

I must deprecate, in a friendly way, the implication of my hon. friend's
question that there is necessarily any difference of policy in this matter between the United States on the one hand and the United Kingdom and France
on the other. I hope that at the conference in question the three governments
will be able to work closely together and that at this conference, as in all
other matters – and this is of the most vital importance to Canada – the
closest co-operation inside the Commonwealth and the closest co-operation
between the United Kingdom and the United States will be reflected once
again.

On 7 August Arnold Heeney, our Ambassador in Washington, discussed the Suez question with Secretary of State Dulles. Dulles appeared to share my doubts that Egypt would accept the sort of solution
which Britain and France insisted upon, and to share my fears that the
British and French governments seemed to be committing themselves
irrevocably to the use of force if political pressure failed, and that the
employment of force would severely strain the Atlantic Alliance and
the Commonwealth. Mr Dulles told Mr Heeney that he hoped Canada
would follow developments very closely, and exercise in London and
elsewhere 'the considerable Canadian influence in the direction of a
peaceful solution of this very anxious problem.'

Although we did not make formal representations on the subject of
our apprehensions, we did attempt to encourage and support every
move that seemed to improve the chances of a peaceful settlement. We
further devoted considerable attention, both in the Department of
External Affairs in Ottawa and in our Missions in London, Washington,
New York, and Paris, to possible developments if the dispute were
taken to the United Nations.

During that first London Conference from 16 to 23 August, we
followed progress with the closest interest. Two plans for settlement
of the dispute were placed before the meeting. A United States plan,
with amendments by Pakistan, Ethiopia, Iran, and Turkey, called for
international control and operation of the canal with 'due regard' for
Egyptian sovereignty and fair payment to Egypt by users. An Indian
plan, which might have been acceptable to Egypt, called for Egyptian
ownership and operation with 'a consultative body of user interests to
be formed on the basis of geographical representation and interests
charged with advisory, consultative and liaison functions.' At the end
of the conference, eighteen nations endorsed the United States plan
and four (India, Ceylon, Indonesia, and the Soviet Union), the Indian

plan. The United States plan was embodied in a 'statement of views' and a five-power committee, made up of Australia, Ethiopia, Iran, Sweden, and the United States and chaired by Australian Prime Minister Robert Menzies, was named by the eighteen to explain its purposes to the Nasser government and to seek Egyptian acceptance of it as the basis for negotiating a settlement of the canal dispute.

On 29 August the Canadian Cabinet agreed that we should publicly support the eighteen-power proposals. The next day, I gave this statement to the press:

The Canadian Government has followed with interest and concern the discussions held recently in London over the Suez Canal and has welcomed the proposal of the eighteen governments, from Asia, Africa, Europe, Australasia and North America, which resulted from the conference.

President Nasser of Egypt has agreed, and his decision in this regard is also welcomed, to receive five members of the conference, under the chairmanship of the Prime Minister of Australia, who have been charged by the eighteen to explain to him and to the Egyptian Government the purposes and objectives of the majority proposal, and to ascertain whether Egypt would agree to negotiate a Suez convention based on it.

It is devoutly to be hoped that President Nasser will accept this invitation to negotiate a peaceful and permanent solution of this serious problem along the lines of the London majority proposal. A failure to do so would involve a very heavy responsibility indeed.

So far as the Canadian Government is concerned, we feel that these proposals are reasonable and satisfactory and deserve our support as a basis for negotiation. They respect not only the sovereignty, the interests and susceptibilities of Egypt, but they also make adequate provision for safeguarding, through cooperative international arrangements with which the United Nations would be associated in an appropriate way, the international character, use and maintenance of the canal.

The Canadian Government understands the view of the users of the canal that this international waterway must be efficiently and impartially operated, not only in the interest of Egypt but also of the states who use it and for whom its efficient operation is economically essential. The canal should therefore be kept free to the maximum extent possible from political interference on the part of any single state. We also understand the desire of Egypt to safeguard its sovereignty and its national dignity.

We feel that the eighteen-power London proposals provide for both these essential considerations and, therefore, form a solid basis for a peaceful settlement of the Suez Canal question which is so important to the well-being and security of all states.

In London on 3 September, I had a private talk with Selwyn Lloyd. Our officials had withdrawn at his request. At one point in a fairly wide-ranging discussion of the canal crisis, he rather wondered whether, if things dragged on, Israel might not take advantage of the situation by some aggressive move against Egypt. He seemed to think that this might help Britain out of some of her more immediate difficulties, but agreed with me when I said that the long-range results and, indeed, even the short-range results of such action would be deplorable and dangerous; that such action by Israel would certainly consolidate Arab opinion behind Egypt; that even Arab leaders who might now be worrying about Nasser's moves would have to rally behind him. It never occurred to me that there was already a plan supported by the French for an Israeli attack on Egypt, and that the British would soon be involved.

In all, it was a very depressing interview. I reported to Mr St Laurent:

'The impression I got from my talk with Lloyd, not only on the Suez matter but on the circumstances surrounding the meeting of the NATO Council on Wednesday, is that the UK Government are not being very skilful in their management of these international problems, even when the policies they may be pursuing are the right ones. Lloyd, for instance, seemed quite surprised when I told him that the manner and place of the announcement that the NATO Council would discuss the Suez question, made from London rather than from NATO in Paris, was the wrong way to proceed and that it would be bound to create unfavourable impressions in certain quarters. He said that it was purely accidental that it came from London because he had been discussing the possibility of the Council putting the subject on the agenda with Ismay [NATO Secretary General] that day and, therefore, the decision was given out here rather than by NATO in Paris. He had no intention of giving any impression that the UK was summoning the Council.

'The same lack of skill seemed to have been shown in the way the earlier British troop movements to the Middle East and the recent despatch of French troops to Cyprus were explained or, rather, were not explained to public opinion. There seems to be a lack of imagination and skill on the part of those who are concerned here with the public relations aspect of UK policy moves. The results are often perplexing for the friends of the UK and indicate, it seems to me, a lack of direction and no sureness of touch.

'I hope I am not being unfair to people here or unduly pessimistic when I say that my impression is that events in the international field are pulling the British Government with them rather than being influenced and directed by that government.'

The British kept referring to the use of force if necessary. I knew Mr Dulles well enough to know, and this was confirmed by the messages we were getting, that he was not going to advise the American government to use force, even if this meant a division of opinion with the British. There was real danger of a misunderstanding; Eden saying: 'Force – we may have to use force,' and Dulles saying: 'Well, force only as a last resort.' It amounted to 'force if necessary but not necessarily force,' with one emphasizing force if necessary and the other emphasizing not necessarily force. While Dulles was talking to the British and the other members of the conference indicating that force might have to be used in certain circumstances, he was at the same time working in other places to give the impression that force would not be used and that they would have to find a way of solving this problem without using force.

On 5 September, I made a statement in the NATO Council reviewing the main features of Canada's attitude on the Suez question. I asked the Council members:

If the present negotiations in Cairo fail or, more likely, if they are inconclusive and Egypt merely takes note of the proposals without doing anything about them, we inevitably ask ourselves, what then? It is a worrying question.

We must, I think, rule out force. I say that not without qualification because otherwise we would not be spending between 40% and 50% of our budgets on defence. But we must rule out force except as a last resort and use it only in accordance with the principles we have accepted in the NATO Pact and the UN Charter.

If the negotiations in Cairo fail, what political action can be taken? Where should it be taken? At the UN? – and how? I feel myself that a majority opinion at the Security Council, even if it is vetoed there as it would be, might be an important and valuable support for subsequent negotiations or action.

By 9 September, Nasser had rejected the Menzies mission proposals as an attempt to restore 'international colonialism.' No doubt it had been a very good idea to talk to Nasser on behalf of the Canal users, but Mr Menzies was not exactly the kind of man likely to create the best impression on Nasser. He was a very strong and able man, but violent in his opposition to what had been done, and publicly so. Thus, he perhaps was not the best negotiator for this particular situation. At any rate, he always claimed, with some justice, that any chance he had of succeeding with Nasser was torpedoed by Eisenhower's statement in Washington on 5 September, that it was unthinkable that the United States would support the use of force. With talk like that in Washington, Nasser was not too worried about what Menzies was saying to him in Cairo, and so the mission accomplished nothing.

Egypt, in turn, suggested a conference of canal users to review the old 1888 Convention. This was summarily rejected by the British Foreign Office. At this point Foster Dulles interjected his scheme for a Suez Canal Users' Association (SCUA). On 12 September, the day Sir Anthony Eden announced in rather strong terms to a special session of the British Parliament a 'tripartite' plan to establish an international users' association, Mr Dulles, through our Ambassador in Washington, sent me his own appreciation of the plan. Dulles said that with the failure of the Menzies' mission to secure Egyptian co-operation, Britain and France had seen no alternatives to force on the one hand or complete capitulation to Nasser on the other. Dulles added parenthetically that he did not think his colleagues had tried very hard to find any other course of action. In these circumstances, he had devoted all his personal attention to developing a 'makeshift arrangement' to provide an intermediary route between the alternatives of force and capitulation in the hope that the association would provide a way of obtaining Egyptian co-operation on a *de facto* basis when it seemed that no scheme could produce Egyptian co-operation on a *de jure* basis.

It was his idea that the Users' Association would serve to keep the London Conference group together as a cohesive body to deal with practical matters and even with some political matters. Dulles believed that the association could take over as the employer of the pilots; it could be the authority to set the traffic pattern through the canal; and that it would be the 'collecting agent' for tolls. It would use the money coming into its hands to pay the pilots and other expenses and to recompense Egypt for expenses which it might incur in the operation of the canal. The continued employment of the pilots was a worrying problem to Dulles, because the United States would not let its ships go through the canal if, as he told Heeney, the Egyptians attempted to put Soviet pilots, for example, on United States ships.

Dulles indicated that Britain and France had accepted his scheme reluctantly. He claimed he had been assured they were 'prepared to act' on 15 September. He went on to say that while his scheme 'did not abound in intrinsic merit' it could, nevertheless, provide some middle ground for a provisional solution and that it had already shown enough merit to induce Britain and France at least to delay military measures. He said he was not sure how the Users' Association scheme would be portrayed by Eden to Parliament. If it was interpreted as a punitive action against Egypt, the scheme would in all likelihood fail. If it was presented as another attempt to bring about the practical operation of the canal, leaving the door open for broader negotiation, it might work.

He was véry clear that the United States would never support the Users scheme (or any other) with force.

I was surprised at Dulles's rather optimistic tone and very sceptical about either the practicability or wisdom of SCUA; everyone that I had talked to in Paris about it confirmed that, in default of the unlikely submission of Nasser, the new arrangement could hardly be put into operation without some kind of clash; that not only would the SCUA scheme not work, but that it probably was never meant to work. Indeed, when the British government asked us to give public endorsement to the plan, we were unable to obtain sufficient detail to permit a satisfactory assessment of its possibilities and, as a consequence, we did not support it. Certainly, Dulles was not prepared to exert any pressure on Egypt and when he, in effect, publicly invited Nasser to reject the SCUA scheme at a press conference in Washington on 13 September, the British leaders with apparent reluctance concluded that there was no basis for a combined Anglo-American approach to Middle Eastern problems. We were later told by a British source that at the end of August, Dulles had agreed with Eden and Lloyd that Nasser was an evil and dangerous influence who should be removed from the Middle East political scene. Following this agreed assessment, a secret meeting took place in Washington between the appropriate British and American officials to examine and report to their respective governments on the ways and means by which this objective could be carried out. Their agreed report began, in the best joint staff manner, by setting forth explicitly the object of the exercise: the elimination of Colonel Nasser. It then went on to suggest the methods by which this objective might be achieved. When the report came to Dulles, he apparently refused to associate the United States with the 'object of the enterprise,' although he is reported not to have objected to any of the methods suggested. It was in this context of Dulles's diplomatic gimmicks that the British received his press statement of 13 September that 'I know nothing about a plan to shoot a way through ... We certainly have no intention of doing so ... If we are met by force ... the alternative for the United States is to send our vessels around the Cape ...'

One must wonder whether Dulles was influenced in his attitude to the British Prime Minister's belligerent posture on Suez by Eden's rejection in 1954, while he was Foreign Secretary, of Dulles's proposals for military action against Ho Chi Minh to help the French in Indo-China. Further, there can be little doubt that the American position against action was affected by the upcoming United States elections of

November 1956. Unfortunately, the Dulles scheme for a Canal Users' Association, artificial solution that it was, while giving a little more time for the forces of negotiation to operate, appears to have been the final move in destroying any basis for successful negotiations. Between 19 and 21 September, a second London Conference was held, attended by the eighteen nations which had supported the US plan at the earlier conference. Fifteen of those nations (excluding Ethiopia, Japan, and Pakistan) accepted the Dulles plan for a Suez Canal Users' Association. Suffice it to say that the proposal was rejected by Nasser.

Meanwhile, on 21 September we announced that Canada had agreed to license the export of the 24 F-86s which Israel had requested, to be delivered at the rate of four per month. Although we were fearful that Britain and France might resort to force, we did not suspect that Israel would become involved with them. We made it clear, however, in our statement that if 'political circumstances changed in a way which would warrant cancellation or postponement of all or part of this order, such action would be taken.'

In a letter to me dated 5 October, Mrs Golda Meir (at this time the Foreign Minister of Israel) expressed the gratitude of the Israeli government for our decision and their regret that it was for arms that they had had to turn to us for help. A few days later Mr Ben-Gurion wrote to Mr St Laurent reaffirming that the Sabre jets would be used solely for defence against aggression. When the Israeli attack on Egypt occurred, none of our jets had been sent and we did not fill the order.

The crisis had by now been raised at the United Nations. On 23 September Britain and France asked for a meeting of the UN Security Council to consider the 'situation created by the unilateral action of the Egyptian Government in bringing to an end the system of international operation of the Suez Canal, which was confirmed and completed by the Suez Canal Convention of 1888.' Next day Egypt asked the Council to consider 'actions against Egypt by some Powers, particularly France and the United Kingdom, which constitute a danger to international peace and security and are serious violations of the Charter of the United Nations.' On 26 September the Security Council adopted both items on its Agenda for its meeting on 5 October.

We were gratified that Britain and France had finally taken the Suez dispute to the UN. We envisaged a Security Council resolution which would not be entirely acceptable to either side, followed by a period of fruitless negotiation, and ultimately a reference to the General Assembly. Initially, Britain and France sought endorsement by the Council of the eighteen-power proposals. This was not forthcoming.

However, as a result of public sessions and closed sessions, and private talks among the Foreign Ministers of France, Britain, and Egypt, and the UN Secretary General, Dag Hammarskjöld, there emerged a resolution unanimously adopted by the Council on 13 October. It laid down six principles as a basis for a settlement of the Canal dispute:

1 there should be free and open transit through the Canal without discrimination, overt or covert – this covers both political and technical aspects;
2 the sovereignty of Egypt should be respected;
3 the operation of the Canal should be insulated from the politics of any country;
4 the manner of fixing tolls and charges should be decided by agreement between Egypt and the users;
5 a fair proportion of the dues should be allotted to development;
6 in case of disputes, unresolved affairs between the Suez Canal Company and the Egyptian Government should be settled by arbitration with suitable terms of reference and suitable provisions for the payment of sums found to be due.

An attempt to link these proposals to the Users' Association was vetoed by the Soviet Union. Discussions between Hammarskjöld and the British, French, and Egyptian Foreign Ministers continued at the United Nations until the Israeli invasion of Egypt.

On 29 October the Israelis moved against Egypt and toward the canal, a lightning thrust. The next day the British and the French moved diplomatically, demanding that both sides agree to a cease-fire, withdraw ten miles from the canal, and stop the fighting. Their intervention, or so the British and French claimed, was to safeguard navigation on the canal. They warned both parties to the dispute that if they did not accept this ultimatum within twelve hours, Anglo-French forces would have to move in and occupy key points to keep canal traffic moving. The Egyptian government rejected this ultimatum. The Israeli government accepted it, on condition that Cairo also accept – which meant a rejection. On the 31st the French and British Air Forces began to bomb selected points in the Canal Zone.

These events came as a complete surprise to us. I was in Ottawa at that time and was worried, as was everybody. The general situation had been worsening between Israel and her neighbours. We feared that Britain, because of her treaty obligations to Jordan, might become involved in a conflict with Israel. Right up until the Israeli attack, which the Israelis regarded as a defensive action to protect themselves, the British government was warning them that if their attack were against

Jordan, the British would have to intervene. When the attack did take place, I remember we felt a kind of relief for the first few hours since the attack was against Egypt. It was a strange business.

Mr St Laurent first heard of the Anglo-French ultimatum from a wire-service report. Needless to say, he was not very pleased about the state of Commonwealth consultations. Probably the ultimatum had been announced in the British House of Commons immediately after Eden sent his messages to all the dominions. When he finally did receive Eden's message, Mr St Laurent rang and asked me to come down to see him at his end of the hall in the East Block. I had never before seen him in such a state of controlled anger; I had never seen him in a state of any kind of anger. He threw me the telegram and said: 'What do you think of this?' It was marked 'Top Secret and Personal, Message from the Rt. Hon. Sir Anthony Eden to the Rt. Hon. L.S. St. Laurent,' and tried to justify the Anglo-French action and seek our sanction of it.

Eden stated that his concern was to stop the fighting and to ensure the safety of the Suez Canal, and that the British and French governments considered the risks of hesitation far greater than the risks of intervention. They had reserved the right to take such military action as might be necessary to compel both Israel and Egypt to cease hostilities immediately and withdraw their troops from the banks of the canal. Eden claimed that this war had to be stopped before it developed into a wider conflict. He counted on our understanding and hoped for our support in their endeavours. There was not much to reassure us in his suggestion that they expected to raise the matter at the UN in 'the most appropriate way.'

Our immediate problem was to let Eden know that he could not count on our support automatically. This was no situation for 'Ready, Aye, Ready.' His telegram had to be answered at once to clear up that point. Mr St Laurent was prepared to send a pretty vigorous answer. Instead, after most careful drafting by the Prime Minister, myself, and my officials, and after meeting with our Cabinet colleagues, a calm and courteous reply – but also a very firm reply, as opposed to what has been claimed was a brutal and unfriendly reply – was sent to Sir Anthony Eden. It was delivered to the British High Commission in Ottawa at 11:30 AM, 1 November 1956. It read:

Thank you for your message of yesterday, which reached me at five o'clock our time, in the afternoon. I understand, of course, that in view of the rapidity with which your government and that of France felt it was necessary to act, it could not be otherwise; but the first intimation I had of your government's intention to take certain grave steps in Egypt was from the press reports of your statement in the House of Commons.

I must add that without more information, and information different from that which we now have, about the action of Israel, we cannot come to the conclusion that the penetration of its troops into Egypt was justified or that the probable resistance of the Egyptians necessitated the decision of the UK and France to post forces in the canal zone. No doubt, however, your own information is much more complete than ours. We now await developments, and information concerning them, with most anxious interest.

In the meantime, we have suspended all shipments of arms to Israel and will endeavour to shape our course in conformity with what we regard as our obligations under the Charter of and our membership in the United Nations. We are never unmindful, of course, in our own decisions, of the very special relationship of close friendship and intimate association which we have with the United Kingdom and with your government. Nor do we forget the vital importance of the Suez Canal to the economic life of the United Kingdom.

You will not be surprised when I tell you that, apart from the danger of a war which might spread, there are three aspects of this distressing situation which cause us particular anxiety. Our misgivings in this respect have already been communicated to some of your colleagues through our High Commissioner, who may have passed them on to you.

The first is the effect of the decisions taken on the United Nations, of which the United Kingdom has been such a staunch and steady supporter. The fact that the action which you took was taken while the Security Council was seized of the matter is, I think, most regrettable, and the result of the Security Council vote last night equally regrettable.

There is also the danger – and I am sure that you are even more conscious of this than we are here – of a serious division within the Commonwealth in regard to your action, which will prejudice the unity of our association. The statement which the Government of India issued this morning is significant evidence of this danger.

Finally, and this is a matter of deep and abiding interest to Canada, the deplorable divergence of viewpoint and policy between the United Kingdom and the United States in regard to the decisions that have been taken, and the procedure followed, is something that will cause as much satisfaction to the Soviet Union and its supporters as it does distress to all those who believe that Anglo-American co-operation and friendship is the very foundation of our hopes for progress toward a peaceful and secure world. That co-operation and friendship, which you yourself have done so much to promote, has now served the world well for many years. It would be a tragedy beyond repair if it were now to disappear, or even to be weakened. It is hard for a Canadian to think of any consideration – other than national survival or safety – as more important. This aspect of the situation is very much in our minds here at the moment, as I know it must be in yours.

I have no desire, of course, to add by any words of mine to the heavy burdens you are already carrying, but I know that you would like me to tell you frankly, and as a friend, of my worries; and this I have tried to do.

At an Emergency Session of the Security Council on 30 October, the United States representative had introduced a draft resolution which called on Israel to withdraw its armed forces behind the established armistice lines; and upon all members 'to refrain from the use of force or the threat of force in the area in any manner inconsistent with the Purposes of the United Nations,' to assist the United Nations in ensuring the integrity of the armistice arrangements, and to refrain from giving assistance to Israel until it had complied with the resolution. The draft resolution was vetoed by France and Britain. A Soviet draft resolution, which embodied the first part of that of the United States (withdrawal to the armistice line) and a Yugoslav amendment asking the Secretary General to report on compliance were similarly defeated.

In the Security Council on the following day, Yugoslavia (because of the deadlock) presented a resolution calling for reference of the Middle East question to the General Assembly, under the Uniting for Peace Resolution. The vote was 7 in favour, 2 opposed (France and the United Kingdom), and 2 abstentions (Australia and Belgium). Since, in this instance, the negative votes did not constitute a veto, the resolution was adopted, although the French and British representatives questioned the legality of the procedure. The vote on the Anglo-French contention that reference to the Assembly would be illegal was 4 in favour (Britain, France, Australia, and Belgium), 6 opposed, 1 abstention (China). A special emergency session of the General Assembly was called for 1 November. Thus, the question was moved from the Security Council to the General Assembly.

Before recounting my activities at the UN Assembly, I want to deal further with the question of the Anglo-French intervention and to make some general observations on why, how, and with what results I became so deeply involved as the Secretary of State for External Affairs of Canada. On 28 September, Lloyd had told me that he himself was 'as ready to bash the Egyptians as anybody,' but 'he had to ask himself where his country and the Commonwealth would stand after the job of bashing had been done.' We now know that while I was talking to Lloyd in London, and while telegrams were being exchanged between London and Ottawa and other Dominion capitals, talks were also going on between the French and Israelis, with the knowledge of Eden and Lloyd, which would lead to military intervention. Yet, when I saw Lloyd, whom I knew very well, there was no hint, certainly none that I recognized, of these discussions; this explains to some extent our subsequent reaction of bewilderment and dismay. If we were in the dark, we were not alone. Many of Selwyn Lloyd's own colleagues were in a darkness almost as stygian.

I find it impossible to discover any sensible explanation for the Anglo-French course of action. On the French side, I think it was in part a reaction against Pan-Arabism, against Egyptian support for the Algerian rebels and the war going on there. There must have been a mixture of many motives for the British; fury at being double-crossed by a man who had seemed to promise so much in the way of new and good relations if they got out of the canal area; a feeling by Eden of personal betrayal in that he had been let down by this 'little tin-pot, fascist' dictator, as some people described Nasser. The depth of Eden's feeling can be seen in the following words from a radio speech he gave shortly after Nasser nationalized the canal: 'If Colonel Nasser's action were to succeed, each one of us would be at the mercy of one man for the supplies upon which we live. We could never accept that. With dictators you always have to pay a higher price later – for their appetite grows with feeding'; no doubt a reflection on Eden's experience in 'facing the dictators,' Hitler and Mussolini, in the 1930s.

Eden must have thought, in a hang-over from the great imperial days: 'All we have to do is to move into Egypt. We have done this before, they will collapse; it can be done in a few hours and will be forgotten.' It was an amazing miscalculation of forces and circumstances. It was not even a good military operation. The only possibility of its success within the terms of reference given by the British to themselves was by a very smooth, quick, and effective operation. It was neither quick nor smooth. The air operation was well done but the mounting of the Armada and the landings hardly seemed much of an improvement over Gallipoli. This ill-conceived and ill-judged enterprise also revealed a complete misappreciation of world response. I believe that the British were quite unprepared for the reaction against them, especially in Washington. The French were more cold-blooded – more realistic, if you like; they seemed prepared to ride out world opinion. But not London. In London there was surprise and shock at the violence of the reaction against what they had done. There was dismay – even in Eden's own party.

There is no doubt that the architect of the affair, at least on the British side, was Eden, who still considered himself Foreign Minister (with Lloyd a kind of Minister of State). It is always difficult to weigh exactly human factors, but no doubt many a battle has been lost because the General had a bad night and a worse breakfast. The Suez operation demanded strong, vigorous health and this Mr Eden did not have.

The reports of secret planning late in October between the British, French, and Israelis in that country house outside Paris, with no one aware of what was going on except for the few people engaged, the secret stratagems – all this was not unlike the conspiracies of the sixteenth century. Throughout the crisis we had tried to persuade the British against the use of force. But the small group who planned the invasion were not to be persuaded, not by the United States which they felt had badly let them down, and, evidently, not by Canada. In fact, we were told by a British official that their bitterness towards us was as great as that towards the Americans, because we had negotiated a wheat sale to Egypt in October. This the British leaders regarded, in their almost irrational isolation, as a 'stab in the back.'

When I attended the NATO Ministerial meeting in mid-December 1956, I had discussions with Eden's three closest collaborators in the Suez intervention: Butler (Conservative party House Leader), Lloyd, and Macmillan (Chancellor of the Exchequer and soon to be Prime Minister). I reported these conversations and conclusions to Mr St Laurent in a memorandum dated 18 December:

'Little is said about what may be the real, less publicized reason for the action, to destroy Nasser, and no one was able to give me any satisfactory answer to my question: "If you had destroyed Nasser, who would have taken his place and would you be better off?" I mentioned on one or two occasions the point that if the destruction of Nasser was the objective, they should have given the Israelis two or three more days to complete the military job which would probably also have resulted in a political crisis in Cairo, then the British and French could have taken the lead in the United Nations in a move to push the Israelis back. Both Butler and Lloyd indicated to me that this was where they made a big mistake, but David Ormsby-Gore, who is Lloyd's Parliamentary Private Secretary and who was present during my final talk with Lloyd last Saturday night at the British Embassy in Paris, would not accept this judgment. He was positive that if the Israelis had been allowed to go on fighting, all the Arab states would have intervened militarily at once and the conflict would have spread all over the Middle East.

'It is a sad reflection on the judgment of those responsible that only now are they beginning to realize the fact that failure was likely from the outset and that the consequences of failure, economically and politically, would be heavy and hard to bear; or that as a result there would be a strong temptation to throw the blame for such failure on others, on the United States, or on the United Nations, or on fate! Yielding to temptation, however, puts an extra strain on the North

Atlantic Alliance and indeed on the whole postwar effort for collective security and international organization.'

On the question of my involvement with this crisis, it will be clear from what I have already written that we had been actively concerned as a member of the UN with events leading up to, and following, the establishment of the state of Israel. We did not seek this involvement, but when circumstances brought it about, Mr St Laurent was willing to accept it as part of the responsibility of UN membership. I supported and applauded his viewpoint.

Canada, in discharging its UN responsibilities, had acquired a good reputation at New York for sincerity and objectivity. We had as much influence on developments there as any power, I think it is fair to say, apart from the Permanent Members of the Security Council.

Therefore, when the fighting began and the UN Assembly was called to deal with the situation, I believed that we would become actively engaged in its activities, and would be asked to take on new responsibilities.

CRISIS AND RESOLUTION

Before flying to New York on the afternoon of 1 November, I talked with my Prime Minister about the problems to be faced. We considered what the UN might and should do to resolve the crisis which could spread far beyond the Suez, which threatened to destroy Anglo-American co-operation, to split the Commonwealth, and brand our two mother countries, Britain and France, as aggressors.

Mr St Laurent agreed, as did our Cabinet colleagues, that we should seize any opportunity to be helpful, while not rushing into rash action. During our discussions, I brought up the possibility of an emergency UN force to police the area of combat and to provide a substitute for British-French intervention, thus giving them a good reason to withdraw from their own stated objective of restoring peace before they could be formally condemned by the Assembly. Mr St Laurent thought that something like this might be necessary, and that I could, if circumstances seemed to warrant it, throw out the idea in a general way, test the reaction to it, and then report back. Cabinet agreed.

My purpose in this initiative, if it proved feasible, was to have the UN take responsibility for bringing the fighting to an end. It was absolutely clear to me that only in this way could Britain and France be extricated from a situation which was becoming increasingly dangerous for them. This was 1956, not 1876, and their course was doomed to failure and ultimate disaster, opposed, as it would be, both by the USSR and the USA, and by the Asian members of the Commonwealth.

For these reasons, I was determined to advocate a policy at the

Assembly, and do everything I could to have it adopted, which would end the fighting before it spread – in short, to establish a UN peace and police force. We were clear on our objectives – although a fog almost prevented my plane from landing at New York, and I barely made the opening of the Assembly debate.

It was an all-night session, lasting until 4:30 the next morning. Basically, there were two items of business before the Assembly. The first was the inscription on the agenda of the item referred to the General Assembly by the Security Council under the 'Uniting for Peace' procedure. The vote was 62 in favour, 2 opposed (France, United Kingdom), 7 abstentions (Australia, Belgium, Israel, New Zealand, Portugal, Turkey, Union of South Africa). The second was a United States draft resolution introduced by Secretary of State Dulles calling upon all parties to the hostilities to agree to an immediate cease-fire and to halt movement of forces and arms into the area. It urged parties to the Israeli-Arab armistice agreements of 1949 to withdraw their forces promptly behind the armistice lines and to observe the provisions of the armistice agreements. It further urged that as soon as the cease-fire became effective, measures should be taken to restore freedom of navigation through the Suez Canal. The resolution requested the Secretary General to observe and report on compliance, and provided that the Assembly should remain in emergency session until the resolution had been complied with.

After some hours, the debate was cut short and the resolution was put to a roll-call vote at the request of the United States. The result was 64 in favour, 5 opposed (Australia, France, Israel, New Zealand, United Kingdom), and 6 abstentions (Belgium, Canada, Laos, Netherlands, Portugal, South Africa). One member (Luxembourg) was absent.

I had to make up my mind very quickly, in the midst of doubt and emotion as the debate unfolded, on what course to follow. I had seen Foster Dulles before the debate opened to ask what the Americans were likely to do. He told me about their resolution, that they were going to push it through and try to get a vote that night. He had become a statesman in a hurry. I was disturbed by this, but it was apparent that there was no way to deter him and I did not try.

We had to sense the atmosphere in New York and, particularly, find out what the British were thinking. (The French were standing pat.) I had seen the British Acting High Commissioner in Ottawa the evening before I left for New York. Now I saw Sir Pierson Dixon, the British Ambassador to the United Nations, an old friend for whom I had great admiration, and told him we were contemplating some kind of initiative. I also talked by telephone with Norman Robertson in London who, earlier in the day, had cabled me that he had been in touch with Sir Ivone Kirkpatrick, the Permanent Under-Secretary at the Foreign Office. He had told Kirkpatrick that I was turning over in my mind the possibility of proposing a cease-fire, to be followed by a major diplomatic conference to deal with the whole context of Middle Eastern and North African questions. He had also told him that, as part of this approach, it would be essential to set up an adequate UN military force to separate the Egyptians from the Israelis pending a stable and peaceful settlement of outstanding Middle Eastern questions.

We had learned in advance of Eden's intention to state in the British House of Commons that 'police action there must be to separate the belligerents and to prevent the resumption of hostilities between them. If the UN were then willing to take over the physical task of maintaining peace, no one would be better pleased than we.' It was not much, but it was something. We took it to mean that Britain and France would be prepared to hand over the 'police task' they had assumed to a UN force strong enough to prevent a renewed outbreak of hostilities between Egypt and Israel pending the conclusion of a peace treaty which would guarantee Israel's existence and integrity. I knew that we would have to have something more to offer than just a diplomatic gimmick to meet Anglo-French requirements; another observer corps would not do. It was also clear to me that if Canada were going to take any initiative in this, we had from the beginning to detach ourselves from both sides. In other words, we could not support the United States resolution and expect to get a sympathetic hearing in Britain, Australia, New Zealand, Belgium, or in one or two other places. We could not oppose it. If we opposed it, our standing with the other members of the Commonwealth, with the Moslem world, and with the United States would simply disappear. We would thus have had no further capacity for any useful service in this emergency, no more than Australia or New Zealand, once they voted against it.

Meanwhile, my official colleagues – and no one ever had better – John Holmes, Geoff Murray, and Bert MacKay moved about and talked to their friends in the corridors and the delegates' lounge asking: 'Well, what do you think should be done?' By midnight we had a fairly good idea that a UN peace-keeping intervention would be well supported. If you like, we had begun to mount a diplomatic operation on the assumption that we might decide to introduce a resolution for a cease-fire, to be policed by a United Nations emergency force, a resolution to contain also a recommendation for a political settlement.

Therefore, after discussing the situation with Mr St Laurent in Ottawa by telephone, I decided not to participate in the debate on the US resolution. I abstained in that early morning vote, but asked for the floor to explain my abstention. I wandered on about how we did not have enough time to consider everything, that a matter such as this could not be hurried. This was not my real reason at all, but it was impossible to explain that I was abstaining on tactical grounds. I did, however, have a chance to express these thoughts: 'What is the use of passing a resolution which brings about a cease-fire and even a withdrawal? What are we withdrawing to, the same state of affairs? In six months we'll go through all this again if we do not take advantage of this crisis to pluck something out – how was it Hotspur put it: "out of this nettle, danger, we pluck this flower, safety" – if we do not take advantage of this crisis to do something about a political settlement, we will regret it. The time has now come for the UN not only to bring about a cease-fire, but to move in and police the cease-fire and make arrangements for a political settlement.' In putting forward the idea of a United Nations emergency force, I said: 'I therefore would have liked to see a provision in this resolution ... authorizing the Secretary General to begin to make arrangements with Member Governments for a United Nations force ... My own government would be glad to recommend Canadian participation in such a United Nations Force, a truly international peace and police force.' When Dulles got up to move adjournment, he said that he welcomed this statement, and he asked the Canadian representative to formulate and introduce a concrete proposal for an international force. I had earlier suggested to him that he might do this if he felt that it was a good idea.

Later that day, 2 November, while Israeli forces seized the Gaza strip after heavy air and mortar bombardment, creating an acute food problem for refugees in the area, I had lunch with Dag Hammarskjöld and his Executive Assistant, Andrew Cordier, in New York. I was accompanied by two of my officials, John Holmes and Bert MacKay. Hammarskjöld was not too enthusiastic about my proposal (although he is reported to have begun to change his mind later that day). Indeed, he was quite cool to our idea of UNEF and very pessimistic about our chances of success. He did not reject the idea but spoke almost entirely of the difficulties. He emphasized the Israeli objections and pointed out that Ben-Gurion considered even the present United Nations observers to be intruders. In the course of this discussion, Hammarskjöld was extremely critical of Israel and its leaders and of Israeli methods of negotiation, particularly their habit of gaining a point, then moving on to gain more. (At one point, he expressed the view that Israel as a state would not last.) He seemed to believe that there had probably been collusion between the French and the Israelis before the invasion, but was very doubtful that the British were included.

One of the reasons for his failure at this point to support the proposal for an international force seemed to be his preoccupation with the Suez Canal negotiations on which he had been working with Messrs Fawzi, Pineau, and Lloyd. Clearly, he was bitterly disappointed that these discussions, which he thought were progressing favourably, had been frustrated by the invasion. He said that the advance towards agreement of the three Foreign Ministers had progressed further than was generally known. The Foreign Ministers had, in fact, gone beyond their instructions, and one of the problems was the difference between their positions and those of their respective Prime Ministers. Hammarskjöld's latest proposals had not been rejected by Fawzi at the time of the invasion. The Secretary General had even taken action to arrange a private meeting in New York between Fawzi and Mrs Meir and had some hope that this meeting might take place. He added that early in July, that is, before the nationalization of the Suez Canal, the Egyptians had approached the British and French about the possibility of negotiations with the Israelis, and had also spoken to him. He expressed his firm conviction that Nasser did not want the Russians to gain control in Egypt and would be cautious in going much farther with them. The Secretary General was much exercised over the situation in the Gaza strip. He believed from his reports that the refugees were being badly treated and that, as they were armed, there might be a terrible massacre. He said that if this did happen he would personally ask the United States to intervene with their fleet.

Sir Pierson Dixon was hardly more encouraging when I saw him again before flying back to Ottawa; he seemed uncertain and dispirited.

I arrived back in Ottawa at 6:45 PM to be met by the press and much urgent business. We had to draft and seek support for our proposed resolution on UNEF. Before reporting to my Cabinet colleagues the next morning at 10:00, I saw Neil Pritchard, the Acting British High Commissioner. Britain and France had informed the UN of their willingness to stop military action provided UN forces moved into the area to keep the peace and provided that Egypt and Israel accepted small Anglo-French forces in the canal area pending arrival of the UN force. I was considering how advantage could be taken of the terms of the Anglo-French reply to initiate police action. I asked Mr Pritchard to ascertain whether his government would be willing to accept at once token UN detachments and a formal relationship with the existing truce supervision organization of General Burns. After Pritchard left, I saw the Egyptian Ambassador for a few minutes, who informed me of the extent of Anglo-French bombing. British and French ground forces had not yet landed in Egypt.

Through every step of the way we were in close touch with Norman Robertson in London and Arnold Heeney in Washington (where Dulles had just gone into hospital with cancer), trying to keep our fingers on the pulses of our two closest friends and allies. Initial reaction to our initiative in both capitals was encouraging.

At the Cabinet meeting that Saturday morning, Mr St Laurent was also encouraging about the possibility of a Canadian initiative through a resolution to create a United Nations force. Our Minister of National Defence, Mr Campney, was enthusiastic. After about an hour's discussion, Cabinet approved in principle a UN police action in two stages. The first or short-term stage would be conducted by troops immediately available, but not exclusively British and French. We would try to get a US contingent sent in and Canada would also help. The temporary force would remain between Egyptian and Israeli forces until a more permanent UN police force could be provided. If the US government thought this approach was in any way promising, we would try to convince the British to agree and to undertake that there would be no Anglo-French troop landings until the UN Assembly had passed the required resolution which we proposed to sponsor with United States support. Alternatively, if they were willing, it might be sponsored by the United States.

While the Cabinet was still meeting, Heeney was instructed to get State Department reaction. They were interested but sceptical. Although they were as anxious as we were to extricate Britain from her present position, it was important that they should not give occasion for a charge of collusion with others to that end. That might deprive them of such influence as they now had. Furthermore, they were doubtful that the landings could be stopped at this stage. The addition of token forces to the Franco-British occupation might be taken as legitimizing the present operation. This would be interpreted as an attempt to bring under UN auspices an action which the majority of the UN opposed.

As a consequence of the US attitude, Cabinet approved in principle a somewhat different approach. The new proposal would have the Assembly create a Committee of Five to consider and report within forty-eight hours upon the immediate establishment of an 'intervention force.' The committee might consist of India, Brazil, Yugoslavia,

Sweden, and Canada (or one of the other 'abstaining' nations). Alternatively, the United States might take the fifth membership thus making all five supporters of the resolution of 2 November. We did not decide that we would necessarily put forward this resolution in its present or any other form. The situation was too fluid. Instead, Mr St Laurent and our colleagues approved the principle of such a resolution and left it to me to carry it out both in the timing and in the exact wording. In short, when I went back to the UN that evening, I had authority to introduce this kind of resolution if and when it seemed desirable.

I left for New York at 5:00 PM, arriving at 6:45 PM. I had, I remember, two or three press men with me on the plane who wanted to talk to me. All I wanted to do was look out the window and think about what I ought to do, how I ought to do it, and what the consequences would be. It was a rough flight, but I was so preoccupied with what was to face me in New York that I forgot to be air sick.

The response of the British government to our initiative had been encouraging. Eden was prepared to accept our draft resolution with a few minor changes. This gave me some confidence that the British (and French) would not begin their landings before the night of 4 November, and that if the Assembly took immediate action along the lines of our resolution no landing would take place while the recommendations for an international police force were being worked out. The Americans were also becoming more positive in their consideration of our new proposal.

Emotions were still running high, however. The Prime Minister of Australia issued a statement supporting Anglo-French intervention as 'the only quick and practical means of separating the belligerents and protecting the Canal.' He added 'that the author of the Suez Canal confiscation and the promoter of anti-British and anti-Israeli activities in the Middle East should now be represented as the innocent victim of unprovoked aggression is, of course, both wrong and absurd.' In this, Menzies' sentiments (as those earlier expressed by the Prime Minister of New Zealand) were in startling contrast to those emanating from the Asian Commonwealth members. An official Indian government statement had described the Anglo-French intervention as a 'flagrant violation of the UN Charter,' adding that it might even lead to war on an extended scale. The Prime Minister of Ceylon had said he could see no adequate justification for either the invasion of Egypt by Israel or the Anglo-French action. The Pakistan Prime Minister declined public comment initially on the intervention of British and French forces, but described the Israeli attack as aggression. Press criticism of the Anglo-French position was violent in all three countries.

The 3 November meeting of the General Assembly was another all-night session, lasting until about four in the morning. Immediately, I began discussions with Cabot Lodge (the United States Permanent Representative), Pierson Dixon of Britain, Arthur Lall of India (and through him the other Asian and Arab delegations), and the Secretary General. Cabot Lodge expressed broad agreement with Canadian views. Indeed, the State Department had evidently taken our initiative to heart and had prepared a draft for him which he felt would be acceptable to the Egyptians and consequently to the Afro-Asian group. His text was simpler than ours and with some minor alterations we adopted it as our own. Dixon was not too happy with the changes but agreed not to vote against it. Hammarskjöld still seemed pessimistic and worried. I can still picture my talking to the Secretary General. He did not think that we could get this going quickly enough to prevent the British and the French from being condemned as aggressors. When he came to see me again at my desk in the Assembly two or three hours later, he said he had changed his mind. He now felt this was our only hope and thought there was a good chance of it succeeding.

Our leg-men in the meantime were working among the senior advisers of the various delegations. In the lounge, in the corridors, interviews were going on, tactics decided, and quick decisions made. We worked quickly to get our resolution circulated informally that evening and, as a consequence, before our resolution was formally presented, John Holmes had learned from Lall that Loutfi, the Egyptian Permanent Representative, had explained our idea to Nasser and that he had agreed to it in principle. So we were in a strong position, as Krishna Menon of India discovered, much to his discomfiture, when he arrived at the UN on 5 November and opposed the force's creation.

There was another draft resolution on the agenda that evening. We knew about it in advance, and its presence was in accordance with our tactics. It was submitted by nineteen Asian and African members. This reaffirmed the United States resolution of 1–2 November (which it noted had not yet been fully complied with), authorized the Secretary General to arrange with the parties to implement a cease-fire and report on compliance within twelve hours. It also requested the Secretary General to arrange for withdrawal of all forces behind the armistice lines.

Following the presentation of the nineteen-nation resolution, I got up immediately to put forward the Canadian draft resolution. I introduced it with the following explanation:

The immediate purpose of our meeting tonight is to bring about as soon as possible a cease-fire and a withdrawal of forces, in the area which we are considering, from contact and from conflict with each other. Our longer-range purpose, which has already been referred to tonight and which may ultimately, in its implications, be even more important, is to find solutions for the problems which, because we have left them unsolved over the years, have finally exploded into this fighting and conflict ...

So far as the first and immediate purpose is concerned, a short time ago the Assembly passed, by a very large majority, a resolution which is now a recommendation of the United Nations General Assembly. And so we must ask ourselves how the United Nations can assist in securing compliance with the terms of that resolution from those who are most immediately concerned and whose compliance is essential if that resolution is to be carried out. How can we get from them the support and co-operation which is required, and how can we do this quickly?

The representative of India has just read to us, on behalf of a number of delegations, a very important resolution which deals with this matter. In operative paragraphs 2 and 3 of that resolution, certain specific proposals are made with a view to setting up machinery to facilitate compliance with the resolution. I ask myself the question whether that machinery is adequate for the complicated and difficult task which is before us. I am not in any way opposing this resolution which we have just heard read. I appreciate its importance and the spirit in which it has been put forward. But I do suggest that the Secretary General be given another and supplementary – not conflicting, but supplementary – responsibility: to work out at once a plan for an international force to bring about and supervise the cease-fire visualized in the Assembly resolution which has already been passed.

For that purpose my Delegation would like to submit to the Assembly a very short draft resolution which I venture to read at this time. It is as follows: 'The General Assembly, bearing in mind the urgent necessity of facilitating compliance with the resolution of 2 November, requests, as a matter of priority, the Secretary General to submit to it within forty-eight hours a plan for the setting up, with the consent of the nations concerned, of an emergency international United Nations force to secure and supervise the cessation of hostilities in accordance with the terms of the above resolution.'

I would assume that during this short period the Secretary General would get into touch with, and endeavour to secure co-operation in the carrying out of the earlier resolution from, the parties immediately concerned – whose co-operation, I venture to repeat, is essential – as well as endeavouring to secure help and co-operation from any others who he thinks might assist him in his vitally important task ...

The Canadian draft resolution was voted on first and resulted in 57 in favour, none opposed, and 19 abstentions (Soviet Bloc (9), Britain, France, Australia, New Zealand, South Africa, Egypt, Israel, Laos, Portugal, Austria). We were very pleased. Although our resolution instructed the Secretary General to report back within forty-eight hours, in fact a United Nations Emergency Force had been created. We did not put it exactly in those terms but that is what we meant. Even Britain and France did not vote against it. They could not very well after what Eden had said in the House of Commons, and the French had to agree. Further, we knew that the British government, in particular, was under increasing pressure from their own officials not only to go along with our proposal but to have Eden say the right thing so that the UN force could get him off the hook.

At 11:30 AM on 4 November, after a little sleep and breakfast, we met at the Secretary General's office. In addition to Hammarskjöld, Cordier, and myself, there were the delegates of Colombia, Norway, and India, plus, of course, Hammarskjöld's Under-Secretary, Ralph Bunche. Our task was the very important one of making certain that our resolution became reality. We worked quickly and well with the emphasis on the urgency of getting our troops into the area.

Hammarskjöld considered that General Burns of the Palestine Truce Supervision Organization would make a good commander for the emergency force. I agreed. He had cabled Burns about this and about the possibility of enlisting everyone engaged in truce supervision work as his staff so that there could be the nucleus of a force in being and on the spot.

We decided to omit from the force permanent members of the Security Council. Mr Eden in his reference to the United Nations force in the House of Commons had expected that the British and French forces on the spot would become part of any UN force. Certainly, I had contemplated this as an interim measure, as had the Secretary General. If Eden had been in New York, however, he would have realized that such a move was not likely to commend itself to the General Assembly. The Afro-Asians would never accept cloaking the Anglo-French occupation of Egypt with UN respectability. The very mention of the idea provoked Lall into saying that the British and French should be regarded as 'untouchables'! Further, it soon became necessary (for other reasons) to debar Soviet participation.

It was understood that if the Canadian delegation put forward a resolution for a United Nations emergency force, we would contribute to it. So during the day, after consulting by telephone with Mr St Laurent in Ottawa, I wrote formally to the Secretary General: 'The Canadian Government has decided to make an appropriate contribution, the details of which will be communicated to you shortly, subject to the required constitutional action which will be put in motion without delay.' That evening Mr St Laurent, in a speech in Toronto for national broadcast, made public our intention: 'The Canadian Government is ready to recommend Canadian participation in such a UN force if it is to be established and if it is thought Canada could play a useful role.' In the meantime, I made it clear to Hammarskjöld that Canada would be very reluctant to participate in the emergency force if we thought it would develop into a long-term commitment which did little more than maintain the unsatisfactory status quo until another explosive situation developed.

The General Assembly met again in Emergency Session on the evening of the 4th to consider the preliminary report by the Secretary General. Canada, Colombia, and Norway sponsored a resolution putting the Secretary General's recommendations into effect. A United Nations Command for an emergency international force 'to secure and supervise cessation of hostilities' would be established. Major General E.L.M. Burns was appointed on an emergency basis as Chief of the Command, and authorized to recruit the necessary officers. At the same time, the Secretary General was to take the administrative measures necessary for the execution of the resolution. The vote approving this resolution was 57 in favour, none against, and 19 abstentions (Soviet Bloc (9), Australia, Britain, Egypt, France, Israel, Laos, New Zealand, Portugal, Turkey, and the Union of South Africa).

In the course of that night, however, Anglo-French forces began their landings in Egypt. What a ghastly coincidence to have Anglo-French troops landing in Egypt at the very time the Soviets were crushing the two-week-old Hungarian people's rebellion. It was as brutal and grim a betrayal of a people as I had ever seen. I became almost as wrought up about the situation in Hungary as about the Suez business, though I had no instructions for any immediate action concerning Hungary, beyond condemning the action of the Soviet Union in the Assembly. If I had not been so deeply involved in Suez, I would have been much tempted to see if we could get a resolution to have a UN Assembly Committee fly straight to Budapest with the UN flag and some men in UN uniforms. This was an emotional reaction. It was a most exhausting time with these two things present in mind and heart. Prime Minister Nehru of India in a speech of welcome to the delegates to the UNESCO Conference in New Delhi declared: 'We see today in Egypt, as well as in Hungary, both human dignity and freedom outraged and the force of modern arms used to suppress peoples and to gain political objectives.'

Some hours in advance of the Anglo-French landings, Sir Anthony Eden had communicated to Mr St Laurent their intention forcibly to separate the combatants to ensure the safety of the canal. Their decision, he claimed, had been difficult, indeed agonizing, but he was sure that they had reached the right one. It was imperative that the British and French not wait upon developments in New York, however laudable, but immediately take a grip of the situation and create conditions under which an emergency United Nations force, once formed, could relieve them of their responsibility. Again, he sought our support for their decision and proposed that a meeting of the Security Council should be convened at ministerial level to try and arrive at a permanent settlement of the Israel-Egypt problem.

Mr St Laurent called me at the United Nations to discuss the Anglo-French action, Eden's pallid explanation, and a reply to the telegram. His telegram, which was approved by our other Cabinet colleagues, expressed a sentiment that I shared completely:

Your Acting High Commissioner personally delivered your message to me about ten thirty our time last night. Shortly afterwards I discussed its substance with Mr Pearson who was about to speak at the General Assembly meeting. I think we have a sympathetic understanding of your and France's position but we still regret you found it necessary to follow the course you are taking. Of course the motives and the known character of the actors do make a difference, but it is unfortunate that the events in the Middle East have cloaked with a smoke screen the renewed brutal international crimes of the Soviets. Many felt their satellite empire was crumbling and that they would not dare challenge world public opinion alone by resorting to the use of their military forces against their neighbours to reverse that trend. However they now say they too are restoring order in the face of inability of local authorities to do so; they may also say that they spare no precaution to avoid civilian casualties, that they give adequate warning so that these populations can submit to their will without suffering from military operations, etc. To you and to us all this is specious but the opportunity for comparisons resulting from what can seem to be disregard of United Nations Charter and the decisions made by its constitutional organs themselves and not by others for them, handicaps us in using world opinion as a check upon their outrageous conduct. We are also much concerned about the reactions of the Eastern members of the Commonwealth and can only hope that events will turn out to be such that the results will come to be regarded by all on our side as much more important than the measures taken to bring about such results, measures which we hope in the end will be brought about under the aegis of the United Nations with the co-operation of the United Kingdom and France acting as influential and helpful members.

During this crisis we have concentrated our thought and action upon seeking some way of resolving matters that would lead finally to some workable solution of Middle Eastern affairs with a minimum of damage to the unity of the Commonwealth and the Western alliance. Our concern with the seriousness of the large issues has led my colleagues and me to offer to have Canadian forces participate in whatever United Nations force is needed to secure an acceptable solution. We will continue to do our best to be of whatever assistance we can in a positive way but I would not wish to leave with you the impression that as seen from here the situation appears other than tragic.

On 5 November the government of Egypt formally accepted the resolution establishing a UN command after the first air drops of British and French paratroops in Egypt had taken place at Port Said and Port Fuad, climaxing several days of bombardment. On that same day, Israel conveyed to the United Nations her unconditional acceptance of the cease-fire which the Assembly had demanded.

As the Secretary General worked to complete his report on the principles on which a UN emergency force should be based, the Security Council met at the request of the Soviet Union who proposed that all member states 'and especially the United States and Soviet Union' should give military and other assistance to Egypt unless military action by France, Britain, and Israel against Egypt ceased within twelve hours. Inscription of this item on the agenda was rejected by a vote of 3 in favour (Soviet Union, Yugoslavia and Iran), 4 opposed (Britain, United States, France, Australia), and 4 abstentions (Belgium, China, Cuba, Peru). The Soviet Union, amid rumours of the movement of Soviet aircraft to Syria, then sent notes to Britain, France, and Israel warning that the USSR was prepared to resort to force if necessary to halt 'aggression' in Egypt. A simultaneous note to President Eisenhower containing pointed reference to the Soviet potential for nuclear warfare suggested that the USSR and the United States should unite their forces to halt Anglo-French intervention in the Middle East.

Britain firmly rejected the Soviet note, observing that if world conditions had been less grave, it would not have been answered at all. President Eisenhower, in his reply to Premier Bulganin, warned that the United States would oppose any Soviet effort to intervene by force in the Middle East, and termed the suggestion of Soviet-United States combined military intervention 'unthinkable.'

In New York the Norwegian Permanent Representative, Hans Engen, and I lunched with the Secretary General, now enthusiastic about the response to the United Nations force proposal and anxious that it not lose impetus. We were preparing a resolution for submission to the Assembly endorsing the Secretary General's second and final report on the formation of an emergency force. The report (and resolution) proposed the setting up of a small committee 'as a kind of Cabinet,' under the Secretary General's chairmanship, for the UN force. We became a member of Hammarskjöld's 'Cabinet' and for the next ten days had steady going, interspersed with some very emotional and difficult moments.

By telephone, Heeney conveyed to me three impressions of his concerning the current attitude of the United States administration:

1 their strong support (indeed enthusiasm) for the UN force and their desire to start planning at once for the United States contribution in terms of transport and logistic assistance;

2 their identity with us in linking provision of the UN force with the two-sided political settlement for Suez and Palestine; and

3 the gap in communications between the United States and the United Kingdom and France during the present crisis; this was causing them to turn more and more in our direction.

He also raised the question whether Canada and the United States should co-ordinate their planning at this stage on their respective UNEF contributions, since the United States had offered to provide us land and sea transport. I told him that I felt it would be a mistake for Admiral Radford and General Foulkes, the Chairmen of the American and Canadian Chiefs of Staff, to get in touch with each other at this stage, but perhaps later on when arrangements for the constitution of the UN force had been developed. There was a risk that the UN force might be given an excessively United States aspect, even though United States forces were not to be formally included.

The next day, 6 November, after the Secretary General had finished his report on which I had worked with him until two in the morning, and after it was announced that a cease-fire was to take effect at midnight, GMT, that night, I phoned Ottawa. I reported that the Secretary General was thinking in terms of a force of about 10,000 in all, to be available as soon as possible to supervise the cease-fire. I said that an added consideration for speed in considering the nature and size of a Canadian contribution was that some of the Soviet satellite states, notably Poland, were already offering contributions. I spoke to Mr Bryce, the Secretary of the Cabinet, regarding the Cabinet meeting to take place the next morning, and expressed the hope that the Canadian government would be able to offer a specific contribution, details to be worked out with the Secretary General and General Burns. I also hoped that the force would be available within ten days to two weeks. Mr Campney decided that he would recommend to Cabinet that the Canadian government offer as its initial contribution a battalion group of between 1000 and 1500 men, to be available within the time-period I had suggested to Bryce.

That evening Mr St Laurent received, in response to a talk that he had had with the Acting British High Commissioner in Ottawa the evening before, a further message from Sir Anthony Eden. He claimed to understand our feelings and anxieties. He had been living with them from day to day; his decisions had been taken only after scrupulous weighing of the moral considerations and with the Commonwealth always first in his mind. The Anglo-French operation, he suggested, had been a life-saving one for the Arabs; without it, Israel would have decisively defeated them one by one. Eden accepted that the British and French had incurred much criticism but he hoped that we would regard what they had done as paving the way for UNEF to become a reality, the consequence of which might now give the United Nations the strength necessary to preserve international law and peace in the world.

On 7 November the Secretary General received firm offers of immediately available forces from Canada, Colombia, Norway, Sweden, Finland, and Denmark (the Scandinavian contingents to function as a single unit). Prime Minister St Laurent announced in Ottawa that a Canadian contribution of battalion strength, with mobile base and full facilities for operation as a self-contained unit, was being made available. The Secretary General's second report had said, *inter alia*, that it was desirable from general experience that countries should provide self-contained units (in order to avoid loss of time and efficiency). In the first period, we thought it was likely that the force would have to be composed of a few units of battalion strength. As finally established, the force might call for adjustment in size and organization. Other important features of UNEF not already mentioned as contained in the Secretary General's report were: that it was 'to secure and supervise the cessation of hostilities' in accordance with the cease-fire and withdrawal resolution; that the force was of a 'temporary nature' and 'limited in its operations to the extent that consent of the parties concerned is required under generally recognized international law'; that the force 'although para-military in nature', was 'not a force with military objectives.'

As a footnote to the history of these times, the original draft of the report by Hammarskjöld and Bunche used the phrase 'to enforce and supervise the cessation of hostilities' and it managed to slip through our revision during the early hours of 6 November. However, I spotted it an hour or so later, just as the draft was going off to be reproduced. We changed it to 'to secure and supervise.' Thank goodness I noticed it, because we would have soon been in the soup if this force had been charged with the job of 'enforcing' anything!

In the debate on the Secretary General's second report (which was approved 64 in favour, none opposed, and 12 abstentions), I offered the following remarks in its support:

My Government has been proud to offer a contribution to this force and steps are now being taken by us to organize it as a matter of urgency. With the acceptance of this resolution – and surely it can be unanimously approved – the ending of hostilities can be confirmed and safe-guarded and work of peace-making begun on a solid UN foundation. Indeed, it has begun, but much remains to be done before it is finished. This is a moment for sober satisfaction, but certainly not for premature rejoicing. Yet it is hard not to rejoice at the thought that we may have been saved from the very edge of catastrophe – and saved, let us not forget, not by threats or blusters, but by the action of the UN. If we draw the necessary conclusions from the manner of our escape and act on them, perhaps we will not in the future have to get so perilously close again. I repeat, however, that much remains to be done, even in the first stage which is now underway. The organization of a UN force, from other than permanent members of the Security Council, is bound to be a task of great complexity and difficulty. We are breaking new ground, we are pioneering for peace, but if we take full advantage of this opportunity, I feel sure we can reap a rich harvest from that ground in terms of peace and security in the area concerned and, indeed, in wider terms as well.

We must now press on with the greater and perhaps even more difficult task of a political settlement; which will be honourable and just, and provide hope for security and progress for millions in this part of the world who have not known them in these troublous and distracting years. This is implicit in the resolution before us and that of November 3, which establish the conditions within which the UN force must operate. Until we have succeeded in this task of a political settlement, our work today, and the cease fire of yesterday – though they give us reason for hope and encouragement – remain uncompleted.

Nevertheless, the fighting has ceased, the process of restoration is to follow, and the work of peaceful settlement pursued in one part of this distracted and dangerous world. We cannot fail to be relieved and pleased about this, and to rejoice in the fact that the UN has made the essential contribution to such a good result.

If we had not acted swiftly and, I think, effectively here, we might have been facing today a conflict which perhaps would have engulfed us all.

I hope that we can pass this resolution quickly so that the UN force can be organized promptly and effectively and moved to the spot without delay.

Surely that is the most urgent and immediate duty for us to discharge at this moment, and I hope that we can do it without delay.

The next day, 8 November, before I flew home to Ottawa, I wrote to my old friend and former Cabinet colleague, Brooke Claxton: 'It has been a confused, dangerous and hectic time down here but there is, I think, a chance of working things out through the proposed UN force. You will know, as an old hand at this game, how much activity there has been for the Canadian delegation, and how wearing it has been. It seems that when there is a UN or NATO critical situation, someone always comes to the Canadian delegation and suggests "You are the people to propose something." Thank God we have Dag Hammarskjöld as Secretary General. He has really done magnificent work under conditions of almost unbelievable pressure. I have been very close to him in the last week, and I know.'

The working out of the legal basis for the operation of the force was extremely complicated, extremely difficult, and extremely important because it was a precedent for similar operations. There was a great deal of discussion in the Assembly about this. To work out the conditions under which the force would operate proved very difficult for the Secretary General, indeed, even more difficult later on. The Israelis would not allow us in any territory occupied or controlled by them and that included the Gaza strip. This was disappointing but not unexpected. Besides, there was nothing that could or needed to be done at that moment, because it was the canal area which we were trying to clear. The UN force was to lie between the two hostile armies, replacing the British and French. We had to get there quickly, but we had to get a legal basis for our operation on Egyptian territory – and this we had to do with a minimum of trouble. On 12 November, before Hammarskjöld left for Cairo, he told me that Nasser had insisted that the UN force should leave Egypt whenever, in the opinion of the Egyptians, their work had been accomplished. Looking back now I might have attached more importance to it than I did. Hammarskjöld, however, did not seem to take this too seriously. I remember reacting quite strongly, but not violently. I said, 'This is going to cause trouble in the future.'

Hammarskjöld said: 'Oh don't worry about it, because I told him that condition was quite inadmissible.' It did not turn out to be inadmissible eleven years later.

We got into difficulty about Canadian participation in the force. This is a story in itself, and the facts have been distorted more than once. No one in Ottawa had expected any difficulties to arise over the Canadian contribution to the force *per se*. We were simply taking our initiative in the UN to its logical end, and doing so with considerable efficiency, when we publicly announced on 7 November that:

To comply with the resolutions of the United Nations, the Canadian Government has agreed to make an offer of a Canadian contingent to the Emergency International UN Force for the Middle East. This proposal is subject to adjustment and/or rearrangement after consultation with the United Nations Commander. Arrangements have already been made for a group of Canadian officers to be available today for consultation with the UN Commander in New York, as soon as he arrives.

It is proposed to offer a Canadian contingent of battalion strength, augmented by ordnance, army service corps, medical and dental detachments, to ensure that the battalion group is self-contained and can operate independently from a Canadian base. The size of the contingent is expected to be over 1000 men.

Canada will be prepared to have this force lifted by the RCAF to the Middle East.

It is proposed to provide this contingent with a temporary mobile Canadian base for the first phase of its policing operations. The Canadian Government is prepared to use HMCS *Magnificent* for the purpose of transporting vehicles and stores to the Middle East and for use as a temporary mobile Canadian base for rations, medical supplies and munitions, fuel and limited accommodation stores. HMCS *Magnificent* will also provide a small hospital to accommodate the sick and injured in the force; accommodation for a force headquarters; and communications between the force and Canada.

I knew that we were going to have some difficulties from the moment I received a telephone message at the Assembly that what Ottawa had in mind for UNEF was The Queen's Own Rifles. I shuddered at this because we were, after all, participating in a United Nations force which was going to move into territory that had been Egyptian and from which the British army was about to be thrown out (or retired as gracefully as possible). Yet here we were sending in The Queen's Own, wearing essentially a British uniform with UN badges. The Egyptians had just been fighting the Queen's Own. When I voiced my misgivings to our Minister of National Defence, his reaction was so immediate and

violent that I did not pursue the subject. In any event, it appeared that
our only alternative to the regiment in question was The Black Watch!
What we needed was the First East Kootenay Anti-Imperialistic Rifles!

The Egyptian reaction to the prospect of Canada's Queen's Own was
entirely predictable. We were forewarned of Nasser's attitude on this
question by our own people in Egypt on 10 November, and by Mr
Cordier in New York. We had earlier in the day informed the Secretary
General that a Canadian advance party of approximately fifty officers
and NCOs would be ready to leave Monday, 12 November, by air the
moment requisite authority was given by Order-in-Council. At Cordier's suggestion, our advance party was delayed twenty-four hours.
Nasser apparently felt that it would be better if there were no Canadians in the force. He appreciated what we had done in New York, but
the Canadian contingent would lead to misunderstanding and, perhaps,
to incidents because it would be very difficult for his people to dis-
tinguish between The Queen's Own from West Surrey and The Queen's
Own from Calgary. We were also English-speaking, and had very
close ties with Britain and France. Therefore, he would prefer Canadians not to be in the force. Our Ambassador in Cairo, Herbert Norman, concluded that it was the constitutional issue (that is, our Commonwealth association) that raised real doubts in Egyptian minds, but
since they did not wish to offend us they stressed the risk of incidents.

In retrospect, this was not an unfriendly gesture on Nasser's part, it
was just being sensible. But at the time, I blew up at the Egyptian
Representative to the United Nations, Dr Loutfi, when he called on me
at the Drake Hotel on the evening of 11 November just after I had arrived back in New York from Ottawa. He tried to explain as delicately
as he could Egyptian misgivings about our participation. It amounted to
a personal appeal on behalf of Fawzi Bey to keep the Canadians out of
UNEF. I considered the Egyptian position outrageous. I informed him
that what he had said had put me in a very difficult, indeed an impossible, position and that I would find it very hard to report this to my
Prime Minister. Canada, I pointed out, had taken an entirely independent and objective position in the United Nations, not an easy thing to
do given our close and friendly association with the British. Having
taken this independent position, it would be very hard for Canadians to
be told that their troops were not considered independent. Canada had
proposed the establishment of the international force and Canadians
had taken up this idea with enthusiasm. Arrangements were already
under way and an advance party would be leaving Canada within

forty-eight hours. If the Canadian contribution were to be refused, this would be a repudiation of the Canadian government's initiative within the UN, and its effect on popular support for the UN in Canada would be disastrous. I admitted that there was a problem about Canadian uniforms, and perhaps some risk that Canadians would be mistaken for English soldiers. However, arrangements were under way to provide all forces with United Nations badges and special pale blue helmets. Furthermore, Canadians were likely to be stationed near the Israeli frontier. They were not likely to be in Cairo or the larger cities, and would have little contact with the Egyptian population. Canada, I explained, would not at all understand a situation in which the force was commanded by a Canadian but Canadian troops were not to participate. In fact, it would not be possible, I suggested, that General Burns command the force if this were true.

The Egyptians were creating general difficulties at the time by attempting to disbar from the force contingents from any country having a collective security arrangement with the British or the French. I suspected that the Russians, for their own selfish purposes, wanted the conflict to be continued and not settled by UN intervention, and had been encouraging Cairo to take a strong stand. It was undoubtedly true, however, that the Egyptians would have been suspicious of the UN force, even if the Russians had not been there to fan their suspicions. They may have thought that with a UN force of varied composition strung along the Suez Canal, their control of that canal would be more difficult to resume. They may also have thought that with world opinion opposed to British and French policy and with promises of help from Russia, they could, through the United Nations, press the British and French for immediate withdrawal irrespective of the entry of a UN force, or, failing that, drive the British and French out by force with Russian help. It appears possible that Nasser and the more extreme people around him were willing to gamble with peace in this sense. Indeed the next day, the Egyptian Ambassador in Moscow announced that more than 50,000 Soviet citizens had 'volunteered' to serve with the Egyptian forces.

Next morning, Monday, 12 November, I telephoned the Prime Minister, the Minister of National Defence, the Secretary to the Cabinet, and, to see if the US would go to bat for us, our Ambassador in Washington, outlining the conversations I had the night before, and emphasizing the necessity for keeping the whole matter completely secret at this stage. It would have been very unfortunate if the negative Egyp-

tian position regarding Canadian participation had leaked out while
there was any hope of clearing matters up, since the public reaction in
Canada would have been one of consternation and anger.

I also advised that we should delay passing the Order-in-Council
permitting troops to go to Egypt under UN command. This would be
an irrevocable step, in that it would demand the summoning of our
Parliament, and could be postponed for a few days without any serious
delay in preparing for Canadian participation. I suggested to Mr Campney that arrangements might proceed as planned, but that the advance
party be held back for a day or two. Both the Prime Minister and Mr
Campney agreed with this position. If there were press enquiries on
why the Order-in-Council had not been passed, we should say merely
that there had been some delay in clearing things with Cairo, and that
General Burns would not now be reaching New York until Wednesday
morning. We wished to have his report, therefore, before passing the
Order-in-Council.

Mr Campney phoned later in the day to say that he was proposing
to issue a press release about the immediate despatch of the airborne
advance force to Naples and the movement to Halifax of The Queen's
Own. I told him that, before anything was issued, I should check with
the Secretary General to make sure that an announcement of this kind
would fit in with his own plans. I therefore went to see Mr Hammarskjöld who, although the Assembly was in session, had left the podium.
He was with Selwyn Lloyd. While I was waiting, Mohammad Mir
Khan, the Pakistani delegate, also arrived to see him in a state of white-
hot indignation at the news that the Indians were acceptable to the
Egyptians as part of the United Nations force while the Pakistanis
were not. Mir Khan expressed himself in violent terms at this attitude
saying that not only should the Pakistanis be welcomed, but that they
should be at the Suez before the Indians, since they had been the first
to volunteer.

I then saw Mr Hammarskjöld who gave me an account of recent developments with Egypt. Most of the major difficulties concerning force
contingents had been cleared up; the problem of the Canadian contingent had not. Hammarskjöld, however, assured me that he would take
a strong stand about the Canadian force when he flew to Cairo on the
14th, and he was reasonably optimistic. He was quite satisfied with the
proposed statement from Mr Campney. Indeed, he said that our Minister could go further and say, if he so desired, that the Canadian plans
as outlined were in accordance with and had the support of the Secretary General. This, I felt, should help to meet any criticism in Canada

that we were acting too slowly. I phoned Mr Campney and gave him the green light on his statement, with Mr Hammarskjöld's addition.

The Secretary General had also shown me the telegram which he was sending to Nasser:

I thank you for your message of today, transmitted both in the course of your most welcome telephone call and through General Burns. I note that we are now agreed to start the operation and will send you separately details concerning the beginning of the airlift.

I share your trust that we all work for the same purpose of speedily ending the present crisis. I welcome the spirit of cooperation in which you on that basis have accepted Danish and Norwegian participation while suggesting a few additions which I for my part find that I should accept. On the other hand I note that you have left the question of Canadian participation open. I maintain my very firm views on the necessity of Canadian participation, but, as I declared over the telephone, I have to accept to discuss the position of Canada further with you when we meet in Cairo.

Agreement thus exists on starting the operation on the basis of the participation of the following countries: Colombia, Denmark, Finland, Norway, Sweden, India, Indonesia and Yugoslavia. The question of additions to this list will be discussed when we meet.

As I was leaving, I received a phone call from Arnold Heeney in the Secretary General's anteroom. He had experienced no difficulty in getting from Acting Secretary of State Hoover strong United States support for the Secretary General's stand in further discussions with the government of Egypt and, in particular, for participation of the Canadian contingent in UNEF. Indeed, Heeney had first broached the matter with Elbrick of the State Department (Hoover was tied up with the Senate Foreign Relations Committee) at 11:45 that morning. At 4:15 PM, Elbrick phoned Heeney to tell him that the US Ambassador to Egypt had already made representations to the Egyptian government in the sense we desired and that the State Department was considering what else they might do to help us.

That evening I saw three Canadian journalists who were attending the Assembly. They had no knowledge of any real problem about Canadian participation and were content with my explanation of the technical difficulties in constituting the force and getting it into Egypt, but, as I recorded at the time, I did not think we could keep the lid on this much longer.

On the day Mr Hammarskjöld left for Cairo to discuss with Nasser and Fawzi Bey arrangements for the admission of the UNEF, the Egyptian Embassy in Moscow announced that it had received instructions to request the despatch of Soviet 'volunteers' to Egypt. I wrote at the time:

'We are at a critical moment in the development of policy here re Egypt and a strong and consistent stand by the United States seems to me to be indispensable to success. An unequivocal and forceful position against Communist "volunteers" is the first necessity. If the Russians and Egyptians are bluffing in this, their bluff should be called and in a way that will impress the Arabs. If they are not bluffing, then it is all the more important that Washington acts firmly to halt their fatal course. This is all the more important now because of inevitable delays and difficulties in getting the UN force into operation, and hesitations and delays and difficulties in the British and French and Israelis withdrawing at once from their present positions. We can, I think, deal at the UN and through diplomatic channels with this latter difficulty, but only the United States Government can take adequate steps to counter, at Moscow and Cairo, the "volunteer" threat.

'These difficulties seem to me to underline the necessity of pressing ahead with the US Resolutions here on a Suez and Palestine settlement. There seems to be some feet-dragging at the moment here on these two matters. I hope the US delegation will get orders to counteract that here. We must take advantage of the present opportunity without delay or we will soon be in trouble again.'

Fortunately, President Eisenhower announced that the United States would oppose, through the United Nations, any Soviet military intervention in the Middle East. On the second question, the foot-dragging continued.

On 15 November advance units of the UN force (ninety-five Danish and Norwegian troops) arrived in the Canal Zone near Ismailia. Soviet Premier Bulganin, in personal notes to Sir Anthony Eden and French Prime Minister Guy Mollet, said the stationing of UN troops in the Canal Zone would violate the Constantinople Convention. He reiterated charges that withdrawal of British, French, and Israeli troops was being delayed to allow for preparation of fresh attacks on Egypt and demanded that Britain, France, and Israel pay reparations to Egypt for war damage. The Arab League meeting in Beirut announced their acceptance of the General Assembly's resolutions and their intention to invoke Article 41 of the Charter, which provides for Security Council sanctions against aggressors, if Britain, France, and Israel failed to withdraw from Egyptian territory.

The Secretary General was now in Cairo. I informed Escott Reid, then our High Commissioner in India, of Canada's difficulties and suggested that he see Prime Minister Nehru about the Egyptian objections to a Canadian contingent: 'The Prime Minister and I think that a word from Mr Nehru to Cairo might clear up any doubts and suspicions that the Egyptians might have and we would be most grateful if he could intervene personally ... Please act as quickly as possible as the matter should be decided within the next forty-eight hours, and in the right way.' Reid replied the same day, indicating that the Indians had needed no prompting in this matter: 'I saw Nehru shortly before one o'clock for twenty minutes. The Indian Government had, about three or four days ago, heard about the possibility of Egypt's objections to the inclusion of Canadians. He had immediately sent a message to Nasser to say that he was much distressed to hear this and expressing the hope that Canada would be among the countries which would be chosen. He had said that "Canada would be a good choice." About a day and a half ago Krishna Menon had sent a very strong message to Delhi from New York with a copy for the Indian Ambassador in Cairo. Nehru repeated several times that Krishna Menon's message was "in very strong language." Thus India had already made two approaches to Nasser. Nasser was naturally in a very excitable mood. India could not hope that Nasser would always do what they asked him to. Nehru said that nevertheless he would immediately get in touch with Cairo again.'

General Burns had now arrived in New York and we had a short talk on 16 November before we lunched with Cordier and Bunche. Burns was firmly of the opinion that the Canadian contingent would be the mainspring of UNEF and considered that it should go forward as contemplated. He felt that it might be desirable to add to the Canadian contribution but that it would be a mistake to subtract from it in any way.

During the past week, Burns had had two interviews with Nasser who told him that Canada and Canadians stood high in his esteem, particularly as a result of the role played by the Canadian delegation during the first Emergency Special Session of the General Assembly. The Egyptians had, however, expressed to Burns reservations about Canadian participation in UNEF. The fear that Canadians would be taken for British troops and that incidents would result was the reason given. However, Burns had some doubts about the real reason. He thought that the Egyptians had been encouraged to suspect that if the Canadians settled down along the Suez Canal the effect would be the same as if the Anglo-French forces had remained. In his assessment,

Burns was close to the opinion of our Ambassador in Cairo. The Egyptians clearly preferred a 'force of neutrals' and particularly a force composed of strong Afro-Asian contingents. This kind of force would, in reality, not have been a UN force but one which Egypt could have dominated. In these circumstances, Burns had concluded that to yield to the Egyptians on the Canadian participation would wreck the purpose and plan for establishing UNEF in Egypt. Burns had suggested to the Egyptians and confirmed to me that if they raised serious opposition to a Canadian contingent, and their objection was sustained, he would relinquish his command of UNEF. He hoped that the present plans for establishing the initial force in Egypt would proceed, even though it would be necessary to await the final word from the Secretary General. Burns was confident that Mr Hammarskjöld would stand firm about the Canadian contingent in his discussion with Nasser concerning the composition of UNEF.

Following lunch, and after reporting my conversation with Burns to Prime Minister St Laurent, I told Cordier that it was essential that we hear from Hammarskjöld as quickly as possible on his negotiations with the Egyptians. He accordingly sent the following message: 'Canadian Cabinet standing by. Situation critical. Most necessary positive reply.' On the morning of the 17th, I telephoned Mr Campney outlining the situation and suggesting certain press releases in case there was no change. However, a telephone call from Norman in Cairo, received around 9:30 AM, gave us reason to hope for a satisfactory result. Though the connection was very bad, a draft message was dictated by Norman and taken down by us. The draft was as follows:

Canada is welcome as a country from which elements of the UNEF be drawn. It is felt that the most important contribution that could be given at the present stage from that country would be air support in the transport of troops from Italy and for the current functioning of the UNEF in Egypt.

The question of ground troops of Canadian origin could best be considered when UNEF can assess its needs at the armistice line. The present situation seems to be one where it is not a lack of troops for the immediate task but of possibilities to bring them over and maintain their lines of communication.

Norman, in his talk, emphasized that the Egyptians appeared to be friendly and co-operative but were, or professed to be, very worried indeed about the arrival at Port Said for stationing on the Canal at this time of The Queen's Own Rifle Regiment of Canada. In my turn, I told Norman how worried we were about the impression we were receiving that the Egyptians were dictating to Hammarskjöld the composition of the UN force, that we could not accept any such principle, and we hoped that it would not be agreed to by Hammarskjöld. With this reservation, however, we were naturally anxious to help Hammarskjöld in his discussions with the Egyptians but we could not ignore the fact that the contribution we had promised had been accepted in New York as the most effective that we could make, and we had been encouraged to proceed accordingly. Norman pointed out that Hammarskjöld had told him that the message in question did not lay down any conditions for Canadian participation, which would have been improper, and that it did not involve any objection to Canadian forces in principle, but was concerned merely with the timing of their arrival and the area of their activity. Norman was to keep in close touch with Hammarskjöld and let us know as soon as the discussions were concluded.

After this telephone conversation, I went to the Secretary General's office. I discussed the situation with General Burns and Cordier. Burns felt that a Canadian battalion was still essential, though he felt also that even more important at the present moment was air transport and administrative headquarters, signals, transport, engineers, medical. If the Canadian government could, as suggested, supply an Air Transport Squadron and the 300 or so administrative personnel due to be flown that weekend, that would certainly be the most effective immediate contribution. The infantry battalion could come later in the light of circumstances. He could conscientiously give a military opinion as Commander of the force that this would be the most effective action on our part at this moment. Cordier agreed. I then talked the matter over with Mr Campney, who thought that the course outlined by General Burns could be agreed to, subject to the Prime Minister's approval. I then talked to the Prime Minister on the telephone, who thought that the suggestions mentioned above would be satisfactory. About noon on 19 November, after the meeting of the Advisory Committee, I spoke privately to Hammarskjöld about his visit to Cairo. I was, of course, mainly interested in the question of Canadian participation in UNEF. Hammarskjöld assured me that he had entered into no agreement with Nasser concerning the composition of UNEF. He had not departed from the position in principle that it was the UN General Assembly and not the Egyptian government which should decide the composition of the force. The Secretary General had, however, recognized that political reality made it desirable to take into account the Egyptian point of view. He had been faced in Cairo with some hard political facts and, in particular, with the fact that Egyptian public opinion was deeply involved.

In speaking to Nasser, Hammarskjöld had been hard-pressed to persuade him that there was nothing suspicious about the inclusion of such a strong Canadian contingent in UNEF. Hammarskjöld thought he had made some headway, but clearly Nasser continued to feel that Egyptian public opinion would be uneasy. However, Hammarskjöld had agreed to nothing which would exclude the sending forward of the Canadian infantry battalion when the UN Commander, having organized the present forces at his disposal, had occasion to consider necessary additions to the force to enable it to cope with expanding functions. There should have been no misunderstanding on this score.

The real problem about Canadian participation still seemed to be that the Egyptian government would have difficulty in explaining to the Egyptian public the situation which would arise, in particular in Port Said, when the British troops had gone or were going, and it appeared that they were being replaced largely by Canadians. Hammarskjöld suggested to me that this situation might ease considerably once the Egyptian government and people had become accustomed to the presence of UNEF and once the force itself had been deployed on its various functions. Specifically, it would be easier to deploy Canadian infantry in the Sinai or along the demarcation line than in the immediate vicinity of the canal, though the latter was not excluded.

In strict confidence, Hammarskjöld told me that his visit to Cairo was the toughest situation he had ever had to face. He had been under considerable pressure. He found Nasser friendly but confident and demanding, expressing a determination to continue the fight if the UN could not produce a solution. Nasser seemed quite prepared to call in the Russians if he had to, although he professed a very strong preference for not doing so. The Secretary General was extremely worried about the situation he found in Cairo. He was convinced that Nasser was keeping in close touch with the USSR and was ready to take advantage of their offers of assistance and advice if driven to it. In Hammarskjöld's view there remained considerable risk in the whole situation. At the same time, he did not ignore the possibility of a good deal of bluff behind Nasser's firmness. All through the crisis period Hammarskjöld never lost his cool.

In fact, our initial contribution to UNEF had been based on the understanding that Canadian 'fighting' troops would be included later. We knew General Burns felt this way and intended to call for The Queen's Own as soon as he needed them. We therefore kept our battalion at Halifax, ready to sail for Egypt on the aircraft carrier HMCS

Magnificent. When no request for The Queen's Own came during the next two weeks it became increasingly difficult to keep them waiting at Halifax and we began to press UN officials for a formal decision to include the battalion in UNEF. However, Herbert Norman telegraphed us on 4 December from Cairo that it was now General Burns' opinion that some other type of contribution from Canada would result in both a better organized and more effective force. It was now obvious that General Burns did not need Canadian infantry, as he had plenty of infantry from other sources, and that the most useful form of Canadian participation would be our highly trained and efficient specialist troops.

Thus ended the tortuous and complex question of the Canadian contribution to UNEF. On 10 December, Acting Prime Minister Howe summed up our reactions in a press release with this dry conclusion: 'We all regret that changes in United Nations plans have not made it possible for the battalion to proceed overseas as planned."

It was disappointing to the government and confusing to the public that our original offer of assistance had altered. I was therefore glad when General Burns wrote me on 24 December, 'as things have worked out the difficulty about sending The Queen's Own Rifles was a blessing in disguise,' since the 'Canadians in the base units have made all the difference in the world in the efficient operation of the administrative side of the military effort. We just could not have done without them.' Yet nobody believed me in the House of Commons when I said that the troops sent were what General Burns wanted. They talked scornfully, as Oppositions do, about our typewriter army, that we were not allowed to have fighting men in Egypt. It was quite embarrassing because I could not get it accepted politically in Canada that they were the most valuable part of the operation because of the essential work they were doing, work that had to be done by forces from one country.

There was much discussion in the Assembly about getting all the British and the French out. The British and the French did not want to withdraw until there was an assurance that the UN could do the job, and this took some weeks. Some people became very impatient about this, especially the Indian representative, Krishna Menon. It required a good deal of persuasion not to have Britain and France condemned as aggressors. They did, however, retire completely before the end of the year. But the Israelis did not, and were not proposing to leave without conditions. While one could sympathize with them, their conditions were not likely to be acceptable to the UN Assembly, and there was no point in discussing a political settlement until the Israelis withdrew to the original armistice lines. There was no longer much hope of progress toward a political settlement in any event. Things can be done under the incentive of terror and fear that can not be done when the fear disappears. There was a time for about a week or ten days, I think, when the Assembly could have passed a resolution providing the basis for a political settlement which could have been imposed by the United Nations. That moment soon passed, once the danger of world war passed. The Israelis knew this, and so fought very hard against withdrawal without conditions. I recall one or two sessions with Mrs Golda Meir about this in the Plaza Hotel. Eventually they did go back, but they stayed in the Gaza strip as long as they could.

I tried to get the Israelis out of the Gaza strip and succeeded by a UN administration. I had hoped that the strip could become a UN enclave for the refugees, but that was not possible. Egyptian civilian officials moved in immediately after the Israelis got out, although no Egyptian troops came with them. Gaza could have been the first territory to be directly administered by the UN. I do wish it had been possible.

The last and most difficult place to get the Israelis to withdraw from was a little town called Sharm el Sheikh. It commanded the entrance to the Gulf of Aqaba, the route to the new Israeli port of Eilat, now very important to their economic life. They refused to move until the last minute and then only after they received what they claimed was a legal and specific assurance (others claimed it was an expression of hope) that free passage through the Straits of Tiran would be ensured when they left. So it was, for a few years.

There was also great argument about opening the Suez Canal and clearing the way for ships. This was effected under the direction of General Raymond Wheeler, a former United States army engineer. One of the interesting byways in this whole situation (it was perhaps more than a byway) was the conviction expressed when the Users' Association was created and the principles established for the international operation of the canal. The Users were absolutely confident, rather arrogantly so, that the Egyptians could not possibly run the canal. They could not produce the pilots, and would have to appeal to the other nations. The Users had only to sit back and the Egyptians would be on their knees saying: 'Please run the canal for us.' That, of course, did not happen. The canal was run just as efficiently after the Egyptian take-over as in the past. I remember a Norwegian shipowner saying: 'Don't worry too much about the details of international control. They'll have to come to us in a few weeks and beg us to run the canal for them because it is a major source of their revenue and they want to make money out of it.' The Egyptians made more money from it than ever did the Suez Canal Company.

ॐ

When I came back to Ottawa I found myself faced with a very difficult parliamentary situation. At first, what we had done received apparently very strong support from the official Opposition. I think it is fair to say that Mr St Laurent, on the basis of private discussions with the Opposition leaders, did not expect any serious division in the House of Commons over our policies on Suez. However, bitter division there was, and we were condemned strongly for deserting our two mother countries. The Conservative attack was led by Howard Green (who in June 1959 was to become Secretary of State for External Affairs). Green accused us of being the 'chore boy' of the United States, of being a better friend to Nasser than to Britain and France, and claimed that our government 'by its actions in the Suez crisis, has made this month of November 1956, the most disgraceful period for Canada in the history of this nation' and that it was 'high time Canada had a government which will not knife Canada's best friends in the back.' Any feeling of exaltation and conceit or euphoria at our success in avoiding a general war in the Middle East (if in fact we had avoided it by our actions) was dissipated for me by the vigour of the assaults on my conduct, my wisdom, my rectitude, my integrity, and my everything else by an embattled Conservative Opposition. It was a very vigorous debate reflected in the general election of the next year. But I have always believed, and I think the evidence proves this, that the great weight of Canadian opinion strongly approved what we had done. Further, I am absolutely certain and will remain certain in my own mind that the New Commonwealth would have soon shattered over the issue had the British not backed down.

On 5 December 1956 I answered a private letter about the Middle East crisis with these words:

'The idea that we have somehow let the British down, in view of the results of their own action, and our efforts to make those results as helpful to them as possible, is pretty hard to take. Personally, I have great sympathy with their frustrations and provocations in the Middle East over recent months and with their impatience at the ambiguous and inconsistent line adopted by Foster Dulles, but how they expected to correct the situation by the kind of action they took, without consultation with anybody and in the sure knowledge that a large majority of the UN would be mobilized by the Asians and Arabs against them, is beyond my understanding. Their announced purpose was to stop the fighting and keep the Canal open, and that certainly, or at least the latter part of it, has not been achieved. Some people say that their real purpose was to overthrow Nasser, and that certainly has not been achieved. Of course, it might be argued that if the UN had not intervened Nasser would be out by now. That might well be the case, and I for one would shed no tears over his disappearance, but the price would have been bitter and irrevocable hostility with the Arab world; the withdrawal, as I think, of the Asian members from the Commonwealth, and an even better opportunity for the Russians to intrigue and extend their influence in the Middle East than they have now. In addition, the British and French would have been saddled with the occupation of Egypt which would have been an insupportable economic and political drain on them, while the majority of the UN would have inevitably condemned them formally as aggressors and tried to invoke sanctions against them, something which we managed to avoid during all the discussions of the last month ...

'While we could not, of course, give them support at the United Nations, we did try to take a stand which would help them out of their difficulties. No matter what Howard Green may say, and others like him, we know that the Government in London are grateful for the line we followed ...'

Nothing, I suppose, could better demonstrate than the Suez crisis the extent to which the United Nations had remained a central factor in our foreign policy. Our problem was, and is, one of long standing, how to bring about a creative peace and a security which will have a strong foundation. It remained my conviction that there could never be more than a second-best substitute for the UN in preserving the peace. Organizations such as NATO were necessary and desirable only because the UN was not effective as a security agency. UNEF was a step in the right direction in putting international force behind an international decision. The birth of that force had been sudden and had been surgical. The arrangements for the reception of the infant were rudimentary, and the midwives had no precedents or genuine experience to guide them.

Although this preoccupation with the organization and strengthening of peace was a deeply personal concern of mine, I was always anxious not to exploit any of our achievements in external affairs for political purposes. I had made a point of emphasizing, in and out of Parliament, that foreign affairs should be kept as far as possible on a non-controversial basis. Our successes were national, not partisan or personal. I must admit, however, that the announcement that I had won the Nobel Peace Prize for 1957 came at the right time, so far as my morale was concerned.

It was 14 October, when, for the first time in our history, Parliament was to be opened by the Queen. Her Majesty had been invited to do this some months earlier by Mr St Laurent, but an election had intervened, and when the day came it was Mr Diefenbaker who sat at the right of the throne and enjoyed the glow resulting from that Liberal invitation.

I was ruminating over these wrong and unhappy twists of fate in the spartan basement office to which I had descended from my ministerial chambers, when the telephone rang. It was a Canadian Press reporter asking me if I had any statement to make. I said: 'On what?' When he informed me that I had just been awarded the Nobel Prize for Peace, I dismissed what I considered to be his attempt to raise my spirits with some impatience. 'You mean,' I corrected him, for I had heard nothing about any award officially, 'that I have been nominated. There are many nominations every year.' 'I mean no such thing,' he replied; 'I'll read you the telegram.' He did and it seemed perfectly clear. As for my comment, my message to the world, it was short and to the point, if somewhat inadequate: 'Gosh!'

I just sat there, hoping that the press report would shortly be confirmed by an official message from the government of Norway. It was, and I ceased to lament my sad situation regarding the opening of Parliament under the wrong auspices. Needless to say, there was great excitement in the Pearson family. And that evening at the state dinner at Rideau Hall, I got almost as much attention as the new Prime Minister.

I accepted the Prize on 11 December 1957. I recall that Scandinavian Airlines diverted a plane from New York to Ottawa to pick us up. It was a wild night, with a blizzard blowing. The plane had to circle for an hour before it could land. I felt sorry for the other passengers who had been expecting a non-stop flight to Oslo, especially so when I discovered that they had not been served their dinner because the airline people had planned a special one to do us honour. This came as a surprise (and a challenge) because my wife and I had eaten at the airport while waiting for the plane to get down. When we were finally airborne it was near midnight, and they started serving this very special, deluxe, unprecedented, seven course Nobel Peace Prize dinner. We were almost to Norway by the time we got through the last course.

The ceremony at the University Aula in Oslo was impressive. Dr Gunnar Jahn, Chairman of the Nobel Committee, presented me with the Prize for Peace and I responded with the customary formal lecture, a portion of which is included here as what I hope is a fitting conclusion to this volume:

'A great gulf ... has been opened between man's material advance and his social and moral progress, a gulf in which he may one day be lost if it is not closed or narrowed. Man has conquered outer space. He has not conquered himself. If he had, we would not be worrying today as much as we are about the destructive possibilities of scientific achievements. In short, moral sense and physical power are out of proportion. This imbalance may well be the basic source of the conflicts of our time, of the dislocations of this "terrible twentieth century."

'All of my adult life has been spent amidst these dislocations, in an atmosphere of international conflict, of fear, and insecurity. As a soldier, I survived World War I when most of my comrades did not. As a civilian during the second war, I was exposed to danger in circumstances which removed any distinction between the man in and the man out of uniform. And I have lived since – as you have – in a period of cold war, during which we have ensured, by our achievements in the science and technology of destruction, that a third act in this tragedy of war will result in the peace of extinction. I have, therefore, had compelling reason, and some opportunity, to think about peace, to ponder over our failures since 1914 to establish it, and to shudder at the possible consequences if we continue to fail.

'The stark and inescapable fact is that today we cannot defend our society by war, since total war is total destruction, and if war is used as an instrument of policy, eventually we will have total war. Therefore, the best defence of peace is not power, but the removal of the causes of war, and international agreements which will put peace on a stronger foundation than the terror of destruction.

'If we could, internationally, display on this front some of the imagination and initiative, determination and sacrifice, that we show in respect of defence planning and development, the outlook would be more hopeful than it is. The grim fact, however, is that we prepare for war like precocious giants and for peace like retarded pygmies ...

'Spinoza said that "Peace is the vigour born of the virtue of the soul."

He meant, of course, creative peace, the sum of individual virtue and vigour. In the past, however, man has unhappily often expressed this peace in ways which were more vigorous than virtuous. It has too often been too easy for rulers and governments to incite men to war. Indeed, when people have been free to express their views, they have as often condemned their governments for being too peaceful as for being too belligerent.

'How can there be peace without people understanding each other, and how can this be, if they don't know each other? How can there be cooperative coexistence, which is the only kind that means anything, if men are cut off from each other, if they are not allowed to learn more about each other? So let's throw aside the curtains against contacts and communication.

'I realize that contact can mean friction as well as friendship, that ignorance can be benevolent and isolation pacific. But I can find nothing to say for keeping one people malevolently misinformed about others. More contact and freer communication can help to correct this situation. To encourage it – or at least to permit it – is an acid test for the sincerity of protestations for better relations between peoples.

'At the moment, however, I am more conscious of the unhappy fact that people are more apt to be united for war than for peace, in fear than in hope. Where that unity is based on popular will, it means that war is total in far more than a military sense. The nation at war now means literally all the people at war, and it can add new difficulties to the making or even the maintenance of peace.

'May I express one final thought. There can be no enduring and creative peace if people are unfree. The instinct for personal and national freedom cannot be destroyed, and the attempt to do so by totalitarian and despotic government will ultimately make not only for internal trouble but for international conflict. Authority under law must, I know, be respected as the foundation of society and as the protection of peace. The extension of state power, however, into every phase of man's life and thought is the abuse of authority, the destroyer of freedom and the enemy of real peace.

'In the end, the whole problem always returns to people; yes, to one person and his own individual response to the challenges that confront him.

'In the response to the situations he has to meet as a person, the individual accepts the fact that his own single will cannot prevail against that of his group, or his society. If he tries to make it prevail against the general will he will be in trouble. So he compromises and agrees and tolerates. As a result, men normally live together in their own national society without war or chaos. So it must be one day in international society. If there is to be peace, there must be compromise, tolerance, agreement.

'Above all, we must find out why men with generous and understanding hearts, and peaceful instincts in their normal individual behavior, can become fighting and even savage national animals under the incitements of collective emotion.

'That is the core of our problem: why men fight who aren't necessarily fighting men. It was posed for me in a new and dramatic way one Christmas Eve in London during World War II. The air raid sirens had given their grim and accustomed warning. Almost before the last dismal moan had ended, the anti-aircraft guns began to crash. In between their bursts I could hear the deeper, more menacing sound of bombs. It wasn't much of a raid, really, but one or two of the bombs seemed to fall too close to my room. I was reading in bed, and to drown out or at least to take my mind off the bombs, I reached out and turned on the radio. I was fumbling aimlessly with the dial when the room was flooded with the beauty and peace of Christmas carol music. Glorious waves of it wiped out the sound of war and conjured up visions of happier peace-time Christmases. Then the announcer spoke – in German. For it was a German station and they were Germans who were singing those carols. Nazi bombs screaming through the air with their message of war and death; German music drifting through the air with its message of peace and salvation. When we resolve the paradox of those two sounds from a single national source, we will, at last, be in a good position to understand and solve the problem of peace and war.'

APPENDIX 1

During December 1950 and January 1951, as I have outlined in Chapter 8, I served on the United Nations Cease-Fire Committee with Nasrollah Entezam of Iran, President of the General Assembly, and Sir Benegal Rau of India. My diary tells the full story of our abortive search for a settlement of the war in Korea.

December 15, 1950 (Friday)
The President asked the two of us, Rau and myself, to begin our 'cease-fire' work by lunching with him. Also present were General Crittenberger [United States Representative on the UN Military Staff Command] and [Ernest] Gross [Deputy US Representative to the UN], representing the Unified Command. At lunch we discussed very informally questions of procedure – how our Committee might operate. Gross was anxious that we should not give the impression we were mediating between two conflicting parties of the same status. We assured him that we would keep that very much in mind. We were one agency of the United Nations and the Unified Command another agency of the United Nations. The other party to the conflict was an aggressor.

Gross also seemed anxious for us to finish our work as quickly as possible and report to the First Committee, which has been called to meet on Monday. Gross was of two minds as to whether, on Monday, the First Committee should start debating Formosa, or whether we should try to postpone its meetings until we had finished our 'cease-fire' work. [John Foster] Dulles [then a Republican member of the US delegation to the General Assembly] apparently wanted to give his reply to Vishinsky's [the Soviet Foreign Minister] charge of US aggression against China, which, he says, he has been prevented from giving for some time. I argued strongly for not proceeding with the agenda of the First Committee until we had finished our work on the 'cease-fire' ...

After lunch we met in the President's office. Gross, who did most of the speaking for the Unified Command, produced a plan for a 'cease-fire' which would be satisfactory to the Unified Command. We discussed this for some time, emphasizing how important it was to keep it secret at this stage. I took the position that we would not confront the Chinese formally with an agreed plan submitted to us by the Americans, but that we should indicate to the Chinese that we had received information from the Unified Command about a plan that we thought reasonable and on which they might wish to comment; or produce some ideas of their own. The Unified Command made it clear that their plan was not submitted for bargaining. Our Committee thought it to be a very reasonable and sensible arrangement, which made a good many concessions to the opposite side, such as representation on the agency for the supervision of the plan ...

After Crittenberger and Gross had left, we discussed our further procedure and decided that we would not rush matters. We would first examine the Unified Command plan and not contact officially the Chinese Communists [a Chinese Communist delegation under General Wu Hsui-chuan was in New York in response to an invitation from the Security Council to discuss Taiwan] until we had some indication whether an official invitation to them to appear before us would be one that they could accept, or whether it might bring forth quick and final refusal. I suggested that we first send them, formally, a copy of the United Nations resolution establishing our Committee, and Rau, who was seeing them tomorrow, would then tell them unofficially that we would be glad to see them whenever they wished. But we should not rush them or put all our eggs in that particular basket. The Chinese Communists here might, in fact, have no authority to talk to us at all.

Meanwhile, the Secretary General had joined us and he said that he had seen the Chinese Communists during the morning and that they had been very tough ... Trygve Lie was a little depressed about all this, especially as he is not satisfied with the way in which our Committee is likely to operate. He does not think much of Benegal Rau, who, he says, does not know how to handle the Communists, or how to talk to them effectively. However, he was pleased that he had been asked to join us this afternoon ...

Trygve Lie then left us to see the Chinese Communists, who had asked for an appointment at Lake Success for 5.30. Later he told me about this visit over the phone, and asked me to join Entezam and Rau at his house in Forest Hills at 9:00 PM.

We found him excited and depressed over the afternoon meeting with the Chinese ... They told Lie that they had already informed Sir Benegal Rau that they did not recognize our Committee and were unwilling to talk about a 'cease-fire,' except on terms already made quite clear to Rau, who should have made them quite clear to us. Unless there were negotiations about a political settlement in Korea, the withdrawal of foreign troops, and Formosa, along lines indicated by Malik, they could not talk about any 'cease-fire.' They used language which, according to Lie, was completely 'Russian,' and very much like Malik's speeches in the First Committee. They complained that they had been sitting around waiting for the question of Formosa to come up; that they had heard on the radio that the Assembly was over, so they were going home to Peking. They asked Mr Lie, whom they thanked very warmly for all his help and courtesy, to get them 'passports' and travel accommodation on a BOAC plane leaving next Tuesday, and to arrange for a press conference tomorrow, Saturday, at 3:00 o'clock, where they would make a statement. Lie said that he pleaded with them not to do this, and that he talked 'very tough' with them. He told them that they were in danger of precipitating war if they broke off like this, because it would be interpreted here that the Chinese Communist Government had no interest in bringing the war in Korea to an end. He asked them to put off their press conference, and to see the Cease-Fire Committee, which, he said, had been working hard all day, and which was composed of men who were doing their best to make peace. The Chinese admitted that the three men were good and trying to make peace, but said that there were other men who were not good and, therefore, there was no hope for these three! In any event, they said these great matters of peace and war would have to be decided on the highest plane. The top men should get together. Lie asked them if they meant Mao, Stalin and Truman, and they indicated that that was the kind of thing they had in mind ...

Lie then asked Rau if the Chinese had not told him their decision that morning. Rau said 'no,' but that they did tell him that they could not negotiate a 'cease-fire' arrangement unless we were willing to negotiate other things as well. Rau had pointed out to them this morning, as Lie pointed out to them this afternoon, that the 'cease-fire' resolution *did* provide for general negotiation, but only after a 'cease-fire' had been worked out. They did not seem to understand this part of the resolution, which Rau tried to impress on them.

Rau then phoned to see if he could go and see the Chinese tonight. They had told Lie that they were going to be in to see Mr Truman on the television. When Rau phoned, however, he was told that they were not in, but would let him know in the morning whether he could see them then. If he does see them he will tell them how shocked he was to hear they were going away so soon; that we would be glad to see them before they go. Our hope was to discuss matters with them before their press conference. We agreed that if they won't see us, we must not consider that this means the end of our work, as they are merely officials of the Chinese Government. We should write them formally expressing our interest in seeing them in respect of this resolution, as representatives of their government, but adding that we would be quite willing to establish contact with their government directly in the matter, or with the North Korean military authorities. We agreed that we should also send a message direct to the Peking Government saying we had not been able to discuss these matters with their authorities here, and that we would be glad to discuss them with representatives of the Peking and North Korean Governments at any place that was mutually satisfactory ...

Lie was very depressed. He said his discussion with the Chinese this evening, and their demand for transportation home, reminded him very much of his interview with the German Ambassador the night the Nazis descended on Norway ...

Lie's view is that they are getting orders from not only Peking, but from Russia. As the Russians are leaving, they decided that they should leave too.

It has been a gloomy day, but I think that too much of this has been caused by the language and attitude of Wu and Company. After all, we shouldn't expect them to be polished and courteous and friendly. But apart from their methods, there is quite enough in the facts of the situation to warrant a good deal of pessimism about the results of our 'cease-fire' work. But at all costs, we must try everything before we admit failure.

December 16, 1950 (Saturday)
This was as interesting a day as yesterday, and about as discouraging. In the early morning, Gerry Riddell [our Permanent Representative] and I drafted a letter to send to the Chinese Communists before they held their press conference this afternoon ... I also worked on a draft of a communiqué which could be given to the press after the Chinese conference, in which the Chinese statement seemed to make such a communiqué desirable. It would emphasize that flat rejection of any discussions by the Chinese Communists here did not necessarily mean the end of our work; that we must try to keep these negotiations going on, even if it means a trip to Peking! This is desirable, both on political and military grounds.

At 11:00 o'clock Entezam phoned me ... Rau had reported to him that his efforts to get in touch with the Chinese Communists had been unavailing. They claimed that they were too busy to meet him during the morning, but would see him that evening ...

I met Entezam and Rau at the former's hotel at noon, and they agreed with my draft to the Chinese with one or two minor changes. We then had it typed and despatched by messenger to the Chinese at the Waldorf, having previously telephoned them that it was coming.

After luncheon we motored out to Lake Success and met in the President's office there with the Secretary General. He said that there had been no indication of softening on the part of the Chinese, who would be arriving any minute for their press conference. We then listened, through a loud speaker in the office, to Wu read his statement to the press. It was not too bad and

did not include any reference to their departure, or to their refusal to negotiate with the Cease-Fire Committee ...

While we were in one room, the Secretary General discussed matters with
the Chinese (after the press conference) in an adjoining room. He found out
that they had not received, or at least read our letter, so he proceeded to read
it to them from a copy which we had given him, and it was then translated
into Chinese. They were very interested, but indicated that they would make
no change in their plans for departure. Lie then asked them if they would
like to see the Cease-Fire Committee, which was meeting in the next room.
They said that they had high regard for the members of the Committee personally, but that this was a political matter which they were not able to discuss with the Committee officially, as they did not recognize the resolution
setting it up. They said, however, that they would like to see Mr Entezam,
as President of the Assembly, not as a member of the Committee. Entezam,
therefore, had a half an hour with them, which he said was devoted largely to
an exchange of courtesies, ardent assertions of Asiatic solidarity, expressions
of appreciation on the part of the Chinese of the motives behind Asian intervention in the Assembly, and of fear that the Americans, however, would
make peace in the Pacific impossible. Entezam claims that he gave them
some good advice, but that he did not talk to them at all about the Cease-
Fire resolution. We will leave that to Rau who is having dinner with them
tonight.

Meanwhile, we decided not to issue any press communiqué, but to tell our
press officer to emphasize to the journalists that our work had not finished
and that, if necessary, we would get in touch with the Peking and North
Korean Governments direct. The chances of this happening are, however,
very slight. It is difficult to see what can be done, but we will be a little
clearer on this point tomorrow when Rau reports about his dinner with the
Chinese.

In addition to sending the letter to the Chinese Communists here, we had
the Secretary General cable it to the Peking Government direct. Wu, according to Trygve Lie, did not seem to worry about us going over his head in this
manner.

December 17, 1950 (Sunday)
Our Indian colleague, who is becoming more and more spiritual and ghost-
like as our work proceeds (it has been a very great strain on his far-from-
robust physique), spent about four hours with his Chinese friends and found
them, as usual, friendly and full of talk about peace and Asian co-operation.
At the same time, whenever he confronted them with the concrete questions
and problems arising out of the present situation in Korea, and in the United
Nations, they did not budge an inch from the stubborn position that they
had previously taken; namely, that all that was required was for the American aggressors to get out of Korea and Formosa and stay out. They insisted

that the 'cease-fire' resolution was merely a trap, and one which they would not walk into. They also indicated that no fire crackers had been set off in Peking at the possibility of our arrival there to negotiate! In fact, they thought we would be wasting our time in going to Peking, which, I suppose, we would. Rau was very discouraged about it all and I think that he is losing most of his illusions about negotiating with Communists. However, he was cheered up by the farewell remarks of the Chinese. They urged him not to give up hope, but keep on working with the other members of the Committee for a 'cease-fire' and peace. Rau seemed to think that this meant that the door was not closed, but, of course, it may only mean that we are to keep on working to get the Americans to alter their 'aggressive' policy.

The three of us then discussed the procedure we should follow at the First Committee tomorrow. After making our interim report (I think Rau should do this) we can try to get the Committee to adjourn until we make our final report ... I suggested that we meet again at 8:30 and get Gross and [Gladwyn] Jebb [the British Permanent Representative to the UN] to attend. I said that I would arrange the meeting. Later I telephoned Gross and Jebb and they will be on hand.

I also had a talk this afternoon with the Secretary General who thinks that we should now call off 'cease fire' negotiations altogether, admit failure, pass the 6-Power Resolution, and then refer the whole question of what action, if any, should be taken against the Chinese, if they continue aggression in Korea, to the Collective Measures Committee set up in the United Action For Peace resolution. I do not know whether Lie is influenced more by his desire to spend Christmas in Norway, or to strike another blow for collective security in the United Nations. He kept warning me that we must now be very careful in the 'Cease-Fire' Committee not to give the impression that we are 'appeasing' the Chinese. I had thought of suggesting that he should come to our meeting tonight, but after talking to him, decided that he would not be much help.

December 18, 1950 (Monday)

We met last night from 8:30 until nearly midnight at the Ritz Towers. In addition to the President, Sir Benegal and myself, there were present also Gladwyn Jebb, Ernie Gross and a colleague from his delegation, and Dayal of the Indian Delegation.

We at once tried to urge on Gross the advantages of discussing and voting on the second Asian Resolution to remove Chinese fears that we were not serious about negotiating Far Eastern issues once the 'cease-fire' had taken place. We pointed out that this did not involve any additional commitment, because, in fact, we were committed to this course of action by the Preamble of the Asian Resolution we had already passed. We also argued that Mr Attlee and Mr Truman, in their communiqué from Washington, had committed themselves to the principle of negotiating with the Chinese Communists. Why, then, not proceed at once with the second Asian Resolution, which would improve the atmosphere and, therefore, help the work of the Cease-Fire Group.

Jebb would have gone even further and amended the Resolution to indicate that in the negotiating committee referred to, there would be included the US, UK, USSR and the Peking Governments ... Gross thought that we were paying too much attention to Chinese Communist suspicions, and that in our preoccupation with their worries about a trap, we were losing sight of the fact that we might be making a trap for ourselves. He said that his government did not intend to back down from the Truman-Attlee communiqué, or to exclude the Chinese Communists from Korean negotiations, but that was a very different thing from specifically including them in a UN resolution at this stage. It is, of course, easy to understand the American position on this point, even though we may not approve of it. A resolution of this kind, which would specifically include the Chinese Communists in a negotiating committee, would, in fact, be a formal recognition of them, and almost an equally formal exclusion of the Chinese Nationalists. Gross was quite certain that Washington could not accept this.

I then tried to argue that we should leave the membership of the negotiating committee entirely open, and discuss and pass on the rest of the resolution. The President of the Assembly did not like this much, as he felt that once the resolution was passed, the names of the states would have to be filled in and we would be almost immediately up against the question of Chinese representation – the main point at issue. We had much talk but made little progress, and at the end of the evening I suggested that possibly we might reach agreement on the following course. When the committee met, the Cease-Fire Group would make its interim report, and in that report emphasize that 'cease-fire' and negotiation were tied together, and as soon as one was arranged, the other would begin; also that in the negotiation, the Chinese Communists would naturally be included in some appropriate form, making reference to the Truman-Attlee communiqué, to show that this was in the minds of those two governments. The US and UK would then support this statement, thereby, it was hoped, removing Chinese Communist fears and suspicions. This suggested procedure was generally approved.

However, when I reached Lake Success this morning, I found that there was great confusion as to how we should act. Sir Benegal had overnight changed his mind on two things. First, he did not want to make the report on behalf of the Cease-Fire Group, as I gathered he had received messages from New Delhi warning him against taking too active a part in our work. In fact, he indicated to me that his Prime Minister had said that if I were not on the Group, he would not be able to continue. Apparently they have some confidence that I will not allow Sir Benegal to get into too much trouble! He also did not think now that we should make a long statement as an interim report, in an effort to argue away Chinese fears. He felt that this might merely produce a debate which would not improve the atmosphere. He felt, therefore, that I should make a short interim statement, merely reading the cable we had sent to Peking, and explaining factually what we had done. After discussing the matter with Gross and finding that, in any event, the US would not be able to support the longer statement along the lines indicated last night, I agreed to do this ... When the committee met, therefore, I made my report, which got a friendly reception, even from Malik, and then after a considerable wrangle we adjourned ...

Meanwhile, after a talk with the Secretary General we decided that Rau should try to see the Chinese once again before they left, and report to us tomorrow. If there is no response from them or from Peking by Wednesday, we will then suggest to the Chairman of the Political Committee that he tell his members that there will be no meeting until January 3rd. By that time we will have our formal report ready, explaining our failure. We also will have a couple of weeks without any United Nations meetings on Korea and this may be helpful. As long as the Cease-Fire Group is formally in session it will, presumably, be a little more difficult for the Chinese to begin their offensive in Korea, or certainly to justify it. It will be more difficult for the US to summon the Political Committee for further and more decisive action against the Chinese. We may have to do that later, but we now have time to think things over and discuss the implications of any further action.

December 19, 1950 (Tuesday)
Rau paid his farewell visit to the Chinese this morning and he told Entezam and me about it at noon. He got nowhere, though on leaving Wu told him that they might be back again after their visit to Peking. This is probably an attempt to befuddle and deceive us, though you never can tell with these chaps. Rau said that he did his best to persuade them that they were making a big mistake in ignoring the cease-fire discussions.

We then talked about the issue of a communiqué along the lines of that worked out yesterday. Entezam and I had doubts of the wisdom of this in view of the uncompromising attitude of Peking. So we agreed to abandon our press statement and, instead, send a further telegram to Peking in an effort to remove the misunderstanding and fears that Wu had expressed to Rau. I agreed to alter the draft press communiqué accordingly. We also agreed to send a final message to Peking Thursday (if we had not heard from them), indicating that we would go ahead next week with our final report, not waiting any longer for their views. I said that I would draft that.

In the afternoon I put these two documents together – and told the US and UK what we were doing. The former won't like it.

We met at Entezam's at 5:30 and I read them the messages. Rau thought our telegram to Peking should be more positive in its assurances that if a cease-fire could be arranged, the Chinese Communists could expect negotiations to begin at once and to be included as members of any UN Committee for that purpose. But I didn't think that we should go too far. After all, we couldn't bind the UN, though we could commit ourselves, and also the Asian sponsors of the Resolution who, earlier in the afternoon, had been consulted by Rau.

Our telegram went off tonight, and I am going to Ottawa tomorrow. Wu & Co. left this afternoon issuing a final statement which did not help – though it might have been worse.

Their mission was certainly a failure and possibly worse, as it may have hardened them in their position, without giving them any understanding whatever of the United Nations or of the United States.

January 2, 1951 (Tuesday)
On my arrival from Ottawa, and after a discussion on recent developments with Riddell, we met the other members of the Cease-Fire Group, Mr Entezam and Sir Benegal Rau, at 11:00 AM, and went over the final draft of our second report with them. Rau's position remained that the report must contain no comment or observations, but be strictly factual and objective. I was equally anxious that the report should not give the impression that we were mediating between two parties of equal status; that the facts should make it quite clear who was responsible for the break-down in the cease-fire effort; and, finally, that we should accept, in our report, the Unified Command's proposals for a cease-fire as a reasonable basis of negotiation.

Rau, somewhat reluctantly, I think, agreed to the changes I suggested to make the above points clear.

He then mentioned the possibility of ending our second report with a statement of principles which, in our opinion and in that of the Committee if it were accepted, might be the basis for a political settlement of Korean and Far Eastern questions. This procedure would re-assure the Chinese that a cease-fire would be followed by political discussions. Entezam and I thought this idea a good one, providing it was made clear in any such statement that the fighting must stop before negotiation could begin; and that we were aware of the fact that a resumption of the fighting might take place any minute ...

Before giving final agreement to the statement, I said that it should be discussed with the Americans, because we did not wish to disagree with them at the Political Committee concerning it. Entezam and Rau agreed to this. Riddell and I, therefore, had lunch with Gross and Ross and showed them the draft of the statement, as well as the final draft of our second report, to which it would be added. They made one or two suggestions for amending the final report, which were acceptable. They also agreed, in principle, to a statement of principles (somewhat to my surprise), but wished to have our draft changed to make it quite clear that the United Nations and Chinese forces were not of equal status and that we were not asking for discussions until a cease-fire had been arranged.

In the afternoon, the Cease-Fire Group met again and revised our statement of principles in accordance with the morning and lunch-time discussions ... Rau, to our surprise, said that he now could not accept the statement without reference to Mr Nehru, and as the latter was flying to London it would be impossible to get such acceptance before the Political Committee meeting on Wednesday. Therefore, we had to give up the idea of making the statement part of our second report, but hoped that it might be produced later as a separate document. I redrafted the statement accordingly.

In these discussions, the primary consideration we had in mind was the desirability of exhausting the possibilities of conciliation, to the satisfaction in particular of the Asian states, before proceeding to any resolution condemning the Chinese as aggressors, and to do so in a manner that would not be made ludicrous by the development of a major military offensive in Korea. The Americans, for obvious reasons, were anxious that neither the Political Committee nor their delegation should appear to be dilatory in the face of Chinese aggression. On the other hand, they seemed conscious of the desirability of being assured of as much support as possible for subsequent Assembly action in regard to Korea ... It seemed to me that, by adding to the Cease-Fire Group's report the statement of principles, or by a separate statement of principles from the Group, and by having this statement communicated to the Chinese by the President, it would be possible to carry through to its final stage the conciliatory process which so many different elements in the Assembly seemed to desire.

Tonight, Riddell and I gave a dinner for representatives of those governments which had land forces participating in Korean operations, and brought them up-to-date on cease-fire developments ...

I suggested to them the possibility of a supplementary statement of principles, and found very general agreement on this. We arranged with the Norwegian delegate that at the meeting on Wednesday he would enquire whether principles for a negotiated settlement had been discussed by the Cease-Fire Group, and, if so, could we make a report concerning them. This would give me an opportunity to reply that we would be glad to do so. Later, Rau and Entezam agreed to this procedure.

January 3, 1951 (Wednesday)
The Political Committee met at 10:45 and Rau submitted our Second Report with a very short statement. Austin made a moderate and restrained speech, in spite of a most violent and provocative attack previously by Malik, and agreed that the 'door should be kept open for honourable negotiations.' This gave Sunde, the Norwegian, a chance to ask his question. I answered it, and we adjourned for 48 hours to give the delegations time to study our report, and the Cease-Fire Group time to prepare a statement of principles. The machinery is now in motion. We *may* have begun something important.

January 4, 1951 (Thursday)
At this stage, the Commonwealth Conference of Prime Ministers in London began to intervene in our Korean cease-fire deliberations.

I also received a telegram from Wrong in Washington expressing the anxiety of the United States authorities and United States public opinion over the inactivity of the United Nations in dealing with the Korean situation in the face of the 'massive attack' which was now in full swing. The State Department, through Hickerson, did not object to the 48 hours delay, but hoped that we would deal with our report on Friday, as well as any supplementary statement of principles, thereby paving the way for condemnatory action by the middle of next week, if the Chinese Communists flouted our cease-fire recommendations.

January 5, 1951 (Friday)

A telegram was received this morning from the Prime Ministers, asking for 'at least a week's delay' on the part of the Political Committee, as they desired to make new proposals for a Korean and Far Eastern settlement. Also, our statement of principles was not only not to be discussed at Friday's meeting, but it should not even be made public.

This message worried Jebb and myself because we felt that neither the United States nor the 50-odd members of a United Nations committee would think much of the idea of a delay while a Commonwealth meeting decided in London what should be done. I sent, therefore, a telegram at once to the Prime Minister, and another to [Norman] Robertson, expressing my view that we could not, and should not ask for a delay beyond a few days; that if we did the United States delegation might withdraw from its agreement to support an 'intermediate stage,' and might insist on proceeding at once to the next stage with a resolution declaring China an aggressor. This is, of course, what we are trying to avoid at the moment, as it would cause a serious split in the anti-communist forces with practically all the Asians abstaining on any condemnatory resolution. They would claim that they had every right to do so if we had not exhausted every possibility of negotiation along the lines of their own (Asian) resolution, introduced some time ago, and now to be replaced, we hoped, by our more suitable statement of principles; more suitable because it combined cease-fire, Korean settlement, and Far Eastern discussions in one package ...

At a meeting of our Cease-Fire Group in the morning, Rau said that he had not yet received approval from Nehru for our statement, but had received an instruction to press for a postponement, which he proposed to ask for. Jebb and I told Rau that it was quite impossible for the Americans to accept a long delay.

We agreed, therefore, that at the meeting I should make a short statement saying that the Cease-Fire Group needed further time for its report and asking for an adjournment until Tuesday. This course was followed, though many of the delegates are grumbling about the delay.

The Americans accept the situation, but reluctantly, and only because they feel that precipitate action at this stage on a statement of principles will not secure for them the maximum of support for the next stage, condemnation, which will follow the refusal of the Chinese (which they expect) to accept *any* statement of principles. Austin is more impatient about delay than the people in Washington and will explode if he is not permitted to make a tough speech before long. It is also quite clear that once the 'intermediate stage' is tried and has failed, the Americans will expect us all to rally round the 'condemnation.' They are already working on the points which should be included in any 'aggressor' resolution and have circulated a memorandum on this subject to various delegations. This has caused much uneasiness as it seems to assume action against the Chinese which cannot, in fact, be made effective without further steps, which might lead us into a futile war. One day soon, we will have to face this problem of Chinese aggression; meanwhile, we can still work on the 'principles for a settlement.' This might be called an honest and determined delaying action. I hope it is not confused and made more difficult by impracticable suggestions from London.

January 6, 1951 (Saturday)
Telegrams and telephone calls to and from London. The Prime Ministers spent most of yesterday on Korea, but, from our distance, much of their discussions seemed unrealistic in that it did not appreciate sufficiently the state of American public opinion, or the facts of war. They emphasized the need for caution, delay and recognition of the Chinese position. Action in our group of three is based on all these considerations, plus the additional necessity of recognizing the mounting feeling of exasperation in the United States, and of not ignoring the principles of the Charter of the United Nations. How to reconcile all these things is the problem.

Mr Bevin has tried to do it in new proposals which he circulated to the Prime Ministers today, which are on their way to us and are apparently to take the place of our statement of principles ...

The confusion in which we had been working was removed by the receipt of a telegram this evening with the details of the Bevin plan. It seems to promise China support for membership in the United Nations, as well as her claim to Formosa, if only she will negotiate, and it does not seem to lay it down specifically that a cease-fire must precede any political discussions, something on which we have always stood firm in our cease-fire discussions.

There is absolutely *no* chance of this scheme getting any consideration in Washington. Nor should it. I don't see how we could support it at all at Lake Success, in view of the stand we had previously taken of no discussion of issues before the fighting stops.

The telegram communicating these new proposals caused some consternation in New York among the Commonwealth delegations (except India) and the feeling was shared in Washington by [Sir Oliver] Franks [the British Ambassador] and Wrong and the Americans, to whom they showed the new plan. It will take far more than a week's delay to get any support for this scheme. Mr St Laurent, in a telegram to me, seemed to appreciate the position more than the other Prime Ministers did. Their instructions were rigid, to get a week's delay (which we couldn't) and then press the United States to give favourable consideration to the Bevin plan. Mr St Laurent gave me more freedom of action, and seemed, rightly, to understand the difficulties of 'keeping in step' with both Washington and India in this matter.

January 7, 1951 (Sunday)
Messages from London have bewildered us by references to Korean talks in the Security Council, a queer misconception. They also indicate, to our surprise, that in the consideration given in London by the Prime Ministers to Korea, there had not been any discussion of our statement of principles as such. Apparently at the Friday meeting the text of our statement was not available for circulation by the United Kingdom or by ourselves as it had not reached London because of some delay in transmission. Nehru certainly had a text, but did not produce it. It was hard to understand this, unless it was due to the fact that Nehru did not wish to discuss any text until he had ascertained the reaction of Peking to it. The draft text, though it was not before the Commonwealth Prime Ministers, certainly was before the government in Peking, but at this stage, Nehru had probably not received their reaction.

The messages from London today, both by telephone and telegram, though they have added to our information have not, certainly, removed our doubts. I, therefore, telegraphed another statement of our position to London, arguing against the effort to secure a week's delay, unless we were willing to run the risk of unfortunate consequences, and also pointing out that the Bevin plan did not seem to us to be an improvement over our own statement of principles. I suggested that the Prime Ministers should forget the Bevin plan and work on the text of our statement, sending to us as quickly as possible suitable amendments ...

January 8, 1951 (Monday)
In the afternoon, the Political Committee held its meeting ... and Jebb made his proposal for an adjournment to Thursday in a very good speech, arguing that it was not unreasonable that we should be given a few more days to complete our statement of principles! He stressed the desirability of looking before we leaped, so that we would all be able later to leap together. No doubt the Americans thought that by this statement Jebb meant that when the time came to leap, all the Commonwealth would leap with the United States into condemnation and sanctions! They may be fooling themselves about this.

Though Wrong had telephoned me from Washington that the Americans would, at best, abstain on any vote for adjournment, and would probably have to express their opposition to it when the time arrived, Austin took the matter very calmly and seemed, indeed, quite happy about the delay. Before the meeting, in fact, when Austin approached me at the committee, I thought it was to express his indignation at the suggestion that we were going to stall along for some days more. Instead, he patted me amiably on the shoulder, and congratulated me on the hard work we were doing in the Cease-Fire Group, and how reasonable it was that we should be given lots of time!!! The same old story of the impossibility of knowing whom to believe in any expression of American policy ...

January 9, 1951 (Tuesday)
At yesterday's London meetings, from the telegrams which we received overnight, and from a telephone conversation with Robertson, it became clear that Nehru would not permit Rau to sponsor our present statement; that it must be changed to recognize the fact that the Chinese talks must include the questions of Formosa and UN membership, the former to be discussed 'in conformity with existing international obligations,' which meant the Cairo Declaration [of 1 December 1943, issued by Roosevelt, Churchill, and Chiang Kai-shek, which stated that Taiwan, ruled by Japan since 1895, would be 'restored' to China and also called for a 'free and independent Korea']. It was agreed that Bevin's Saturday plan should be given up, and that the Prime Ministers should examine our statement of principles ... However, further messages from London indicated that the changes suggested by the United Kingdom to our statement made it practically a new resolution ... with the cease-fire part omitted ...

Our first reaction was one of surprise and consternation, and I conveyed my feelings to the Prime Minister at once. I emphasized to him again that there did not seem to me to be a chance in the world that the United States would accept any plan which abandoned the idea of a cease-fire before discussions. Possibly the Prime Ministers had assumed that there must first be a cease-fire, in which case I thought that something might be worked out along the lines of their suggestions. Jebb, however, thought that the message was a clear abandonment of cease-fire before negotiation, and Sir Benegal Rau was inclined to agree with Jebb's interpretation. The correctness of this was later confirmed in a message from London, which stated definitely that the Prime Ministers did not intend that a cease-fire should be a pre-condition of negotiations, which pre-condition had, after all, been rejected already by Peking. It was pointed out, however, to us that the new resolution might be so worded as to suggest a cease-fire simultaneously with the beginning of talks. The British Embassy in Washington then discussed with the Americans the London proposals on the basis of this interpretation and found, as I was sure they would find, that the Americans would have nothing to do with it. Likewise, in London that part of it which condemned Chinese action in Korea met with Indian disapproval. I hope, therefore, that we won't hear anything about this second new approach from London, and that we can still stick to our statement of principles with suitable amendments.

Meanwhile, Jebb and Rau had lunch with me today, and I went over with them the revision of the draft statement of principles in the light of suggested amendments from London. We altered it to include specific references to Formosa and recognition; with the additional words in the introduction, 'taking account of the Cairo Declaration, the Charter of the United Nations, and the resolutions of the General Assembly affecting these problems.' This should certainly appeal to the people in London, though it will not be very popular in Washington ...

It now became of first importance to find out whether Nehru would authorize Rau to associate himself with the new amended statement in case it was acceptable to Washington. We have as yet no assurance on this point. If Rau drops out, and this is possible, Mr St Laurent agreed that Entezam should introduce the amended statement on behalf of the two of us. Mr Robertson reported this to me by telephone, and said that it should be fully understood that the Prime Minister did not wish to have me back away from the position I had taken in regard to the most recent statement of principles. This is very encouraging ...

After this telephone conversation with Robertson, Riddell and I saw Gross to get his views on our amended draft. He was worried about it, especially about the specific reference to the Cairo Declaration in the preamble, as well as Paragraph 5. I agreed, therefore, and Rau subsequently concurred, to take such a reference out of the preamble. He was also very worried about the omission of the phrase 'under the United Nations' in paragraphs 3 and 4, and we substituted (Rau later agreeing) 'in accordance with United Nations principles.' Finally, he did not like a specific reference to Formosa and United Nations representation in two places. I agreed, therefore, to remove that in the introduction.

Gross is sending the revised text to Washington, but could give us no assurance that it would be acceptable there. I telephoned Wrong and asked him to do his best to get the Americans to accept these changes. They will at least find them more agreeable than the proposals telegraphed today from London.

Dean Acheson was dining with Wrong tonight and this gave the latter an opportunity to take up with the Secretary of State the most recent British proposals and our amended draft. Acheson's reaction to the former was similar to that reported by the British Embassy, which had discussed them with other United States officials. The amended draft statement of principles, however, did not get a bad reception ...

January 10, 1951 (Wednesday)
Wrong telephoned this morning that the United States will accept our draft statement of principles, providing Rau will join Entezam and myself in putting it forward. This is really a very great triumph for us, as the text went even further, in some respects, than the amendments suggested from London.

I telephoned this news at once to London with the additional information that if Nehru is not in a position to authorize Rau to sponsor our statement, even as now amended, then the United States would feel that they were freed from their commitment to support it. Nevertheless, they would still support the statement in its earlier form, even if it were put forward only by Entezam and myself. (We have authority to do this.) The Americans, however, made it clear that support of any statement of principles must not itself be interpreted as precluding them from taking further steps later which they consider desirable, if the Chinese Government should either reject the statement or ignore it. I made a strong plea to London that Mr Nehru should now authorize Rau to associate himself with the statement. In any event, we must know about this by tomorrow morning.

The Americans let us know today through Wrong that they expect the Political Committee to complete its action on the 'intermediate step' this week, and that after a reasonable interval of four or five days, it should then take up the United States condemnation proposal, if one is required. The British Ambassador in Washington, however, and Jebb here, have not yet received from Mr Bevin authority to drop yesterday's 'new proposals' and to revert to the statement of principles. This is strange. As Wrong put it, however, in a telegram today, 'The chorus of protests from New York and Washington should, however, have brought about its (the new proposal's) demise.'

The United Kingdom people will probably get their new instructions tonight, because in a telephone conversation with Mr Robertson this evening, I learned that the Prime Ministers' conference had now agreed on the statement of principles in its final form, though they hoped that certain changes could still be made ...

Mr Nehru was still worried about the beginning of Paragraph 5 – 'As soon as a cease-fire has been arranged ...' He thought that this might be construed by the suspicious Chinese as an American device not to begin political discussions until every detail of the cease-fire arrangement had been formally adopted, and this might take some time. I agreed that I would try to get these words in Paragraph 5 altered to remove this fear, and later I suggested to Gross the substitution, 'As soon as a cease-fire has been agreed on ...' If this could not be done, I told London that the three of us could interpret the original words in a sense which might remove Chinese fears that they would be used unduly to delay discussions.

Mr Robertson worried me by saying that Mr Nehru had not, however, agreed, when the meeting closed in London, to authorize Rau to support the statement, but would make up his mind within the next hour or so. As we meet at 3:00, we didn't have much time.

I at once telephoned Washington to indicate the interpretations that the Indians desired ... I also asked them to do their very best to press on the United States authorities the fact that they should now not merely abstain, but vote in favour of the statement of principles, if the Indians would sponsor it ... Both Mr Wrong and Mr [George] Ignatieff [then Counsellor at the Canadian Embassy, Washington] will do their best to clear up this point, and I will see Gross here about it. Abstention would not be good enough, as the Chinese would use it as an excuse for not paying any attention to the document, on the ground that the Americans had not accepted it.

After these talks, just before lunch, Rau phoned to say that his Prime Minister had agreed that he should sponsor the statement of principles, but he might have to make some interpretative remarks. I told him that I was going to try to get the first line of Paragraph 5 changed, in a way which would meet one of Mr Nehru's points. He seemed pleased about this and I, in turn, am very pleased that he will be able to sponsor the statement.

Wrong then phoned from Washington to say that Hickerson would take responsibility for agreeing to the change in the first words of Paragraph 5.

Finally, just as Riddell and I were leaving for Lake Success with our precious document in its final form – agreed to by Rau and Entezam over the telephone – a message arrived from Washington that Messrs Austin and Gross had been instructed not merely to adopt an attitude of 'acquiescence with good-will' to our statement, as had been reported by the British, but definitely to vote in favour of it.

Hickerson told Wrong that never before had the State Department been subjected to such arm twisting. He said they would take it from nobody but Canadians!

Riddell and I then motored out to Lake Success and got the statement through the secretariat mill, just in time for the opening of the meeting.

In the afternoon, I presented it to the Committee in a very short speech. Malik bitterly attacked it, while Austin gave it his blessing. Rau made his interpretative statement ...

Later in the day I sent a message to the Prime Minister asking him to urge on Nehru the importance of having Panikkar [Indian Ambassador to China] support and explain the statement in Peking. Otherwise, it would be misrepresented by the Russians. I also got David Owen, who is acting as Secretary General of the United Nations, to cable the text at once to the United Nations representative at Shanghai, who could then re-telegraph it to Peking. It is, I think, important to get it into the hands of the Peking authorities as quickly as possible. Of course, the Indians had already sent the earlier draft to Peking.

January 12, 1951 (Friday)
A difficulty has arisen over the form in which our statement should be approved by the Political Committee, and who should sponsor any resolution of approval. It was our opinion that the resolution should be very short, merely noting, with approval, our statement and forwarding it to Peking for their consideration ... In conversation with Jebb last evening, I suggested that the Cease-Fire Group should not itself sponsor any resolution, because it would be approving its own statement, but that Jebb should try to collect 5 or 6 sponsors and draft a short resolution along the lines indicated above. The sponsors might include a Latin American, a Scandinavian and a couple of Asians.

Meanwhile, I sent another message to London asking Mr St Laurent to impress on Mr Nehru how important it was that Rau should support and vote for any resolution of endorsation.

This morning Jebb telephoned me that he had been trying to arrange a sponsoring group for an endorsation resolution, but was having great difficulty. The Asians, or at least some of them, were anxious to be the exclusive sponsors, and were also anxious, he said, to amend the statement itself before it went to Peking, with a view to removing the stipulation that a cease-fire must actually take place before any negotiations begin. This, of course, is a fundamental part of the statement, and without it the Americans naturally will not support it. Apparently they, the Asians, have been influenced by Rau's interpretative remarks yesterday ... I told Jebb that there were only two courses now that seemed to me to make sense. One is that the Asians alone should sponsor the resolution as it stands, or that the Cease-Fire Group itself, notwithstanding the disadvantages of this course, should introduce the sponsoring resolution.

I then telephoned Rau to confirm, if possible, Jebb's fears. Rau was somewhat reassuring. He said that it is true the Asians had been talking about the question of a resolution and its sponsorship, and had come to the conclusion that the sponsors should not include any country which had forces fighting in Korea, as the Chinese might use this as an excuse to state that the resolution and the statement were primarily for the purpose of extricating such forces from their present difficulties. I told Rau that this seemed to me to be not unreasonable, and I suggested to him that he use his influence to have a resolution sponsored by four or five countries, such as Mexico, Sweden, Syria, Burma, and possibly Indonesia. Rau said that he would try to do this. He did not think that the Asians would try to amend the statement, and in this respect was less pessimistic than Jebb. I mentioned to him the possibility of the twelve Asians who had sponsored the earlier resolution now sponsoring the statement of principles. He said that India was one of these, but that he could not take this action without consulting Nehru. So we returned to the idea of the group of five.

I passed this on to Jebb and he seemed to think that sponsorship by countries not fighting in Korea would be satisfactory, and he agreed to try to get agreement on that basis. He was having a meeting for this purpose at noon.

This meeting was apparently not able to work out any satisfactory arrangement, so later in the afternoon, at Jebb's suggestion, and apparently as a last resort, Rau persuaded [Abba] Eban [then Israel's Permanent Representative to the UN] to introduce the sponsoring resolution alone. Eban did this at the end of the afternoon, and it will be discussed tomorrow.

January 13, 1951 (Saturday)
Everything should have gone smoothly today, but the contrary was the case. The difficulty arose over the fact that the resolution sponsoring the state-

ment and referring it to Peking 'for their observations' has been sponsored by Israel. This was enough to arouse the ire and opposition of the Arabs, who, one after another this morning, recanted their earlier decision of approval, and began to find fault with the resolution. This gave encouragement to other doubters, and when, by the end of the morning, amendments were submitted by El Salvador and Dr Tsiang [Nationalist Chinese Permanent Representative to the UN], which would have completely destroyed the statement (one would have substituted Nationalist China for Communist China), things looked dreary and discouraging. Something had to be done during the lunch hour, and done quickly. As soon as we adjourned, I saw Malik of the Lebanon, who had been leading the Arab filibuster, and tried to persuade him to adopt a more reasonable course; not to allow Arab hostility to Israel to wreck a course of action which they themselves had warmly supported. Malik said that the Arabs were having a meeting during the lunch hour and he would see what he could do to straighten things out.

I then got hold of Eban, Jebb, and Padilla Nervo of Mexico, who, with Riddell and myself, went to the Hidden House (an appropriate place) for lunch and discussion. Nervo came up with an ingenious idea. He suggested that we abandon all discussion of the Israel resolution and get back to the statement of the Cease-Fire Group, which should be put to the committee by the chairman as a document on which we would vote, first for and against. After all, it was the first item on our agenda! This would do two things. It would remove the Israel-Arab difficulty, and also avoid the necessity of voting on any amendments. It was essential to do this latter, because Austin had told me before lunch that he could not vote against any amendment to substitute Nationalist China for Communist China. American abstention on this issue in any vote before the committee would, of course, wreck our statement, because it would confirm Chinese suspicions that the Americans were trying to trick them.

Nervo also promised to persuade the chairman as to the rightness of this course, and Eban agreed that if the statement of principles was carried, he would withdraw all of his resolution except that paragraph which referred the statement to Peking.

At 3:00 o'clock, therefore, Nervo raised his point of order, the chairman accepted it, and, somewhat cavalierly, put the statement of principles to the vote at once without discussion and without amendment. It was carried against the protest of several members over what they considered – and not without some reason – arbitrary and unconstitutional procedure. However, the main thing is that fifty delegations voted for the statement. Then after a long wrangle ... the Norwegians put forward a short resolution, simply asking the Secretary General to transmit the document to Peking. Eban, therefore, withdrew his own resolution completely. The Norwegian resolution was carried and there were only one or two more hurdles to overcome. One was a suggestion by my neighbour, Santa Cruz, the Chilean, that we should set a time limit for a reply from Peking. I talked him out of this as it would have been interpreted as an ultimatum. Now we can sit back and see what happens in Peking during the next few days. And I can go to Ottawa.

January 19, 1951 (Friday)
On reaching New York this morning, I found that a meeting had been arranged at the United Kingdom delegation to consider the draft resolution on Korea proposed by the Americans ...

Jebb had been instructed to press for division of the condemnation resolution into two parts so that agreement might be reached on the measures to be taken under the second part of the resolution before action was taken in the Assembly. However, he was prepared to accept without amendment the language of the first part of the draft resolution, in which a finding of aggression was contained.

A revised text resulted from our discussions which all those present agreed to refer to their governments. Gross and Ross persistently held out against efforts to qualify in any material degree the finding of aggression against the Chinese and resisted any language which might imply a commitment never in any circumstances to carry United Nations action beyond the borders of Korea, though they were prepared to state, publicly if necessary, that they did not consider a draft resolution as in any way constituting an authority to the Unified Command to undertake operations of any kind elsewhere than in Korea.

The Americans seemed genuinely anxious to reach an accommodation with other delegations, but they are severely restricted by the rigid instructions they are now receiving. It seemed to me on some occasions that the way in which they expressed these instructions reflected a determination in the State Department to remain free to take strong action against China, if, in their opinion, the circumstances and the military situation in Korea warranted such action ...

After the meeting of the Political Committee, I attended a meeting with United States, United Kingdom, French, and Australian representatives at which Gross reported the views of Acheson and the State Department on the amendments we had suggested in the morning. Acheson is being very firm, and I don't think we can co-sponsor a resolution along the lines he insists upon. Gross said that the State Department felt it was absolutely necessary to table the resolution tomorrow (Saturday). I said we would not be in a position to sponsor the resolution under these circumstances, but that did not mean that we would oppose it or even abstain in the vote. I explained that if we were not sponsoring, I would feel freer to explain our position and interpret the resolution.

Gross asked what we would think of the United States sponsoring the resolution alone. I supported this but Shann [Australian Delegation] and Lacoste [French Delegation] thought the absence of co-sponsors would have a bad effect and would influence the vote in support. Gross himself thought the effect on American opinion would be bad. When Jebb asked what the American attitude would be if amendments were proposed, Gross said that they would not accept them. He was obviously under instruction to be decisive. He recognized that they might lose support in some quarters if they persisted with their own draft, but he said they were being pressed very hard in the other direction by the Latin Americans. His attitude was that the United States was prepared to go through with the kind of resolution they wanted regardless of the amount of support they received.

When Gross explained that the American people considered any further talk of principles of negotiation as 'churning over the same kind of weakness,' I said again that there was a psychological factor to be considered on the other side. Many other peoples considered that the condemnation of China was a very important step which might have very far-reaching consequences, and in judging those consequences they had to take into consideration the statements of very important people in the United States, such as General O'Donnell [Commander of the United States Bomber Command in Korea] who has just made a very bellicose statement about action to be taken against the Chinese. Gross made a rude comment about General O'Donnell, and again showed understanding of the difficulties that others might have. I am afraid such understanding, however, here and in Washington, is very much subordinated to the necessity the Americans feel of satisfying Congress and public opinion by following a tough condemnatory line with China.

I think myself that if they introduce their resolution with a list of co-sponsors, practically all Latin Americans, they will be making a big mistake. Much better for them to put it forward alone and see how much support they can get.

January 20, 1951 (Saturday)
... When we reached Lake Success at three o'clock this afternoon we learned that the Americans had changed their minds and would introduce the resolution alone. They have recognized what seemed pretty obvious to the rest of us, that their position was not strengthened by their association with a handful of Latin Americans and other small states with the obvious abstention of the United Kingdom, France and ourselves. Austin introduced his resolution in a brief and mild statement and was supported by the representatives of Greece, Turkey and assorted Latin Americans. Jamali of Iraq, however, advocated another attempt to find a peaceful settlement and said that the twelve Asian and Arab nations were revising their original resolution. Rau likewise advocated further attempts at conciliation. He considered Peking's reply as 'partly acceptance, partly non-acceptance, partly a request for elucidation and partly a set of counter-proposals.' In his speech he included a remarkable reference to the Commonwealth. He pointed out that Indian leaders had rebelled against British authority in India but that this fact had not prevented Britain from negotiating with these leaders. As a result, the

prestige of the United Kingdom had never stood higher in India. India was a partner in the Commonwealth, and the Commonwealth had become a great moral force in the world. It inspires somewhat ironic reflections, that India would use this argument in these circumstances.

January 21, 1951 (Sunday)

Today was largely spent in drafting a statement which I intend to make tomorrow on the resolution. It will be a long statement putting forth candidly the reasons why we do not think the United States resolution is timely or wise but cannot vote against it. There is no doubt that the Chinese are committing aggression, and if we are asked whether we agree with this description of their activities we cannot say 'No.'

After the draft had been virtually completed Peter Stursberg of the CBC telephoned to say that Gross had made a statement to the press this morning in which he appears to have reversed United States policy with regard to Formosa. Gross appears to have implied that the United States would not discuss the future of Formosa without the participation of Nationalist Chinese representatives, thereby apparently contradicting Paragraph 5 of our statement of principles. This is extremely unfortunate, as it will certainly confirm the fear, not only of the Chinese in Peking, but of our Asian and Arab friends, that the United States is not sincerely interested in a peaceful settlement and is indeed endeavouring to sabotage efforts in that direction. If it was necessary for Gross to make such a statement, he should surely not have done so without letting some of the rest of us know. This action certainly requires some revision in those parts of my draft statement in which I paid tribute to the sincerity and good intentions of the United States.

January 22, 1951 (Monday)

This morning's press reports of Gross's press statement are far from reassuring. We have communicated, however, with the Embassy in Washington who report that the State Department appear to be embarrassed and are insisting that Gross's comments were in no way intended to alter United States policy. The statement appears to have been a truncated version of a speech which Gross made at Roanoke, Virginia. There is no doubt, however, that the statement has left a bad taste. It could not have been worse timed and could conceivably have been a deliberate attempt to make certain that there would be no acceptance of our offer by the Chinese Communists.

Late in the morning Jebb telephoned to tell me in strict confidence that a message from Chou En-lai had just been passed through their facilities to Rau and that the Indians were requested by Chou En-lai to pass it to Mr St Laurent. Shortly afterwards Rau got in touch with me and sent the message around to the hotel. It is a reply to the enquiry, which Mr St Laurent had suggested to Mr Nehru, that Panikkar might make in Peking about the interpretation of certain parts of the Peking reply of last week. This further interpretation from Peking is not entirely clear, but there is no doubt that it is considerably more favourable to our point of view than what seemed to be the intent of the original message.

By the time we had read the message and I had discussed it with Ottawa, there was no time to concert our tactics with Rau or with any of our other friends. When we reached Lake Success about three o'clock we discovered that Rau intended simply to read this reply and request postponement for further consultations and to allow delegations to obtain new instructions. The British were concerned because no advance warning had been given of this development to the Americans, and Jebb took it upon himself to show Gross the telegram. The Americans, needless to say, were upset by the reference to Mr St Laurent in the telegram and considered that we have been up to no good with the Indians behind their backs. I don't see why they should complain. In the first place, there was no point in consulting them as to their views on our request for further elucidation because they had already made clear that they had no doubts in their minds as to the meaning of the Chinese reply. They had even produced a precipitate rejection without consulting any of their friends. Furthermore, as the reply was addressed to Rau, I did not consider it my place to pass it on. The Americans were not unaware of the fact that Mr St Laurent had been in touch with Mr Nehru and was seeking through this channel further information, because I had reported as much to Gross and the others present at last Friday's meeting in New York.

The meeting started off well with a brief statement by Rau in which he merely read the text of the latest reply from Peking and asked for a forty-eight hour adjournment. Several of the Latin Americans were so taken by surprise that they implied they would drop their prepared statements and accept a postponement. There were signs, furthermore, that the Soviet group were caught off guard. The Byelo-Russian next to me leaned back to his colleague behind him after Rau had finished speaking and muttered in Russian, 'Very interesting,' in a tone which indicated that he could not have been more surprised. Tsarapkin [USSR Delegation] dished up the conventional rehash of last week's Pravda editorial without adding any new ingredients in the light of developments. It is possible that the meeting would have adjourned shortly with general agreement on a postponement of some kind if [Carlos] Romulo [Philippines Delegation] had not intervened to ridicule the new Peking reply, to introduce doubts as to its authenticity and question the propriety of considering a communication addressed to only one member. The Greek and Turkish representatives also opposed postponement but in more candid and respectable terms. After the issue had been thoroughly obscured, Austin broke loose with an ill-tempered and abusive statement. He ridiculed the communication from Peking as 'not much more than a postal card' and with bumbling sarcasm attacked those who attached any importance to it. He grossly insulted Rau and Fawzi Bey of Egypt, and in general put on one of the worst performances of his career. So angry were most members of the committee that when a vote was taken on the motion for a 48-hour adjournment immediately after Austin's outburst, the motion passed by 27 in favour, 23 against, with 6 abstentions. It was one of the most severe moral defeats the United States has had. Austin should find little comfort in the support he received, which was confined largely to Latin America and countries like Greece and Turkey which are very much dependent upon the United States. In opposition, on the other hand, were the British, the Western European countries, ourselves and most of the Americans' reliable allies. None of us is at all happy about this division in the ranks at this time, but Austin by his attitude and tone left no alternative.

This is one of the most serious divisions we have had with the United States on policy and I thought it best, therefore, to return to Ottawa this evening to discuss the matter fully.

January 23, 1951 (Tuesday)
Shortly after I reached Ottawa this morning I received a message from Riddell concerning a meeting he had just had with Rau. Rau had asked Riddell to see him to discuss the next step in the Political Committee as the result of the most recent communication from Peking. Rau gave Riddell a copy of a draft resolution, the text of which Riddell immediately sent me. This draft resolution took note of the most recent reply from Peking; and recommended the immediate convening of a Seven-Power Conference (France, the UK, the US, the USSR, Egypt, India and Peking) to obtain further clarifications of Peking's reply and to see whether, on the basis of these clarifications, further negotiations could take place for a cease fire and a Far Eastern settlement. The resolution was drawn up in very vague terms and contained no provision for a time limit for a reply from Peking, if the resolution were adopted.

In his conversation with Riddell, Rau said he had received clearance from his government to propose this resolution in the Political Committee, and that the other eleven Asian-Arab states were prepared to be associated with him in proposing it ... Rau told Riddell that he had no idea what the reaction of the US Delegation might be to this resolution, and he indicated that he hoped I would be prepared to discuss it with the Americans. He also asked Riddell to let him have my comments on the resolution before the Asian-Arab group met this afternoon.

Riddell pointed out to Rau that the draft resolution might appear to go counter to the principle which we had previously adopted, namely that agreement on a cease-fire must precede a negotiating conference. Riddell said we had always recognized that the cease-fire itself might have to be a subject of negotiation, and that it had never been specified where the negotiations regarding the cease-fire should take place; but he added that it might create difficulty to summon the Seven-Power Conference before any commitment had been given, even in principle, to a cease-fire.

Riddell asked Rau whether he and his Asian colleagues had considered, as an alternative, the possibility of proposing a rather more precise formula providing for a Seven-Power Conference to establish an immediate cease-fire; to arrange for a withdrawal of troops from Korea; and then to proceed with the discussion, by stages, of other Far Eastern problems along the lines agreed to in the Cease-Fire Principles adopted on 13 January. Rau said that they had considered propositions of this kind and indicated that he and his Asian colleagues might be prepared to amend their draft along these lines. He added that he did not himself have instructions which would enable him to do this, but he thought he might be able to obtain the necessary clearance. He said that, if it were my view that a course of action along these lines were preferable, he and his Asian colleagues would seriously consider proceeding in that manner. He added that there were certain disadvantages in this course of action which should be borne in mind. A communication to the Chinese along the lines suggested would necessitate a delay for reply. The reply would probably be equivocal and a further delay might be necessary for more clarification. He said that the principal advantage of his draft resolution was that it would get around the delay and frustration caused by the sequence of communications back and forth across the Pacific. Riddell then told Rau that he would get in touch with me immediately and inform him of my views.

Meanwhile two messages from the Embassy in Washington indicated the sharply unfavourable reaction by the State Department to the events yesterday in the Political Committee, and the apparently uncompromising opposition of the United States Government to any effort to seek further clarification of the most recent Chinese reply. The gist of these two messages was that the United States was determined to press on with their condemnation resolution as soon as possible, and that they still insisted on the idea of an unconditional cease-fire as a necessary prerequisite to any subsequent negotiations. The US also expressed sharp impatience as to the manner in which the Chinese reply had been elicited, and they refused to accord this message the status of an official answer to the UN. Finally, these messages from Washington quoted Hickerson to the effect that he would be less than frank if he did not say that the State Department had been surprised that we had not consulted with them before making an approach to Peking for clarification of the latter's original reply. Hickerson said he quite realized that governments were at liberty to make approaches of this kind, but he thought the US should have been consulted. He added that any negotiations with Peking should be under UN auspices, and under conditions approved by the General Assembly, and not under the auspices of a 'select group of governments.'

On receipt of Riddell's message concerning his conversation with Rau, I prepared a rough draft of an alternative resolution somewhat along the lines Riddell had mentioned to Rau ...

I instructed [John] Holmes [Head of United Nations Division in External Affairs] to telephone this draft immediately to Riddell and to ask him to emphasize to Rau our interest in a Seven-Power Conference and in seeking further clarification from Peking. Riddell was also asked to inform Rau that the latter's draft would not do from our point of view as it was drawn up in much too general language and did not contain a time limit for a reply from Peking. Riddell was asked to let Rau know that we hoped that an alternative resolution on these lines might be sponsored by the Asians, and that we, for our part, would emphasize to the United States Delegation that it was a forty-eight hour 'take-it-or-leave-it' proposition so far as Peking was concerned. It was also indicated to Riddell that, if the Asians were not prepared to accept this draft, I might incorporate the substance of it as a general suggestion in the speech I was going to make in the Political Committee.

In the afternoon, after receiving my views and the draft resolution I had prepared, Riddell got in touch with me before he approached Rau again. He pointed out that, in view of the uncompromising attitude of the United States towards any further attempts to seek clarifications through Panikkar, we might wish to retain more freedom of action in regard to the sponsorship of any draft resolution. If, however, he were to communicate the details of our tentative draft resolution to Rau, he might be forced into the position of entering into a redrafting job as a sort of twelfth member of the Asian group. Such an implicit commitment of Canadian co-sponsorship or support might prove embarrassing, particularly as it might well be difficult to get the Asian group to accept all the points contained in our draft. I agreed with Riddell that there were strong arguments for retaining our freedom of action in this matter and that the best thing was to let Rau know our views without, however, committing ourselves to co-sponsorship of any resolution.

After this conversation, Riddell then told Rau that he had heard from me to the effect that I was in favour of seeking further clarification of the Chinese position by some method and that I thought a resolution along the lines he had previously indicated to Rau this morning might prove a useful method of doing so. Riddell added, however, that the effect of such a resolution would be lost if it were opposed uncompromisingly by the United States, and that we had no idea at the moment whether the United States would be prepared to acquiesce in a resolution along the lines we had suggested, or even in any modification of such a resolution. It seemed necessary, therefore, before a decision could be taken as to the method by which a further clarification could be sought from the Chinese, to determine whether the United States Delegation might modify the position which it was now taking. Riddell added that, in any case, I felt very strongly that any resolution of this type should have a 48-hour time limit for a reply from Peking. Apparently Rau did not comment at any length on these points, but left the impression with Riddell that the Asian group, who were going to meet a few minutes later, would go ahead with their own resolution substantially in the form previously indicated.

January 24, 1951 (Wednesday)
Before leaving Ottawa to return to New York I sent a message to Wrong regarding the queries raised by Hickerson and Rusk yesterday, concerning

our role in seeking further clarifications of Peking's reply. I sent this message to confirm oral instructions I had given over the telephone to Ignatieff last night. I told the Embassy to explain to the State Department that our enquiry for clarification in no sense amounted to a negotiation with the Peking Government. We were puzzled by the obscurities in the first Chinese reply and we had no channel through which to seek clarification; so the Prime Minister quite naturally asked Nehru if Panikkar might be able to find out the real intentions of the Chinese. We assumed, as no doubt everyone else assumed, that Panikkar and the other representatives in Peking would be trying to find out what the Chinese meant by their reply. We were very much surprised ourselves that the reply came back in the form of what seemed to be a direct answer to Mr St Laurent from Chou En-lai ...

I see no reason at all why we are under any obligation to give the Americans full details of an informal exchange of messages with another Commonwealth Government. As for consulting the Americans about the enquiry, they had made themselves so clear on the subject of the Chinese reply, even to the extent of producing a precipitate rejection, that there was really no point in asking for any clarification of their views. We had certain doubts about the meaning of the Chinese reply but they obviously had none.

In view of this I consider that we have no reason at all to be apologetic about our actions so far as the State Department is concerned. I also told the Embassy, when they spoke to the State Department, to make it very clear that we were not passing on any blame whatever to the Indians ...

We have also now received a copy of the instructions sent from the UK Government to Jebb. He is instructed to try to persuade the US not to press their resolution to a vote until further clarification had been received regarding Peking's reply. If unsuccessful in this, he is to request a vote on the US resolution, paragraph by paragraph ...

In India today Nehru broadcast a statement sharply critical of the US, and said that the American proposal to name Peking as an aggressor 'cannot lead to peace.' He added that 'it can only lead to intensification of conflicts and might perhaps close the door to any attempt at solution by negotiation.' This statement has received a lot of publicity in the US and has, understandably, been bitterly criticized.

In my absence Riddell attended the meeting of the Political Committee at 3:00 PM today, where Austin pressed for adoption of the US resolution as being essential to preserve collective security. He said that 'if any one of us is attacked, each of us would in that situation desperately ask the United Nations to provide the unified support of every other government in the world to meet the attack. How can we bring that about for our own countries? Only by a determination to take united action to support each other faithfully and vigorously when an act of aggression occurs.' Austin also referred to the additional reply by Peking read by Rau at the meeting on Monday, and dismissed it as being 'another rejection' of the UN cease-fire principles ...

I reached New York late this evening.

January 25, 1951 (Thursday)
A meeting of the Political Committee took place at 3:00 PM today. The first
speaker was Rau, who gave his version of the three questions submitted to
the Peking Government as a result of the message from Mr St Laurent to
Mr Nehru. Rau's version of these three questions is as follows:
1 Do the foreign troops referred to in paragraph 1 of the Chinese reply include Chinese volunteers?
2 Do the Chinese insist that negotiations on broad political issues should
   precede a cease-fire?
3 Is formal recognition of the Chinese Communist Government as spokesman of China in the United Nations a pre-condition to agreement to a
   Conference?
Rau then repeated Peking's answers to these three questions which he had
given at the meeting of 22 January. Rau also formally introduced the revised
Asian-Arab resolution which had been distributed yesterday. In doing so
Rau emphasized that this revised text was a re-draft of the Asian-Arab resolution of 12 December 1950, and that, accordingly, it should have priority
in the voting over the US resolution ...

During the day we also received from the Israeli Delegation, on a confidential basis, a number of suggested amendments to the US draft resolution. The first of these amendments was to paragraph 2 of the US resolution; it would alter the phrase which said that Peking had 'rejected all' UN
proposals to read that Peking had 'not accepted' these proposals. Another
amendment was to the last paragraph of the US draft resolution and would
have the effect of mentioning specifically that the cease-fire principles of 13
January continued to be the policy of the United Nations. However, by far
the most important Israeli amendment was to the paragraph in the US resolution concerning the Collective Measures Committee [of 14 nations, set up
by the 'Uniting for Peace' resolution to study and report on political, economic
and military methods which could be used to strengthen peace and security].
This amendment would make it clear that the Committee composed of the
members of the CMC would not submit a report regarding additional
measures unless the Good Offices Committee, referred to elsewhere in the
resolution, had reported failure in its efforts. It is not yet clear whether the
Israelis intend to submit their suggestions as formal amendments or whether
they wish to use them only as a basis for discussion with other Delegations.

January 26, 1951 (Friday)
At a meeting of the Committee this morning I was the first speaker. I made
a lengthy statement giving our views on this general question and specifically on the two resolutions. The following is a summary of my statement:
I started out by analyzing the history of the efforts of the first Cease-Fire
Group, leading to the statement of principles adopted on 13 January, Peking's reply of 17 January and the subsequent clarifications received through
the Indian Ambassador in Peking. I then said that, in view of this last reply

from Peking, the Canadian Delegation believed that it would be wise for the Political Committee to consider a specific programme for a negotiated settlement which would, 'on the one hand lead to the fulfilment of United Nations objectives in Korea and, on the other, to a peaceful settlement of outstanding Far Eastern issues.' I then outlined six points which we considered might have been the basis for such a programme. These points are as follows:

1 An immediate conference consisting of the US, the UK, France, the USSR, India, Egypt, and the Peking Government.

2 The first order of business of this conference would be the appointment of a Cease-Fire Committee consisting of representatives of the US and the Peking Government, and a representative of UNCURK [United Nations Commission for the Unification and Rehabilitation of Korea, established by the Assembly on October 7, 1950], to arrange a cease-fire on the basis of the cease-fire principles agreed to on 13 January.

3 Once the cease-fire had been achieved the conference would consider 'a peaceful solution of Korean problems.' This would include arrangements for the withdrawal from Korea of all non-Korean armed forces including, specifically, all Chinese nationals and armed forces.

4 Discussion of other Far Eastern problems (Formosa and Chinese representation) could then take place in the conference in accordance with paragraph 5 of the January 13th cease-fire principles.

5 Governments with special interests in these Far Eastern questions (other than the seven governments referred to above) would be invited to participate in the discussion of specific questions.

6 If this programme were adopted it should be transmitted by the United Nations to Peking immediately, with a request that a definite positive or negative reply should be made by that government within 48 hours.

I made it clear that we were not submitting any definite proposal at the present stage, but that we were throwing out these suggestions for whatever use they might be to other Delegations.

I then referred to the two resolutions before the Committee. So far as the Asian-Arab resolution was concerned I said we could not support it because, if this resolution were adopted, it might follow that general negotiations would take place before a cease-fire had been agreed to. This, in our opinion, would sacrifice a basic principle which we had adhered to all along – namely, that a cease-fire should precede negotiations on other issues.

I then referred to the US resolution. I said that a decision was difficult regarding it, if we accepted the obligations of the Charter, and in view of the implications as to where the resolution might lead us. I pointed out that the duty of the United Nations would not be discharged merely by joining in moral condemnation of an aggressor. I said that, even in the present difficult situation, Canada believed in continuing efforts to find a peaceful and honourable solution of the United Nations' differences with China. We believed that the door should be held open for further negotiations if there was any reason to think that they might be successful.

Nevertheless, I said that we would support the US resolution because we could not deny the fact that Chinese forces were participating in aggression. I also pointed out that the resolution was in no sense a declaration of war – limited or unlimited – against China. If this were the case the Canadian Delegation would not support it.

I said that some features of the resolution did not carry our conviction, and that, although we would support the resolution as a whole, we would reserve our position regarding amendments submitted to it which, in our judgment, would improve it. I then summed up our position by saying that we considered that the presentation of this resolution was 'premature and unwise' at a time when the possibilities of negotiation with China had not been exhausted. We would, however, support the resolution, if pressed to a vote, because its main purport was to record a fact which could not be denied – namely that Communist China had assisted the aggressors in Korea. I added that our support for this resolution was easier for us in view of the fact that it had been submitted by the United States, which was taking the leadership 'in the defence of freedom everywhere.'

The other point I made in my statement was that, in our judgment, this resolution, if adopted, 'does not give the Unified Command or its Commanders in Korea any authority to take action which it and they do not already possess.' My purpose in making this statement was to secure from the US Delegation a definite statement on the record that the adoption of this resolution would not give MacArthur any authority to extend the war.

The only other substantial statement made this morning was by Eban of Israel who spoke very much along the same lines as I had done. He also urged that every honourable method for peaceful negotiation should be exhausted before the United Nations condemned Peking as an aggressor, and before consideration was given to any 'additional measures.' Eban spoke in the sense of his Delegation's amendments, (given to us yesterday) but did not, at this stage, submit any formal proposals ...

After my statement this morning, first Jamali of Iraq, and later Sir Benegal Rau told me that the Asian Group would be considering this afternoon an amendment of their resolution to incorporate the points which I had made. They both asked me how I felt about this. I said that we ourselves were not proposing any new resolution or any amendments to existing resolutions, but that naturally, any suggestions made by our Delegation could be utilized by any other Delegation, if it saw fit. I pointed out to them both that, in making our suggestions regarding a programme of cease-fire and negotiation, I had had in mind that this programme might be taken up by the Good Offices Committee immediately it was established. I agreed, however, that, if these points were incorporated in the Asian resolution, it would probably command more support than it would at present. One objection to this course was that if the Asian resolution was voted on first, and defeated, with the amendments now suggested, it might be a little more difficult for the Good Offices Committee later to put forward these suggestions to the Peking Government. This, however, was not a difficulty of any great substance, in my opinion. Sir Benegal then asked me point-blank whether we would support the Asian resolution if it were amended along the lines of our suggestions. I said that that would entirely depend on the form of the resolution as finally agreed to by the Asians. It would certainly be difficult for us to oppose it, and it might even be drafted in a way which would command our support if, in fact, it were voted on first. This points up the importance of the question as to which of these two resolutions should be given priority in the voting.

After the morning meeting (there was no afternoon meeting), Gross of the US Delegation told me that the UK had proposed to them certain amendments to their resolution which would have the effect of suspending action by the CMC until the GOC had reported to the Assembly. The US Delegation forwarded this suggestion to Washington, where it was considered this morning at a Cabinet meeting, and was rejected both by the President and by Acheson. Washington, however, *has* agreed to an alteration of their resolution by which the CMC, in its work, would take into consideration the report of the GOC. Gross did not think they would go any further than this.

Afterwards I had lunch with Jebb, who explained to me the latest attitude of his Government towards the US resolution and their present belief that, if it could be amended along the lines of the Israeli proposal, and if it could be made clear that there would be no consideration of 'additional measures' until the GOC had reported, the UK could support it. On the other hand, if these amendments were not accepted, they would vote against the US resolution and they believed that several other delegations would support them in this course. I suggested to Jebb that the American reluctance to accept these amendments might be lessened if a timelimit was given for the work of the GOC – say three or four weeks – and he said he would pass on this idea to London. I also pointed out to him that the amendment which the Americans *had* agreed to accept did, in fact, seem to furnish what the UK wished, because it would mean that the CMC (or the new committee of the same membership) could be suspended until there was something to report to it from the GOC. Jebb was interested in this and said that he hoped his Government might, in the light of this interpretation, be satisfied with the US amendment, if Washington would not accept anything else.

So far as we are concerned, I think we should support the UK and Israeli amendments to the US resolution if they are submitted or, alternatively, the US amendment, if that is all we can get. I should add that the Americans have also agreed to accept the change to paragraph 2 (suggested by Israel) which would alter the words 'has rejected' to 'has not accepted.' This would make it possible for us to support this paragraph on which, in its present form, we would abstain.

I think that if the US resolution can now be put in an amended form, incorporating the UK and Israeli ideas, it will obtain a very large majority. Otherwise, I think it will just barely obtain two-thirds majority – as there may be at least 20 voting against or abstaining.

My feeling is that things are at the moment moving in a better direction and that there is still some possibility of adopting a resolution which, by combining a moral condemnation with stronger provisions for a cease-fire and negotiation, will command a very great measure of support. This would, of course, be the most desirable result and we will do our best to bring it about.

January 27, 1951 (Saturday)
Another meeting of the Political Committee took place this morning ... the most important statement was that made by Austin in which he referred to my statement of yesterday and gave a categorical assurance that, in the view of his Government, the adoption of the US resolution would not give the Unified Command 'any additional authority which they do not possess.' Austin also indicated that his Delegation would be prepared to accept a modification of paragraph 2 of their resolution by altering the words 'has rejected all' to read 'has not accepted.' Furthermore, Austin implied that the US would be prepared to accept an alteration of paragraph 8 to make it clear that the new committee, composed of members of the Collective Measures Committee, could defer its report regarding additional measures in the event that the Good Offices Committee reported progress. In view of the fact that Austin's statement followed immediately after Malik's [Charles Malik, Chairman of the Lebanese Delegation], it seems evident that the US and the Lebanese Delegations have reached agreement and that Lebanon will shortly submit formal amendments to these two paragraphs, which will be acceptable to the US. It also seems obvious that the US Delegation will acquiesce in having the Asian-Arab resolution voted on first.

There appears to have been considerable reaction in the press to my statement of yesterday outlining the suggested Six-Point Programme for a cease-fire and negotiation. In particular, press comment in the United Kingdom seems to be favourable although the English newspapers show a tendency to treat it as a formal Canadian proposal, rather than as the informal suggestion which it was. There is also a sympathetic editorial in today's *Washington Post*, but generally speaking the US press reaction has, as anticipated, not been favourable ...

I spoke tonight to the Prime Minister over the telephone, and he agreed that I should stay here at least until Monday, in the hope that a vote will be taken that day in the Political Committee. Mr St Laurent also considered that, in view of the more flexible attitude shown by the US in the last few days, particularly in Austin's statement of today, we could give their resolution stronger support than had been previously expected. He also hoped that the UK and France would now be able to support the US resolution.

Today at lunch, and later at dinner, Rau discussed with me ways and means of facilitating the work of the GOC, once the US resolution was adopted. We both considered that there might be some merit in delaying confirmation of the resolution by the Plenary Assembly until the GOC had

had an opportunity to pursue its work for a short time. The President could then decide when the Plenary Assembly should be convened. Such a procedure would mean that no formal and final action would be taken *at once* against the Chinese.

Meanwhile, Entezam has told both of us that he is going to ask Rau and me to form the GOC. I told him that this might be difficult for me, as I could not continue to be in New York. He said, however, that, in his view, the Good Offices Committee need not do the actual work of negotiation itself, but could establish some machinery to this end, and merely supervise that machinery by occasional meetings. We also discussed the possibility of appointing to the Good Offices Committee someone of the calibre of Ralph Bunche [Principal Director of the UN Department of Trusteeship and winner of the Nobel Peace Prize in 1950] to act as Secretary or Agent-General, and Entezam seemed to favour this idea.

Entezam strongly stressed to Rau and me that he did not want to take on this job again unless he had the same group with him; and both of us agreed to refer the matter to our Governments. In view, however, of India's general position concerning the US resolution it does not seem probable that the Indian Government will authorize Rau to serve on the GOC.

January 28, 1951 (Sunday)
We have today received, through Mr Chipman, the text of a telegram from Panikkar to Mr Nehru reporting a meeting yesterday between Panikkar and Chou En-lai. In view of the fact that Panikkar's message refers specifically to Canada Mr Nehru asked that a copy of this message be transmitted to Mr St Laurent. Panikkar's message attributes to Chou En-lai the belief that Canada altered its original position because of United States pressure, and that, by weakly yielding to this pressure, we are endeavouring to trap the Chinese as well as to appease the United States. In view of the fact that Panikkar's own comments on Canada's attitude do not appear to have gone far to dispel this impression of the Chinese, we are preparing a message to Chipman for transmittal to the Indian Government, in order to set the record clear. This message will point out that, from the beginning, we have made it clear that if a resolution condemning China for assisting the aggression in Korea were put to the vote we would have to vote in favour of it, even though we might consider it premature and unwise. Our whole effort throughout has been to urge the United States to suspend action on its resolution, but without success, and it has now become evident that any formal motion to suspend such action would not now receive the necessary support in the Committee. For this reason we have recently been trying to get the United States to modify its resolution and to agree to a flexible interpretation of it, and here we *have* had some measure of success. In this sense we have been putting more pressure on the United States than they have applied to us. As to the Asian resolution, we do not consider it satisfactory in its present form because it does not fully recognize a principle we have

adhered to all along – that is, that the fighting must stop before subsequent political negotiations begin. In transmitting this message to Chipman we are not sanguine that it will have much effect on the opinion of the Peking Government, but it may at least dispel any illusions regarding our position which are still present within the Indian Government itself.

Following my telephone conversation with Mr St Laurent last night I tried to get in touch today with Jebb to discuss with him the more co-opera-tive attitude shown by the US in the last two days, and to express our hope that the UK would now be able to support the US resolution. Jebb was out of town, but Riddell passed on our views to Coulson and I telephoned them to Wrong for transmission to Sir Oliver Franks.

January 29, 1951 (Monday)
This morning I learned from Wrong that the United Kingdom Delegation have now received instructions to support the US resolution with the amend-ments suggested by Lebanon on Saturday, which will no doubt be formally submitted today in the Political Committee. United Kingdom support for the US resolution is, however, based on the condition that, once the resolution has been adopted, the Good Offices Committee will immediately attempt further peaceful negotiations with Peking, taking into account the Six-Point Programme which I outlined on Friday. After receiving this information from Wrong we got in touch with Lacoste of France, who said that his Dele-gation had also now received similar instructions to support the US reso-lution.

Meanwhile, reports in the Press indicate that MacArthur made yesterday in Tokyo one of his all-too-familiar and embarrassing statements. He is re-ported in the *Herald Tribune* as having said that 'the stake we fight for now is more than Korea. It is a free Asia.' If this report is true, this is certainly a most deplorable speech by a man holding the position of United Nations Commander, particularly at the present time. I asked Mr Wrong to try to secure the text of MacArthur's statement and he replied later this morning saying that the State Department have no such text, but that they believe the report in the *Herald Tribune* is substantially correct. Wrong also in-formed me that the British Embassy had been instructed by London to make representations to the State Department regarding this statement and he asked me whether he should do likewise. I have asked him to express to the State Department our regret and anxiety that the United Nations Com-mander in the field should make such a statement, which bears no relation to the purposes of United Nations intervention in Korea. Coming at this time, on the eve of the vote on the US resolution before the Political Com-mittee, it is particularly unfortunate. I also asked Wrong to recall to the State Department that, on Saturday, Mr Austin confirmed, on behalf of the United States Government, my assumption that their resolution gave the Unified Command no authority that it does not already possess. If General MacArthur thinks he has authority under any United Nations resolution, not merely to defeat aggression in Korea, but to liberate Asia from Communism, (to use his reported words), he is, in our view, profoundly mistaken. While this may be a most desirable objective, it is certainly not one for which the armed forces of the United Nations can be used in *present* circumstances.

I have also received a message from Heeney [my Under-Secretary in Ottawa] to the effect that the Prime Minister told him that, if Rau accepts the President's request to act on the Good Offices Committee, he (Mr St Laurent) feels it would be virtually impossible for me to refuse. If, however, Rau does not accept this assignment, Mr St Laurent believes that this might indicate the Indian Government's conclusions that the Good Offices Committee's efforts would be fruitless; in the latter eventuality Mr St Laurent believes that I might refuse to serve on the Committee on the grounds that a new membership might have a better chance of success.

(Subsequently Rau did in fact receive instructions from his Government not to serve on the Good Offices Committee, and, a few days later, on 7 February, I informed Mr Entezam that I also would not be able to serve on the Committee. In my letter to Entezam I mentioned my inability to spend very much time in New York and also the fact that, as Rau was unable to serve, it might be better if he – Entezam – chose two new men to work with him. Shortly afterwards Entezam named Padilla Nervo of Mexico and Grafström of Sweden as the two other members of the Good Offices Committee.)

Two meetings of the Political Committee took place this morning and afternoon at Lake Success. Prior to the meeting Malik of Lebanon circulated the two amendments he had outlined at Saturday's meeting. The first of these was to amend paragraph 2 of the US resolution to read that the Peking Government had 'not accepted,' rather than had 'rejected all,' UN proposals for a peaceful settlement. The second and most important amendment was to the eighth paragraph of the resolution and authorized the new Committee, charged with considering additional measures against China, 'to defer its report if the GOC, referred to in the following paragraph, reports satisfactory progress in its efforts' ...

At this afternoon's meeting, Malik of Lebanon formally submitted his two amendments and repeated that he would support both the Asian-Arab resolution and the US one. He also insisted again that the Asian-Arab resolution should be voted on first ... This meeting was concluded with an unsuccessful effort on the part of the Soviet bloc to obtain a postponement for twenty-four hours on the grounds that they had not received instructions from their governments concerning the revised Asian-Arab resolution ...

January 30, 1951 (Tuesday)
Three meetings of the Political Committee took place today – morning, afternoon and evening – before the US resolution was finally adopted by a vote of 44 in favour, (including Canada), 7 against and 8 abstentions ...

At the beginning of this afternoon's meeting Rau of India, in answer to an obviously pre-arranged question from Fawzi Bey of Egypt, said that the Indian Government had been informed that the Asian-Arab resolution was regarded in Peking as 'providing a genuine basis for a peaceful settlement.' The Indian Government further understood that, if the Asian-Arab resolution were adopted, the Peking Government would be willing to co-operate in negotiations for a settlement. On the basis of this, both Egypt and India, supported by other Asian states, made strenuous efforts to defer a vote on the two resolutions on the grounds that at least another twenty-four hours were needed to consider this 'new information.' Eventually, however, a Turkish proposal calling for closure of debate and an immediate vote on the two resolutions was adopted by 36 in favour (including Canada), 17 against (the Soviet bloc and the Asian states), and 5 abstentions.

After the closure of debate, and prior to the voting, I again explained the Canadian position on the two resolutions. I said that we would abstain on the Asian resolution. We could not vote in favour of it because it did not 'embody the essential principle that there must be an end of fighting before there can be a discussion of political questions.' We could not, however, vote against it because it emphasized the necessity of securing a settlement by negotiation, which we had always supported. So far as the US resolution was concerned, I said that we would support it, as amended by Lebanon. In our view the resolution, as amended, did not close the door to peaceful negotiations. Furthermore, we could not dispute the fact that the Peking Government had engaged in aggressive action in Korea. I repeated, however, that we still considered it was 'premature and unwise' to force a decision on this resolution until all methods of peaceful negotiation had been 'completely exhausted.'

Before the vote, and after defeat of his proposal for postponement, Sir Benegal Rau made a bitter speech urging rejection of the US resolution. He said his Delegation wanted it placed on the record that 'when the world was marching, in our view, toward disaster, we – most of the Asian powers – did all we could to halt that march.' He argued vehemently that, if the US resolution were adopted, tension in the Far East would be perpetuated and 'the atmosphere for successful negotiations would be vitiated.'

At the meeting of the Committee this evening, and following the closure of debate, voting first of all took place on the Twelve-Power Asian-Arab resolution. It was rejected by a series of individual votes on portions of the resolution and, consequently, under Rule 128, no vote was taken on the resolution as a whole ...

The US resolution was then adopted with the results given above. Prior to the vote on the resolutions as a whole the two Lebanese amendments were adopted by separate votes ...

Subsequently, on February 1, the General Assembly adopted this same resolution by a vote of 44 in favour, 7 against (Burma, India and the Soviet bloc) and 9 abstentions ...

※

APPENDIX 2

While I was President of the United Nations General Assembly, a great deal of my time and energy were taken up with the Korean affair. In Chapter 8 I told how I found myself caught between Krishna Menon of India and Dean Acheson of the United States as we tried to work out a formula which would bring hostilities to an end. I kept a detailed diary of those days.

The first delegate to approach me ... was Krishna Menon of India, who indicated that he was dealing with Korean questions for his delegation and wanted to discuss with me how the Assembly could assist in bringing about an armistice. He thought that it would be useful if he and one or two of the other delegates could have private talks with me on this matter. I told him that I was at his disposal, as I would be at the disposal of any other delegate, including the Russian, who might wish to see me about this matter. After running over several names, we decided that, for the first meeting at least, there should be only the two of us plus Padilla Nervo of Mexico and Mr [Paul] Martin [then Minister of National Health and Welfare] of our delegation. We met for the first time on Monday, October 27.

Before this meeting, however, I had discussed with members of our own delegation in a general way the possibility of putting forward a resolution which, without going over past history in Korea, or specifically endorsing efforts to bring about an armistice there, or attempting to impose on the Communists any proposals which had previously been put forward by the Unified Command and rejected, would embody a specific and concrete solution for this one problem of prisoners of war. It was felt that by isolating this problem in this way there was a greater chance of finding a satisfactory and acceptable solution to it. It was also felt that while the principle of full repatriation could be agreed on, as required in the Geneva Convention, the use of force for this purpose would have to be excluded, but that this exclusion might be put in a form that the Communists could possibly accept, if they really wanted an armistice. It was recognized also that any such specific resolution must not be in conflict with the 21-power resolution which the Canadian delegation had sponsored, and the principles of which we supported.

Before the meeting with Menon, Nervo and Martin, referred to above, I had discussed in general terms an approach along the above lines with Selwyn Lloyd of the UK delegation, and Dean Acheson. Lloyd was generally favourable; in fact, the idea was one which the UK could support ...

Acheson was non-committal and was more concerned with another idea which I had put forward to him very confidentially as something which had been running through my mind and which was related to an armistice. I asked him what he would think if, as President, I made an appeal to the Communists and to the Unified Command for an immediate cease-fire while the Korean question was under discussion at the Assembly. Just as in the Middle Ages, we had the Truce of God, so we might now have a Truce of the Assembly. Acheson was quite disturbed by this idea, apparently thinking that I might spring it on the Assembly without warning. I told him I had no intention of doing this, but would be glad to get his more considered reaction. This was on Friday, October 24, and as he was leaving for Washington next day, he said he would discuss it with people there. The result of the discussion of this particular matter in Washington was entirely negative. The Pentagon especially thought that it was a most dangerous suggestion and would do far more harm than good if accepted ...

On Monday evening [October 27] we met Menon and Nervo, and we had a long and somewhat rambling discussion of the best line to follow in order to achieve an armistice. At this discussion, Menon put forward at some length ideas which he had previously advanced at a Commonwealth meeting. Unfortunately, he is not very clear or decisive in expressing his ideas, and is inclined to be somewhat tortuous and metaphysical in his reasoning. He has, of course, a good deal of sympathy with the Chinese Communist point of view, but is, I think, sincere and well meaning. Selwyn Lloyd earlier had told me that Menon should not be discouraged from his pursuit of an armistice. I agreed, but added that it should not be forgotten, in any talks with Menon, that there might be other Indian advice going to New Delhi from New York, and also that he might be unduly optimistic in his interpretation of the information he is getting from Peking via his government. In any event, the Indian government is our sole source of contact with Peking and I think that we should exploit that channel to the limit without having any illusions either of the possibility of final success, or of receiving always responsible and accurate information.

At our talk on Monday evening, Menon and Nervo, as far as one could gather, were in pretty close communion, though somewhat vague in their ideas. They both, however, entirely agree, and we did not demur, that the right of repatriation must be admitted, that Chinese Communist suspicions that we had any reservations on this score should be removed, and that we should not attach too much importance to polemics on either side. Menon feels that once this unqualified right of repatriation is established, the Chinese will agree that the exercise of the right in individual cases may be extended over many months, while the prisoners are making up their minds and that force during this period would not be exercised either for repatriation or retention. This, however, would require that during this period when reluctant prisoners are not exercising their right, they should be removed from the custody of either side and turned over to a neutral agency which would ensure that no pressure would be brought to bear on them of any kind.

I tried to persuade Krishna Menon to put his ideas on paper, or at least to get them clarified. We also encouraged him to keep the lines open to Peking and to give us an assurance as soon as possible that his government would back or, indeed, initiate a resolution or proposal along the lines we had been discussing ...

On Thursday afternoon, October 30, Menon came to see me again and told me that he had had further information from New Delhi and that things were proceeding satisfactorily. He was reasonably optimistic that if no wrong moves were made here the Chinese might accept a prisoner of war solution that would be agreeable to us ... I told him of the lines along which we were drafting Mr Martin's statement on Korea for the First Committee, which I thought would be helpful. He indicated that the point of view which Mr Martin was expressing at Commonwealth [delegations] meetings had already been helpful ...

I had invited Gross and Ross to luncheon on Saturday, November 1, with Messrs Martin and [Jules] Léger [my Assistant Under-Secretary] of our delegation. Shortly before lunch hour Selwyn Lloyd phoned to see whether he could join us as he had been discussing Korean developments with the two Americans. We spent a couple of hours on the Korean question and outlined to the Americans our views. I emphasized that as the 21-power resolutions would not receive much Asian-Arab support and would certainly be turned down by the Communists, we should have our next move very clearly in mind. To Ernie Gross the next move was an easy one, namely, a resolution which would recommend further economic, diplomatic, and possibly military pressure on the Chinese. This, of course, is the fundamental difference between our positions. Gross thinks that such pressure, steadily and continuously exerted, is our best hope for an armistice and peace in Korea. We think that we should make a further effort along the lines indicated above to bring about an armistice by negotiation, which would at least have the merit of exposing the Communist position even if it were not successful in other respects. The Americans are strongly of the opinion that whatever may be the merits of this approach, we should not at this stage complicate or confuse the issue by the introduction of any other resolution than the two [the 21-nation resolution and a Russian one] before the Committee ... we outlined to the Americans some ideas that we were thinking of putting in our speech, which, though they would be in general terms, might encourage some other delegation to introduce a resolution which would embody them. We were thinking, of course, of the Indian delegation.

While we were discussing this matter a telephone call came for Gross from Nervo to the effect that his government had decided to submit at once a resolution to the First Committee embodying their own particular proposal for sanctuary in third countries for unwilling prisoners. Gross tried his best to persuade Nervo to postpone the introduction of this resolution, but Nervo was acting on instructions from Mexico where, as a matter of fact, a press conference announcing the resolution was being held that afternoon. It appears that President Aleman, who is going out of office in a couple of weeks, wants to make one final, dramatic move which may, as it has been cynically observed, win him a Nobel Peace Prize!

On Monday, November 3, Menon came to see me again in my office to say he had had further communications from his government and that he thought it would be useful now if I could hold another discussion with himself, and possibly the three ex-Presidents of the Assembly who were here – Nervo, Entezam and Romulo. I agreed so far as the first two were concerned, but I expressed the view that if Romulo were at this time introduced into our talks, they might receive more publicity than we would desire and, therefore, we had better confine our meeting to the four of us plus Mr Martin. He agreed ...

One of the difficult, indeed perplexing aspects of this whole problem is the relationship between the Indian and other Asian delegations, and, indeed, between Menon and the head of his own delegation. It may be that not only delegations but individuals are acquiring a vested interest in their own ideas, and a corresponding suspicion of other people's proposals as likely to interfere with their own work as peacemakers. For instance, the Mexicans are now tied to their own resolution which is, in its turn, tied to their President, while Menon himself, a complicated character, is, I feel sure, caught up by his own role in this matter and worried about interference in the performance of that role by others.

In the afternoon of Monday, Mr Martin made his statement before the Political Committee and it went over very well. It is true that the ideas included in that speech in regard to a new approach to the prisoner of war question were pretty carefully expressed, but certainly the delegates appreciated their importance. Our care in this matter was due partly to our wish not to be tagged with firm 'Canadian proposals,' and partly to pave the way for the necessary resolution which should come from India later.

Tuesday morning, November 4, Martin, Menon, Nervo and Entezam met me in my office and we canvassed the whole position. Menon was more optimistic than previously about the Chinese reaction to our new approach of continuing repatriation under neutral control. His government had apparently been receiving some encouraging reports from Peking. He even went so far as to suggest that possibly the Chinese might accept a fifth member of a neutral commission as umpire in case of disputes. He might, I pointed out, be an Indian! However, we discovered real difficulties over the relationship of the Mexican proposal to our own ideas, and also to the priority to be given to the various resolutions in the First Committee. Things would be so much simpler if there were only the 21-power and Russian resolutions before the Committee, but that is not now the case. Menon said that it was clear beyond any doubt that if we first passed the 21-power resolution, which would be considered by the Chinese as a slap in the face, then all hope of agreement by them to a subsequent UN resolution on the prisoner of war issue only, along the lines we had been discussing, would be removed. Therefore, it became vital to put the 21-power resolution *after* the others. I accepted this point, but reminded the others that the Americans might object strenuously to it. I also gave them an assurance that I would do my best to persuade those concerned in the First Committee to so order their business that a resolution along the Indian lines, which might command the most possible support, would be put first ...

In this connection there was a good deal of discussion about the role of the President in this whole question. Nervo was inclined to exalt the importance of that role and to encourage presidential initiative. He even suggested that I might fly to North Korea with the new proposal, which he hoped the Assembly would adopt. I was a little startled by this! ...

This business is now becoming very tangled and complicated, and we will have to proceed very carefully if anything is to be accomplished; especially as the news of these discussions and negotiations is beginning to leak, and the press are beginning to talk about it. I think that my next step is to have a talk with the Americans. Whether they will be able to talk tomorrow to anybody remains to be seen! [The US presidential election was taking place on 4 November 1952.]

This afternoon, Eban of the Israel delegation came to see me concerning their intervention in the Korean debate. He said they had been studying previous statements, especially the Canadian statement, and felt the time had come to collect all the various ideas and put the good ones together in the form of a resolution. For that purpose, he showed me a draft. Eban is a very clear-headed and intelligent fellow, and his draft is an admirable one. However, I persuaded him not to put it forward tomorrow as a resolution, but merely to incorporate it in his statement as a succession of points which might be included in a later resolution. We will never get anywhere in this matter if the committee is deluged with resolutions. On the other hand, it might make it easier for the Indians to have their ideas put forward by other delegations which they, the Indians, can later pick up. This will help them not only here, but possibly with New Delhi, and even with the Communists. Eban's statement, in this form, may, therefore, be helpful.

I have also been urging Menon to report Korean developments here as sympathetically as possible to the Chinese in Peking, through their Ambassador. This is a very important part which the Indians can play, but whether they will be willing or able to play it effectively, I don't know. I wish that Menon would let me see the telegrams exchanged between him and his government instead of reading me excerpts from them. One of these days, after I have given him six or seven cups of tea, his special passion, I will ask him to do so!

There is one aspect in these informal talks which we have not considered very exhaustively but which has been very much in my mind. We must be careful not to take any action which would repudiate the Unified Command negotiators at Panmunjom, or would take their mandate away from them. I think, however, that we can avoid this difficulty if we agree on certain things here which, in advance, we have cleared, at least in principle, with both sides in Korea, and then ask the armistice negotiators at Panjunjom to meet again and solve the prisoner of war problem on the basis of our decision here.

On Wednesday and Thursday there was too much concentration on the results of the United States election to concentrate on Korea as well. The US delegation are taking the position that a change of Administration means no change — at least for the time being — in their functions and policies in regard to the UN or Korea, or anything else. However, this conclusion does not impress other delegations very much. Dean Acheson is in Washington and when he returns on Thursday will probably decide how far the Americans can go at this time in discussing new Korean resolutions with other delegations. Meanwhile, Krishna Menon has continued at Commonwealth meetings to explain his Korean ideas with the others, on the basis of a written document which he has finally produced and read, though he has not circulated it. I gather that the Australians and New Zealanders do not think too much of his draft. He feels that they are not going to support him.

Thursday afternoon, November 6, he phoned to see if he could again discuss matters with me and Selwyn Lloyd. For that purpose we had a meeting in my room at the hotel on Friday morning (November 7). He had been going over his draft in the light of observations made at the Commonwealth meetings mentioned above, and wanted to discuss certain changes with us. It appears that Lloyd and Menon had made contact with Ernie Gross of the American delegation the day before and told him the lines along which they were thinking. Menon seems to think that Gross's reaction was discouraging.

The Menon draft, as it stands, is all right in principle, but will need a good deal of careful consideration in detail. There are two points which will particularly worry the Americans and some other delegations. First, the absence of a provision for immediate transfer of those prisoners who are willing to be moved. The Americans will think that until the whole process is completed their own men may deliberately be kept back. Secondly, they will think, and, indeed, others will, that the use of the neutral commission consisting as it does of two Communists, a Swede and a Swiss, will give the

Communists endless opportunities for delaying tactics; that it will never come to agreement on anything. If, therefore, the armistice comes into effect without the proposed umpire being appointed, the only result will be a cease-fire without any real progress in carrying out the other stipulations. Menon was quite reasonable on both these points and agreed that it was desirable to appoint the umpire before the armistice came into effect.

Menon also feels that the Americans have some reservations in regard to his authority to deal with this matter in view of the fact that the head of his delegation is Madame Pandit. This gave me an opportunity to suggest delicately to him that any reassurance about Madame Pandit's full support for his own efforts would be useful. I told him that I would be glad to see the Chief of his delegation at any time, either alone or with him, to go over these questions with her.

This afternoon Krishna brought Madame Pandit to my office without much notice, and I was considerably embarrassed by the somewhat blunt implication that they were there to remove any difficulties and doubts about Krishna's position or authority. Madame Pandit was quite emphatic that he had the complete confidence of the head of his delegation and in Korean matters was completely responsible for the carrying out of the policy of that delegation. She told me to tell this to the Americans and I agreed to do so.

The opportunity soon came, because immediately after our meeting on the 38th floor of the Secretariat, I went to the hotel where Menon, Lloyd and I had our first more or less formal talk on the Menon draft with the Americans – Ernie Gross, Ward Allen, and a chap from the State Department. Gross raised many detailed objections to the Menon proposals. I think these were well-intentioned and were a sincere desire to explore difficulties, but they irritated Menon, who gets impatient over details, expecting us to be so caught up by the magnificence and significance of his total concept that we should not waste too much time on details. Furthermore, Menon and Gross are not kindred spirits. All in all, it was a somewhat sticky meeting ...

What they [the Americans] do not seem to understand is the vital importance of getting an Indian resolution which rejects the use of force in moving prisoners on the order paper. If the Communists accept such a resolution, even if it is full of risks, the fighting at least stops and the prisoners can begin to move. If they do not accept it we will at least have committed the Indians finally to our side on this issue and with them all the other Asian delegations. I would have thought that this was a matter of the highest possible importance to Washington, but they do not seem to recognize it as such ...

Early Saturday morning (November 8), Krishna Menon phoned me. He was very downcast and anxious to see me at once. He feels that the Americans are being obstructive and difficult, and I suspect is on the verge of dropping the whole business. I couldn't see him until the afternoon when I did my best to put him in a better frame of mind, and encouraged him to persist in the course he has begun. He reacts warmly to a little praise and encouragement.

Menon was particularly disturbed by the cross-examining attitude taken by Ernie Gross and the fact that Gross had had with him two American experts and, also, that Selwyn Lloyd had had two officials with him. I told him not to worry too much about this, that we all appreciated what he was trying to do. I told him also that I would be in a better position to help if he would leave with me a copy of his draft proposal, which he did. I then said that I would try to see Acheson in the morning and go over his points one by one. Menon thought this would be helpful, but felt he could not authorize me to show the text of his proposal to Acheson as all the members of his own delegation had not seen it. However, there could be no objection to my referring to it. He also indicated that if I wished him to join Acheson and me tomorrow morning, he would be willing. This, however, would not, I think, be a good idea ...

Sunday, November 9. I saw Dean Acheson this morning and went over the Indian proposal, point by point. He had already been pretty well briefed in regard to it by Ernie Gross and by Selwyn Lloyd, but I was able to give him more details. He was not unsympathetic and told me that they had been in touch with Washington concerning it. In fact, he read a message which had been sent to Washington to which he was awaiting a reply. If that reply was favourable, they would be able to accept the Indian ideas in principle, but they would certainly wish to have some changes made to the draft. Particularly, they felt it was unwise to spell out the membership of the repatriation commission. We should leave that to the armistice negotiators in Korea. I tried hard to persuade Acheson, first, to adopt a sympathetic attitude toward Menon and his idea, and secondly, to convince the people in Washington that Menon's proposal, or something like it, was bound to go to the Assembly, and probably be passed there. I also emphasized how great an advantage it would be – this is the point I have been driving home whenever the opportunity arises – to have the Indians put forward a resolution on Korea which all the rest of us could accept. Even if the Communists turned it down, this would be a great step forward. If, on the other hand, a cold and unsympathetic attitude toward the Indian effort resulted in their withdrawal from the whole enterprise, they would probably say later that they had done their best to bring about a satisfactory prisoner of war solution, but that this had been made impossible by the attitude of the United States. That, of course, would be playing right into the hands of the Communists.

I told Acheson that there were two ways by which reasonable American ideas could be incorporated into the Indian proposal. He could see Menon himself and try to persuade him to make the necessary changes, or this could be done by Selwyn Lloyd or myself or both. Acheson felt that the latter course was very much to be preferred, especially as he did not know Menon very well, and, in any event, Madame Pandit had already been discussing Korea with him, having met him only yesterday ...

As Eden and Selwyn Lloyd were seeing Acheson at lunch, I told Selwyn Lloyd over the telephone the results of my talk with the Secretary of State. Somehow or other we must bring this matter to a head within the next few days, so that the Indian delegation can make public its resolution, but in a form which the Americans can support. That is the one chance for success at this Assembly so far as Korea is concerned.

During Monday and Tuesday, Menon was apparently working on his draft and trying to make it more acceptable to the Russians and the Americans, without, however, apparently showing either of them a copy of his text. He was loath to let anyone but Lloyd and me have a copy, and this makes it more difficult to get agreement. I saw him for a moment on Tuesday (November 11) to find out whether, in the light of Vishinsky's implacable and entirely negative speech Monday morning, he was disposed to abandon the whole effort, but I was agreeably surprised when he said that he had no such intention. He still thinks that even if the Russians will have nothing to do with his proposal, the Chinese Communists might. As a matter of fact, he is more worried about the Americans than the Russians. He was anxious for me to make arrangements for him to see Acheson alone, as he is determined not to talk with the American officials, and I did this this evening at the Press Correspondents' dinner. I also promised Menon that I would redraft his own proposal in language I thought was clearer and more precise and which would make more of an appeal to delegations. Before I did this, however, I felt it was my duty to let the Americans see his draft, though I did not give them a copy of it. It is useless for Acheson to talk with Menon until he has at least seen the document in question. Menon, of course, does not know this ...

When I saw Menon on Wednesday he was very discouraged. He had had an hour with Acheson during the morning, but felt that he was getting nowhere, and had come to the conclusion that the Americans simply did not want an armistice. He was also worried that the British would follow the American line. Acheson this morning had given Menon a draft of the kind of resolution which they could support, based on the message which he had showed me on Sunday, and which apparently the Pentagon will take. This, however, is no good to Menon, as he is positive that the Communists will have nothing to do with it, because it only recognizes that there shall be opportunity for repatriation rather than the right of repatriation itself. I think that the Americans are being unnecessarily sticky in all this, and I told Menon that we still supported his viewpoint. I also showed him my redraft of his draft, and he accepted practically all the changes. I encouraged him to produce his draft and told him he would get a good deal of support for it. Paul Martin went further and said that we would support it. Of course, we are getting on very dangerous and slippery ground now. If the Americans come out definitely against it, and we support it, that will be an open break between us on Korea.

I promised Menon Wednesday afternoon (November 12) that I would try to see Eden and persuade him that the new draft should be backed by the British, and that they should do their best also with the Americans. So after the Assembly sessions today (Wednesday), I went up to the Waldorf where I found Eden dressing for dinner. I perched on his bed, and went over the new draft with him, which he seemed to think was pretty good. They also had been working on a new draft and he told me to look at it during the evening and see if we couldn't combine our points, get Krishna Menon to accept them in the morning, sell them to Acheson, and get the whole thing out as an Indian resolution tomorrow evening. ...

On Thursday, November 13, I was asked to meet Acheson and Eden at the latter's room at the Waldorf at 11:30 in the morning. As it happened, there was a plenary on that morning, but I gave the chair at 11:15 (somewhat to his surprise) to [Andrei] Gromyko [Deputy Soviet Foreign Minister] as a Vice-President, and left for the Waldorf. Incidentally, Gromyko found himself sitting beside the Secretary General on the podium, and could not avoid shaking hands with him. Possibly they will become a little more friendly to Trygve Lie now that he is leaving [the Secretary Generalship] – or is he!

When I got to the Waldorf I found not only Eden and Acheson, but Schuman (France), Spender (Australia), and Webb (New Zealand), with officials. Saul Rae [my Special Assistant] was with me.

Acheson had just left Menon, after a very unsatisfactory talk with him. There are no points of mental or spiritual contact between the practical, incisive, clear-headed Dean, and the vague, metaphysical, missionary Menon. Acheson made a vigorous onslaught on the Indian ideas and said they were completely unacceptable to the United States. We should stand by the 21-power resolution and resist these efforts to divide us! Spender backed him strongly, even though, admittedly, his Minister had taken the opposite line yesterday in private talks before he left for Australia. It was a shocking example of Spender's irresponsibility, because he admitted that his view, which he put forward so strongly, was not that of [Richard] Casey [Australian Minister for External Affairs]. Webb and Schuman were more cautious, but obviously influenced by Acheson's arguments. They seemed to agree, at least in part, with him that our best course would be to amend the 21-power resolution to introduce some of the Indian ideas. I, however, took the opposite position and defended the Indian proposals as valuable in themselves, and especially valuable as coming from India. I hoped that we would take them as our basis, and consider any necessary changes. Eden seemed to agree with me, though he was careful not to intervene in the discussion, either very often or very emphatically. Toward the end of the meeting Schuman seemed to come around to our point of view. Acheson was, I think, quite disturbed at this division of opinion, which he may justifiably blame on me. I am going to be in the Americans bad books again!

In the afternoon, I met Selwyn Lloyd and Krishna Menon at the former's hotel room, and we went over Menon's draft with a view to making changes in it which would help meet the American objections. Menon was very reasonable about the matter and accepted most of the changes ...

On Monday morning, November 17, Menon came to see me in a state of depression and irritation with the Americans, whose opposition to his resolution had now been made clear to him. I told him that we would stand firm, especially as he had accepted some changes last night which improved the text and would help the Americans ... Menon thinks, however, that the British and others will now yield to American pressure.

The 21 sponsoring powers have now begun to meet and discuss the Indian proposal, the text of which was circulated this afternoon. I will not attend, as I have been dealing with this matter as President of the Assembly up to the present, at least formally. Paul Martin will speak for us, as he did today.

In the meeting today the Americans attacked the Indian proposal vigorously in an effort to rally all the others present to their position. Acheson himself did the talking on one side and Martin, I gather, was the leading protagonist on the other side. They have set up a sub-committee to go into the question further.

The Polish Foreign Minister came to see me this afternoon and I gave him an excuse to talk about Korea, which he took. He refused to commit himself on the Indian resolution, but said merely that it certainly deserves serious consideration. What Menon really hopes for, I gather, is that the Communists and the USA will give the resolution a friendly abstention and everybody else will vote for it. That would, he thinks, give it the best chance for success in Peking.

This afternoon, the Americans called a press conference where Gross, in a most tendentious and one-sided way, I am told, attacked the Indian ideas and their proposal. I can't understand what the Americans hope to gain by these tactics, and shall do my best to put the other side of the case; indeed, I have already begun to do so, to delegations and journalists when opportunity offers.

On Tuesday, November 18, our friend Krishna once again came in to see me. He is to speak tomorrow and I had, at his suggestion, drafted him some notes for his statement. He was very grateful for them. We are worried that he will not make a very good case for his resolution and that he may even confuse rather than impress listeners, or that he may be too provocative against the Americans. However, he has promised to do his best to avoid these dangers.

The sub-committee of the 21 met during the day and Selwyn Lloyd told me, and Martin confirms it, that it was a much better meeting than yesterday, and that the Americans were less unfriendly to the Indian resolution. They have submitted several amendments, most of which should be acceptable, but one will be very difficult. This is the sticking point of the whole matter. They, the Americans, wish to change the last paragraph to make it clear that all prisoners who, after 90 days, will not accept repatriation will be freed. Menon cannot accept this as he pointed out to me this afternoon, because it would remove any possible chance of the Communists giving the resolution favourable consideration. However, he is considering a change in the last paragraph, which will remove the impression that prisoners who have not been repatriated will be detained indefinitely or, alternatively, he may put something in his speech which will bear on this matter. If this last paragraph can be altered somewhat, it should remove any valid reason for American opposition to the resolution. Nevertheless, that opposition will, I think, persist as, for some reason or other, they disapprove of the whole Indian intervention in this matter. They are certainly not showing any imagination or understanding of the importance of such a development ...

Today I had lunch with the editors of *Look* as the guest of Mike Cowles. We talked about the Indian Korean resolution and it was interesting to note that every person at the table said that if they had to vote on it they would vote for it. I suspect that in Washington this afternoon this has been one of the subjects of conversation between Eisenhower, Truman and Acheson, and I wonder whether Acheson's position will be more or less accommodating when he returns to New York tonight ...

At 12:00 o'clock today (November 19), Eden, Lloyd, Menon and Paul Martin met with me in my office on the 38th floor. Eden had just come from a very tough and not too pleasant hour with Acheson and was a little shaken by the stiff and uncompromising attitude he encountered toward the Indian resolution. The Americans will not have it as it stands, but before they attempt to amend it, especially paragraph 17 of the proposals, they demand to know that the British will stand by them. They have emphasized the serious and unhappy consequences of a split on this issue, and have put Eden 'on the spot.' Eden explained this to us, and then we devoted the rest of our time to persuading Krishna to include in his speech this afternoon a reference to paragraph 17, which would make it quite clear that indefinite detention was not implied in that paragraph; that the disposition of remaining prisoners would have to be taken in hand as a UN responsibility and some provision looking toward their eventual release must be made. Lloyd scribbled a few paragraphs for Menon along these lines, but all we could get was an assurance that Menon would not forget this difficulty in his statement which, unfortunately, is to be made without a text or, indeed, without notes, except possibly those which I have given him. There is really nothing much we can do now until Krishna has spoken, and we must hope that his speech will not close the door toward some reasonable changes to paragraph 17. If it does, I think that the British will be forced to take the American position in regard to that paragraph, but that doesn't mean that we have to.

We also talked about tactics after Krishna has spoken. I shall try to get the chairman to adjourn the meeting at once, and I have persuaded Entezam, who was to speak next, not to do so or raise at this time the point of priority for the Indian resolution. This will have to be faced, but Eden is very worried that if it were brought up at this moment, it would further antagonize the Americans, and I suppose he is right ...

After lunch, Eden came up to see me again. I had mentioned to him this morning, very confidentially, that the suggestion had been made that I should try to see Eisenhower before he goes to Korea to brief him on our side of this prisoner of war issue. Eden told me that he had been on the phone with Eisenhower last night and discussed matters with him, but only briefly. It now appears that Eisenhower phoned him again at lunch time and asked him to a private luncheon tomorrow. He, Eisenhower, was being pressed by his people to issue a statement today, emphasizing the importance of the principle of non-forcible repatriation and giving the impression that the Indian resolution implied a breach in that principle. Eden was able to tell him on the phone that no such implication was justified, but Ike apparently has been given the Pentagon view on paragraph 17 that indefinite detention of prisoners is, in fact, the exercise of force to get them back home. Eden got some reassuring remarks from Eisenhower about the necessity of the Americans, the French, the British and Canadians keeping in step on these matters, and he gave Eden the impression that he would welcome further information concerning this particular issue. That is why the luncheon tomorrow may be so very important, especially as Ike will be leaving for Korea shortly. At the luncheon, Eden is going to bring up the question of a private and informal talk between Eisenhower and myself, though this may not now be necessary.

Krishna made his speech this afternoon (November 19) and I sat listening to it in my office through the 'box.' He is not a clear speaker and is inclined to wander all over the place – partly because he refuses to use any kind of text – but he was objective, unprovocative and, at times, quite moving. When he came to the explanation of paragraph 17 of his resolution, he included the various phrases about the importance of indeterminate detention which we were so anxious to get on the record. That was very satisfactory.

Before he finished, Trygve Lie came into the office with some very secret information which had been conveyed to him by a reputable person – apparently a UN official – who had just got back from Korea. This was to the effect that the American military do not want to be involved in the resumption of armistice negotiations following the Indian resolution, because they were all set now for a big offensive, especially an air offensive, which they thought would end the war. I would have put this information aside as mere rumour were it not for some of the developments of recent days. Trygve wanted to talk to Eden about his information, so when Eden came up to my office after Menon's speech, I steered him down the corridor for a few minutes while Lie passed on the above to him for what it might be worth ...

Eden now has to decide if and when he will speak and what he will say. He is seeing Dean Acheson later in the day and unless he changes his mind, as a result of this interview, will speak tomorrow at 3:00 o'clock and give

Menon's proposal a favourable reception, while suggesting an interpretive amendment to paragraph 17. He is not looking forward to his talk with Acheson, who seems to inspire a certain amount of apprehension in him. These are two people who shouldn't be left alone in the same room to argue ...

On Thursday afternoon, November 20, I saw Eden in my office at the United Nations, as he was worried about the inability of the Indians to agree on some clarifications to their resolution which would make it easier for the Americans to accept it; as well as about the stiff and critical attitude of the Americans to the Indian proposal. I told him that I was going to Ottawa with Acheson the next day and would not be available here for mediation work for a couple of days. He was disappointed about this and, after some further talk, I decided that possibly I had better forego the Ottawa trip, even though I was to be host at the dinner on Friday. I then saw Acheson, explained my difficulties, and expressed the hope that if I had to stay behind, he would not think I was being discourteous. I was worried about this, especially as we had been disagreeing so strongly and officially here over Korean matters. But he was most friendly and understanding and only sorry that my work here might prevent me getting a change in Ottawa. I phoned the Prime Minister and he took the same position. So after much soul-searching I decided to stay behind, and Maryon went along alone with the Achesons to act as hostess at the dinner ...

During the day (Friday) a meeting of the sub-committee of the 21-power group was held at which the Americans brought strong pressure to bear for a prior acceptance by all the sponsors of the 21-power resolution of the amendments which the Americans consider necessary before they give any pledge to support the Indian resolution or even to give it priority. Gross was, I gather, not very tactful in the way he argued in favour of this; the pressure was too obvious. However, the British, the French and ourselves are not to be moved by these tactics, which were repeated later in the day at a full meeting of the 21 powers.

In the afternoon I saw Eden again. He is becoming increasingly irritated by the American tactics. Their pressure is being exercised not only in private meetings, but in public by telling the press about the 'serious rift' between London and Washington, and by creating an atmosphere of tension and crisis. This must please the Russians if nobody else. Eden is, I think, worried that Menon and the Indians may become stiffer and stiffer as American pressure grows, and there will be less possibility to get them to accept reasonable changes ...

On Saturday I had lunch with Eden and Lloyd and Paul Martin in my room, when we decided to persist in our efforts to bring the Indians and Americans together in regard to amendments. We also decided, however, that if the worst came to the worst and the American amendments went too far to be acceptable to the Indians, we would vote for the Indian proposal as it stood, come what may.

While Eden was with me I telephoned the Prime Minister to make sure that Acheson's talks in Ottawa had not altered the position of our own government in this matter. Mr St Laurent talked to me for some time and reassured me that the position remained unchanged and they would continue to back me in the line that I was following. Acheson had made a pretty impressive case for firmness, etc., but had not persuaded the Prime Minister or his colleagues that our own policy and tactics were wrong.

This afternoon a strange incident occurred. Gross called on Eden having previously informed the press that he was going to do so, and having given the impression that his visit was a critical one, and that he was going to give the British something in the nature of an ultimatum. Eden was intensely annoyed at this way of conducting delicate diplomatic negotiations. He told me about it afterwards and indicated that it would have the contrary effect on him to that which the Americans desired.

I spent a good deal of Sunday (November 22) with Lloyd and later with our own delegation. There was an important meeting of the 21-power group in the evening and we discussed the policy we should follow in the face of what is likely to be more American pressure. Mr Eden decided not to forego a day in the country with Eisenhower for the meeting in question, the background of which were exaggerated stories in the Sunday papers of 'crisis' and 'serious splits' ...

The explosion at the 21-power meeting did not develop as the Americans fortunately (probably because Dean Acheson had returned from Ottawa and took charge himself) adopted a much more reasonable and conciliatory attitude. He even stated that press accounts of the 'rift' were 'grossly' exaggerated! ...

Monday was a busy day for me. At 11:45 I saw General Eisenhower and took advantage of the opportunity to mention Korea and the Indian resolution ... I went from my talk with Eisenhower to the Waldorf where I saw Dean Acheson and found him friendly and relaxed after his Ottawa visit. He is coming round to the necessity of not trying to push impossible amendments at the Indians or going too far in the 'arm twisting' of friends. I told him that we were still trying to get the Indians to accept those changes considered essential by Washington, but that he should be under no illusions that this can be done easily. He seems to feel that, of the '21,' only the French, British and ourselves are supporting the Indian position but, at the same time, appears grateful for my efforts with Menon, concerning whom his opinion is no higher than before. Personalities, as always, are of considerable importance in solving these problems ...

This afternoon in the First Committee, Vishinsky, to our great surprise, and even before Acheson spoke, damned the Indian resolution all over the lot and was almost as hard on its author. Everyone wondered why he had gone out of his way to do this, and thereby, once again, bring the rest of us closer together. Possibly it was because the Indian initiative is making too much of an impression in Peking.

Acheson was to speak after Vishinsky and, in the circumstances, it seemed to me a great chance for him merely to contrast the violence and unreasonable attitude of Vishinsky with the friendly and constructive approach of the rest of us to the Indian initiative; that a long, legal analysis of Menon's proposals, with pleas for their revision, was now out of place and unwise. I sent word to him to this effect, but he went ahead with his prepared speech, which, while logical and even brilliant, and impressive in its demands for changes to the Indian draft, was not, I think, what was required in the circumstances. Both its praise of Menon himself and its use of Menon's own speeches to prove the necessity for further 'clarifications' to the Indian draft, were bound to make our Indian friend uneasy.

Tuesday, November 25, I had a farewell lunch with Eden. He is leaving for England happier than he was a couple of days ago. Afterwards, with Paul Martin, I saw Menon on further changes to paragraph 17. He wants to continue our talk tonight, but I have about reached the end of my resources with him, also our tea is running out, so I think I will leave him to Selwyn Lloyd.

This afternoon, the '21' agreed to give priority to the Indian resolution, so this hurdle is over.

Tonight, at midnight, I had just got to sleep when Lloyd phoned to say that, after a Homeric struggle, he had persuaded Menon to accept amendments to paragraph 17, either giving the United Nations ultimate responsibility, without qualification, for the 'hard core' of POWs, or adding 'and ultimate disposition' after 'care and maintenance.' This is quite a triumph.

This morning, Wednesday November 26, things went off the rails again. Menon, who visited me early in the morning, repented that he had given in last night to Lloyd ...

Dean Acheson, with whom I discussed the matter later in the morning, unfortunately said that Washington – particularly the Pentagon – preferred the alternative and shorter version of paragraph 17 ... they were very irritated with Menon at suggesting further changes, and in withdrawing from the agreement which he had made last night ... Lloyd and I had to bring them together, and quickly, as Dean Acheson insisted on a final and irrevocable decision before the meeting of the Committee was over ... Acheson was in the Committee while these negotiations were going on, and Menon was in my office. Messages were exchanged back and forth. Pretty hectic!

To make assurance doubly sure on this tacit agreement about the change [of the period during which prisoners would be repatriated] from 60 to 30 [days], I scribbled out the following paragraph, which Gross read to Acheson in the Committee, who agreed, and then later I read to Menon, who also, somewhat reluctantly, agreed: 'If it is moved by a member of the Committee that '60 days' in paragraph 17 be reduced to '30 days,' the Indian delegation will take the position that they will leave this change for the Committee to decide and will abstain on any vote concerning it. If this amendment should be carried by the Committee the Indian delegation will vote for the paragraph 17 as amended in this way and will not feel that such a change would cause them to vote against or abstain on the whole resolution.'

It was just as well that I did this, because a couple of days later when the vote was being taken, Menon was inclined to think there was no such agreement, and he was free to vote against the Danish amendment reducing the period from 60 to 30. However, I flourished this pencilled paragraph at him and he agreed to stand by it. Menon, though he may be a difficult person, does not break his word ... Late Wednesday night I mentioned to Menon that I might send a telegram to his Prime Minister, putting the developments of recent days in proper perspective and attempting to remove the impression that the resolution, as now amended, meant a surrender to the Americans. I had also the purpose in mind, though I did not mention this to Menon, of finding out whether Menon's worries and his insinuations that his government was thinking about withdrawing from the whole initiative were justified. I thought that if I could explain the position to Mr Nehru, I might get a reassuring and positive reply from him which would remove any excuse for Menon to weaken or withdraw ...

On Friday morning I showed him the reply from Mr Nehru which was completely satisfactory from my point of view. It certainly removed any excuse for Menon withdrawing or even weakening. However, at the First Committee this afternoon when the vote should have been taken, he made a plea for an adjournment until Monday, even though I had begged him to accept a compromise for adjournment until Saturday only. He tried to argue with the Committee that he needed further instructions from his Government, but after Mr Nehru's telegram, I knew myself that this was not his real reason. What he wanted was delay in order to prepare his own speech and recuperate from his exhausting labours of recent days ...

During the morning, in an effort to help Menon, I had tried to persuade the Americans not to oppose a delay until at least Saturday, or even Monday, if the Indians absolutely insisted. This irritated them, but they were disposed to be co-operative. Unfortunately, however, at a luncheon I gave during the day, at which Dean Acheson and Madame Pandit were both present, she went up to Dean and urged him to make sure that the vote on the Indian resolution took place during the afternoon. You can imagine what Acheson said to me when he had finished with Madame Pandit! I must say that I felt badly let down by Menon on this particular issue. However, he got his delay and the Americans will have to make the best of it. I doubt whether any harm will result, though it would have been better to have pushed the thing through this afternoon.

I was freed from Menon's ministrations on Saturday until the evening, when he dropped in to tell me about his day in the country with Mr Vishinsky, who brow-beat him a good deal and told him that India had joined the imperialist camp and would have to take the consequences! He certainly has

Menon worried. He wanted me to help him on his speech for Monday where-
in he is disposed to take a strong anti-American line in order to prove that
India's position remains neutral. I told him that this would be foolish,
though there was no reason why he shouldn't explain as emphatically as
possible his own resolution in terms which would prove that it was far
removed from the Unified Command proposals at Panmunjom.

During the day I received telegrams from Peking and North Korea in
which the Communists come out strongly for the Soviet resolution and abuse
the Americans. However, the language was not as violent as usual, and the
telegrams make no mention whatever of the Indian resolution. There may
be some significance in this.

On Sunday we worked over some ideas for inclusion in Menon's speech,
especially in the direction of proving that it was an honest compromise between the two points of view. He [Menon] dropped in to see Lloyd and me
this evening and seemed quite grateful for our assistance. Unfortunately,
he is still tempted by the idea of making at the last minute further changes
which would meet the Communist position, but I think we argued him out
of this as unwise and unnecessary. Also, I think we have persuaded him to
vote against the Soviet amendments as any other course would be interpreted as a repudiation of his own resolution.

On Monday afternoon he made his speech, a long and rambling dis-
course but which had some good material in it. Vishinsky then made a
vicious assault on what he called the Indian 'rotten compromise.' Afterwards
the vote was taken and was unanimous in favour of the Indian resolution
except for the Soviet bloc. This was a most happy and satisfactory conclusion. I phoned Dean Acheson this afternoon and he is very satisfied with
developments and now thinks that the delay over the weekend, far from
doing harm, may have done good. All that remained now was to dispose of
the Soviet resolution. This was done Tuesday morning ...

... the Plenary [Session of the Assembly] (December 3) went through
smoothly and the resolution, after a good enough speech by Menon, was
adopted by 54 in favour, 1 abstention, and 5 against. It was a dramatic
moment when the roll call was taken, for the resolution, I am sure, represents a very important step, even though it is not likely to bring about an
armistice at this time. It is the basis from which we start in the future, and
it is a United Nations basis in the best sense of the word, with the Asians
and Arabs solidly behind it.

The next problem was how to get the resolution to Peking and Pyongyang
[the North Korean capital]. I had a press conference after the resolution was
passed, and I was asked a lot of questions on this point. I indicated that it
might be delivered personally by someone acting on behalf of the President
(I had the Indians in mind), or it might merely be cabled. I thought myself
that the first course would be the better as the Indian Government, through
their representative in Peking, could explain the resolution when they delivered it. I therefore cabled Nehru to see if they would take on this job.

This resulted in an exchange ... which clearly explains Nehru's reluctance to act as requested. He puts up a strong case for sending the message direct by cable. I had thought that it would be more impressive and courteous to have it delivered by hand, but, as Nehru points out, the Communist Foreign Ministers might take the other view, namely, that my unwillingness to address them directly by cable was a slight! We decided, therefore, to send the message by cable, without anybody's intervention. I decided also, however, to send an explanatory memorandum, though the Americans did not think much of this idea. This took a bit of drafting, as it had to be pretty carefully done. In the end, the resolution and the explanatory note were cabled on December 5, and I can now sit back and wait for the reply. If and when it comes, it will probably be a pretty blunt and tough refusal.

It came (at least the Peking reply came) on December 15 and was as anticipated above. However, it was not in either abusive or even excessively belligerent terms. My first reaction was to submit the reply with a very short report to the Assembly immediately, but after discussing it with some of my friends, I decided it would be better to hold it off to the end of the week so as not to precipitate a discussion which, at this time, would do more harm than good. If this course were challenged by the Russians, I could say that I was still awaiting a reply from the North Koreans, and did not wish to report on one without the other. Menon was quite happy about this procedure and somewhat to my surprise agreed that a debate at this stage would be unwise. I also decided not to make any statement in submitting the two replies to the Assembly, but merely to circulate them as a formal UN document. As it happened, the North Korean reply did not come in until December 18 and on Saturday afternoon the two replies were circulated officially to the members of the Assembly without any covering statement. As we expected to adjourn on Sunday afternoon, it was not likely that this course would precipitate a debate at this stage in our proceedings.

The best tribute to the effect of the Korean resolution on the Russians is the fact that on Saturday evening, they attempted to efface that effect by closing the session with a debate on another Korean item, on which they thought they would get more support. For this purpose, late Saturday night the Russians phoned to see if they could come around to see me at once on a very important matter. I had some suspicion what it was and decided not to be rushed that way, and said that the earliest I could see them would be 11:00 o'clock on Sunday, December 20. Shortly after the Russians phoned [Andrew] Cordier [the Secretary General's Executive Assistant] got in touch with me to say that they had sent to him a new item for inclusion in the agenda about the massacre of prisoners of war in Pongam camp. It was this that they wished to talk to me about. They wanted a meeting of the General Committee before the Assembly Sunday afternoon in order to get this item included in the agenda for immediate discussion.

At 11:00 AM Sunday, December 20, Zorin [another Deputy Soviet Foreign Minister], with an interpreter, called at the Drake. He is a smooth and slippery customer, but as tough as he is smooth. He was obviously speaking on strict instructions from Moscow. He read the proposed item, and 'insisted' on a meeting of the General Committee before the General Assembly. I told him that this would be difficult if not impossible as some members of the General Committee could not attend until later in the afternoon. I mentioned particularly the British and the Americans. Zorin, however, said that he insisted on a meeting at 2:00 o'clock, and if I did not call it, they would bring the matter up at the beginning of the Plenary session. I told him that they had the right to ask for a meeting of the General Committee, but no right to decide at what hour it would be held. I would summon it for as early an hour as possible, and would phone him back shortly. I then discussed the matter with two or three delegations and the Secretariat, and we agreed that it would be unwise to give the Russians any excuse to say that we were trying to block the inclusion of this item in the agenda; therefore, we should hold our meeting at 2:00 o'clock even if Gross and Lloyd were not there. This was done. The wind was taken out of Gromyko's sails by no one objecting to the inclusion of his item in the agenda. This should have prevented any debate, but Gromyko was not going to let this opportunity go by, so he made a speech insisting not only on its inclusion, but on its immediate discussion when the Assembly opened. There was strong objection to this, and by 3:00 o'clock when the debate was still raging, I told the General Committee that if they could not come to a decision at once, I would adjourn the meeting as the Assembly was to be in session at 3:00, and reconvene them after the Assembly session. This, of course, did not suit Gromyko at all, so he agreed to the wording 'immediate discussion at the present session,' without specifying whether this was to be at the beginning or the end of the session. After the meeting, I told the Russians that if they would accept the inclusion of this item at the end of our agenda, I could guarantee them that the Assembly would continue in session until it was reached, even if we had to go on all night. This should have satisfied them, but it didn't, for at the beginning of the meeting, Gromyko demanded that his new item should be given priority over all the others. I ruled that this could not be done and was sustained by the Assembly. We therefore proceeded with our regular business and did not reach the Soviet item until midnight. There was an hour between 7:00 and 8:00 when certain delegations were free to work out tactics in connection with it. It was decided not to oppose its inclusion on the agenda or immediate discussion. The Americans had a promise from the Latin Americans and the Arab-Asian group that they would sit it out to the very end, so that this Russian propaganda item could be disposed of before the Assembly adjourned. What the Russians hoped, I think, was that either they would not be given an opportunity to make their speeches on the alleged murders of prisoners of war, in which case they could say they were gagged; or the item would come up for discussion so late that many of the smaller delegations would not be in their places and a vote against the item, therefore, would be small. It did not work out this way for them. Gromyko made his hour's speech, which was as vicious an attack on the Americans as I have ever heard at the United Nations. All the other Communist delegates spoke in the same manner and at length. The US, UK, Canadian and other delegations rejected their resolution. The debate dragged on but no one showed any sign of weakening or going home. Personally, to set a good example, I remained in the chair from 8:30 [PM] until 4:50 [AM] without a break! The Russians, I think, must have been disappointed when the vote finally took place, as every delegation was present, even though a good many of them were asleep! Whether asleep or not, they voted, and the result could not have been very satisfying for Gromyko. 45 delegations voted against his proposal, 5 in favour, and 10 Asian and Arabs abstained. It would have been, of course, better if this latter group had voted against the resolution also, but I think they were glad to have an opportunity to abstain to show that they were not irrevocably committed to the anti-Communist side. The excuse they gave was that there had not been time to investigate the Russian charges, and, therefore, while they could not be accepted, they could not be summarily rejected. However, even with the 10 abstentions, the Russians did not succeed in pulling off a last minute propaganda coup.

The epilogue to this story is a tired little group of Canadians packing up at the Drake Hotel at daybreak, driving to LaGuardia airfield, boarding an aeroplane during a wild and stormy dawn, and flying home to Ottawa, somewhat the worse for wear, but in time for Christmas peace and cheer.

INDEX